D0858064

RIT - WALLACE LIBRARY
CIRCULATING LIBRARY BOOKS

OVERDUE FINES AND FEES FOR <u>ALL</u> BORROWERS

*Recalled = $1/ day overdue (no grace period)
*Billed = $10.00/ item when returned 4 or more weeks overdue
*Lost Items = replacement cost+$10 fee
*All materials must be returned or renewed by the duedate.

Plato's Sophist

The publisher gratefully acknowledges the generous support of The Wilbur Foundation in making the Carthage Reprint Series available.

Plato's Sophist

The Drama of Original and Image

Stanley Rosen

Carthage Reprint
ST. AUGUSTINE'S PRESS
South Bend, Indiana
1999

Manufactured in the United States of America.

Library of Congress Cataloging in Publication Data

Rosen, Stanley, 1929–
    Plato's Sophist : the drama of original and image / Stanley Rosen.
        p.   cm.
    Originally published: New Haven : Yale University Press, c1983.
    Includes bibliographical references and index.
    ISBN 1-890318-63-9 (pbk. : alk. paper)
    1. Plato. Sophist. 2. Sophists (Greek philosophy).
  3. Methodology. 4. Ontology. I. Title.
    B384.R67 1999
    184—dc21   99-13195
                                                                         CIP

∞The paper used in this publication meets the minimum requirements of the American National Standard for Information Sciences—Permanence of Paper for Printed Materials, ANSI Z39.48-1984.

To the Memory of
Robert Earl Charles
ἀνὴρ καλὸς κἀγαθός

CONTENTS

Acknowledgments   ix
Prologue   1
  Orientation   1
  Dramatic Phenomenology   12
  The Dramatic Context   16
  The Predicationalists   29
  Eidetic Numbers   48

ACT ONE: DIAERESIS   59

SCENE ONE: Gods and Philosophers (216a1–218b6)   61
EXCURSUS: Diaeresis in the *Philebus*   70
SCENE TWO: Hunting the Sophist (218b6–219a3)   84
SCENE THREE: The Angler (219a4–221c4)   91
SCENE FOUR: Division and Multiplication of the Sophist
(221c5–226a8)   100
SCENE FIVE: Nature and Work (226b1–231b8)   115
SCENE SIX: Summary of the Diaereses (231b9–e7)   132

ACT TWO: IMAGES   145

SCENE SEVEN: The Problem of Images (232a1–235c7)   147
SCENE EIGHT: Diaeresis Once More (235c8–236c7)   170
SCENE NINE: The Problem of Non-Being (236c8–239d5)   175
SCENE TEN: Another Look at Images (239d6–241c6)   186
SCENE ELEVEN: Precise and Imprecise Myths (241c7–245e5)   204
SCENE TWELVE: The Battle of the Giants (245e6–249d8)   212

ACT THREE: FORMS   227

SCENE THIRTEEN: Identity, Predication, and Existence
(249d9–252e8)   229
SCENE FOURTEEN: The Eidetic Alphabet (252e9–255c7)   245
SCENE FIFTEEN: Non-Being (255c8–259d5)   269
SCENE SIXTEEN: False Statement (259d6–264b8)   291
SCENE SEVENTEEN: Diaeresis Concluded (264b9–268d8)   309

Epilogue.   315
Works Cited   333
Index of Greek Terms   337
Index of Passages Cited   338
General Index   339

ACKNOWLEDGMENTS

This book has its proximate cause in a series of seminars on the *Sophist* given over the past fifteen years at Penn State University and the University of Nice. I owe a good deal to the students in these seminars and want to thank them collectively for their many contributions to my understanding of Plato. The antepenultimate draft of my study was prepared in French, to be delivered in a seminar at the University of Nice in the spring semester of 1981. The challenge of having to think and speak about Plato in three different languages at once had the same effect on me as is exhibited in the well-known *mot* of Dr. Johnson: when a man knows he is to be hanged in a fortnight, it concentrates his mind wonderfully. I am extremely grateful to the philosophical faculty at the University of Nice for their hospitality, and especially to Professors Dominique Janicaud, Alain De Lattre, and Jean-François Mattei. I want also to. thank Professor Pierre Aubenque of the University of Paris, chairman of the committee that issued the invitation to visit Nice, who also kindly invited me to speak before his seminar at the Sorbonne.

Three good friends, each a distinguished Plato scholar, took on the onerous task of reading the penultimate draft of this study in its entirety. They corrected numerous errors and made a variety of objections to existing formulations which have led to several extensive changes, especially in the Prologue but in other places throughout the manuscript. Without the generous help of Aryeh Kosman of Haverford College and David Lachterman and Mitchell Miller of Vassar College, this would have been a much more imperfect book than it in fact is. Each was continuously prepared to place at my disposal his philosophical acumen and erudition. I have not always been able to follow their suggestions, and they should in no way be held responsible for my own errors and opinions. Nevertheless, they have made substantial contributions to the final version of this book. Let me also thank here the anonymous reader of a still earlier version, who persuaded me of the need to discuss the secondary literature on the *Sophist* more extensively than I had. This is the place to make a further remark. A number of my views on the *Sophist* are different from those which seem to be widely accepted by contemporary students of Plato. In particular, one of the major themes of this study is that one cannot employ, or assume, the paradigm of predication to explain the Eleatic Stranger's doctrine of formal elements and their combinations and separations. In order to make the strongest possible case for my approach, I have thought it wise to analyze at some length a number of the most distinguished contributions to ways of reading Plato that differ from my own. A close study of these books and essays proved invaluable to me in formulating my own views. The fact that my analysis of the secondary literature is often critical should in no way obscure my debt to the authors involved. Plato's text is extraordinarily difficult, sometimes perhaps intractable. I have done all that I can to make my own interpretation persuasive and to engage in elenctics without eristics. If I have not succeeded in this respect, the failure is unintentional, and I apologize in advance to those concerned.

As usual, my colleagues at Penn State University have supported my work with generosity and understanding. And finally, my special thanks to Maureen MacGrogan, my editor at the Yale University Press, who did so much to make this book possible, and to Anne Mackinnon for her judicious editing of the final version of the manuscript.

PROLOGUE

ORIENTATION

Plato's *Sophist*, like any of his dialogues, may be approached from two more or less contrasting perspectives.[1] For purposes of convenience, I shall refer to these as the ontological and the dramatic perspectives. The dramatic perspective regards the dialogue as a unity, and more specifically, as a work of art in which the natures of the speakers, as well as the circumstances under which they converse, all play a part in the doctrine or philosophical significance of the text. The most obvious motivation for the adoption of this perspective is the dialogue form itself; perhaps the most important textual justification is the discussion of rhetoric and writing in the *Phaedrus*, and to a lesser extent, in the *Republic*.[2] From this standpoint, it is not finally satisfactory to dismember the *Sophist* into a collection (even a heap) of fragments and to study just those fragments which seem to contain "technical" discussions of a "philosophical" as opposed to an "artistic" nature. A comprehensive understanding of the "technical" passages, to the extent that such is possible at all, depends, according to the partisans of the dramatic perspective, upon grasping their function within the organic dialogue. In terms of the discussion in the *Phaedrus*, the perfect writing is alive to the extent that it accommodates its speech to the nature of the "listener" or

1. With the following remarks, cf. the interesting article by Y. Lafrance (1979). I agree with him that one cannot contrast "la lecture continentale" and "la méthode analytique" in the way that he criticizes. I link them together as distinct versions of an approach that cuts across Lafrance's own distinctions with respect to Plato scholarship.
2. *Phaedrus* 257b7ff; *Republic* III, 392c6ff.

1

reader. The dialogue thus represents the intentions of the speaker with respect to this or that presentation of a technical doctrine.

In slightly different terms, the power or work of discourse is ψυχαγωγία, which we may translate as the guidance or education of the soul (including one's own). But souls differ in nature, and can be led only through different kinds of speeches. Let us call the knowledge of which speeches lead which kinds of soul "philosophical rhetoric." The dialogue, regarded as a dramatic unity, is thus an image, albeit one of a peculiar kind, of the author's comprehensive intentions. It is via the dramatic form of the dialogue that the author accommodates his doctrines to the natures of different readers (*Phaedrus* 271a4–272b6). Since rhetoric in this sense (as opposed to the mere persuasiveness of sophistical rhetoric) is a τέχνη, in the precise sense that it is based upon genuine knowledge of natures or forms, we must extend the sense of the term "technical" to include the dramatic form of the dialogue itself, as well as such "technical" issues as being, non-being, falsehood, and the like. (It should not escape our attention that part of the art of rhetoric is knowing when to keep quiet: *Phaedrus* 272a4). That philosophical rhetoric is indeed a τέχνη is emphasized in the *Phaedrus* at, among other passages, 272b7–274b5. There is then a close connection between philosophical rhetoric and diaeresis, or the division and collection in accordance with kinds, a method that will play an important role in the *Sophist*. Philosophical rhetoric, as rooted in a knowledge of kinds or forms, speaks the truth, if in an accommodated sense. Sophistical rhetoric speaks the likely. This distinction also figures prominently in the *Sophist*. We note that, whereas "the likely" (τὸ εἰκός) must differ from the truth in that it is not based upon a vision of forms, nothing is said in the *Phaedrus* of a "logical" or analytical nature to explain how we "see" forms. To the contrary, the language is accommodated or rhetorical in the extreme on this point. Socrates employs imagery to describe the perception of forms. Unfortunately, we cannot distinguish between philosophical and sophistical images unless we have ourselves perceived the forms. Once again, this is a problem of the utmost importance in the *Sophist*.

This last difficulty is alluded to indirectly by Socrates when he says that perfect speech may be impossible, but if it is possible, it must be addressed to gods, not to human beings (*Phaedrus* 273e4ff). Socrates does not say that the gods will reply; he does not identify perfect speech as dialogue. Certainly there are no conversations between philosophers and gods in the Platonic dialogues (although the possibility is raised that the Eleatic Stranger may be a god). Such conversations are apparently the subject matter for comedies, or dramas, but not for dialogues. This establishes an interesting difference between "drama" in the usual (Greek) sense and philosophical dialogue. If properly worked out, it should go some way toward erecting a distinction between poetry and philosophy. But that distinction, for Plato, does not preclude the use of poetry (for example, of philosophical rhetoric, or dialogues) by the philosopher.

We need to make one more point with respect to the discussion in the *Phaedrus*. A writing is perfect to the extent that it imitates the speech of a living person; in other words, writing is inferior to conversation. More than one reason is given to explain this inferiority. For example, reliance upon writing weakens the memory. Perhaps the most important reason, however, is this. Writing is like painting; at least this is true of those writings whose form is monologic. Just as a painting does not answer the questions put to it by its viewers, so too a monologue does not reply to the questions of its readers. (I note parenthetically that the difference between paintings and writings will play an important role in the *Sophist*. With the passage in the *Phaedrus* (275c5–276a9), one should carefully compare *Philebus* 39a1ff.) Whereas the philosophical rhetorician knows when to be silent, monologues are always silent; that is, they lack this knowledge. The relation of this point to the previous remarks about analyzing "technical" passages in isolation from the whole should be plain. The extraction of certain passages as philosophically important, and the disregard of the context, hence of the dialogue as a unity, is an interpretation on the part of the reader. This is not to say that interpretations are unnecessary. But surely it is prudent, and hence reasonable, to ground one's interpretation in that provided by the author. The comparison between philosophical rhetoric, or dialogues, and living conversation is intended to make the point that the dialogue form contains Plato's interpretation of the significance of the "technical" (in the narrow sense) themes discussed by his characters. It does not replace a technical analysis of those passages, but it supplements such an analysis.

I turn now to what I call the ontological perspective. As the term suggests, the primary concern of this perspective is with the technical content of the dialogue; in the case of the *Sophist*, this content is understood as a theory of "being," in one sense or another of that term. However, the extent of these senses is not so wide as to include the dramatic, mythical, or "literary" elements of the dialogue. Though they may vary on other matters, representatives of the ontological perspective agree upon the need to enforce with rigor the distinction between philosophy and poetry, sometimes called the distinction between the ontological and the ontic. In either case, however, the distinction is based upon a conviction that philosophy is a science, or (to put it with slightly more caution) that philosophy is scientific. As I have just noted, this conviction is originally joined to the equally fervent belief that philosophy must be distinguished from poetry. Unfortunately, the virtual identification of philosophy with "conceptual analysis" or "technical thinking" (even by those ontologists who reject technical thinking as ontic, or as wedded to a conception of being as *produced*) leads inevitably to a blurring, and perhaps to an erasing, of the distinction between philosophy and poetry.

This last point requires more careful elaboration. Let us here inspect the two main schools in our century of the ontological perspective. These are the phenomenological and the analytical schools. I use the term "phenomenological" in the sense of the early Heidegger, for whom it designates the method of the science of being. I refer to Heidegger rather than to Husserl because Husserl was not concerned with Greek philosophy, or with the history of philosophy in general, with some exceptions (for example, Galileo, Hume, Kant). For Heideggerean phenomenology, Plato enjoys a crucial (if somewhat pejorative) role. To this, one could add that the great majority of phenomenologists in contemporary philosophy derive, either directly or indirectly, from Heidegger's revision of Husserlian phenomenology. Apart from Heidegger's interest in Plato, there is another reason which makes his version of phenomenology more important to the student of the *Sophist* than is the Husserlian phenomenology. Despite his emphasis upon phenomenology as a scientific method, hence as a laying bare or uncovering, and so a kind of exact describing of what shows itself, Heidegger unites the descriptive task of phenomenology with the task of interpretation. I shall return to this point below, but its significance is already visible in Socrates' comparison between painting and monologue in the *Phaedrus*.

By "analytical," I refer to those students of Plato who follow primarily in the tradition of Frege, but secondarily (and not negligibly) in that tradition as modified by the later Wittgenstein, Austin, Ryle, and others. There is an interesting analogy between the Husserlian and Heideggerean phenomenology on the one hand, and the Fregean and "ordinary-language" analysis on the other. Whereas it would be technically wrong to say that Heidegger "subjectivizes" Husserl's "objective" or scientific phenomenology, it is nevertheless true that Heidegger makes the method of ontology a function of *Dasein* (or what used to be called human nature), which is in turn interpreted in terms of historicity and temporality. It is open to discussion whether Husserl himself finally was led to a subjectivist doctrine (as for example in the thesis of the transcendental ego understood as intersubjectivity). But the pervasive intention of Husserl is to give a scientific description of the "phenomena" (in his sense of that term), and not an interpretation which is rooted in the historically conditioned nature of human thinking. Heidegger's "science" of human nature is intrinsically a doctrine of the interpretation, as distinguished from the description, of the "phenomena." This becomes especially evident in the later Heidegger, and in the unending progeny of hermeneuticists spawned by these later writings.

With respect to the formalists and the ordinary-language analysts, a similar point obtains. Frege's devotion to a mathematical science, rooted in exact concepts and eternal senses, has been gradually diluted, not to say dissolved, by the "hermeneutically" inclined ordinary-language philosophers, for whom one's language (including its categorial structure) is a horizon and a historical creature. This creature shapes whatever is thought or said within that language and so is as contingent as the language itself. One may therefore observe a serious flaw in analytical Plato scholarship. Its practitioners tend to employ formal logic and set theory on an *ad hoc* basis in explicating the technical doctrines of Plato's dialogues. But they normally do not inform us about the ontological status of their formal techniques. Are these techniques "Fregean" in the sense of being eternally valid, and in that sense are they simply the rectification of Plato's attempt to achieve an eternally true doctrine? Or are these techniques merely "up-to-date," and so the currently fashionable, but soon to be replaced, tools for producing concepts, and hence presumably having nothing to do with (what I shall later define as "official") Platonism? Differently stated, was Plato a Fregean, and so a Platonist, or was he a late Wittgensteinian? In terms taken from the *Sophist*, does Plato acquire or produce being? As we shall see very shortly, this is a critical question, since, on the Stranger's explicit doctrine, it is the sophist, but not the philosopher, who asserts that man produces being.

The phenomenologist of the Heideggerean variety tends not to be interested in the dialogue form,[3] with the exception of certain iso-

3. An important exception here is H. G. Gadamer.

lated passages like the myth of the cave, which are employed to establish the ontological interpretation, that is, to support an ostensibly "average" concept of being as a *res, Vorhandenes, Seiendes,* or thing. The same point can be made in an apparently opposite manner. The phenomenologist *exaggerates* the unity of the Platonic dialogue, or reads all parts of it as contributing to a homogeneous concept of being. However, this amounts to a failure to allow any independent status to the dramatic or ontical elements in the dialogue; it amounts to a denial that Plato had a more nuanced doctrine of being than the phenomenologist allows. I cite a typical statement of this position from Heidegger's 1927 lectures, *The Basic Problems of Phenomenology*:

> As early as antiquity a common or average concept of being came to light, which was employed for the interpretation of all the beings of the various domains of being and their modes of being, although their specific being itself, taken expressly in its structure, was not made into a problem and could not be defined. Thus Plato saw quite well that the soul, with its logos, is a being different from sensible being. But he was not in a position to demarcate the specific mode of being of this being from the mode of being of any other being or non-being. Instead, for him as well as for Aristotle and subsequent thinkers down to Hegel, and all the more so for their successors, all ontological investigations proceed within an average concept of being in general.[4]

This "average concept of being," as Heidegger goes on to state, is that of the εἶδος or what is shaped, and hence *produced*, by *Dasein*.[5] Two pages later, Heidegger generalizes: "Ancient ontology performs in a virtually naive way its interpretation of beings and its elaboration of the concepts mentioned."[6]

I will not here cite sample passages from the analytical ontologists, as I plan to subject their characteristic doctrines to close scrutiny in what follows. Suffice it to say that, in one sense, the analytical thesis is the inverse of the phenomenological thesis. According to the latter, Plato adheres to an average concept of being. According to the former, there are instead to be found in Plato attempts to eliminate such a general concept (culminating in the pure detached

4. Heidegger (1982), p. 22.
5. Ibid., p. 108.
6. Ibid., p. 110. For a detailed criticism of Heidegger's interpretation of Plato, see Rosen (1969), chap. 5.

forms of the "middle" period) in favor of more sophisticated articulations of syntactical structure. In another sense, however, these two theses are the same. For the analyst, the "general concept" of being is now that of predication (although, as we shall see, part of the apparent Platonic doctrine of being is assimilated into the modern notion of identity). Furthermore, whereas the late Plato is more "sophisticated" than the early Plato, this sophistication is just a naive, because ancestral, anticipation of doctrines to be given their perfected form by Frege and his successors. Finally, both phenomenologists and analysts tend to agree that being is for Plato produced. I say "tend," because the analysts make no explicit pronouncements on this crucial point. But if being is a "concept," and more specifically if being is just the fact of possessing a certain predicate, since a predicate is a linguistic distinction, being is finally a linguistic construction. One could object to this that predicates correspond to properties, but this objection is beside the point. On the analytical interpretation, it is exactly the case that *being is not a property*. To the contrary, being is how we talk predicatively, and so, which properties we choose as significant, or even which properties become significant for language users like ourselves, in our historical epoch, and so on.

It is of striking interest that both ontological schools have been decisively influenced by Aristotle. Whereas it is true that the Eleatic Stranger speaks of a science of dialectic or diaeresis, he does not speak of a science of being, or of an ontology. It is Aristotle who first puts forward a science of being *qua* being. And it is Aristotle who first develops a doctrine of predication as one of the pivotal features of how we talk about being. In other words, Aristotle points out that "being is spoken of in many ways" (πολλαχῶς λέγεται τὸ ὄν), but he attempts to grasp comprehensively these ways in one (or perhaps two) scientific discourse(s). Plato makes no such effort to reduce the ways in which we speak of being to a science, or even to two sciences of ambiguous relation. One of the theses of the present study is that it is not the naivete of Plato, but perhaps of his interpreters, to reduce being to an average concept. Aristotle's rejection of the dialogue form is at the same time an attempt, or part of an attempt, to transform the various senses of being pointed out by Plato in his dialogues into a homogeneous or general and conceptual account. The first step in reading Plato is to put aside our Aristotelian spectacles. To this extent, and in a sense that requires considerable modification, I prefer the dramatic to the ontological perspective.

Let me now turn to the needed modification. The most striking dramatic feature of the *Sophist* is the difference between the Eleatic Stranger and Socrates. This difference is both personal and doctrinal or methodological. Plato draws our attention to this difference by the dramatic connection between the *Theaetetus* and the *Sophist*. We are expected to listen first to Socrates' interrogation of the brilliant young mathematician and then to the discussion between Theaetetus and the Stranger. Our first impression is that the Stranger is, so to speak, a prototypical Cartesian who rejects the history of philosophy in its entirety, as he makes apparent in his account of his predecessors (including Parmenides), in favor of the universal method of diaeresis. A more careful reading leads us to modify this impression. The use of diaeresis in the dialogue is problematical and is explicitly subordinated to an investigation of pure "concepts" or "senses" together with an analysis of natural language that reminds us of Frege. Whereas one cannot agree that the Stranger is primarily concerned with problems of "reference and predication,"[7] the comparison with Frege is at certain points valid. Putting to one side for the moment the exact nature of the Stranger's positive teaching, it is evident that he is guided in his analytical work by mathematical principles of reasoning. These principles indeed issue in a positive and highly technical doctrine that is explicitly stated. This fact sharply distinguishes the Stranger from Socrates.

At this stage in our reflections, there is a sense in which the dramatic and the narrowly technical features of the *Sophist* coincide. It now becomes necessary to read the text in two different "directions." Suppose that we begin with a close dissection of the narrowly technical doctrines of the Stranger. Very far from articulating an ontology or science of being understood as a general concept of εἶδος, the Stranger proceeds in a variety of ways and uncovers various senses of "being." Despite the exercises in linguistic analysis, the Stranger does not explain these senses by means of a theory of predication. Instead, he begins rather arbitrarily (and not at all by way of diaeresis) with an incompletely specified "alphabet" of pure forms, which is accepted by Theaetetus without surprise.[8] These elements are said to combine with one another to form the fundamental structures of intelligibility and, derivatively, of rational discourse. The Stranger uses at least two models, neither of them predicational, to illustrate the combinatory process, and a variety of verbs. In addition to the alphabet of forms, the Stranger treats the being of images and "being" (οὐσία), or "the whole" (τὸ πᾶν), understood as

7. Owen (1971), p. 225.
8. Perhaps this is because of his earlier conversation with Socrates; cf. *Theaetetus* 185c4ff.

the living and divine cosmos. Nowhere does he unify these senses of "being" into a discursive account or scientific λόγος. The closest he comes to offering a comprehensive definition of "being" is when he speaks on behalf of a sect of his predecessors, the improved materialists. And this definition of being as *power* is itself never developed into a comprehensive or general account. But even if it were, it could be equivalent neither to εἶδος on the one hand nor predication on the other.

Let this suffice for the moment as an indication of the diversity of the Stranger's methods and doctrines. I have intentionally omitted the use of diaeresis from this sketch because, as is to some extent obvious, and as closer study confirms, the method of diaeresis, despite the praise bestowed upon it by the Stranger, plays no role in the development or statement of his narrowly technical doctrines. The most that can be said for diaeresis, as it is actually employed by the Stranger, is that it serves as a method for exposing the many aspects of the nature of the sophist, which aspects are directly visible to us in daily life, if they are visible at all.

This reference to diaeresis serves as a transition to the second direction in which we must read the *Sophist*. Our scrutiny of the "inner" nature of the Stranger's doctrines leads us "outward" toward the occasion and circumstances under which these doctrines are elaborated. Given the diverse procedures of the Stranger, what is the connection between his narrowly technical doctrines and the mathematical aura of the dialogue as a whole? To what extent is the *Sophist* a mathematical drama? And how are we to understand the shift from Socrates to the Stranger as the principal speaker in our mathematical drama (if that is an accurate description)? What is the mathematical basis, if any, of the nature of the sophist, the definition of which is the pervasive theme of the dialogue? Is not the sophist, as a human type, the antithesis of a quasi-mathematical form? Let us grant that, in order to define the sophist, we require an explanation of the nature of likeness, and thus of the difference between accurate and inaccurate images, or more generally, of the difference between images and originals. It soon becomes evident that no such explanation is provided by the Stranger. The distinction between the sophist and the philosopher cannot be made on the basis of a "scientific" or "technical" definition. Would we not have done better to pursue the definition of the sophist in terms of the art of rhetoric in its practical dimension or, in other words, on the basis of the distinction in the *Phaedrus* between philosophical and vulgar rhetoric?

The Stranger's treatment of the puzzles of being, non-being, and false statement is intimately connected to the puzzle of the nature of likeness. If we cannot distinguish between originals and images, our direct perception of pure form is not sufficient to resolve the paradoxes of natural language identified by the Stranger; it is not sufficient to supply a λόγος of non-being (and hence of being). Once we have understood the technical inadequacies of the Stranger's views, both internally and as a basis for defining the sophist, we are led to ask why the Stranger proceeds with a "technical" paradigm of sophistry. Is the sophist a false geometer, or something entirely different? Assuming for the moment that we had a precise mathematical grasp of formal structure, and hence of sound linguistic behavior with respect to being and non-being, would this resolve the problem of sophistry? Is sophistry a τέχνη in the narrow sense, or is it a comprehensive interpretation of the significance of τέχνη? Is not sophistry an interpretation of the good life, and in this sense an imitation of philosophy?[9]

By reasoning of this sort, we are led to encompass the entire dialogue, and in this manner to return to the point at which we began our survey: the difference between Socrates and the Eleatic Stranger. Can the shift from the former to the latter be understood as a signal from Plato of a shift in his own thought? How we answer this question will depend upon a number of factors. Not the least of these is the fact that advocates of a shift in Plato's thought are usually also believers in the importance of the order of composition of the dialogues. The *Philebus*, however, was written after the *Sophist*, and in it Socrates is once more the main speaker. Whereas there are some differences in emphasis between the Socrates of the *Philebus* and, say, the Socrates of the *Republic*, it is hardly the case that, in the *Philebus*, Socrates continues the doctrines and methods of the Eleatic Stranger. Beyond this, it will not be difficult to show the methodo-

9. One finds occasionally in the secondary literature the view that Plato does not intend seriously the Stranger's "refutation" of sophistry via the συμπλοκὴ εἰδῶν, e.g., Peck (1952); Marten (1967), pp. 223–24; Kojève (1972), pp. 169–70. However, these authors do not explain adequately (or at all) why Plato assigns these defective analyses to the Stranger. My own view, to be developed in the text, may be stated summarily as follows: the character of the Stranger is Plato's way of providing a philosophical commentary on the charges levelled against Socrates by his Athenian accusers. The Stranger in effect charges that Socrates is a sophist with no positive doctrine, who corrupts the Athenian youth. The Stranger attempts a technical refutation of sophistry which is also the expression of a positive doctrine of his own. This refutation fails on technical grounds; but the very attempt to reduce sophistry, and thus philosophy (of which sophistry is a fantasm), to τέχνη is an error. I have no doubt that Plato was aware of all this, as is apparent in the Stranger's tacit recantation in the *Statesman*. None of this, however, means that the Stranger's technical doctrines are sheer irony, or that they do not require the closest analysis.

logical deficiencies in the Stranger's way, or somewhat more accurately, his recommended way, of pursuing the sophist. On at least
one crucial point, it is patent that Plato must have been aware of
the inadequacy. Whereas the difference between the sophist and the
philosopher is that of worse and better, the Stranger asserts that, as
partisans of diaeresis, we must ignore the difference of worse from
better and concentrate exclusively on the difference of like from like
(that is, of like "kinds" or like "looks").

This pervasive problem is accentuated if we contrast the *Sophist*
with the *Protagoras*. At *Protagoras* 319a4, Socrates makes a clearly
ironical attribution to the sophist of the τέχνη of politics. I shall
have more to say about this point below. Here the following introductory remark is in order. Socrates' usual procedure (and the *Protagoras* is no exception to this general rule) is to deny that sophistry
is a τέχνη or genuine knowledge. He does, however, regularly (if not
invariably) treat sophistry as a practical or political activity closely
akin to oratory. If there is a scientific analysis of sophistry, then it
must take its bearings from the nature of rhetoric. In a sense, the
Stranger does this; but the difference between his treatment of rhetoric and that of Socrates is plain by a comparison of the *Phaedrus*
and the *Sophist*. According to Socrates, a genuine understanding of
rhetoric entails not just knowledge of the forms (via diaeresis), but
also, and comprehensively or in a regulative sense, knowledge of the
human soul. According to the Stranger, knowledge of the nature of
sophistry does not require an understanding of rhetoric so much as
of the structure of natural language. Hence it requires an understanding not of the human soul but of forms and syntax. In dramatic
terms, this is closely connected to the Stranger's relative lack of
interest in the nature of his interlocutor, especially in contrast to
Socrates. Socrates is interested in himself, and more generally, in the
differing kinds of human souls, as well as the different kinds of
speeches which are required to "guide" or "educate" them. Despite
his doctrine of the ideas, Socrates is anything but an ontologist, in
the sense of one concerned primarily, if not exclusively, to develop
a doctrine or a general concept of being. I have already indicated that
the Stranger is also not an ontologist in this sense. Yet he comes
much closer to being a man of pure theory than does Socrates in the
Sophist (but not, we should remember, in the *Statesman*).

To draw one immediate inference from these observations, the
difference between Socrates and the Eleatic Stranger is reflected in
the difference between the dramatic character of the *Protagoras* and
of the *Sophist*. Is there any evidence to persuade us that Plato, the

author of both dialogues, gave up his interest later in life in the human soul and philosophical rhetoric, on behalf of a proto-Fregean philosophy of language? The evidence that we have, to over-simplify for the sake of initial clarity, is the *Protagoras* and the *Sophist*. Even if one gives some credence to the hypothesis of a development in Plato's interests and views, he never disowned his earlier work in the manner of Kant or Bertrand Russell. Nor is there any evidence of such a radical shift in views, or *any* such shift, in Aristotle. But it is hardly necessary for us to resolve this issue by turning to Aristotle. What we need to do instead is study the Platonic dialogues; in the immediate instance, we need to study the *Sophist*, all of it, and in minute detail. It should soon become evident whether the *Sophist* disavows the dramatic format, and whether Socrates is no longer of crucial significance to an understanding of Plato's teaching.

DRAMATIC PHENOMENOLOGY

I said previously that I prefer the dramatic to the ontological approach to the *Sophist*. It should now be clear that this does not require a suppression of the narrowly technical themes in the dialogue. On the contrary, it requires their meticulous analysis, both in themselves and as elements in a comprehensive dramatic structure. In this section, I should like to clarify this view from a somewhat different angle and to introduce a term to describe my reading of the *Sophist*. The term in question is *dramatic phenomenology*. Whereas a dialogue is not a "drama" in the sense of a poetic play written to be performed in the theater, it has a manifestly dramatic form. A dialogue is a poetic production in which mortals speak neither to gods nor to heroes, but to each other. At the same time, there is a hierarchy of mortals within a Platonic dialogue that is rooted, not in the contingencies of birth but in the natures of diverse human souls. Similarly, a dialogue is not a phenomenological description, but an interpretation of human life. As a poetic production, it so orders its scenes of human life as to provide an indirect commentary on the significance of the speeches delivered within those scenes. Adapting a distinction of the Stranger's to our own purposes, we may say that a dialogue is centrally concerned with the better and the worse, the noble and the base.

It may be possible to give a phenomenological *description* of a philosophical dialogue, but a dialogue is not itself such a description. Dramatic phenomenology is the artistic reformulation of phenomenological descriptions of speeches and deeds within the context of a unified statement about the good or philosophical life, and hence about the noble as distinct from the base. Such a unified statement is an interpretation of human life. It is not an ontologically neutral interpretation, or one that does nothing but render explicit the intentional, uncovering, or hermeneutical, and hence temporal and historical, nature of *Dasein*. This is of course not to deny that a philosophical dialogue uncovers something about human nature. But, to repeat, the intrinsic unity of this uncovering is not that of an "average concept of being." It is that of the superiority of the philosophical to the nonphilosophical life. Such a unity is entirely compatible with, and in fact requires, representations, or images, of the most diverse types of human existence, hence of the most diverse human speeches.

No interpretation will be uniformly acceptable to all competent persons. Perhaps the same is true of a phenomenological description. In principle, however, the intention of the orthodox phenomenologist is to provide a scientific or "objective" description that is the same for every person who is able to see the object from the perspective of the phenomenologist himself. This perspective is again in principle accessible to every person able to undergo the askesis of phenomenological purification. Despite their initially scientific pretensions, Heideggerean interpretations, as we have already noticed, inevitably evolve into *historical* perspectives; and the perspective of a past historical period is no longer accessible in principle to anyone able to undergo the phenomenological purification. Not even a precise study of the relevant documents can overcome this historical shift in perspectives. How one interprets the past is thus a function of one's vantage point. To a limited but noticeable extent, there is an analogy here with mathematical interpretations. A mathematical interpretation, like those in the natural sciences, is judged finally on pragmatic grounds. These grounds, however, cannot be purely technical. What counts is the intention of the investigator. We construct models in order to understand something. The value of the model resides finally in the value of what it enables us to understand, and so, in our intentions.

The problem of the relativity of interpretations applies with special force to a Platonic dialogue. To say that Plato's doctrines are exactly the same as the views of his principal dramatic figures is to say that an exact description is an explanation. It amounts, perhaps unintentionally, to the thesis that in order to understand the *Sophist* all we need to do is read it aloud, without making any slips of the tongue. But this will not do. As an interpretation of the episodes it recounts, a dialogue is an image of images. An image looks different from different perspectives. If Plato possessed a homogeneous doctrine of a fundamentally scientific nature which he wished to communicate in a univocal and explicit manner to all readers, then his choice of the dialogue form betrays a singular incompetence. This is not a charge with which I care to associate myself. Nor is it necessary to take such a charge seriously, as a reflection on the nature of the dialogue form makes evident.

I want to connect this problem of the relativity of interpretations with one of the most important themes in the *Sophist*: the distinction between acquisition and production. The Stranger attempts to define the sophist as a producer of false (i.e., inaccurate) images. A false or inaccurate image fails to reproduce accurately the proportions of the original. A true image does reproduce those proportions accurately. This distinction gives rise to a variety of technical problems, which will be examined more closely in the following pages. Let us note here one main problem with respect to true and false images. If the true image exhibits the exact proportions of the original, then *qua* image of that proportion, it seems to be the same as the original. But if the false image exhibits proportions which are not exactly those of a given original, they remain proportions, hence presumably the imaged proportions of some other original, from which in turn they cannot be distinguished. In other words, we have to disregard the medium in which the image is manifested as here irrelevant. Either the image *qua* proportion is the same as the original or it is different from it. If it is the same, then there are no images but only originals that recur. If it is different, then it cannot be a true or accurate image. On either alternative, it follows that the distinction between truth and falsehood is impossible to maintain. We have no discursive access to original or to genuine being, except in the sophistical sense that every statement is true. Philosophy is then assimilated to sophistry. The sophistical thesis is thus the assertion that man produces being in his capacity as talking animal.

Let us introduce the following distinction between orthodox, or "official," and unorthodox, or "unofficial," Platonism. Official Platonism may be equated here with the thesis that human beings in general, and philosophers in particular, have access to the true natures of things. Platonism in this sense asserts that vision of pure form is the acquisition, not the production, of truth. Unofficial Platonism is the doctrine that follows from the assimilation of philosophy to sophistry. It is the version of Platonism that is read into the dialogues explicitly by the Heideggerean phenomenologist and implicitly by the analytical ontologist who assimilates being into the linguistic function of predication. Whereas I reject the technical content of these two versions of "unofficial" Platonism, I am very far from dismissing their thesis (explicit or implicit) as indefensible. At least with respect to the analytical version, one could say that I take it more seriously than do those who, perhaps unintentionally, imply it. The thesis becomes defensible, not by a close study of the Stranger's narrowly technical doctrines, but rather from a reflection on the nature of the dialogue.

A dialogue is a production, and more sharply stated, an image of images. Whereas some of the subordinate images may be of pure forms, the same is not the case with the comprehensive image. As an image of images, the dialogue represents a determinate perspective from which Plato understands the whole. But is it an accurate image (an icon) or an inaccurate fantasm? In considering this question, we may assume that Plato means exactly what he says. His intention, so to speak, is *iconic*. There are, however, two restrictions intrinsic to the execution of the intention which we may call *fantastic*. The first is pedagogical. Sound pedagogy, as the *Phaedrus* explains, requires that all speeches, and hence comprehensive speeches especially, must be accommodated to a variety of possible listeners. Not everyone can understand the philosophical life in the same way, because we do not all understand life in the same way. Even those of us who would agree that there is a distinction between the noble and the base, or between philosophy and sophistry, would not draw the distinction in the same place. This is the second restriction: life itself is "fantastic" in the Stranger's sense that it adjusts its presentation of original proportions to accommodate the differing perspectives of its audience. The metaphor of an audience is of course not entirely sound; we live life, we do not observe it. But the difference between living and observing simply accentuates the fantastic nature of the phenomena of the everyday. The world as it appears is a sophist, continuously changing its looks as we interrogate it.

Each Platonic dialogue, to vary our formulation, is an image of the soul. The soul is in turn a microcosm or image of the whole. But the whole is not a formal structure. In the *Sophist*, the Stranger refers to the whole as a god. Whatever this may mean, each human being is a part of the whole who interprets it as a whole. This is true of all of us, but especially of the philosopher, and especially of the philosopher who attempts to provide a λόγος of the whole. The relativity of interpretations stems most directly from the varying na-

tures of human beings. To a certain extent, the philosopher over-
comes this relativity by the comprehensiveness of his λόγος, which
(at least in "official" Platonism) draws its strength from direct perception of pure forms. But the overcoming of relativity in the interpretation or evaluation of the shifting looks of the whole is not the
same as the overcoming of the shift in looks. Even if we accept the
official doctrine of forms or ideas, phenomenal experience does not
cease. And there are many beings to which no pure form corresponds. One such being is the sophist. In sum, a unified interpretation of the whole includes a perception of its largely perspectival
nature.

One consequence of the nature of the whole is the impossibility
of mathematicizing philosophy altogether. There is no Platonic system or science of the whole. There is no science of being. Being is
spoken of in many ways, and there is no one sense of "being" that
serves to provide a paradigmatic or focal meaning for the others. By
the same token, if we enlarge our own perspective to include all of
the Platonic dialogues, then Socrates and the Eleatic Stranger (to say
nothing of Timaeus and the Athenian Stranger) are two aspects of
the philosophical nature. They are two images, and indeed two *fantasms*, of Plato. If I may employ a slightly exaggerated but not outrageous metaphor, Plato exists as the "ontological difference" between Socrates and the Eleatic Stranger. This ontological difference
does not, however, terminate in a discursive ontology. No matter
how sophisticated our logical techniques, when we speak of the
whole, we must have recourse to images. This is why the thesis that
man produces being is both defensible and of crucial importance.

THE DRAMATIC CONTEXT

It is now time to look a bit more closely at the dramatic nature of
the *Sophist*. I begin with a general observation that follows from
what has already been said. Philosophers cannot be defined or identified simply on the basis of their logical or argumentative powers
and techniques. If these powers and techniques culminate in the
production of being, then, by the thesis of official Platonism (and
the leading schools of contemporary Plato interpretation share this
thesis), their possessors must be sophists. In a more positive vein,
we know from such dialogues as the *Republic* that the philosophical
nature, in addition to possessing a strong intelligence and memory,
is marked by courage, temperance, and justice. In a typical passage
(VI, 487a2–5), Socrates also includes "splendid and graceful behav-

ior" among the philosophical attributes, as well as a love of truth. The validity of an argument is not affected by the character of its propounder. But sophists are also capable of constructing valid arguments. The difference between the better or just λόγος and the worse or unjust λόγος is not in their formal validity so much as in the uses to which they are put. The discussion of the philosophical nature in the *Republic* is of special interest to the student of the *Sophist*, because in it Socrates unites closely excellence of character and mathematics as the basis of higher education. As Socrates says at IV, 400d6–10, λόγος itself follows the ἦθος of the soul, hence the importance of a musical education for the guardian class. By "musical," of course, is meant a combination of song, dance, and the fine arts, all of which are marked by harmony and measure, or in other words by mathematical properties.

There is another aspect to the connection between music and mathematics on the one hand, and philosophy and politics on the other, as Socrates develops these in the *Republic*. Let us grant for the moment the thesis of official Platonism that mathematics is the study of the eternal order of the cosmos. As was just noticed, music, the training of the character, is itself marked by mathematical properties. But this does not mean that the study of pure mathematics in itself trains the character. It rather points to a set of properties which are common to mathematics and music, but expressed, thanks to these τέχναι, in different modalities or dimensions of the human soul. Music provides the critical primary training of the character of the soul, a character which is *followed* by λόγος, and hence by pure mathematics. In other words, the ends or goodness of pure mathematics are provided by music. Music is thus "political" in a sense that mathematics is not. In terms of the individual, music guides or regulates mathematics in the pursuit and the accomplishment of the good life.

Taking this reflection one step farther, music trains the soul by producing icons of the original forms of the virtues of the free man (III, 401a7–c9). Socrates introduces this point by way of the case of letters, a paradigm which is also used by the Eleatic Stranger. The main point, however, is this: we cannot recognize images of letters unless we know their originals. The function of music is thus to direct the soul toward the intellectual perception of the forms of the virtues. Music is thus both productive (a making of images) and erotic (it directs the soul away from beautiful bodies to beautiful or pure forms). The discussion of music is thus followed immediately by a discussion of sexual eros (III, 402e3ff). We can relate this discussion to a slightly earlier passage. As a consequence of their poetical and musical education, all of which is discussed well before the introduction to the mathematical or narrowly philosophical education, the guardians become what they must be: "makers [δημιουργούς] of the freedom of the city" (III, 394b9–c1).

These remarks should suffice to make plain that for Socrates, or differently stated, according to the thesis of official Platonism in its "classical" statement, poetical and musical production regulate the theoretical sciences within the philosophical life. Production, however, is subordinated to acquisition, "acquisition" meaning here the orienting intellectual perception of pure forms. Without that perception, we cannot identify the images of originals; in other words, we cannot distinguish icons from fantasms. Unless it can be shown that the originals are themselves produced, as for example by the τέχνη of conceptual analysis or by "theory construction" in the contemporary sense, it cannot be said of Platonism that it teaches implicitly the producedness or artifactual nature of being. But conversely, unless it can be shown that the originals are *not* produced, acceptance of the thesis of official Platonism remains an act of faith or vision. This act of vision cannot be confirmed by the logical and mathematical τέχναι if these are taken in the modern or productive sense. But even as understood by official Platonism, namely, as nonproductive τέχναι, they are rooted in a pretechnical perception of form, ratio, proportion, and the like, which perception regulates the technical dissection and construction (or analysis and synthesis) of mathematics. A mathematical proof does not demonstrate the originality of the formal structure it elicits. The determination of the originality of mathematical paradigms is not a technical matter.

Even if we assume (as I do not) that there is a fundamental shift in Plato's thinking, represented by the shift from Socrates to the Eleatic Stranger, what holds true for the doctrines of Socrates also holds true for those of the Stranger. Whatever the Stranger says or believes, it is not mathematics but poetry and music which guide the soul in its pursuit of excellence. Order, proportion, or harmony is the root of both mathematics and music (taken now as including poetry), but this root puts forward its branches in two quite distinct ways. Second, the Stranger must also be bound by the fact that both music and mathematics perceive or intuit their regulative paradigms. The Stranger, like Socrates, is faced with the dilemma of demonstrating the "acquired" nature of the paradigms, even though acquisition is not demonstration and tends, as τέχνη, to cover over what is acquired by a secondary, produced form.

Before we relate these observations more directly to the dramatic details of the *Sophist*, something should be said of Socrates' treatment of poetry or mimesis in the same passage of the *Republic* that we have been discussing above. This treatment is based upon the problematic principle that regulates the entire political investigation, namely, the principle of the division of labor. According to Socrates, human nature is cut up into small pieces; each man has a definite nature or talent, so that no one can imitate many things nobly or do all those things of which imitations are likenesses. There must then be a separate imitator for tragedies, comedies, and so on (III, 394e1–395b7). It should be immediately obvious that Socrates, or more fundamentally, Plato himself, violates this principle in the case of imitation. In a distinct but related sense, one could say that the philosophical statesman also violates the principle, and hence the definition of justice, by minding everyone's business.

There is something unjust about perfect justice, or, with respect to our main concern, about the Platonic dialogues. Plato imitates all his characters, whether philosophers, sophists, statesmen, mathematicians, or even women or evil men (cf. III, 396a7). Still more generally, Socrates distinguishes two kinds of poetry, narrative and mimesis. In narrative, the poet speaks throughout, without pretending to be his characters. In mimesis, the poet assimilates his manner of speaking in each case and as much as possible to the person he announces as the speaker (III, 393b6–c10). Mimesis is thus self-concealment; it is practiced by the authors of tragedies and comedies (III, 393c11–394b2). The "moderate" or "measured" man (μέτριος ἀνήρ), in other words the man of temperance or good character, will not engage in mimetic poetry but will restrict himself to imitating in narrative the speech and deed of good men, especially when the good man is acting steadily and sensibly, but less so when he is unsteadied by illness, erotic love, drunkenness, and so on (III, 396b10–e3).

It should not be forgotten that these views are expressed by Socrates within a specific dramatic context of their own. Nevertheless, they are of considerable interest to us on several counts. To begin with, it is plain that Plato himself violates the restrictions on imitation at all periods of his development, including that of the *Sophist*. So far as I am aware, however, advocates of a "developmental" interpretation of the dialogues do not suggest that the later Plato jettisoned the ethical or practical teachings of his middle period in their broad outlines. Second, even if Plato had changed his general views of ethics and practice (a possibility for which there is no evidence),

Socrates' words would retain their interest for us. In other terms, Socrates continues to be the "antithesis" to the Eleatic Stranger, and his views on the education of the soul, or more specifically, of the mathematical soul of youths like Theaetetus, must be compared with the views or procedures of the Stranger. It is up to us not merely to understand the views of the Stranger, but either to choose between him and Socrates, regardless of Plato's development, or else to show how Socrates and the Stranger represent two differing aspects of a unified Platonic teaching and practice.

The link between mathematics and music, or between philosophical dialectic and knowledge of the soul, and thus between philosophy and rhetoric, is evident in the *Phaedrus* and the *Republic*. In the *Phaedrus*, diaeresis plays the central role assigned to mathematics in the *Republic*, but the general point is the same.[10] This is so despite the fact that the *Republic* tends to denigrate eros and exalt moderation, whereas the *Phaedrus* praises eros and divine madness. In both dialogues, the central problem is knowledge of the soul and *paideia* or ψυχαγωγία. It is easy to see that this problem is also pivotal in the dramatic structure of the *Sophist*. However, there is a relative neglect of pedagogical music in the *Sophist*. In accordance with this, rhetoric is treated in a fundamentally pejorative manner. The Stranger apparently advocates diaeresis and knowledge of pure form, but not a philosophical rhetoric rooted in diaeresis and knowledge of pure form. We should not be surprised to find that the Stranger is not interested in the souls of individual human beings, or at least not in the same way as Socrates (cf. *Statesman* 308e4–311a2). The Stranger lacks the peculiar combination of erotic and political music that is so prominent a feature of Socrates' nature.

The background prominence of mathematics in the *Sophist* is directly reflected in the Stranger's behavior, but not in that of Socrates. This is evident from a comparison between the *Theaetetus* and the *Sophist*. The main part of the *Theaetetus* records the conversation on the day prior to that depicted in the *Sophist*. In the earlier conversation, the personnel are the same, except for the absence of the Eleatic Stranger. Theaetetus is introduced to Socrates by the mathematician Theodorus, who is the youth's teacher. The body of Theaetetus looks like that of Socrates, who asks whether the same is true of their souls. The subsequent conversation is explicitly dedicated to the task of finding the answer to this question about

10. What Socrates describes as diaeresis in the *Phaedrus* should not automatically be identified with diaeresis as practiced by the Stranger, just as there is no reason to identify diaeresis in the *Sophist* and *Statesman* with what the Stranger calls "dialectic" in the former dialogue.

Theaetetus's soul (145b1–c6). It is just possibly implied that Socrates is the original and Theaetetus the image, although this way of putting the point is obviously inadequate. If Theaetetus and Socrates have resembling souls, they must both be images of something else, presumably of the paradigmatic philosopher.

In the opening scene of the *Statesman*, the sequel to the *Sophist*, Socrates observes that he has interrogated Theaetetus "yesterday" and has just been listening to his interrogation by another. Socrates thus establishes the continuity of the conversations from his own standpoint (*Statesman* 257a1–258b2). He has now completed his inspection of Theaetetus's soul (although he does not tell us his conclusion). It is now right to inspect Theaetetus's companion, Young Socrates. Socrates thus calls our attention to the fact that the two young interlocutors of the trilogy *Theaetetus, Sophist*, and *Statesman* present us with images of his body and name. The deeper question is of course whether they also provide images of Socrates' soul. At a still deeper level, the same question applies to the soul of the Stranger. The question is thus whether the soul of Socrates is visible in the trilogy.

Socrates differs from the Stranger in a variety of ways, of which the most important from the present standpoint concerns their interest in the soul. Socrates cares about the individual nature of the youths with whom he converses, whereas the Stranger is relatively indifferent to this consideration. By the same token, Socrates speaks a good deal of himself, and especially of his erotic skills and attachments. This is especially plain in the *Theaetetus*, which stands in sharp contrast to the Stranger's silence on personal matters in the two following dialogues. One point may be mentioned here as representative of the contrast. Socrates claims especially to admire and to seek out Athenian youths of spirit and keenness. The Stranger, on the contrary, is perfectly willing to converse with Athenian youths or with any others, provided that they are patient and will give him no trouble (*Sophist* 217d1–3). Furthermore, the Stranger prefers to deliver monologues on philosophical topics, rather than engage in brief responses or exchanges with an interlocutor. Socrates, as is notorious, claims to be unable to deliver or to follow long speeches, and regularly underlines the importance of arriving at agreement in conversation. In sum, the Stranger has no interest in the philosophical rhetoric described in the *Phaedrus*. This fits nicely with the narrowly technical nature of the positive doctrine he elaborates in the *Sophist* (although it is not quite so appropriate to the Stranger's doctrines as expressed in the *Statesman*).

To this we may add that the Stranger has no apparent interest in the Socratic doctrines of eros and divine madness. He never says that he knows only that he does not know. He communicates a positive doctrine of a highly technical nature. And even where he seems to be practising irony, as for example in the long diaereses, there is no trace of Socrates' urbane playfulness. The somewhat pompous seriousness of the Stranger's discursive style is presumably a sign of his association with the austere Parmenides. It is also surely connected to the fact that Theodorus, Theaetetus, and Young Socrates are all mathematicians, a human type identified by Socrates as extremely serious and lacking in humor. This last point may be illustrated by a consideration of Theaetetus and Theodorus.

In the *Republic*, Socrates says that mathematicians are men who dream that they are awake (VII, 533b6ff). Whatever its other meanings, this ambiguous remark is intended to suggest that mathematicians regard themselves as unusually sober or, in the contemporary idiom, "hard-headed," and certainly so in comparison with playful speculators like Socrates. By referring to this self-estimate as a dream, Socrates indicates its limitations. Plato regularly presents mathematicians in a serious vein and in a context free of praise for eros and madness. Theodorus of Cyrene, a sober man of advanced years and a well-known geometer, who is also Theaetetus's teacher, is said by Socrates not to tell jokes (*Theaetetus* 145c1). According to Theodorus himself, he is not experienced in dialectic, which (like Callicles in the *Gorgias*) he regards as appropriate for youths, not for mature men such as himself and, hence, Socrates (*Theaetetus* 146b1–7).

Theodorus describes Theaetetus as the most remarkable of all his students. The youth is extraordinarily intelligent, as we ourselves can see from his account of his mathematical discovery. What is perhaps most remarkable, furthermore, is that he combines exceptional gentleness and bravery with his capacity to learn easily what would be difficult for others. As Theodorus says, most quick-witted persons have sharp tempers, and are unstable and manic rather than brave. But Theaetetus moves toward learning "smoothly, without stumbling, effectively, and full of gentleness," like a stream of crushed oil (*Theaetetus* 143e4–144b7). In addition, Theaetetus, like Socrates, is ugly, a fact which may have contributed to insulate him from experience in matters of love. In the *Sophist* (222d10), the Stranger says to him, "You have never turned your mind to the kind of hunting practiced by lovers." In general, Theaetetus's nature is a rather good example of the previously noted description of the philosophical nature in the *Republic*. He is apparently even less erotic than the young philosophers in the *Republic*, who are allowed to kiss a beautiful youth as a reward for bravery in battle.

There is another way in which to appreciate the different relation between Socrates and mathematics on the one hand and the Stranger and quasi-mathematical analysis on the other. The Stranger's visit to Athens coincides with the trial, and so shortly precedes the death, of Socrates.[11] When the Stranger is brought into his presence, Socrates suggests that the visitor may be a refuting god rather than a mortal. Presumably refutation is divine because it leads to the replacement of worse with better views. It is better to know that one does not know than to believe falsely that one knows. But this is a general truth; it does not follow that Socrates is in fact refuted by the Stranger. What should be evident from the considerations already presented is that the differences between the Stranger and Socrates amount in dramatic terms to an attempted refutation of the latter by the former.

The difference between Socrates and the Stranger is not one having to do with knowledge of the mathematical τέχναι. To a large extent, it is also true that the Stranger and Socrates share the same principles of λόγος or analytical thinking. It is not even finally correct to say that the Stranger's interpretation of sophistry is radically different, on the essential points, from that of Socrates. This is perhaps best seen in Socrates' treatment of Protagoras in the *Theaetetus* as an "epistemologist" or author of a theory of sense perception. Socrates infers as the main consequence of the Protagorean doctrine that "if all things are changing, every answer to any question whatsoever is correct" (Theaetetus 183a4ff). This conclusion may also be summarized in the thesis that knowledge is sense perception. In other words, perceptions are not, in this view, "images" of unchanging paradigms, but rather the *production* resulting from the collision of the perceiver and external flux. This is the same as the thesis attributed to sophistry by the Stranger, namely, that there are no images, but only originals, and hence no difference between "true" and "false." Socrates differs fundamentally from the Stranger, however, in his regular procedure, followed even in the *Theaetetus*, of attempting to give a political or ethical refutation of sophistry. The epistemological refutation in the *Theaetetus* cannot be sustained for two reasons. First, we need not accept Socrates' interpretation of

11. Cf. Miller (1980), pp. 2, 8. I agree with Miller that the trilogy provides "a distinctively philosophical version of Socrates' trial." I disagree with the initial thrust of his later remark: "Condemned by the nonphilosophical many, he seeks 'philosophical judgement' . . . from the learned few."

the maxim "man the measure." Second, Socrates himself fails to arrive at a discursive account of knowledge, and so is not in a position to distinguish between epistemic truth and falsehood. But none of this need affect the adequacy of his practical criticism of sophistry.

By concentrating upon the attempt to provide a technical or "theoretical" refutation of sophistry, the Stranger implicitly rejects Socrates' recourse to practical refutations. We can state this even more sharply. Socrates was widely regarded by his fellow Athenians as a sophist, and this is surely one of the underlying premises in the accusations of Meletus and Anytus. As we shall see, the Stranger arrives at a definition of sophistry in one of his diaereses that is unmistakably intended to apply to Socrates. Socrates is a "noble sophist," but a sophist nonetheless. The reason for this charge is as follows. Socrates pretends to have no positive doctrines and spends much of his time in aporetic conversations with the future leaders of Athens, conversations which can only deepen their perplexity and leave them prey to the twin wolves of skepticism and cynicism. This behavior vitiates his practical refutation of sophistry, which is not rooted in a positive technical or theoretical analysis. It cannot be verified effectively or publicly by competent observers employing a reliable method. The Stranger's thesis, as I understand it, is thus very close to the contention of Hegel, another devotee of systematic knowledge. Socrates is guilty as charged. Whereas Hegel regarded this guilt as tragic, the Stranger makes no such judgment.

The philosophical indictment of Socrates, then, is that he has betrayed λόγος. Instead of remaining silent, or obeying the Athenian *nomos*, Socrates both states publicly that he has nothing to say and reduces to absurdity the statements of others. Or, he presents us with political fairy-tales, the wishes or prayers of just men, as in the *Republic*. Wishing, however, is no substitute for positive doctrine, just as the praise of mathematics is not a mathematical resolution of the puzzles surrounding being and non-being. How does Socrates reply to this indictment? In the *Sophist* and *Statesman*, he makes no audible reply.[12] In general, though, the reply he gives in the *Apology* is a fair account of his public behavior, as this is visible in the dialogues. Socrates claims to live the philosophical life, even though he lacks knowledge. He does not claim to lack opinions. Since Soc-

12. David Lachterman suggests that the shift in the Stranger's behavior from the *Sophist* to the *Statesman* is due to his recognition of the technical failure of his refutation of sophistry, and so of Socrates. I shall have more to say on this later in this study.

rates knows the mathematical and other τέχναι, this amounts to an assertion that technical or quasi-mathematical knowledge is not coextensive with philosophy. It amounts to a vindication of the wishes or dreams of good men.

At this point, the narrowly technical and the dramatic dimensions of the *Sophist* coincide. We have to determine whether the Stranger's positive doctrine is technically sound, and whether it refutes sophistry in a technical way. It may be that the Stranger is guilty of the reverse of Socrates' crime, namely, of technicism. I close this discussion of the dramatic nature of the *Sophist* with a warning. In the *Statesman*, the Stranger launches a powerful attack, unprecedented in Plato, against τέχνη, which he says must be entirely subordinate to sound judgment or φρόνησις (295a9ff). This looks very much like an acceptance of the position of the "know-nothing" or political Socrates. If anything, the Stranger goes farther than Socrates. If the rules of all the arts may be suspended in accordance with the sound judgment of the philosopher, then positive doctrines are inevitably transformed into rhetorical constructions. Our account of the difference between Socrates and the Stranger is valid for the *Sophist* only. It is a separate task to understand the *Statesman*.[13]

In the *Statesman*, the Stranger follows two distinguishable routes in his analysis of the royal art of politics. The first is technical and productive; it makes use of diaeresis or conceptual analysis, myth or poetry, and the productive metaphor of weaving. The second is practical and nonproductive; it subordinates τέχνη to φρόνησις and brings into prominence the pratical sense of the fitting, or a kind of nonmathematical measure that is akin to sound judgment. Contrary to Socrates' usual procedure, however, the Stranger does not associate sophistry with politics, not even as an inaccurate image of statesmanship. In the *Sophist*, the Stranger does agree with Theaetetus that no one would consult the sophist if he did not promise to teach us how to dispute concerning *nomos* and the entire political sphere (232d1ff). But this point is submerged in a list of topics about which the sophists teach disputation. The list includes virtually everything; we see here that the sophists copy the philosophical concern with the whole. Furthermore, in the course of the dialogue, the Stranger transforms the art of disputation into the art of producing fantasms, a step that leads him in turn to the narrowly technical themes of non-being, being, and true and false statements.

If we compare dialogues like the *Gorgias* and *Protagoras* with the

13. For a step in this direction, see Rosen (1979).

Theaetetus, we see that Socrates employs both theoretical and practical refutations of sophistry. I have already commented on the theoretical refutation in the *Theaetetus*. The doctrine of sense perception attributed by Socrates to Protagoras is one which entails that
man produces being. This interpretation follows from an earlier passage in the same dialogue, where Socrates classifies all earlier thinkers, sophists included, with the sole exception of Parmenides, as
members of the army of the partisans of comprehensive genesis.
According to Socrates, the general of this army is Homer (152d1ff).
In his subsequent analysis of the doctrine of comprehensive genesis,
Socrates shows it to be a materialist cosmogony in which body and
soul, as well as learning and care or practice, are generated from
corporeal elements. This coincides with the interpretation of Protagoras's maxim that man is the measure. Just as sense perception
generates beings, so poetry generates interpretations of human life.
The same point is made in the myth assigned to the great sophist in
the dialogue to which he gives his name: *Protagoras*. According to
this myth, which is told at the instigation of Socrates, the laws are
conventional, like spelling and writing (326c8–9). Justice and the
laws are like "the other human inventions" (τεχνήματα; 327a8–b1).
Protagoras thus contradicts his earlier assertion in the same myth
that "justice and shame" were a gift from Zeus (322c2ff). Perhaps
Zeus supplied man with a sense of justice and shame as protection
against the absence of natural justice and natural laws. More likely,
however, the reference to Zeus is part of Protagoras's "exoteric"
teaching. Protagoras claims that all sophists prior to himself concealed their art in order to avoid the jealousy of the unwise. Among
those whom Protagoras includes as concealed sophists are Homer,
Hesiod, and Simonides, but no philosophers (316d3ff). In the *Theaetetus*, in the same passage in which he names Homer the head of
the army of genesis, Socrates asserts that Protagoras concealed his
true teachings from the many (152c8–10). If the analysis of "man
the measure" presented by Socrates is to be taken as the revelation
of Protagoras's true teaching, then the statement in the myth of
Protagoras that justice and the laws are manmade must be the sophist's actual doctrine.

The upshot of these passages is that Socrates treats sophistry as
productive, just as the Stranger does. But the Stranger identifies
sophistry as a productive τέχνη, whereas Socrates does not. This
emerges most sharply in the *Gorgias*, in which Socrates says that
the sophist and the rhetor are the same, or very nearly the same
(520a6–8). Perhaps the slight difference betweeen them comes to

this: the rhetor (as represented by Gorgias) emphasizes the persuasive power (δύναμις) of his art (see *Gorgias* 455d6ff), whereas the sophist emphasizes his knowledge (cf. Protagoras's reference to his μάθημα at *Protagoras* 318e5, shortly before Socrates attributes to him the political τέχνη). However this may be, Socrates classifies rhetoric and sophistry under the rubric of flattery. Each copies a τέχνη, but is not itself one, because it cannot give a λόγος of the nature of its methods or the cause of each thing under its jurisdiction (*Gorgias* 465a1ff).

Rhetoric copies the τέχνη of (the administration of) justice, whereas sophistry copies the τέχνη of law giving (464b2ff). What Socrates says of rhetoric is presumably also true of sophistry: that it is "an image of a part of politics" (πολιτικῆς μορίου εἴδωλον; 463d1ff), a kind of acting or playing the part of the original it copies (464c7ff), a non-technical "knack" (ἐμπειρία καὶ τριβή) of a soul that is good at guessing, is brave, and is by nature clever at dealing with mortals (463a6–c8). Sophistry, despite its similarity to rhetoric as a "knack," is evidently more comprehensive: like philosophy, it attempts to found the whole by imitating the law-giver. Nevertheless, the knack of the sophist is that of the rhetor. Gorgias defines this "knack" (as Socrates calls it) as political persuasion aiming at freedom for oneself and rule over one's fellow citizens (452d5ff; 454a6ff). Socrates identifies it as the "demiurge" of persuasion (452e9ff).

To sum up, sophistry is productive but nontechnical, and it is an image of the fundamental political art of law giving. For our purposes, the two main consequences of this discussion are as follows. Sophistry, first, is not the imitation of technical propositions in the narrow sense, but of the comprehensive political art; hence, it is an interpretation of the good life. Second, contrary to what is claimed in the *Phaedrus*, rhetoric is not a τέχνη. This is also contrary to the facts, since rhetoric follows procedures that can be taught and that are more systematic than those of many an activity classified as technical by Socrates. Despite Socrates' contention that the rhetorician acts the part of the administrator of justice, one cannot act the part of a rhetorician unless one possesses the art of rhetoric. There is a difference between the art of the actor and the art of the rhetorician: the former must be able to memorize his lines and to deliver them in a convincing manner. But the rhetorician must be able to *produce* his speeches on the basis of what Socrates disparagingly calls his "cleverness" (463a8) at understanding and responding to the many kinds of human soul.

Why does Socrates deny (or alternatively, conceal his agreement with] the view that sophistry is not merely productive, but a τέχνη as well? It should be remembered that this term is employed throughout Plato with a certain amount of equivocation. Sometimes it applies to such humble activities as shoe making and carpentry, sometimes to "practical" arts like politics, and sometimes to "theoretical" arts like geometry and arithmetic. Neither Socrates nor the Stranger distinguishes explicitly between the theoretical and the practical arts. Instead, for both, some arts are productive and some are not. As the *Gorgias* shows, Socrates includes politics under the productive arts. In very general terms, a τέχνη is an activity that follows a method to some definable goal and that may be taught.[14] The method of the τέχνη may thus be separated from its goal or its human value. This, I think, answers our question. A technical problem requires a technical solution.

There is, however, no technical solution to the problems raised by sophistry. If, however, one appeals to practical considerations as well as to the ordinary human perception of morality, it is possible to carry out a double-pronged attack against sophistry. On the one hand, Socrates argues that sophistry is counterproductive or does not make man blessed. On the other hand, he employs rhetorical devices to make us ashamed of surrendering to sophistry. The Stranger, however, takes a different tack. He gives a primarily technical interpretation of sophistry because he is prepared to offer a technical solution to the problems raised by sophistry. In this sense, the Stranger is a prototypical version of the late modern analytical philosopher, who rejects nontechnical formulations of practical or moral judgments as "impressionistic," to say nothing of recourse to the rhetoric of shame. This is the Stranger's refutation of Socrates. The *Statesman* is in effect the Stranger's recantation.

The next step in our preparations for the study of the *Sophist*, I suggest, is to consider paradigmatic versions of the analytically oriented approach to our dialogue. We do so not in any spirit of vulgar polemic but in agreement with the thesis that it is urgent that we understand the Stranger's technical doctrines correctly. Thus far, I have argued that the ontological approach to the *Sophist*, of which the analytical version is in my opinion the most fruitful, errs in disregarding the dramatic context of the narrowly technical passages. Let us now look at the other side of the coin, in order to see whether prevailing views on the technical passages themselves are sound.

---

14. Cf. Kube (1969), p. 16. This is a valuable general study of τέχνη as it is used by Plato and his predecessors.

THE PREDICATIONALISTS

In what follows, I give pride of place to representatives of the analytical school of Plato scholarship. This is advisable for two reasons. First: the Stranger is obviously not a phenomenological ontologist, nor, on the basis of what has preceded, can the phenomenological thesis be sound that Plato had a "general concept of being." However, whereas it should be clear by now that one cannot understand the *Sophist* without taking into account the dialogue as a whole, evidence has been presented to confirm the thesis of a relationship between the Stranger and late modern philosophical analysis. The question is now to determine how far this relation extends. Granted that there are indeed prototypical elements of "Fregeanism" in the Stranger, is he fundamentally concerned with reference and predication? Second: I have learned a great deal from the study of the analytical writings on Plato, and what follows, even where I disagree with the essay under discussion, is intended to acknowledge my indebtedness. One preliminary word: the reader may wonder, as he peruses this section, why there is no treatment of the work of G. E. L. Owen and Michael Frede, perhaps the two most prominent representatives of the "predicationalist" interpretation. The reason is supplied by their prominence. I have decided to postpone my analysis of their studies of the *Sophist* until I come to the relevant section of the text. In this way their views, and my own, can be contrasted more directly with what Plato wrote, while at the same time I adhere to my principle of treating the Platonic text as a unity. The present section, then, is not the only place in which the reader of this study will find a treatment of the secondary literature.

I shall here be concerned primarily with the problem of the forms and their manner of combination. The majority view today is perhaps that the Eleatic Stranger explains formal combination by developing a theory of predication. There are some who continue to deny this, following to one degree or another in the footsteps of F. M. Cornford. Cornford denies that the forms are predicates (Cornford 1935, p. 259).[15] In this vein, he says that "no satisfactory account of the relations of Platonic Forms can be given in terms of Aristotelian logic" (p. 268). Again: "the goal of Dialectic is not to establish propositions ascribing a predicate to all the individuals in a class. The objective is the definition of an indivisible species—a Form—by genus and specific differences" (p. 269). The result of dia-

---

15. Cf. Lafrance (1979), pp. 33–34, for an excellent if brief rebuttal of the analytical reading of the *Sophist* as an exercise in predication.

lectical division is thus an ἄτομον εἶδος "because the process of division can be carried no further" (p. 270). Some of these "uncuttable" or atomic forms constitute what Plato calls "very wide" or "important" forms, of which examples (in Cornford's translation) are: existence, motion, rest, sameness, and difference. These are not categories or *summa genera*, and not a "class, either of entities or predicates" (pp. 275–76). Instead, they are "Forms or Natures" (p. 276). They are very wide because they either "pervade and blend with every other Form and with one another" (such as existence, sameness, and difference) or "divide the field of existents between them, and exclude one another" (such as motion and rest [p. 277]).

In Cornford's account, then, forms are not predicates and dialectic is not logic. Dialectic is ontology, "for the Forms are the realities (ὄντως ὄντα)" (p. 266). These realities are either compatible or incompatible with one another. Cornford calls the relation of compatibility "blending" (p. 278). He thus distinguishes between formal relations and the relation of individuals to a particular form: "this whole account of the blending or mutual participation of Forms cannot be directly applied to the old problem, raised in the *Parmenides*, of the participation of individual things in Forms" (p. 297). A technical distinction between formal combination or participation and the predicative relation between individuals and forms is that "'participation' as between Forms is a symmetrical relation" whereas predication is not (pp. 256–59). It follows from this that the form "being" is not the copula.[16]

On certain general points, Cornford's interpretation seems to me to be either right or on the right track. I agree that forms are not predicates. Since "being" (my *being*) is itself a form, it could not possibly be the copula. The distinction between the formal and the predicative relation is therefore sound, as is the equivalent distinction between ontological combination and the participating of instances within a form. I also agree in part with Cornford, if not necessarily for his reasons, on two further theses. First, the middle section of the *Sophist* "may be understood as showing that Plato, though he still held that the Forms must be changeless, has become aware that he ought not any longer to speak as if the Forms were the whole of Reality" (p. 246). In my own terms, there is a difference between the eidetic alphabet, one element of which is "being" (τὸ ὄν), and the whole, or "being" in the sense of the living and indeed divine, cos-

---

16. One may note parenthetically that, on crucial points, Cornford follows J. Stenzel (1961); cf. pp. 72, 83, 95.

mos (οὐσία). Second, Cornford is right to say that "the whole question" concerning images, "what sort of existence the image has," is not solved in the *Sophist* (pp. 322–23).

My major disagreements with Cornford may be summarized as follows. It will not do to refer to ontological combination as "blending," even though the Stranger himself uses this word at one crucial passage (to be discussed in the text of this study), since this violates the integrity of each unique formal element. I also cannot agree that ontological forms are reached by dialectic in the sense of diaeresis (cf. Stenzel 1961, pp. 72, 101). At least I can find nothing in the *Sophist* to support this conclusion. To the contrary, diaeresis is applied to the sophist, not to "Forms." The forms (letters of the eidetic alphabet) are literally *asserted*; that is, they are taken as self-evident and, in that nontechnical sense, as accessible to intellectual perception. It is a pervasive thesis in the secondary literature that the Stranger arrives at his forms by diaeresis. We shall see that there is no evidence in the text for such a thesis. Cornford, to continue, despite his distinction between combination and predication, takes the "very wide Forms" (his translation of μέγιστα γένη) too widely. Consider page 300: "We can also make statements about individual things. But it is true that every such statement must contain at least one Form—one of those 'common terms' (*Theaet.* 185) which are necessary to all thought or judgement about the objects of direct perception." My view, however, is that the "very wide" forms underlie, or are embedded within, the "deep structure" of all intelligible relations (and hence of all intelligible statements), but do not appear directly in all such relations or statements. As a specific example, "Theaetetus sits" contains no reference to a "very wide" form. On another point, the distinction between logic and ontology, whereas I sympathize with the motives underlying this distinction, I believe it to be based upon too narrow a conception of "logic." Ontological combination is on the one hand a "formal" ingredient in logic (that is, it is implicit in formal structure as such), and on the other, as a relation, it is suitable for logical analysis. Finally, Cornford's view of ontological combination as a symmetrical relation needs to be studied further.

I will comment on this last point by way of an important paper by J. L. Ackrill, "Plato and the Copula: *Sophist* 251–259" (in Vlastos 1971). Ackrill holds that "there are, of course, many different *ways* in which things or persons may be associated or connected, and many of these ways involve nonsymmetrical relationships" (p. 216). Ackrill gives a preliminary example involving the cardinal virtues: justice, courage, wisdom, and temperance are *subordinate* to virtue. But this example, to be pertinent, requires us to extend the μέγιστα γένη in a way that is not sanctioned by the *Sophist*. Nothing is said by the Stranger to suggest either that there are atomic forms corresponding to the virtues or that his own examples of such forms can be classified as superordinate and subordinate. Let us therefore consider instead Ackrill's analysis of statements incorporating the Stranger's own examples.

Ackrill contends that "κοινωνεῖν followed by the genitive (e.g., θατέρου) is used where the fact being asserted is that some εἶδος is (copula) such-and-such (e.g., different from . . .), that is, it is used to express the fact that one concept *falls under* another. The dative construction, on the other hand, occurs in highly general remarks about the connectedness of εἴδη, where no definite fact as to any particular pair of εἴδη is being stated" (p. 220). In other words, the dative construction with a combining verb does express the general symmetrical notion of "connectedness," whereas the genitive construction does not.

However, Ackrill's grammatical distinction is based upon a philosophical interpretation of the relations in question; one cannot infer or validate the interpretation from the grammatical distinction. We need therefore to consider specific statements. Ackrill takes two of Cornford's own examples. The first is (in Cornford's translation) "motion exists." Ackrill rightly objects as follows. If the relation between the two forms here is that of "blending," with no reference to the copula, then absurdity follows: "For if 'Motion blends with Existence' means 'Motion exists', then 'Existence blends with Motion' must mean 'Existence moves'" (p. 217). I have already noted that Cornford's use of "blending" is unfortunate, although not for the same reason as is averred by Ackrill. My main reply to Ackrill is that he has not correctly translated the Stranger's statement, or at least the technical form of a statement like the one he cites. "Motion exists" must first be rephrased as "change is." Let us adopt the convention, to be used throughout this study, of italicizing English words that designate forms introduced by the Stranger. The correct analysis of this statement is then: the form *change* combines with the form *being*. There is no copula here, and the result is a symmetrical relation. Furthermore, no absurdity follows, since it is perfectly correct to say that the form *being* combines with the form *change*. The real problem here is another one: we do not know what such a "combination" means, and this is perhaps what led Ackrill and many others to take it to mean "predication."

We might symbolize "change is" as "*change* * *is*," where " * " designates ontological concatenation, but this does nothing to provide a definition of "concatenation." I can bring out another aspect of the obscurity of the Stranger's theory by considering Ackrill's second example. Ackrill cites "Motion is different from Rest," which he agrees is equivalent to "Rest is different from Motion." However, he provides a "dialectical" analysis of the first statement as follows: "Motion communicates with Difference from Rest." He adds that if "communicates with" stands for a symmetrical relation, then "we must be prepared to say that 'Motion communicates with Difference from Rest' is equivalent to 'Difference from Rest communicates with Motion.'" Taking the symmetrical communion as between motion and difference from rest, we arrive finally at the equivalence of "Motion is different from Rest" and "Difference from Rest moves" (p. 218).

In the first place, Ackrill packs two forms into the expression "Difference from Rest." It is not the case that motion, a unique form, communicates with difference from rest, a second unique form. The correct analysis is as follows: the form *change* combines with the form *being*, as do the forms *otherness* and *rest*; furthermore, *change* combines with *otherness* with respect to *rest*. The puzzle here is in the expression "with respect to," implied by the "from" in Ackrill's "different from. . . ." What does "from" mean here? Every form is "different from" every other form. But in order to express the difference between two forms, we need to refer to a relation of four forms. The third form, *being*, may be disregarded in this context. There is then no problem about symmetry. Just as *change* combines with *otherness* with respect to *rest*, so too *rest* combines with *otherness* with respect to *change*. What we want to know, nevertheless, is how we can see the "otherness" of "change" *with respect to* "rest." Given the complex web of formal relations, how can we pick out the pertinent combination in each case? I believe the answer is, by intellectual perception. Certainly no answer of any kind is offered by the Stranger. But whether or not my suggestion concerning intellectual perception is sound, there is no reason to interpret "combines . . . with respect to" as a predicative relation or, specifically, as "partaking of" *qua* "subordinate to." So we still require some theoretical explanation, if any exists, of the linguistic data gathered by Ackrill.

Ackrill is a distinguished representative of the view that there is a doctrine of predication in the later Platonic dialogues. He is also a distinguished Aristotle scholar, and one is tempted to infer that he has read Plato through Aristotelian spectacles. In any case, I find myself in closer agreement with that great opponent of the Aristotelian interpretation of Plato, H. Cherniss, at least with respect to the five examples of pure forms in the *Sophist*. Cherniss says: "the relation of the ideas to one another is that of implication or compatibility and its opposite, not that of principle and derivative or of whole and part" (1944, p. 46). And although there is no application of diaeresis in the *Sophist* to a pure form (an "idea" in Cherniss's terminology), Cherniss may be correct in other cases in saying that diaeresis "appears to be only an aid to reminiscence of the idea" (p. 47). It should be noted here, however, that whereas the μέγιστα γένη explicitly identified in the *Sophist* are (as I shall argue) "pure forms" in the sense that they are not divisible into constituent forms, there is no reason to assume that this holds true for *all* uses of εἶδος, γένος, or ἰδέα in the Platonic corpus. I also sympathize with the statement of R. E. Allen (in Allen 1967, p. 46) that Plato's forms constitute "a theory of predication without predicates." In his exposition of this thesis, Allen is primarily concerned to refute the charge of self-predication levelled against the forms. He distinguishes between "derivative designation" (something is *F qua* "causally dependent upon *the F*") and "primary designation" ("*F*" is used as a synonym of "the *F* itself" and "*F*-ness"). So "to state that *F*-ness is *F* is to state an identity" (p. 46). Allen (in my view, rightly) says that the forms are not commutative universals, but originals (or standards). Thus, particulars resemble forms as mirror-images do a real object (pp. 53ff). However, this leaves unexplained the relation between original and image, as well as the mode of being of an image.

My objection to the predicationist theory is directed primarily to the failure by its representatives to distinguish between atomic forms and the parts of speech in true and false statements. The atomic forms are not predicates; but this does not exclude the normal use of what we now call "predication" in the construction of statements about empirical objects or events. It is of course entirely plausible to assume that there must be a connection between the discussion of the combination and dissociation of pure forms, on the one hand, and the analysis of false statement, on the other. However, one of the cruces of interpretation is to determine precisely what this connection is. When the Stranger turns to false statement, the only example he gives is that of the directly disconfirmable assertion "Theaetetus flies." There are no atomic forms in this assertion, and the attempt to assimilate its elements into forms of any kind, whether atomic or compound, leads to serious difficulties, and indeed, to absurdity. We know that "Theaetetus flies" is false by looking at Theaetetus, not at forms, whether singly or in combination.

Ackrill's paper represents what one may call the "ordinary-language" approach to the sense of the forms in the *Sophist*. My next example, although still drawing upon the resources of natural-language grammar, turns upon a technical distinction which utilizes the machinery of logic and set theory. In "An Ambiguity in the *Sophist*" (Vlastos 1973), G. Vlastos discerns two kinds of predication in the central passages of the dialogue, which he holds are confused by Plato. According to Vlastos (pp. 273–74), we may distinguish between what he calls "ordinary" and "Pauline" predication. Ordinary predication is defined as follows:

$$B \text{ is }_{pp} A \; = \;_{df} B \; \epsilon \; A.$$

In ordinary predication, an adjective A is predicated of an abstract property B. Hence A is true of the class or abstract property B, but not of the instances of B. The second kind of predication is defined as follows:

$$B \text{ is }_{pp} A \; =_{df} N\{(x)[(x \; \epsilon \; B) \rightarrow (x \; \epsilon \; A)]\}.$$

N is Vlastos's symbol for the necessity-operator of modal logic. In Pauline predication, the adjective A is predicated necessarily of B's instances, if there are any, but not of B. Hence the definition for Pauline predication may be rewritten as:

$$B \text{ is }_{pp} A \; =_{df} N \; (B \subset A).$$

After defending the validity of the distinction, despite the fact that Plato does not mention it (pp. 281ff), Vlastos goes on to indict the author of the *Sophist* of a logical confusion. "We are in the presence of a writer whom we know to be scrupulously truthful," Vlastos says (though he does not explain how we know this, nor for that matter, if we did, how we would reconcile it with our view of the writer of a drama, who must attribute views to imaginary characters). Since Plato does not say that he knows the ambiguity, whereas if he did know it he would see that a sentence he calls false is in one sense true, we may infer that he uses sentences which can be analyzed in terms of the above-defined uses of predication, intending in each case just one of those meanings, "utterly unaware of the alternative reading" (p. 283).

I will ignore Vlastos's theses on Plato's honesty and his reference to the Eleatic Stranger as "Plato's mouthpiece" (p. 311). My sole concern here is with the accuracy of his technical analysis of the passages in question, which occur in the *Sophist* at 252d and 256b. Vlastos sees in each of these passages the assertion, said to be false, that "motion is resting." According to Vlastos, at 252 the (denied) assertion that "motion is resting" is in fact an instance of Pauline predication, and so is false, because it attributes "rest" to the instances of the form "motion" (pp. 274, 278–79). We should note that the assertion, if it is made at all, is contained in a speech by Theaetetus, not by "Plato's mouthpiece," as a refutation of the general claim that all things have the power to combine with each other (πάντα ἀλλήλοις . . . δύναμιν ἔχειν ἐπικοινωνίας). If the claim were true, Theaetetus points out, then "change itself would come entirely to a stand, and rest on the contrary would itself move, were they to come together with each other" (κίνησίς τε αὐτὴ παντάπασιν ἵσταιτ᾽ ἂν καὶ στάσις αὖ πάλιν αὐτὴ κινοῖτο, εἴπερ ἐπιγιγνοίσθην ἐπ᾽ ἀλλήλοιν). The Stranger then asks: "But is this impossible by the greatest necessities, that change should stand still and rest should change?" (. . . κίνησίν τε ἵστασθαι καὶ στάσιν κινεῖσθαι;). Theaetetus replies, "How could it not be?" (252d2–11).

In this passage, there is no discussion of the theory of forms; Vlastos in fact explains "itself" in the passage as not specifying the forms motion and rest (pp. 279ff). I am not sure that he is right about this, since both Theaetetus and the Stranger could be thinking of what will be defined technically as forms, even though they have not reached that level of explicitness. However, the passage is extremely difficult, and the sense of "itself" is not crucial to my analysis of Vlastos's procedures. If we read over the exact wording of the passage, we see that there is no reference to predication. The general claim under inspection speaks of a δύναμις ἐπικοινωνίας, a "power to combine." The only phrase in the balance of the passage that refers to this power is ἐπιγιγνοίσθην ἐπ᾽ ἀλλήλοιν, "were they to come together." And the passage as a whole makes it clear that "they" (motion itself and rest itself) are "things" (included in πάντα), not grammatical terms, like predicates. How we speak about "things" is one thing; how "things" come together is another. There is no explicit statement in this passage that "motion is resting." But I grant at once that it is important to know how we are to understand our statements about whether "motion itself" combines or comes together with, or fails to come together with, "rest itself." One cannot, however, infer a theory of predication from the concatenations and separations of "things." It is therefore both premature and beside the point to ask whether "motion is resting" is a sample of ordinary or Pauline predication.

Nevertheless, let us now allow the statement "motion is resting" as a sound inference from our passage, and ask ourselves which type of predication it illustrates, and with what consequences. If this is a

case of Pauline predication, then, by Vlastos's formal definition,
"—— is resting" defines a set A, of which the set B, "motion," is a
proper subset. But this produces no formal contradiction, since it
merely tells us that all members of B are also members of A, or that
whatever moves also rests. This could very well be true, contrary to
Vlastos's interpretation. On the other hand, suppose that "motion
is resting" is an instance of ordinary predication. By Vlastos's formal definition, the statement then means that the adjective "resting" is predicated of the set "motion." This, as Vlastos himself points
out (p. 276), is true. If then either Theaetetus or the Stranger uses or
implies the statement "motion is resting" at 252 (and at 256), in just
one of its possible meanings, how are we to decide which reading is
correct, especially since Vlastos assumes that Plato was unaware of
the distinction? Vlastos opts for Pauline predication, but as I have
just shown, that does not guarantee falsehood.

We turn now to 256b. Here the Stranger is indeed discussing his
doctrine of formal elements. He asks, "if change itself partook
somehow of rest, would it not be absurd to call it standing itself?"
(Οὐκοῦν κἂν εἰ πῃ μετελάμβανεν αὐτὴ κίνησις στάσεως, οὐδὲν ἂν ἄτο-
πον ἦν στάσιμον αὐτὴν προσαγορεύειν;). I note that the denial of
"motion is resting" does not occur in this passage, either. Perhaps
more important, Vlastos assumes without argument that "partook
of" means "has as a predicate." Again, there is no discussion here of
the parts of speech, but precisely of pure forms. And since "change
itself" is without dispute an atomic form, then change cannot "partake of" the atomic form "rest" by including the form *rest* in its
own formal structure. To do this would not be to receive an "abstract property" (in Vlastos's terminology), but to lose its nature or
atomic simplicity, and thus (absurdly) to become instead the form
"standing itself," or *rest*. So, the Stranger does not say, and cannot
be taken as implying, that the assertion "'motion' is a proper subset
of 'rest'" is false. As I noted above, this assertion might be true. The
main point, however, is surely this: to predicate A of B is to say one
of two things. Either A is an accidental property of B or A is an
essential property of B. (The fact that contemporary philosophers of
language may not accept the distinction between accidental and
necessary predicates is irrelevant, but one may note that modal logicians normally do make this distinction.) However, at the level of
pure formal combination, there cannot be any accidental predication, because there are no contingent combinations. To make a necessary predication is here to attribute a complex structure to what
has been defined as entirely simple in its nature. *Change* could not

assimilate *rest* without being dissolved (as a form). But the subset relation employed by Vlastos does not carry out this dissolution.

I have discussed Vlastos's paper at length as a representative of studies in which concepts from logic and set theory are applied directly to the task of explicating Platonic doctrines.[17] Needless to say, if one proceeds in this manner, one will quite naturally discover a theory of predication in the transformed Greek text. I have also disagreed with the manner in which Vlastos arrives at his English formulations of what is being said in the text, hence too with his assumption that one can disregard entirely the dramatic form of the dialogue in attempting to understand Plato's teaching. The technical apparatus in Vlastos's paper is of course relatively simple, but this enabled us to make a reasonably close analysis of the steps involved. There are numerous studies of Plato in which much heavier formal machinery is applied to the Platonic texts, and I cannot here provide comparably detailed analyses of such works. Instead, I want to make some general remarks, which follow directly from what has been said about Vlastos's paper, and then to analyze crucial passages from a book-length study of "conceptual realism" as it is presumably illustrated in Plato, Aristotle, and Russell (to say nothing of Cantor and Frege). What is of importance is whether it is legitimate to analyze the Stranger's discussion of pure forms in the language of set theory and the predicate calculus. What I deny is that set theory or quantification logic is an appropriate tool in this carefully defined task. These tools may or may not be useful in explicating other aspects of the themes of the Platonic dialogues. Certainly the first step is to state clearly, in English or any other natural language, what these themes are.

I have discussed elsewhere some of the technical problems that arise from the assumption that contemporary mathematical analysis is the best, and theoretically neutral, manner in which to dissect any philosophical doctrine (cf. Rosen 1980). Here I will limit myself to points that are immediately pertinent to the theme at hand. I note first that if the forms are predicates, then *being* must be as well. This, however, goes directly contrary to the standard interpretation of "being" as "existence," and hence as the existential quantifier.[18]

17. Cf. Cantor (1932), p. 165, n. 2. Cantor here takes his sets to be akin to the "mixed" sets in the *Philebus*. However, see also note 19 below.

18. As the term "standard" is intended to convey, I am here disregarding free logics, substitutional quantification, and other deviations, now receiving much attention, from the main consensus among analytical philosophers and mathematical logicians from Frege and Russell to Quine. I take no sides in this controversy. For further discussion, see Orenstein (1978) and Williams (1981).

The theoretical conclusion that being is not a first-level predicate is in fact *built into* modern logic and set theory. It is not a self-evident metaphysical truth, and it is nowhere asserted by Plato. Recourse to logical analysis of the theory of forms thus constitutes at worst a flagrant self-contradiction, and at best a procedure that requires elaborate theoretical defense.

Let us come at this problem from a slightly different angle. Predicate logic and set theory incoporate three main senses of "is": identity, predication, and existence. The form *being* is not responsible for what we call "self-identity"; the latter follows from the form *sameness*. The statement "whatever exists, is the same as itself" would have to be rewritten, if it could be expressed at all in the Stranger's theory, as "$\forall x \ (Bx \rightarrow Sx)$, but the variable x ranges over instances of forms, not forms. Differently stated, universal quantification makes no existential commitment to an x that is B and S (in the immediately preceding case), but it is nevertheless true that if any x's did exist, they could not be forms *qua* atomic letters, or elements in the Stranger's formal alphabet. One might be tempted to say the opposite, and thus establish the so-called paradox of self-predication. But this paradox cannot be applied to the pure forms of the *Sophist*, regardless of what is the case elsewhere, since no form can combine with itself. Furthermore, to allow forms as values of x would give rise to nonsensical cases like *"change is being* implies that *change is sameness"* as a true instantiation of the above universal formula. One cannot predicate a predicate of a predicate. In short, the uniqueness of each form makes it impossible to quantify over them. One might conceivably be tempted to try an existential formula like this:

$$\exists ! x (Fx \ \& \ Bx \ \& \ Ix)$$

or "there exists a unique x such that x is a pure form, x exists, and x is identical with (= the same as) itself." We have already seen, however, that the existence of the objects represented by x cannot be the same as the existence (actually, the being) represented by *being*. To say that one form takes *being* as a predicate is thus a confusion of types. In sum, if we define x at the outset as ranging over forms, then either forms are predicates or they are not. If they are, we cannot write Bx. If they are not, then we cannot write anything.

Considerations of this sort, which could be multiplied, show that *being* is not representable by identity, predication, or existence. It is worth noting separately that the combination of *being* and *sameness* cannot be written as $B \in S$ without using the doctrine of predication, and also that such a designation transforms the pure forms of the Stranger into extensional concepts. I note that a unique individual cannot be an element in another unique individual. Similarly, $B \subseteq S$ goes beyond the Stranger's instructions, because it makes B ingredient to the conceptual structure of S, and this is wrong. In other words, whereas it may be true that the elements of B (existing things, other than forms, which derive their existence by way of ultimate combination with *being*) are also elements of S (things that are the same as themselves, thanks to ultimate combination with *sameness*), B is still not a subset of S. I say "it may be true" that elements of B are elements of S. Strictly speaking, of course, this cannot be true, since in fact *being* and *sameness*, as unique elements, have no elements themselves. The language of set theory, like that of quantificational logic, is the wrong language to apply here.

I do not go so far as to say that the theory of formal elements cannot be formalized at all. Perhaps, with sufficient ingenuity, one might devise an algebraic structure that would use as a basis the alphabet of pure forms, and as the operation, concatenation. For example, one theorem in such an algebra might be

$$B \star S = B.$$

We should note, however, that $\star$ cannot be a binary operator, since *otherness* will not combine with one form only. Another possibility for formalizing the Stranger's theory might be some type of combinatory, or quantifier-free, logic. However, it is not my intention to explore these possibilities. My intention is to understand, as carefully as possible, the Stranger's doctrines. Since nothing is said in the *Sophist* to warrant the view that the Stranger conceives of his forms as "formalizable" (in the modern sense of the term), I leave this investigation to others.

There can be no doubt at all that Plato was strongly influenced by mathematics in the development of his philosophical views. The Stranger's conception of discursive thinking is governed by three more or less explicit principles (enunciated in the initial formulation of the problem of talking about non-being), which are either the same as, or very similar to, principles of mathematical reasoning. I call these the principles of enumerability ("to be is to be countable or nameable"), reference ("a significant term is the name of an object"), and noncontradiction. This is not the place to go into detail about the nature of these principles, but one has only to state them to see that, for the Stranger, mathematics is the prime example of λόγος in the sense of ἐπιστήμη. No effort to untangle the threads of the discussion in the *Sophist* can be adequate if it does not consider the implications of mathematics for Plato's teachings. Such a consideration, however, can hardly start with the consequences of assumptions underlying modern logic and set theory as technical tools; that is, we cannot begin by reading these assumptions into the Platonic text.

Here is one example of what I mean. The reduction of geometry to algebra in modern mathematics may encourage the temptation to overlook the difference between geometry and arithmetic as paradigms of rationality in Plato. The specific visibility of a geometrical form is not captured by its Cartesian coordinates. In other words, logic and set theory beg the question of the ontological and phenomenological nature of the forms. And, once this nature has been reinterpreted as sets or predicates, the branches of mathematics just named allow us to study, or to believe that we are studying, the *relations* of the elements, but not the elements themselves. To use the crucial Platonic word, we are not studying the *natures* of the elements, because we no longer believe in the Platonic doctrine of nature. This shift in focus, together with the plain fact of the importance of mathematics for Plato, leads many scholars to overlook the difference between Plato's concerns and those of Cantor, Frege, and Russell. It is supposed either that the concerns were in the two cases the same, or else that Plato's concerns can be clarified, made sense of, by restating them in terms of the concerns of Cantor, Frege, and Russell. This supposition leads to slovenly thinking in both directions. For example, the designation "Platonism" is used too frequently to designate the philosophy of mathematics of Cantor, Frege, and Russell, when "Kantianism" might often be better applied.[19] Conversely, Plato's problems are replaced by one version or another of modern problems. As an example of this kind of interpretation, I cite the massive treatise by R. Carls, *Idee und Menge* (Carls 1974).

---

19. Consider the following passage from Dauben (1979), which first quotes Cantor on the power set as "a definite set, comprised of nothing but units, which exists in our mind as an intellectual copy or projection of the given set $\overline{M}$," and goes on to say, apropos the development in Cantor's thought: "In dropping all reference to concrete objects, a certain homogeneity of presentation was achieved by defining sets as collected elements of intuition or thought. There was no longer any attempt to differentiate between the concrete reality of the numbers of sets on the one hand, and the intellectual or abstract reality of sets and their corresponding transfinite numbers on the other. At last Cantor accorded sets and transfinite numbers equal status as mutually existing in the intellect." And again: "If all the elements of his set theory existed on the same level, with the same reality as thoughts and images of the mind, then there was no dependence upon real objects of any sort" (p. 171).

In its historical comprehensiveness and attempt to assimilate Greek thought into modern terminology, Carls's work goes beyond any work in English known to me. The main thread of the book is a detailed analysis of the formal doctrines of Plato and Aristotle on the one hand and Russell on the other (with many references to other nineteenth- and twentieth-century "platonists"). From our own standpoint, the crucial purpose of Carls is to establish a similarity between the Greek and early modern doctrines, which he jointly calls "conceptual realism" or "extreme realism," and to study the paradoxes which this realism engenders, as a basis for a more adequate categorial ontology. Thus a pivotal thesis in Carls's investigation is that Platonic forms are classes or abstract objects, defined intensionally as "wholes" rather than as "alls" or "sums" (p. 62). He takes it for granted, however, that the relation between any two of these objects is class inclusion or exclusion, and so the epsilon relation, of set theory. Thus "being" and *being* are understood indiscriminately as ϵ. This, however, leads immediately to the identification of two problems in the Platonic doctrine.

First, an extensional criterion is needed for determining the identity of abstract objects corresponding to predicative expressions (p. 63). In this way, Carls unwittingly shows us that he makes no distinction between atomic forms like *being* or *change*, and forms like "—— is an equilateral triangle" (to use his own example). Even further, he collapses the difference between the ontological and phenomenological nature of an equilateral triangle and the predicate "—— is an equilateral triangle." Second, Carls identifies two paradoxes in conceptual realism, corresponding to the sharing of one form in another and the membership of an instance in a class (= form). He collapses these two paradoxes into one, however, by treating them both in the language of sets. In other words, the "sharing" in both cases is designated by the set-theoretical ϵ-relation (pp. 100–02, 108–09, 112–14).

This procedure already makes it impossible to distinguish the doctrines of sharing and participating, as well as to identify the problems peculiar to each. Thus, Carls notes that the ϵ-relation between concrete individuals and abstract entities can itself be reified to an abstract entity, such that other abstract entities can again stand to the reified ϵ-relation *in* the ϵ-relation. But this paradox arises from Carls's assumption that the ϵ-relation correctly mirrors both ontological relations in Plato, one between forms, and the other between a form and its instances. So far as I can see, Carls does not consider the alternative possibility, namely, that not all forms are, or correspond to, predicates, and therefore that two distinct relations or senses of "being" are at stake. Carls also poses a paradox for Plato at the level of pure forms or ideas. Ideas share neither in their opposites nor in themselves. Therefore (and I here simplify Carls's notation to bring out the main point sharply) the following situation obtains. Let I_1 and $\neg I_1$ stand for an idea and its opposite, respectively. We then have:

$$I_1 \notin \neg I_1$$
which entails
$$I_1 \in I_1$$

by the law of excluded middle (pp. 113ff).

Again, it is easy to see that this version of paradox cannot apply to atomic forms, since they are simple elements which cannot be members of themselves. Second, there is no atomic form corresponding to what Carls calls "the opposite" of a given form. *Rest*, to take the most plausible case, is not the negation of *change*, but a totally distinct form. It is true that *rest* is not an element in the essential structure of *change*. However, this has nothing to do with their concatenation, which proceeds by way of joint combination with *otherness*, and not via syntactical operations such as negation together with the epsilon relation of set theory. There is, indeed, one problem in the Stranger's doctrine that may be inferred from Carls's analysis, but which cannot be symbolized in his formal language. Each form other than *being* derives its "being" through combination with *being*. But *being* cannot combine with itself. Similarly, each form other than *sameness* derives its sameness through combination with *sameness*. Yet *sameness* cannot combine with itself. How do we account for the "being" of *being* and the "sameness" of *sameness*? If the reply is, via self-predication, this is again a reading-into the text of a doctrine for which there is no evidence. But further, if the "sameness"of *sameness* derives from "self-predication," why not say that *change* may be self-predicated so as to attribute "change" to the pure form? The thesis of self-predication cannot be applied on an *ad hoc* basis. If it holds for one form, it must hold for them all. But the Stranger clearly does not believe that the forms change. Even if we argue that the formal relations are revealed to us by grammar, there is nothing ungrammatical about the expression "*change* changes." But the grammatical soundness of the statement turns upon the difference in kind between the name of a form and a verb designating the power of that form. We must then decide on semantical grounds whether the statement in question is true. And

this requires us to decide whether the thesis of self-predication is
true; that is, whether it is asserted, intended, or implied by the
Stranger. I see no evidence to support any of these possibilities. But
that does not resolve the problem indicated above.

There is another problem implicit in the Stranger's doctrine, but
not one which I have found discussed in the secondary literature.
The thesis of ontological combination provides us with a strong motive for claiming that if *being* (for example) derives its sameness via
the form *sameness*, then despite their distinctness to intellectual
perception, their ontological condition is not just that of a combination, but of a *blend*. In this case, perhaps, *being*, as an ingredient
in the blend, could derive its "being"through what it contributes to
the blend as a whole. (Note that this is not an impredicative definition, since we are not defining *being*, but suggesting that it shares
in its own power by way of the application of that power to a blend
in which it is contained.) More plausibly, the "being" of the blend
would have to be understood in some other way, perhaps as *Wirk-
lichkeit* ("actuality") in the Hegelian sense (of which *Sein* ["being"]
is a dimension or ingredient). In other words, we are led, not to a
doctrine of predication, but to a *dialectical logic*.

I am not suggesting that Plato was a proto-Hegelian, nor am I attempting to blur the difference between the usual Platonist and Hegelian senses of "dialectic."[20] The question here is of the philosophical implications intrinsic to the Stranger's doctrines as he develops
them. No one has ever perceived, or defined discursively, the pure
form *being*, the existential sense of "is," or the existential quantifier, in and by itself, apart from all other formal elements. We begin
with a blend of heterogeneous "looks," which, despite their hetero-
geneity, are defined via their difference from each other, as well as
through their self-identity or intrinsic sameness. This is as true of
cognitive and sensuous perception as it is of language. Perceptions
of individual elements occur by a concentration upon one "look" or
another. But this process of concentration itself depends upon the

20. In this connection, the following passage from Hegel is of interest: "Wir haben
bereits vorläufig bemerkt, dass der Begriff der wahren Dialektik ist, die notwendige
Bewegung der reinen Begriffe aufzuzeigen, nicht als ob sie dieselben dadurch in Nichts
aufloste, sondern eben das einfach ausgedruckte Resultat ist, dass sie diese Bewegung
sind und das Allgemeine eben die Einheit solcher entgegengesetzten Begriffe." [We
have already remarked provisionally that the concept of true dialectic is to point out
the necessary excitation of the pure concepts, not as if the excitation were to dissipate
the concepts thereby in nothingness; but, indeed, the simple expressed result is that the
concepts are this excitation, and the universal is indeed the unity of such juxtaposed
concepts.] Hegel adds that Plato does not have full consciousness of the fact that
dialectic in this sense is present in his dialogues. Hegel (1962), pp. 60–61; cf. p. 81.

presence of the given "look" within a web of relations, that is, upon its place within a "one differentiating itself." And exactly the same is true of language.[21]

The Stranger's own metaphor for his pure forms is that of an alphabet. This metaphor raises a number of problems, of which I mention here just one: an alphabet is itself a dialectical structure in that it is a unity of differences. The discreteness of the letters of an alphabet as symbols is posterior to the articulation of the continuum of sound, which is, as sound, self-identical throughout its elements, yet differentiated in them. Indeed, the discreteness of letters in an alphabet precludes the interpretation of "spelling" or ontological combination as predication. When we take the letters c, a, and t, and combine them into the word "cat," *we do not predicate one letter of the other two.* The letter c does not acquire the property of "a-ness" through such a combination. But it also makes no sense to think of c, a, and t as ontologically discrete, self-subsistent and self-intelligible entities. Disregarding here the conventional aspect of any alphabet, the fact is that individual letters are visible as individual, and as letters, only via their function within the alphabet taken as a differentiated unity.

We do not put the world together from discrete formal elements, but neither do we simply take the world apart into discrete formal elements. At no time, whether in our everyday experience or in our philosophical analyses, are we ever in the presence of discrete formal elements, except by an act of concentration or abstraction (or intentionality), which itself functions only thanks to the self-maintenance of the network of formal combinations. Formal elements are not intelligible "in themselves." Why then should we not argue that a careful and detailed analysis of the Stranger's doctrine, however odd or even repugnant it may be to dedicated Platonists, leads or points toward the inevitability of a dialectical logic in something like the Hegelian sense of the term?

It is easy, and false, to reply that such a dialectical logic would destroy mathematics, or that it is refuted by the success of mathematics. Mathematics as an analytical, or even more generally, as a rational, procedure functions at a different level from dialectical logic. Mathematics "works" precisely because it ignores dialectical implications; that is, it works because it does not think through the question of its own ontological nature. It is in this sense, and this sense alone, that one could say that mathematics is ontologically neutral.

21. On this point, cf. the paper by Peck (1952).

In my opinion, the ontological implications of mathematics—that
is, of the entire process of formalism, and not simply of the values
of the variables under quantification—are inconclusive. They point
us in more than one direction, which is one reason why we have
diverse "philosophies of mathematics," in the contemporary sense
of the term. I do not believe that any thorough, rigorous deduction
or argument, whether immanent or transcendental, will ever persuade us to accept either a dialectical or a nondialectical ontology.
None of this justifies our ignoring the fundamental problem, however, and least of all when we are studying a seminal work like Plato's
Sophist.

It is when we think through the implications of the patent importance of mathematics for Plato that we are led to consider the dialectical consequences of the nature of formal intelligibility. One
should not rule out the possibility that the true nature of Platonism
is to *avoid* deciding between a dialectical and a nondialectical ontology. We are able to entertain this possibility when we read each
dialogue as a whole, as a drama about human beings, not simply as
a treatise on semantics or epistemology.

To be still more specific, we must not commit the error of supposing that mathematics is the sole model of reasonableness in Plato.
I say "reasonableness" in order to make a distinction between the
rationality of ἐπιστήμη and the sound judgment or intelligence of
φρόνησις (which even in Plato is often used to designate what Aristotle later codifies as "practical intelligence"). Plato was not Leibniz, let alone Rudolf Carnap. As an influential example of the thesis
with which I am here disagreeing, I cite K. Gaiser's *Platons ungeschriebene Lehre* (Gaiser 1963). This study is filled with interesting
and suggestive material, but its pivotal assumption about the nature
of Plato's philosophy appears to me to be wrong. Gaiser argues that
the fundamental presupposition of the whole Platonic philosophy is
the analogy between the total construction of reality and the special
domain of mathematics (p. 22). According to Gaiser, the soul, like
the objects of mathematics, exhibits the whole; thus mathematical
structure and psychic capacity (νόησις and αἴσθησις) are two aspects
of one and the same thing (p. 25). Gaiser thus claims that, for Plato,
there is a mathematical model, not just for the separate domain of
being of ideal forms, but for the total construction of reality (pp. 49–
50). If this is true, then human phenomena, and hence the soul, are
either mathematizable or irrational; they are not merely nonepis-
temic, but are incapable of being studied reasonably. Among the many
problems this raises for Gaiser, I note his view that philosophy is for

Plato marked by historicity. Would Gaiser claim that the intelligible structure of historicity is mathematical?

It is plain enough from the myths in the dialogues that Plato did not regard it as possible to construct a mathematical model of the whole. Gaiser's thesis depends, other things aside, on his understanding of Plato's unwritten or "esoteric" teaching. I want to say only one thing about this view. It stands or falls on the interpretation of the Platonic dialogue. These are dramas or philosophical poems, and some of the most important speeches in these dialogues are myths. According to Gaiser, Plato's esoteric teaching is not different from that of the dialogues, but more systematic and exact (p. 8). Perhaps so. But is a systematic and exact interpretation of a myth, and indeed of a drama, a mathematical λόγος? Gaiser, of course, does not reduce mathematics to set theory and the predicate calculus. Nevertheless, the paradigm of a mathematical model of the total structure of the cosmos is simply not adequate to the phenomena.

I close this section with one last point. As the reader will see, I claim that the diaereses in the *Sophist* cannot be understood as instances of mathematical or quasi-mathematical reasoning, but instead as constituting a kind of phenomenology of everyday life. They serve to make vivid the problem of the sophist, not to provide us with a scientific definition of the sophist. Two of the most interesting papers I have seen on the nature of diaeresis are by J. M. E. Moravcsik (both published in 1973). I quote here from the more recent study, in *Exegesis and Argument*.

> To begin with, the divisions provide us with an anatomy for definitions, or at least unique characterizations, of the Forms. The method not only answers the question, what are definitions about? but also the question, what configurations make a definition true or adequate? At the same time, in so far as we find Forms as parts of several other Forms, or as an entity that can have other Forms as parts, the uniqueness of each Form can be expressed by locating it on a conceptual map that traces the interrelationships. [p. 326]

Now the only diaeresis that occurs in the *Sophist* is that of the sophist. Moravcsik must then believe that there is a form corresponding to the sophist, that is, to sophistry, as well as to the productive and acquisitive arts. I will not quarrel with this thesis here. Instead, I note that the diaereses are manifold, internally inconsistent, and mutually exclusive. It remains to be seen whether these attributes are part of the Stranger's pedagogical rhetoric, designed to prepare

Theaetetus for an ever deeper understanding of the nature of the sophist, or whether they testify to the undefinability of the sophist. Only a detailed analysis of the text will allow us to choose between these alternatives. But one thing can be said immediately. It is surely puzzling, if Moravcsik's account of diaeresis is correct, that in the entire corpus of Plato, the only two extensive applications of diaeresis are to human types: the sophist and the statesman. Despite the many positive references to diaeresis scattered throughout the dialogues, not even in the *Philebus* do we find any examples of diaereses leading to definitions of noncontroversial forms like those described in the middle-period dialogues or those in the *Sophist*. Moravcsik's paper is valuable because it rules out extensional or set-theoretical models of diaeresis (p. 338), and because he makes the sound observation that "the notion of predication as such does not play an important role in the divisions" (p. 342). But it is, for all its rigorous terminology, not sufficiently grounded in the text. Moravcsik constructs a picture from many small references to a wide range of dialogues; he then builds up a theoretical account, not of this or that dialogue, and certainly not of the diaereses in the *Sophist*, but of his own construction.

EIDETIC NUMBERS

Applications of modern analytical techniques to the Platonic text are ultimately derived from, or indirectly influenced by, Aristotle's criticism of Plato. In this section, I want to consider the attempt by twentieth-century scholars to understand the Platonic doctrine of the division and combination of forms on the basis of Aristotle's contention that these forms are eidetic numbers. This attempt is of interest to us for more than one reason. It seems to be justified by the direct testimony of Plato's greatest associate. Furthermore, if the attempt is successful, it apparently does justice to the ambiguous yet unmistakable link between Plato's dialectical doctrines and his interest in mathematics, but without imposing anachronistic views onto the dialogues. There seems to be an intimate connection between what Plato means by "giving a *logos*" (λόγον διδόναι) and the mathematical notions of proportions or ratios. In the *Philebus* (in a passage to be considered at a later place), Socrates unites the process of formal analysis with counting, and in the *Republic* (VII, 524d2ff), Socrates emphasizes the importance of arithmetic, geometry, and astronomy as preparations for philosophical dialectic. For example, at 525c8–e5, he states that "calculation" (λογισμός) leads the soul upward and "forces it to converse [διαλέγεσθαι] about the numbers themselves [περὶ αὐτῶν τῶν ἀριθμῶν]." Finally, if it can be shown that forms are in some sense numbers, or at least that they possess certain mathematical properties, perhaps we can resolve the puzzle of the nature of eidetic combination, namely, the puzzle of how forms can combine without losing their intrinsic and mutually distinct identities.

There is indeed something attractive, and up to a point, illuminating, about this attempt to understand Platonic dialectic by means of an arithmetical paradigm. However, in my opinion, it is doomed to failure. In the first place, there is something deeply unsatisfactory about the effort to explain Platonic doctrines on the basis of hostile interpretations provided by another philosopher. Second, as the proponents of this attempt themselves admit, there is no direct confirmation of the Aristotelian thesis of eidetic numbers in the Platonic dialogues. If we wish to take Aristotle's reports as accurate, then we must make a distinction between the published dialogues and an ostensible "secret" or "unwritten" Platonic teaching to which Aristotle is supposedly referring. This procedure gives rise to more puzzles than it purports to resolve. Not the least question is this: if Plato wished these views to be kept secret, why did Aristotle make them public? How are we to distinguish Aristotle's interpretation of these "secret" views from their genuine nature? That this is no trivial question is obvious from the philological analysis of Aristotle's interpretations of the pre-Socratics. Third, the attempt is unsuccessful on internal technical grounds.

The thesis of eidetic numbers apparently goes back in modern times to Hermann Cohen. More recently, it has been developed by a line of scholars that includes Julius Stenzel, Otto Toeplitz, Oscar Becker, and Jacob Klein. I shall formulate my discussion in terms of a critique of the interpretation by Klein, with some extended remarks about other scholars in the footnotes. All citations from Klein will be from the 1968 English translation of his German monograph of 1934–36. In order to consider the thesis of eidetic numbers, we shall have to anticipate a portion of the *Sophist* that will be studied later in its proper context. I shall be as brief as possible. In general, we are concerned with Klein's interpretation of what the Stranger calls μέγιστα γένη (*Sophist* 254d4–6), namely, the "greatest" or "most important" kinds, of which *being, sameness, otherness, change,* and *rest* are explicitly named and discussed. Klein takes these kinds to be principles of eidetic numbers, or eidetic numbers themselves, in other words, forms which possess certain numerical properties. I am primarily concerned with the greatest kinds, but I note here that my criticism of Klein is in my view applicable to other versions of forms or ideas, whether in the *Sophist* or elsewhere in Plato. As a corollary to this point, it is important to note at the outset that we cannot understand what the Stranger says about the greatest kinds on the basis of, say, Socrates' discussion of ideas in the *Phaedo* or *Republic*. There is no general concept of a form or idea in the Platonic corpus. Each version of the ostensible theory of forms must be studied in its own right, not assimilated into a nonexistent comprehensive doctrine.

To continue with Klein, Plato presumably developed the doctrine of eidetic numbers for two closely connected reasons. The first reason is the belief that only what is entirely stable can possess genuine being and be genuinely known. Since numbers exemplify the requisite stability, they must give us a clue to the nature of pure intelligible form in the nonnumerical domain as well (cf. *Republic* VII, 529b3–5). The second reason has to do with the problem of the combination of elements of intelligible structure. Formal elements like *man* and *horse* must be able to combine with an element like *animal*, without dissolving the integrity of each element in the combination. The paradigm to be adopted is that of the combination of numbers. Thus, for example, the numbers *two* and *three* (italics designate "the numbers themselves") combine into the number *five* with no sacrifice of their independent identities, but with the addition of new properties (such as even or odd) which they may lack independently. What we must now try to decide is whether this paradigm is applicable to nonnumerical forms.

We begin more directly with Klein's discussion of the admission by Theaetetus in the *Sophist* that being (not yet the form, but a kind of vague generalization on "beings") is both change and rest. This is puzzling in at least two ways. First, it is not *prima facie* clear whether being is one, two, or three. Second, it has also been admitted that change and rest are altogether opposite to one another. It is thus easy to see that this result leads to contradictions, if we leave it as it stands. The first step in supplying the needed revision is to raise three possibilities concerning the greatest kinds. Either none of these elements combines with the others, or all combine with each other, or some combine and others do not. The Stranger establishes that the third possibility alone is acceptable. At this point, Klein says:

> But the very formulation of this possibility indicates the arithmos structure of the genē; for what is it but the division of the

whole realm of *eidē* into single groups or assemblages such that each *eidos* which represents a unique eidetic "unit" (ἑνάς), i.e. a "*monas*" (*Philebus* 15A–B), can be "thrown together" with the other ideas of the same assemblage, but not with the ideas of other assemblages? [p. 89]

However, this rhetorical question is somewhat misleading, as Klein himself points out. Assemblages of idea-monads into a formal genus cannot be exactly like the assemblage of numerical monads into a pure or formal number because of a fundamental difference between the natures of the respective kinds of monads. A number for Plato is a definite (and so finite) collection or assemblage of units. Empirical or practical numbers, used for counting up individuals of definite kinds, employ the kind in question, say "man" or "fruit," as a standard of measurement. The units are then the individual men or pieces of fruit which we count by that standard. Pure or theoretical numbers, however, must also be assemblages of units in some definite amount, but they cannot be assemblages of empirical objects. Theoretical numbers are accordingly definite assemblages of pure, homogeneous units, which are accessible to the intellect alone. As homogeneous, these units are free to combine with one another without restriction. The monads in the number *eight* are indistinguishable from the monads in the number *ten*.[22] Thus the

---

22. The passages in Plato upon which Klein bases his interpretation are *Republic* VII, 526a1–7, and *Philebus* 56d–e; in Aristotle, *Metaphysics* M6, 1080a20ff. Becker (1931), pp. 464–65, points out similarly that, according to Aristotle (*Metaphysics* M6–9, etc.), eidetic numbers differ qualitatively and in their inner structure from mathematical numbers. He accepts the thesis of Stenzel (1959; reprint), p. 117, that the Idea-numbers order, in accord with their *Stellenwert*, the unfolding steps of diaeretic development. However, he holds that Stenzel's own schema of the cardinal numbers of mathematics can explain Stenzel's view that the lowest step of diaeresis involves all the higher steps. According to Becker, idea-numbers are "diairetische Geflechte, deren Knoten die 'Monaden' sind . . . " [diaeretical webs, the knots of which are monads . . .] (p. 469). This leads him to the conclusion (following Aristotle) that the monads of the idea-numbers correspond to the ideas (p. 487). Thus, interpreting *Philebus* 15a–b: "Das Atomon Eidos ist also, diairetisch gesehen, unzerlegbare Monas . . . und doch Vieles (πολλά) und insofern ἀριθμός" [The uncuttable form is therefore, seen diaeretically, a nondecomposable monad, and yet many (πολλά), and thus ἀριθμός] (p. 493). So the idea-number is the δεσμός binding monads into a specific idea. This all seems to founder on the fundamental difficulty that superordinate or "larger" (i.e., "binding") idea-numbers must contain their subordinates in a way that is ruled out by the uncombinability of ideal number-monads. R. Mohr (1981) has recently developed what is in a way the converse of the position common to Becker and Klein. He interprets *Philebus* 56d9–e3 and 59d4–5 together with the other passages cited at the beginning of this note to arrive at the thesis that, in *Republic* VII and *Philebus* 56ff, Plato (i.e., Socrates) is referring to ideas of numbers, but not to eidetic or to arithmetical numbers (pp. 623–24). As Mohr reads *Republic* 526a, then, the passage tells us

number *eight* can enter together with the number *ten* into the community of the number *eighteen*, without loss of identity ensuing for
the constituent numbers, hence with no commingling of heterogeneous units. More generally, any arithmetical number can combine
with any other arithmetical number to form a community in which
none of the participants loses its identity (something that is not true
for empirical or practical numbers).

As Klein observes, the units of eidetic numbers, as distinguished
from those of theoretical numbers like *eight* and *ten*, cannot form
such a community. They are not free to combine with one another
indiscriminately:

> Their "monads" are *all* of different kind and can be brought
> "together" only "partially," namely only insofar as they happen
> to belong to one and the same assemblage, whereas insofar as
> they are "entirely bounded off" from one another ... they are
> "incapable of being thrown together, in-comparable" (*Sophist*
> 253d9).

Each of the monads of an eidetic number is itself a form (or idea);
consequently, each is unique. How then can these unique monads
combine into again unique eidetic numbers without losing their
identities? And how can these same numbers themselves combine
with other such numbers while at the same time preserving *their*
identities? Klein continues:

> The notion of an "arithmetic" structure of the realm of ideas
> now permits a solution of the ontological *methexis* problem (cf.
> *Parmenides* 133A). The monads which constitute an "eidetic
> number," i.e., as an assemblage of ideas, are nothing but a con-
> junction of *eidē* which belong together. They belong together
> because they belong to one and the same *eidos* of a higher order,
> namely to a "class," a *genos*. But all will be able to "partake" in

---

that some numbers, namely, Ideas of numbers, "though they differ in kind, nevertheless, in respect to their internal content, do not vary from one to the next." That is,
"each Idea of number has no parts" (p. 623). Whether or not this is the correct interpretation of Plato's "number theory," it is plain that the proposed ideas of numbers
do nothing to explain formal combination. An interesting aspect of Mohr's brief but
rich paper is his thesis that the ideas of numbers are ordinal rather than cardinal (p.
621). This point was anticipated by A. Kojève in his brilliant, idiosyncratic, and totally neglected "Hegelian" reading of Greek philosophy. "Mais les nombres *ordinaux*
sont précisément tels que Platon dit être les Nombres idéels" (p. 101); of course,
Mohr is speaking, not of mathematical or eidetic numbers, but of ideas of numbers.
A few lines before this, he says, "Et ce point ... coupe court à toute la critique aris-
totélicienne des Idées-nombres."

this *genos* (as, for instance, "human being," "horse," "dog," etc., partake in "animal") *without partitioning it among the (finitely) many eidē and without losing their indivisible unity only if the genos itself exhibits the mode of being of an arithmos.* [pp. 89–90]

This passage gives rise to two questions. Did Plato actually hold the version of a doctrine of eidetic numbers attributed to him by Klein? And is this version, or the doctrine in general, a genuine solution to the ontological *methexis* problem?

The second question can be answered in the negative without any hesitation. Aristotle presents an exhaustive and convincing refutation of the doctrine of eidetic numbers in Book M of the *Metaphysics*, and Klein is well aware of this. He says that Aristotle develops "the many contradictions which must arise from the transfer of the *universal* character of the countable as such to the *eidē*, each of which has a special nature" (p. 92). In addition, Klein regularly observes that Plato has no discursive or dianoetic account of the eidetic numbers that is rigorous and complete. However, I believe that we must go beyond Klein's admission. A careful scrutiny of the passages cited by Klein from the dialogues shows no explicit statement at all of the thesis he attributes to Plato. Looking at the matter from the other side of the coin, J. Annas says of the four relevant passages in Aristotle's *Metaphysics* (A6, 987b11–25; A9, 992b13–17; M7, 1081a5–17; N4, 1091b26), "In all four passages there is a single structure of argument: the identification of Forms and numbers is not presented as a report of what Plato actually said but as the conclusion of an *argument*. Forms *must* be identical with numbers, because they both come from the same principles" (1976, p. 67).

I have no space here to attempt an independent verification of Annas's conclusion or to analyze every passage in Plato that bears upon Klein's thesis. Some of the Platonic passages, however, and all of those that occur in the *Sophist*, will be subjected to the necessary analysis in order to confirm that Klein's thesis does not apply to them. In the present context, we can do two things. First, we may consider very briefly Aristotle's main objection to, or refutation of, the doctrine of eidetic numbers that he himself attributes to Plato. Second, I will show why the technical basis of Klein's interpretation does not apply to the forms introduced by the Stranger in the *Sophist*.

What I take to be Aristotle's main refutation of the doctrine of eidetic numbers occurs in *Metaphysics*, M7. Aristotle says there that either the units in the eidetic numbers are combinable and without

any differences from each other (συμβληταὶ καὶ ἀδιάφοροι), or else
they are different in different numbers. In the first case, there can be
mathematical but not eidetic numbers. For example, by hypothesis,
there is only one eidetic number corresponding to each relevant positive integer. Let us pretend, for the sake of specificity, that *three* is
the eidetic number of man. But there are many "threes" and no reason why one rather than the others should be the "idea" or eidetic
number *three*. On the other hand, if the monads differ in differing
numbers, then, say, the eidetic number *ten* will contain ten units
peculiar to itself; let us call them "ten-units." But *ten* also contains
two fives, and so, two sets of "five-units." To expand upon this a bit,
if *five* is supposed to share in *ten* without altering the nature of either,
then the ten "ten-units" of ten are now joined by two sets of "five-
units." So the original ten units are now twenty units. Aristotle
himself observes that, in fact, the units of numbers are all the same.
This gives rise to a dilemma for Platonism. If ideas were numbers,
they would be neither addible nor inaddible: as numbers, they would
have homogeneous elements and so be addible; but, as addible, they
would no longer be ideas (M7, 1081a5–1083a20).

The puzzles raised by Aristotle concerning constituent units hold
good even if we reject Aristotle's tendency to interpret Platonic forms
as though they were Aristotelian genera and species.[23] This is clear
when we turn to the pivotal step in Klein's argument, namely, his
thesis that the γένος is not partitioned via participation by other
forms. It is true that, say, the arithmetical number "seven" does not
lose its unity or identity as "seven" through the partition of its identity into seven constituent units. But Klein's thesis requires Plato
to believe that the eidetic number of the γένος "animal" does not
lose its unity or identity as that γένος despite the participation of its
various species. The analogy, however, cannot be sustained. We may
agree that "animal" is no less "animal" merely because dogs, horses,
men, and so on, participate in it. But each species of animal (each of
the formal elements of "animal," or *animal*, in my notation) is an
animal by virtue of this participation, whereas each "seven-unit" of
seven is not itself a "seven" (or a *seven*).

Suppose that we conceive of "seven" as the equivalence class of
all sets containing exactly seven elements. On this basis, which is
of course foreign to Plato, each set in the class is as good a representation of the form *seven* as any other, while at the same time it
preserves its independent identity as a unity. But again there is no

23. Cf. *Metaphysics* Z4, 1030a11–14, and Ross (1966), vol. 2, p. 170.

analogy with nonnumerical forms, because there is no discernible difference between one member set of the equivalence class and another, whereas dogs and horses are distinguishable members of the γένος "animal." This shows us that Platonic forms are not extensional entities, like numbers or sets in an equivalence class. The peculiarity of numbers, whether by the Platonic or modern view, is that, even if we attribute objective existence to them, their elements or they themselves can be combined in various ways without damage to their independent entities. In modern set theory, this is expressed as the "transitivity" of sets defining natural numbers. The so-called eidetic numbers attributed to Plato are not sets; they are defined not extensionally but intensionally. And yet, their ostensibly arithmetical feature, namely, that they consist of units, cannot be interpreted arithmetically without in effect instituting a kind of extensionalism which interferes with the properly intensional nature of the units and the eidetic numbers themselves. But in the case of horses, dogs, human beings, or any other nonarithmetical phenomenon, this process of combination and separation can take place without alteration of the elements *only in our thoughts*.

If, then, a paradigm for the *methexis* problem (understood as that of the combination of pure forms) is required, then surely thinking, in the everyday sense of the term, is the appropriate one. We go wrong, however, if we attempt to take the additional step of assimilating our thoughts to numbers. Such a step takes us away from forms as looks to forms as ratios or proportions in the mathematical sense. And this in turn is a crucial step on the path away from the forms of the Platonic dialogues toward modern mathematical logic. It should therefore be carefully noted that, when I state in the following pages that a λόγος is a "ratio" of forms, I am speaking in a metaphorical sense of the term. The metaphor is rooted in the Stranger's distinction between accurate and inaccurate images on the basis of whether these do or do not exhibit the precise proportions of the originals. This distinction makes sense only with respect to visual images of measurable bodies. Yet the distinction between accurate and inaccurate images is carried over to apply to statements, that is, to linguistic images. The statement "Theaetetus sits" is thus presumably a ratio between the form "—— sits" (in the contemporary notation) and whatever form corresponds to "Theaetetus." It should be obvious that this has no arithmetical meaning. There is no proportion $m : n$ that conveys the deep structure of "Theaetetus sits." If we think this through, we come to the conclusion that the statement "Theaetetus sits" is not an image of formal combinations in any kind of arithmological or proportional sense. As we shall see, that leaves unexplained what it means for forms to "combine" with one another. The doctrine of forms provides no explanation of the formal or semantical structure of true or false statements. And yet, a λόγος is in one of its senses literally a "ratio," a sense which seems to fit the point about accurate and inaccurate representations of proportions of originals.

I said above that Klein's point about the nonpartitioning of a γένος does not hold good, even if we disregard the Aristotelian tendency to take Platonic forms as genera and species. However, it is another defect of Klein's interpretation that he does seem to follow Aristotle here. For example, on p. 93 he says:

> The relation of family "descent" between the higher and the lower ideas corresponds to the *"genetic" order of the eidetic numbers*. The "higher" the *genos*, i.e. the less articulated the eidetic number, the more original and *"comprehensive"* it is. In this order the "first" eidetic number is the eidetic "two"; it represents the *genos of "being" as such*, which comprehends the two *eide* "rest" and "change."

On this account, it looks as though *being* is the *summum genus*. This conflicts with the Stranger's assertion that *sameness* and *otherness* also combine with every form. But more seriously, on Klein's view, *being* possesses an inner structure consisting of *rest* and *change*. And this certainly violates the Stranger's insistence upon the independence of each of the most important kinds. Klein cannot be right in his assertion that there is a generic unity of *being, change,* and *rest* that is derived somehow from the nature of *being*.[24] As he himself points out (p. 98), comprehensive unity must share in, and so be derived from, the principle "the One," which is not the first in the series of numbers, but is ostensibly the Good, and so, is beyond being. The discrepancy between these two passages should have directed Klein toward the difference in the *Sophist* between *being* understood as a formal letter or γένος, and "being" understood as the whole. Unfortunately, such was not the case.

One last comment is in order. Klein, like the more orthodox scholars whom he criticizes on other points, takes diaeresis in the *Sophist* (as elsewhere in Plato) to be a training in division according to genera. This activity, says Klein, is necessary to the philosopher "if he is to reach the primal 'genetic' order of eidetic numbers" (p. 97).

24. Cf. Lachterman (1979), pp. 112–13.

Klein's understanding of diaeresis is based upon a conflation of many passages from different dialogues. More specifically, Klein conflates Socrates' discussion in the *Philebus* with the Stranger's procedures in the *Sophist*. In other words, he does not honor distinctions among the dialogues, insisted upon in his later commentaries on individual dialogues, by considering each one as an independent unity. Closely connected with this failure is a consequent inability to distinguish between the philosophical doctrines of Socrates and the Stranger. This failure is also present in his commentary on the *Sophist*.[25]

This concludes our prologue. We are now ready to turn to the *Sophist*.

25. Klein (1977).

ACT ONE

DIAERESIS

Gods and Philosophers

(216a1–218b6)

Our drama may be divided into three acts, each of which corresponds to a main theme in the unified story. I will subdivide each act into a number of scenes, again corresponding to dramatic indications of shifts in the action or conversation. The opening scene does something more than introduce the main speakers in this conversation. As is usual in a Platonic dialogue, it provides us with subtle indications of the problems to be discussed and the context within which they are to be understood. By "context," I mean the dramatic context of the world of the Platonic dialogues, and only derivatively the historical world of fifth-century Athens. It would be a lapse in literary tact to read a drama as a historical document. The conversations presented in the dialogues are dramatic inventions by Plato, not stenographic reports of actual events. It is of no interest to us whether conversations like these "actually" took place; in the deepest sense of the term, they are "actual" conversations presented to us in an artistic form by Plato. The dialogues are what Plato has "actually" chosen to say to us, and it is on this basis that we have to understand him.

In dramatic terms, the main theme of the prologue is the encounter between Socrates and the Eleatic Stranger. As we shall see from the explicit words of the text, this encounter poses the question of the nature of the philosopher. The crucial aspect of this question is whether philosophers show themselves plainly to ordinary human beings or appear in a disguised form. This in turn prefigures the technical question of the distinction between original and image. The problem of the visibility of the philosopher is the context within which we attempt to capture the sophist. A second theme in the prologue is less clearly developed, but discernible, and it bears directly on the dramatic event of the trial of Socrates. Has the Eleatic

Stranger come to praise Socrates or to punish him, and if the latter, for what crime? Finally, we may note that the prologue turns upon a number of diaereses, of which the first is the distinction between Socrates and his friends, on the one hand, and the Stranger, on the other.

The Stranger, as his name makes evident, does not belong to the Socratic circle. Theodorus indicates this distinction in his opening speech: "According to yesterday's agreement, Socrates, we have ourselves come, in an orderly way, and we bring also this Stranger" (216a1–2). Theodorus, a citizen of Cyrene, thus mediates between the Stranger and the citizens of Athens. Although himself a foreigner, Theodorus has close ties with Socrates thanks to his profession as teacher of the mathematical sciences in Athens. We never learn the Stranger's proper name. One could say that we are presented with the challenge of identifying him, provided that this is not misunderstood as an invitation to speculate upon his "historical" identity. The question "Who is the Stranger?" has no historical significance. To the reader of Plato's drama, this question is a more accessible version of the question "What is the Stranger?" Theodorus tells us that the Stranger is a philosopher and companion of those associated with Parmenides and Zeno (216a2–4). Even if we are to take Theodorus's identification as valid, we still do not know what it means to be a philosopher. If we did, of course, there would be no need to enter into conversations on the nature of the sophist, and thus, of the philosopher as well. There is no reason to doubt Socrates' high regard for Parmenides, but a companion of a philosopher is not necessarily himself a philosopher, even assuming that we know what a philosopher is.

Socrates responds in such a way as to accept Theodorus's identification while at the same time raising a question about it. He does this by way of a tacit reference to Homer (*Odyssey* XVII, 485–87). Does Theodorus (whose name, incidentally, means "gift of god") bring us a god rather than a stranger? The surface meaning of this urbane query is that philosophers are like gods among ordinary mortals. However, the deeper sense of the question turns upon a link between the anonymity of the Stranger and the deeds of Odysseus in the Homeric passage just cited. Odysseus has returned to his home disguised as a beggar. He is struck and abused by Antinous, who is in turn reprimanded by one of the "proud young men" courting Penelope: "gods looking like strangers from afar become all things and wander about the cities, viewing human hybris and righteousness." If the proud young man is to be believed, gods are like sophists, who will later be described by the Stranger as assuming all disguises. More generally, we may divide gods from strange mortals on the basis of names or even of essential attributes, but this division does not in itself enable us to identify gods when they walk disguised among mortals. To anticipate, technical diaeresis is one thing, sound judgment in everyday life is something else again. Our knowledge of the natures of things is not in itself sufficient to enable us to distinguish between originals and images. As we shall see, this is because images, even those which are technically inaccurate, look like the originals. We therefore require knowledge of images as well, and especially in those cases where it is not a straightforward matter to check them with the original. Furthermore, if "gods" stand for "philosophers," then, at least according to Socrates, they distinguish between hybris and righteousness. That is, they distinguish between better or worse, and not merely between looks or "forms." Finally, Socrates tacitly compares himself to the proud young man and Theodorus to Antinous. Perhaps Theaetetus is Penelope; as always for Socrates, the hunting of gifted youths is a kind of courtship (216a5–6).

Socrates continues: "Homer says that the gods, especially the god of strangers, accompanying those mortals who share in righteous reverence, look upon the hybristic and orderly deeds of mankind. Perhaps this one who follows you may be one of the powerful, a kind of refuting god who comes to watch over and refute us who are weak in discussions" (216a6–b6). Philosophers, like gods, are hard to distinguish, but one can make this suggestion about them: whereas righteous gods punish the sins of mortals, one philosopher appropriately punishes another by refuting his defective arguments. Socrates thus makes an important correction in the passage from Homer. According to the proud young man, disguised gods view human hybris and righteousness. According to Socrates, gods also refute, or in other words, punish, and thus distinguish between better and worse. It is certainly true that Socrates administers the punishment of refutation to his contemporaries. As a direct consequence of this activity, he is widely regarded as hybristic, a charge leveled against him by Alcibiades in the *Symposium* (215b4–9), and one to which Socrates alludes at least indirectly in the *Apology* as the motive underlying his accusation by Anytus and Meletus. In sum, if the Stranger is a god, he will both distinguish mortals by their looks or natures and administer punishment or judge their merits. The Greek term διαϰρίνω, which will shortly play a pivotal role in the diaereses, can signify both of these classifying activities. It should also be noted that, in the diaeresis section, the Stranger will identify refutation as the art of the noble sophist, a person of ambiguous nature whose description will remind us of Socrates. By raising the prospect that the Stranger is a refuting god, Socrates so to speak defends himself in advance, or places the same charge of noble sophistry against the Stranger.

This by-play is clearly lost on the sober Theodorus. He replies that the Stranger is more moderate than those who devote themselves to disputations or eristics (τὰς ἔριδας). He thus shows us that he cannot distinguish between eristics and elenctic, or between immoderate and moderate refutation. This is another instance of his unfamiliarity with dialectic (*Theaetetus* 146b1ff). If we look ahead once more to the impending diaereses, we see that it follows that Theodorus cannot distinguish between the ignoble and the noble sophist (cf. 226a1–4). The distinction in question turns upon the criterion of better or worse, not simply upon the separation of like from like. This lack of perception may extend itself to the task of distinguishing philosophers from nonphilosophers. Without questioning the intrinsic truth of the matter, then, we are at least entitled to mistrust Theodorus's assurance that the Stranger is, although not a god, a philosopher, and hence divine (216b7–c1). As a mathematician, Theodorus is not a specialist on the human soul, to say nothing of gods.

In his response, Socrates is both more playful and more cautious.[1] He warns Theodorus that it is not much easier to discern (διαϰρίνειν) the family (γένος) of philosophers than that of the gods. This distinction implies that the philosopher is not a god, as Theodorus had claimed a moment ago. But it underlines our need for caution in accepting Theodorus's assessment of the Stranger's nature. This is another amusing example of the difference between classifying by names and by direct perception of genuine examples of the relevant classifications.

Socrates goes on to distinguish between the genuine philosophers and those who are molded in the look (πλαστῶς) of the philosopher, or in other words, between the original and the image. The originals, "assuming all sorts of fantasms, because of the ignorance of the others, 'wander through the cities,' looking down from above on the lives of those below. To some, they seem to be of no worth; but to others, they are most worthy of all" (216c4–8). This is a highly charged

---

1. Cf. 216b7 with *Theaetetus* 145c2 and also Klein (1977), p. 7.

passage. The internal quotation is again from the *Odyssey*, XVII, 485–87. Once more, Socrates introduces terms which will later play a technical role in the Stranger's discussion. I have alluded above to the distinction between accurate and inaccurate images, or (in their Greek names) between icons and fantasms. It follows from the Stranger's analysis that the sophist is a fantasm of the philosopher. In Socrates' statement, the genuine (ὄντως) philosophers disguise themselves with "fantasms" (Socrates employs the participle φανταζόμενοι); he does not say what kind of images are employed by the "look-alikes," as we may perhaps call them. Socrates, of course, does not associate himself with the Stranger's technical use of "fantasm." Nevertheless, we are entitled to notice that Plato introduces several of the Stranger's technical terms into the opening remarks of Socrates. Perhaps Socrates would deny the possibility of distinguishing between icons and fantasms. And here is another curious point. In his first use of the quotation from Homer at 216a6ff, Socrates distinguished between the god of strangers, who is said only to look, and the powerful gods who refute, that is, judge or punish; he also distinguished there between gods, the powerful of whom refute, and mortals, who share in righteous reverence (not the same thing as refuting). In the present use of the Homeric passage, the philosophers look down upon human lives, whereas residents of the cities, the nonphilosophers, judge the images of the philosophers (but not the originals) as worthy or unworthy. So the genuine philosophers are here assimilated "upward" to the god of strangers, whereas the refuting gods are assimilated "downward" to the nonphilosophical citizens.

The two main points in this complex passage seem to be these: (1) it is not just sophists, but genuine philosophers, at least according to Socrates, who disguise themselves when they 'wander through the cities' or mingle with the nonphilosophical public; and (2) gods refute, but philosophers do not. The second point is much more puzzling than the first, since it is surely plain that Socrates engages in the art of contradicting those who claim to know, but who in fact do not. Is this not a form of refutation? Or is the point that there is more than one form of refutation, and that not all these forms are philosophical? Perhaps Socrates rejects in advance the Stranger's punishment or refutation of himself. Needless to say, we are very far from knowing just what it is about Socrates, if anything, that the Stranger would refute. The unsympathetic reader could object that I am making heavy weather of urbane banter and reading significance into what is too slight to support my suggestions. I reply that I am doing nothing more than drawing out the sense of the words actually spoken by Socrates and signalling to the reader those points lying ahead at which these senses will assume their full significance.

Thanks to their fantasms or disguises, the philosophers seem to the city-dwellers to be statesmen, sophists, or madmen. Socrates now takes the critical step in engendering the main discussion. He would like to learn from the Stranger what his fellow countrymen (οἱ περὶ τὸν ἐκεῖ τόπον; 217a1)* think of these things, and what names they use. I call the reader's attention to the apparently innocuous distinction between supposing (ἡγοῦντο) and naming (ὠνόμαζον). This will be of importance in a short time. Theodorus replies to Socrates' query: "What things?" Socrates explains: "sophist, statesman, philosopher" (216c8–217a3). He thus replaces the term "madmen" in his initial tripartition with the term "philosopher." Thus far the Stranger has said nothing. Perhaps his silence is a judgment upon Socratic playfulness. Certainly this playfulness is lost on Theodorus, who does not even understand exactly what needs to be explained with respect to the three natures just listed. Socrates tells him by way of a question: Do the Stranger and his associates consider sophist, statesman, and philosopher to be three names for one, two, or three families? Again, there seems to be some distinction between natures as apprehended and as named. Theodorus assures Socrates that no envy (φθόνος) will prevent the Stranger from responding (217a3–10).[2] Theodorus judges that the Stranger is free from eristics, the spirit of punishment, and envy. We could rephrase this by saying that Theodorus attributes to the Stranger the nature of the pure theoretician, as he understands that nature. Socrates, however, regards the divine nature of philosophers as compatible with an unwillingness to speak to mortals, as was already made plain in his citation from Homer.

The Stranger now speaks for the first time, not to Socrates, but to Theodorus. He confirms that he is free from envy and adds that it is not difficult to say that three families are intended, one for each of

*The Stranger does not explicitly identify himself or his friends as disciples of Parmenides, although this is certainly implied in later passages. I have decided to retain the conventional title "Eleatic Stranger," but call to the reader's attention that "Eleatic" need not necessarily mean "Parmenidean" in the conventional or unqualified sense.

2. Cf. the "mathematical" error committed by Theodorus at the beginning of the *Statesman* (257a1ff). For the distinction between names and natures, see also Zadro (1961), pp. 45–54.

the names just mentioned. To say clearly in each case "what it is" (τί ποτ' ἔστιν), however, is no small or easy deed (217b1–3). Theodorus responds that he and some others (no doubt including Theaetetus and Young Socrates) had been asking the Stranger a similar question on the way to the present appointment. The Stranger, however, declined to answer them, although "he says that he has heard thoroughly the entire issue and not forgotten it" (217b4–8). This little passage makes two points. First, either the Stranger wants Socrates to hear his speech, or else Socrates possesses powers of persuasion, not limited to words, which are lacking in the others. Second, the Stranger's remark, as reported by Theodorus, plainly implies that what we are about to hear is the repetition of the Eleatic doctrine, and not of a doctrine originated by the Stranger. Those who regard the Stranger as Plato's "mouthpiece," while at the same time expressing confidence in Plato's scrupulous honesty, are surely faced with a problem here. How can the Stranger be Plato's as well as the Eleatic mouthpiece? If we say that Plato is here indulging in dramatic license, what is the exact extent of that license? How do we know the contexts in which the license may be applied and in which it is invalid?

It seems to me fairly evident that the Stranger's doctrines, as we are about to hear them, are not attributable to any known Eleatic school. It is equally evident that we do not know, and cannot prove conclusively, to what extent, or in what sense, the Stranger is a lightly disguised Plato. We may arrive at hypotheses on this point after we complete our analysis, or at least a sufficiently large portion of that analysis, but we have no right to assume anything at all about Plato's self-identification with the Stranger before carrying through our analysis. We may be predisposed to believe that Plato sympathizes with the speeches assigned to his main character. But this is not an assumption that works universally in the interpretation of drama, and it should not be applied without extreme caution to the study of a Platonic dialogue. One point may be safely made. The initial impression we receive is that the Stranger will repeat a doctrine he has heard and learned from others. On the other hand, as we trace his path through the discussion with Theaetetus, we will find him hesitating, wondering what to say next, and admitting to errors or unsatisfactory steps in the conversation.

At 217c1–2, Socrates addresses the Stranger directly for the first time.[3] He asks the Stranger not to refuse their initial request, or in

---

3. 217c1–2 "scans as iambic verse" according to Cornford (1935), p. 166, n. 1.

other words, not to be an ungrateful guest. Socrates adds: simply tell us whether you prefer to explain by a long monologue or by questioning someone? He then recalls that, while still a youth, he once witnessed the old Parmenides engaged in a splendid use of the procedure of questioning. No doubt this is intended to persuade the Stranger to emulate the procedure of his ostensible master. Socrates does not mention that he himself participated in the aforementioned discussion. In the *Parmenides*, the method of questioning is described as "gymnastics," an exercise, or a preliminary and youthful step toward serious or adult philosophical investigation (*Parmenides* 135c8ff). The Parmenidean exercise is quite different from the procedures about to be adopted by the Stranger (217c1–7).

The Stranger replies that his method of dialogue is easier to employ with someone who causes no trouble and is patient or tractable. Otherwise, he prefers monologue. This is quite different from Socrates' often-stated preference for short speeches (or questions and answers), as well as from his keen interest in the nature of his potential interlocutor. We may also recall that, in the *Parmenides*, Socrates was impatient and troublesome in his conversations with Zeno and Parmenides, the former of whom compared him to a Spartan hunting dog (128b7–e4). By contrast, in the long exercise itself, the respondent was a youth with the suggestive name of Aristotle, also chosen so as to give Parmenides as little trouble as possible (*Parmenides* 137b6–c3). It looks as though Eleatics are not fond of contradiction (217d1–3). Socrates assures the Stranger that everyone present will respond tractably. But by a division of old from young, and of Theaetetus from the other youths, he indicates his recommendation to the Stranger (217d4–7). Socrates wants the inspection of Theaetetus's soul to be combined with the elaboration of the Stranger's doctrine. One may infer from this nuance that Socrates anticipates and does not fear the nature of the "refutation" which he is about to undergo.

To all of this, the Stranger replies that a kind of shame (αἰδώς τίς; cf. 216b1) prevents him from delivering a long speech, as though he were showing off. Evidently he would prefer to do this, but yields instead to the procedure of question and answer. However, he says that he must in fact speak at length, since the nature of the topic is not revealed by the question in which it is posed. In other words, the Stranger implies that, despite the question-and-answer format of his discussion with Theaetetus, he will regard it as a kind of monologue. This lends some support to those who argue that, in the *Sophist*, Plato has abandoned the lively interplay of question and answer that characterizes the genuinely dramatic dialogues of his earlier period. It does not confirm, however, the thesis that Plato is no longer writing a dialogue. Neither does it prove that Theaetetus's responses will be lacking in interest to the careful reader. It does, however, show that the Stranger conceives of his submission to "shame" as a matter of mere form. It would be inappropriate and even boorish for a guest not to gratify "you and the others" (another diaeresis). The Stranger then accepts Theaetetus as his partner in conversation, especially since he has himself conversed previously with the youth (and so presumably knows him to be tractable; 217d8–218a3).

Theaetetus's first speech, although on the surface polite and tractable, causes a slight difficulty for the Stranger. The youth asks whether it will gratify everyone if the Stranger does as Socrates suggests.[4] This reasonable question echoes Theaetetus's reticence of the previous day (Theaetetus 144b10–c6). I will not press the point, but I detect a slight note of irritation in the Stranger's reply: "it is likely that there is nothing more to be said about that." If Theaetetus is pained by the length of the conversation, he must blame his comrades, not the Stranger. Presumably the content of the discussion will cause Theaetetus no pain. Theaetetus replies that, if he tires, Socrates' young namesake will share the burden (cf. Statesman 257c2ff). The Stranger answers in the same tone as before. That is your private affair; the ensuing discussion is in common with me (218a4–b6). The distinction between "private" (ἰδίᾳ) and "common" (κοινῇ) will assume some importance in the immediate sequel.

---

4. Burnet destroys the point here by transforming the question into an assertion, with no textual justification.

Diaeresis in the *Philebus*

In the next scene, we shall study the method of diaeresis as it is introduced by the Stranger. The present excursus is intended to assist the reader in assessing the nature of diaeresis. If we approach our task by way of the secondary literature, we receive the impression that this method is a kind of mathematical analysis of pure formal structure, and that it is regularly employed in the Platonic dialogues to arrive at precise definitions of individual forms.[1] Very frequently, these interpretations of diaeresis take their bearings by Aristotle's references in the *Metaphysics* to the so-called eidetic numbers of the Platonists. But whether or not Aristotle is the guide, and regardless of whether Euclidean geometry, the theory of proportions, set theory, or mereology is identified as the appropriate paradigm, one thing is true of the accounts in question. An interpretation of diaeresis is inferred from the application of some formal, quasi-mathematical technique to an amalgamation of fragmentary passages from the Platonic corpus. It is the exception, rather than the rule, to find an interpretation of diaeresis, however elaborate, in which a meticulous analysis of the relevant texts (to say nothing of the dialogues as a whole), precedes the application of the techniques, hypotheses, and constructions of the interpretation itself. The student thus proceeds to analyze the details of his own interpretation rather than of the Platonic texts. This is true so frequently, and re-

---

1. An extreme dissent from the dominant view is filed by J. Findlay (1974) on the topic of diaeresis in the *Sophist*: "It is strange that such a jejune procedure should have been thought by some to represent an important *Entwicklung* of Plato's mature thought, and a great advance on the vaguer methodology of the *Republic*" (p. 257). Whereas I do not subscribe to Findlay's depreciation of diaeresis, this is because I do not regard it as a quasi-mathematical method of formal analysis. My own approach is much closer to those of E. M. Manasse (1937) and S. Benardete (1960) and (1963).

gardless of whether the interpreters are philologists, analytical philosophers, or members of the phenomenological school, that I take it as evidence of the common assumption that the literary form of the dialogue is of no importance to the task of philosophical analysis.[2]

Our primary concern is with the *Sophist*, which we shall study in detail. Nevertheless, I believe it will be helpful if we preface our study of the *Sophist* with a close analysis of a passage in the *Philebus*. This passage is of interest to us now for the following reasons. First, it contains an extensive description of the method of diaeresis or dialectic, placed in the mouth of Socrates, and in a dialogue universally agreed to belong to the last period of Plato's authorship. By comparing what Socrates says about diaeresis with how the Stranger employs it, we can test the widely held view that the Stranger is not merely Plato's mouthpiece, but that he is chosen to introduce a new and final stage in Plato's thought. The second reason is the converse of the first. Since Plato returns to Socrates as his ostensible mouthpiece in the *Philebus*, we shall be able to decide whether there are variations in Plato's late doctrine of diaeresis, corresponding to the differences between Socrates and the Eleatic Stranger. Third, the method described by Socrates in the *Philebus*, although quite obscure, explicitly refers to numbers and counting, as the passages on diaeresis in the *Sophist* do not. It is the *Philebus* passage, together with some remarks in the earlier *Republic*, which provides the strongest support for the Aristotelian account of eidetic numbers, and thus to the view that there is a mathematical basis to diaeresis. Our primary concern will be to determine whether the *Philebus* supports the view that diaeresis is by its nature mathematical, or that it may be "formalized" in the contemporary sense of that expression.

It would take us too far afield to enter into a discussion of the dramatic structure and the main themes of the *Philebus*. However, not to do so will put my analysis of the pertinent passage on the same footing as the majority of interpretations of diaeresis in the secondary literature. I can thus show that, even and especially by concentrating our attention on the description of diaeresis, with no consideration of the general literary nature of the *Philebus*, the "formalist" interpretation of diaeresis is not supported by that dialogue. We start with Socrates' assertion at 15a1ff of the serious problem of

2. One analytically oriented author who takes the text seriously, and who as a consequence makes many valuable observations, is K. Sayre (1969). This is one of the best studies on Plato in English.

diaeresis. When we "posit" (τιθῆται) an ungenerated unity such as "mortal," "ox," "beauty," or "the good," there is a serious argument about the diaeresis of these units (τούτων τῶν ἐνάδων). Do they possess genuine being (that is, "are they truly?", ἀληθῶς οὔσας)? If so, how can they be both altogether stable as solitary or separate units, while also dispersed in their unlimited generated instances (ἐν τοῖς γιγνομένοις αὖ καὶ ἀπείροις εἴτε διεσπασμένην καὶ πολλὰ γεγονυῖαν θετέον, εἴθ' ὅλην αὐτὴν αὑτῆς χωρίς)? Do they become multiple, or does each remain itself even though "multiplied," as it were, in its instances?

The solitary units posited by Socrates are presumably forms, in some if not in all ways analogous to the "ideas" in the *Republic*. There is no reason to assume that these forms are indivisible elements in the sense of the eidetic letters of the *Sophist*, as the reference to their possible division reminds us. Socrates does not distinguish here between units corresponding to living things and those corresponding to (what we would call) abstract properties. He says nothing about the nature of these units, although later he will employ the term ἰδέα (16d1), "idea" or "form," when describing their diaeresis. We know only that each is a "one" (for example, βοῦν ἕνα) with respect to a "many." Protarchus (the main interlocutor) agrees with Socrates that the problems of one and many are to be investigated, and Socrates then poses the question where they are to start in the complex war of conflicting views. He himself makes the following suggestion: "We say that one and many are brought together" (or "come to be the same") "by speeches" (or "by reasonings," ταὐτὸν ἓν καὶ πολλὰ ὑπο λόγων γιγνόμενα; 15d1ff). This certainly implies that the units are distinct in themselves, as independent of rational discourse. What we talk about, then, is not the same as how we talk about it. Discourse about units is already a "coming-together" of units into an articulated manifold.

It remains to be seen whether the structure of this manifold is the same as, or otherwise capable of making accessible to us in an undistorted way, the natures of the distinct units. Socrates claims only that one and many "run around" or "circulate" always in each of the things we say. This aspect of language brings pleasure to young men, but also a kind of technical enthusiasm or delight in analytical puzzles (15e1ff). Protarchus requests instruction from Socrates on how youths like himself can avoid these perplexities. He asks for a "better" or "more beautiful" road (ὁδὸν δέ τινα καλλίω), and Socrates agrees to describe the most beautiful road he knows, of which he is a lover (ἐράστης), even though it often deserts him (16a4ff). As a final point, I note that Socrates speaks, here as elsewhere in the passage we are studying, of "one and many," not of *the* one and *the* many. He seems to be referring to the common property of being countable, and not to ontological principles. He does, however, refer to *the* one and *the* many at 14c8.

The beloved road is not hard to point out, but it is extremely difficult to follow. Nevertheless, every discovery of a technical nature has come to light on this road (πάντα γὰρ ὅσα τέχνης ἐχόμενα; 16b4ff). The first main point made by Socrates is that we unite one and many by talking about them. It is obvious that discourse about oxen does not unite oxen with the unit "ox." Socrates must mean that the relation between the unit (or form) "ox" and the individual, generated oxen is made accessible to us through language about the nature of oxen. This is not the same as to say that the unit "ox" first becomes accessible to us through discourse; and in fact, Socrates never says that. Instead, he always speaks of our "seeing" or "grasping" the formal unit. Still, once we have seen the unit, discursive analysis of it, and therefore of its relation to its instances, is necessary. The discursive structure is thus not identical with the eidetic structure, even if it should turn out that their ratios are the same. I am using "ratios" here in an extended or metaphorical sense, to refer to the combinations or patterns of elements in the respective structures. The subsequent discussion of counting these elements has nothing to do with a quasi-Pythagorean attribution of numbers to the elements themselves. Socrates leaves undiscussed the problem of whether the ratios in discourse are images of the eidetic ratios. This will be one of the most important issues in our study of the *Sophist*.

We may also observe that words are themselves generated individuals, but the multiple occurrences of the word "ox" are not instances of the form "ox." It is existing oxen, not their common name, which instantiate this form. Furthermore, the discernible properties of empirical oxen (mammal, four-legged, etc.) are presumably themselves instances, not of the formal unit "ox," but of elements of this unit, which are thus themselves forms: "mammal," "four-legged," and so on. Hence our diaeresis of the form "ox" will be a spelling-out of the elements ingredient in that form. These elements will themselves be forms. This is presumably the basis for the theory, considered previously, that the relation of the elements to the complex unit is like that of smaller to larger natural numbers.

The listing of essential or defining properties is certainly a function of λόγος, and so of the discursive and calculative intellect. Λόγος is then the spelling out of the link between one and many, and of the way in which this link is assimilated from intellectual perception into knowledge or understanding. Language itself requires unity for coherence and manyness for intelligibility. The structure of speech must have some connection with units and pluralities like "ox" and oxen, without which connection, speech *about* these would be impossible. But the structure of speech cannot be the same as the structure of units amongst themselves, let alone of units and their empirical instances. Speech is not a web of *the* "ox," *the* "mortal," and so on. It is *another* web, somehow the same and other (the problem of original and image in the *Sophist*), which, when we lay it over the web of units, somehow makes the latter accessible to our discursive intelligence. When we speak today of "formal logic," we refer to the structure of speech, whether or not we believe in the separate existence of the units of that structure. We also believe that formal logic is "ontologically neutral," or in other words, that it is a web possessing the marvellous capacity to elucidate any ontological one-in-many. This belief, however, is based upon a distinction between the natures of the units whose structures we study and the "ratios" or formal relations of those units. "Form" means for us not the phenomenological form—the "ox," the "mortal," and so on— but the relations that obtain amongst anything we choose to discuss.

We speak of "formal logic," and indeed, we often point out that the term "formal" is redundant, since logic deals exclusively with forms. Yet, Socrates separates, as it were, form from logic. In fact, Socrates does not refer to "logic" at all, but rather to two distinguishable phenomena: λόγος or discursive reason, and a ὁδός, or road, which we all too easily translate as "method," which discursive reason must take if it wishes to understand the problems of one and many. Socrates says that all technical discoveries have been brought to light on this road. A τέχνη is normally a rule-governed process, or one which may be described in a step-by-step way and so taught to others. By its use, we modify preexistent materials to bring something into being that would not exist without our work. These things are called "artifacts." But τέχνη is also used by Plato as a model for, and even as synonymous with, ἐπιστήμη, or reasoned knowledge as distinct from belief and opinion. This kind of knowledge is διὰ λόγου or depends upon the discursive, calculative intellect. It is not clear whether the technical character of ἐπιστήμη entails that even this knowledge possesses a "constructive" or artifactual dimension. Neither is it clear in the passage under analysis in what precise sense Socrates employs the expression πάντα ὅσα τέχνης ἐχόμενα. It has not yet been answered by Socrates whether the units he posits "truly are," that is, whether they are eternal beings or technical concepts. If the road along which we isolate formal units is itself a τέχνη, and if the structure of language, within which we gain access to one and many, is not perfectly transparent, then the results of diaeresis may be modified, like any other technical product, by human work, even if they are not entirely manmade.[3]

Socrates' account of diaeresis leaves this most difficult question open, and indeed, does not even address it explicitly. But it is implicit in the language he uses to phrase his account of diaeresis. We can also say with confidence that it is an anachronism to refer to Socrates' road as "logical analysis," and question-begging to describe it from the outset as "conceptual analysis." Furthermore, whereas we may be able to formalize the results of diaeresis, diaeresis is not itself the exhibition of "logical structure" in the contemporary sense of the expression. With these conclusions in mind, let us return to the text.

As it seems to Socrates, the road is a gift from the gods to mortals, a gift which is presented to us "together with a most bright fire" by some Prometheus (16c5ff). In other words, visibility along the road is not the same as the road itself. Even if it should be right to speak of the road as a "method," we still have to see how to apply the method, and this cannot be done merely by applying the method. It is far from clear that any definite method, with a definite set of rules, is being referred to here. The reference to firelight may be a complement to, or even a revision of, the discussion of the good in the *Republic*. One thing at least is certain. The reference to firelight is no more "literary trimming" than is the reference to the "beautiful road." It is an ingredient in Socrates' account, and, like each other ingredient, it has to be understood, not ignored or translated into contemporary terminology.

The ancestors hand down to us, from their proximity to the gods, a saying "that the things which are said to be always are composed from one and many" (ὡς ἐξ ἑνὸς μὲν καὶ πολλῶν ὄντων τῶν ἀεὶ λεγομένων εἶναι), "and possessing them in a connate limit and unlimitedness" (πέρας δὲ καὶ ἀπειρίαν ἐν αὑτοῖς ξύμφυτον ἐχόντων; 16c8ff). Two points require comment here. First, the things which "are from" one and many are said "to be always." Socrates does not say that the beings to which he refers are generated or come to be, and hence "exist." He says rather that they possess an internal structure, namely, a structure of one and many. These beings are complex manifolds: each is constituted of a plurality of units. If each such

3. Cf. Prologue, n. 19.

internally differentiated unit is "one mortal," "one ox," and so on,
then none is a pure formal element like *being, sameness, otherness,
change,* and *rest* in the *Sophist.* These last are "uncuttable" or atomic
forms.[4] They contain no elements, and Socrates does not mention
them, whether as complex units or elements. But whether or not he
is thinking of them, his method of "counting" cannot be applied to
uncuttable elements, although it may well terminate with them. In
the Stranger's discussion, we *begin* rather than terminate with formal atoms.

Second, it seems that "limit and unlimitedness" are introduced
here as distinct from "one and many." Limit and unlimitedness are
connate with one and many, or rather with the beings constituted of
one and many. However, it is not at all clear what "unlimitedness"
refers to here. The unity of a complex, like the unity of each element
in a complex, is, or serves as, a limit. But if the complex is also
unlimited, then presumably its analysis will never terminate, and so
we shall never be able to arrive at a λόγος or ἐπιστήμη of the complex. Since we are discussing forms rather than generated instances,
we cannot explain "unlimitedness" as a reference to matter (which
is not a sharply distinct notion in Plato in any case).

Since these things are so ordered, "we must always posit a single
look for everything and look for it—we'll find one there—" (δεῖν . . .
ἀεὶ μίαν ἰδέαν περὶ παντὸς ἑκάστοτε θεμένους ζητεῖν—εὑρήσειν γὰρ
ἐνοῦσαν—; 16c10ff). Socrates does not "deduce" the complex, and
hence both the limited and unlimited nature of his formal units,
from axioms or principles. He accepts them on the basis of a "saying" or as a gift from the gods. No doubt this is metaphorical language, but that is precisely the point. Metaphors have to be understood, not disregarded or replaced by anachronistic and inaccurate
terminology. The sense of the metaphor is that we are *given* complex forms as visible. This is our starting point. The starting point
is not with transcendental metaphysical principles, but with the
natural "looks" of things around us: mortals, oxen, beauty, goodness. However, it is not clear what to make of the need to "posit" or
"suppose" (θεμένους; cf. 15a2ff: τιθῆται, τίθεσθαι) a single look or
form for everything. We must not read doctrines of German Idealism
into the text. Perhaps Socrates means only that we are justified by
our immediate experience of heterogeneous looks to suppose that
there is one such look common to all those things that look alike.
Things that "look alike" (my expression) are not only "like" each

4. I am not using "uncuttable" or "atomic form" in the sense associated with J.
Stenzel, namely, as the last (and least extensive) class reached by a diaeresis. In my
usage, a form is an atom if it cannot be analyzed into constituent formal elements.

other *qua* many, but are also "like" the common look that enables us to take them together.

Even if this is right, it remains all the more true that diaeresis *and* the expectation of complex formal unities are rooted in divine gifts, firelight, or the pretechnical diversity of everyday life. The same could be said for mathematics and modern formal calculi, but it hardly follows from this that diaeresis is a formal calculus.

Let us catch our breath at this point. Whether because we cannot address our intelligence to the problem in any other way, or thanks to the divine firelight, we suppose that many oxen look like the formal unit "ox," and so on. Second, we suppose that formal units like "ox," "mortal," "beauty," "good," and so on, are each themselves one and many. Each unit is one, and each of its many constituent elements is one. Third, we suppose that limit and unlimitedness are connate with one and many in the things that are always. Finally, we suppose that in all cases there is a single form—namely, wherever looks show themselves to us, wherever intelligibility has already begun (that is, prior to our "technical" analysis). The expression "in all cases" refers then to the entire visible world. Whatever is visible is so thanks to a single form for each collection of look-alikes.

To continue: we may suppose that the single form is there, but that does not guarantee that we will find it. At least Socrates implies this when he says: "if we get hold of it" (16d4ff). Let us then further suppose that the single form is indeed grasped. Socrates here shifts from the language of sight to that of touch, but it would be unwarranted to see here a reference to "conceptualizing" in the modern sense. The etymology of "concept" leads back to the paradigm of grasping, but we cannot move in the reverse direction and attribute to Socrates a doctrine of concepts on the basis of his use of a touch metaphor. Socrates probably means that we can pursue our path along the road of diaeresis when we have looked very carefully at, and in that sense, secured, our vision of the starting point. He promptly reverts to the metaphor of sight: "after this we must look for two, if such there are, and if not, for three or any other number." In other words, we must see how many formal elements are contained in each complex unit. Socrates says nothing about deduction or any other type of discursive (let alone formal) operation. There is no reference to λόγος here, but only to looking and grasping. Socrates' description is not that of mathematical analysis, but *of an analogue to sense perception*. Thus, counting is a subordinate aspect of seeing.

Another type of difficulty surfaces in the continuation of the pas-

sage. We must look at each of the elements just discerned once more
in the same way. In other words, the elements of our complex unities themselves have constituent elements. Nothing is said, however, about the nature of elements at each level. No examples are
given. There is nothing to justify a "theory of types," and no basis
for applying any set-theoretical terminology, inasmuch as we have
no axioms by which to form sets, let alone identify elements. Socrates says nothing about a hierarchy of natures. For all we know to
the contrary, what is in one case an element of an element will in
another case be an element, or even an original complex unity. We
are merely instructed to look at each element "until we can see, not
only that each unit with which we began" (τὸ κατ' ἀρχὰς ἕν) "is one
and many and unlimited, but how many it is" (ἀλλὰ καὶ ὁπόσα).

The original unit must be the complex: "ox," "mortal," and so on.
If it is unlimited as well as many, this can only be because it has a
limited plurality of elements, each of which contains a limited plurality of elements, and so on in an unlimited way. But there is an
insoluble problem here. The "first-order" elements (relative to our
starting point) of the complex unit must be limited in number. Otherwise, the complex will lack a visible unity; it will be unlimited,
and hence not visible as the given unit. But if there is an unlimited
series of levels of formal elements, then there can be no λόγος or
ἐπιστήμη, no "final enumeration" or "summing-up" of the original
complex. On the other hand, if we attribute the unlimitedness in
question to the matter of the generated individuals (in some quasi-
Platonic sense of "matter"), we then confuse, and indeed dissolve
the initial distinction between, the one and many of "single form"
and its generated look-alikes. Someone might claim to see in our
passage a reference to the principles, reported by Aristotle, of the
one and the indefinite dyad. I have already noted that Socrates does
not speak of *the* one or *the* unlimited in our passage (but cf. 23a9,
24a2–3, for τὸ ἄπειρον). But this apart, another reason can be cited
for rejecting the proposal in question. If there are two principles, the
one and the indefinite dyad, then multiplicity arises by the "articulation" or "differentiation" of the indefinite dyad through the influence of the one. But this leaves altogether unexplained the difference between the plurality of forms and the multiplicity of generated
instances. In Aristotelian language, it leaves unexplained the difference between form and matter.

Socrates then warns Protarchus: "We must not apply the form of
the unlimited to plurality before we see its entire number, the number between the unlimited and the one" (τὴν δὲ τοῦ ἀπείρου ἰδέαν

πρὸς τὸ πλῆθος μὴ προσφέρειν πρὶν ἄν τις τὸν ἀριθμὸν αὐτοῦ πάντα κατίδῃ τὸν μεταξὺ τοῦ ἀπείρου τε καὶ τοῦ ἑνός; 16d7ff). Reference to the "form" of the unlimited, if it is taken literally, rules out the view that the unlimited is the indefinite dyad, since forms are produced in this case by the action of the one *on* the unlimited dyad. Furthermore, if each original complex (what is presumably meant here by τὸ πλῆθος) has an eidetic number *between* the unlimited and the one, in what sense is that complex itself "one and many and unlimited"? The only way to dissolve this difficulty is by assuming that there are two different kinds of unlimitedness, one for eidetic numbers and one to represent the "stuff" or residue that remains after we have identified the eidetic number of any given complex. But is this a solution, or a doubling of the original difficulty?

The sentence I have been studying concludes as follows. Once we fix the eidetic number of the "plurality," "we can then assign each one of all these into the unlimited and bid them adieu." Which "of all these" ones are we discarding, and into which unlimited? I cannot answer these questions, nor is it part of my task to do so. I have taken the reader step-by-step through the description of what Socrates calls "dialectic" as distinct from "eristic" (16e4–17a5), and now ask him to tell me whether there is any evidence in the text of a mathematical analysis of formal structure. One is of course free to speculate about how to revise Socrates' account so as to make it compatible with a contemporary formalism. But one is not free to impose onto the text what is not there, or to infer from it what it will not yield.

Protarchus, naturally enough, does not understand the account given by Socrates of dialectic. Socrates goes on to provide him with two examples: spelling and musical composition. These examples are also employed by the Eleatic Stranger with respect to his alphabet of forms. We will be well advised to see how Socrates constructs his examples.

The first example is that of the letters of the alphabet, which we were taught as children. "Sound, which issues from the mouth of all and each of us, is a kind of unit [ἐστί που μία], but also unlimited in number" (17a6ff). Sound is a one and many, but it is not a metaphor for the complex formal unit ("one ox," etc.) of the previous passage. It is rather the "stuff" common to all letters (and here Socrates seems to approach a version of what Aristotle will later call "intellectual matter"), but more generally, to the indefinite number of noises produced by the action of the mouth upon the continuum of sound. Human activity thus differentiates our "one" into a "many" (if "unlimited" is here synonymous with "many"). In one sense, this activity is natural; but since different "mouths" articulate the continuum of sound into different alphabets, the activity is also technical. An alphabet is an artifact. Socrates does not refer here to spelling as a τέχνη, but he shortly calls it "being grammatical" (τὸ γραμματικόν), and this is referred to as a τέχνη at 18d1–2. Music will be called a τέχνη in a moment. The activity of the mouth may be analogous in some way to the activity of intellectual perception that picks out formal units from the web of phenomena; but this seems forced, since we perceive music with the ear, not the mouth. In any event, we are not told whether or, if so, to what degree the elements perceived are also human productions.

Socrates concludes his initial statement of the example of spelling as follows: "None of us is wiser than another in these things whether because we know its unlimitedness or its unity. But that it is of such a kind and amount, it is this which makes each of us grammatical." So even if there were a reference here to the principles of the one and the indefinite dyad, we should not be wise by knowing them. What we need to know is how words are spelled. Thus words, not letters, are analogous to the complex formal units of the previous discussion. Letters must then be the elements of compounds. This account is far from exhaustive. We might suggest, on the basis of other dialogues (for example, *Theaetetus* 203ff), that syllables are the "first-order" elements of words, whereas letters are elements of elements. In this case, our analysis terminates after a finite number of steps, but it begins and ends in a perception of the relevant entities.

Whereas we count the letters as we distinguish the spelling of each word, we are not "deducing" the letters from the word, nor are we "predicating" one letter of another. Up to a point, Socrates' description of the diaeresis is similar to Descartes's account of his universal method in the *Regulae*. In Descartes, the human intention or will plays a decisive role in determining what is to count as a significant complex. The problem which we are interested in solving thus provides at least the context within which we select what is to count as an "element." In the example of spelling, there is no reference to the will or human intention, but the metaphor of the alphabet communicates a dimension of contingency to the complexes and elements of analysis. Spelling follows rules which are not natural but are conventional, artifactual expressions of man's nature as the talking animal.

The analogy between Socrates and Descartes breaks down precisely at the point of mathematizing or formalizing. In the Cartesian methodology, we shift our attention from the "look" or phenomenological nature of the elements to their proportions or ratios. The method symbolizes these ratios, not the looks of their elements, which of course become invisible if they are replaced by schematic letters or constants. Counting, or *ordo et mensura*, is in Descartes a generalized version of mathematics. Counting in Socratic dialectic is an ordinary arithmetical operation, subordinate to the primary task of seeing the looks of things, that is used if necessary to ensure that we have completed the perceptual task in each case. To put this in another way, it would be pointless, even if it were possible, to formalize the rules of spelling, since these rules are not only conventional but contingent and open-ended. Old rules change, and new rules must be devised as the language grows. But this is not the heart of the matter. We have to see *what* we are counting, and vision cannot be formalized. References by Socrates to counting are thus in themselves no justification for taking the formal complexes as eidetic numbers. It remains to be seen whether the relation between, say, "mortal" and its presumed elements, such as "rational," "two-legged," and so on, is that of the natural numbers.

We turn next to the τέχνη of music, with respect to which sound is also one (17b11ff). The case of music is much more complicated than that of spelling, since sound is now modified by pitch, scales, rhythms, measures, and so on. Further, there are "modifications" (πάθη) in the bodies of the dancers that correspond to the "scales" (συστήματα; 17d2) of musical sound. The greater complexity of music makes the process of counting much more important than in the case of spelling, if we are to distinguish the elements of each "system" or scale. References to number are thus more frequent and more emphatic in this passage than in the previous discussion of spelling. But there are the usual references to "seeing" or to mental "taking in" (for example, καὶ ἅμα ἐννοεῖν; 17d6). One might contend that sounds can be replaced by symbols (as in the musical score) that lead the technician back to the original sounds, whereas this is not true of the looks of things. We can move from letters to words by way of rules of spelling, but no rules will take us from words to beings, unless we start with a knowledge of the beings for which the words stand. However, the same is true in the case of music. If we have not first learned how to symbolize sounds, we will never be able to read a score. We can, however, become mathematicians without any views about what, if anything, our symbols stand for.[5]

5. The fundamentally mathematical nature of Plato's conception of music means, of course, that the rules of musical analysis are not conventional in the same sense as are those of spelling. The ratios of music are natural as the ratios (combinations of letters) of spelling are not. See, for example, the discussion of music in *Republic* VII

The example of music concludes with the same lesson as the example of spelling. We have to grasp mentally the systems of one and many, or in other words the rules (my term) by which the elements combine. Our thinking is left indefinite if we cannot arrive at a definite number in each of the indefinite instances of plurality. Protarchus and Philebus are pleased by this beautiful passage (17e7), but Philebus still does not see the application of dialectic to the problem of pleasure and the good life. Socrates, however, is not done with his account of the road itself. He reiterates his previous conclusion: "If someone were to get hold of any unit, he must not look straightaway to the nature of the unlimited but to some number" (οὐκ ἐπ᾽ ἀπείρου φύσιν δεῖ βλέπειν εὐθὺς ἀλλ᾽ ἐπί τινα ἀριθμόν); "so too conversely when someone must necessarily get hold first of the unlimited, he must not look straightaway at the unit but must think of a number possessing in each case some plurality, and conclude from all into one" (τελευτᾶν τε ἐκ πάντων εἰς ἕν; 18a6ff).

In this restatement, the following points emerge. (1) We do not begin by counting, but by "looking" or "thinking," by an initial perception of the relevant formal complex. (2) Once we have perceived the relevant complex, we must start counting its elements. No rule is provided here for counting, any more than for determining which complex is relevant. (3) Only when necessary should we begin with the unlimited; however, since we can do so if needed, the unlimited has a nature; that is, it is accessible to the calculative intelligence, *and is therefore limited or definite.* Can this sense of definiteness be numerical, given the uncountability of the indefinite? Only if the "form" or "nature" of the unlimited is itself limited, or countable, even though the unlimited itself is not. In this case, we have a distinction between "form" and "content" that does not hold good of other forms. Other forms have formal elements, but here, the "content" of the form or nature of the unlimited is not itself a form. (4) The unlimited seems to be distinct from plurality, or in other words, we seem to have a tripartition of "one/many/unlimited." (5) In all cases, we are to begin with an appropriate number or plurality intermediate between unity and unlimitedness. I take this to mean that we are to disregard initially the unity and the (possibly) indefinite number of elements of the given complex, but to begin with its "surface structure" of primarily visible elements. We take our bearings by the phenomena.

and Cornford's remarks on *Timaeus* 35b–36b in Cornford (1937), pp. 66–73. I shall discuss the role of music in the *Sophist* in considerable detail at a later stage of this study.

I shall end my discussion of the *Philebus* at this point. Socrates goes on to reconsider the example of letters by attributing their discovery to some god or godlike man, possibly Theuth, as the Egyptians say. Despite the subsequent differentiation of the letters into vowels, semivowels, and mutes, no substantially new points are made. We have now carefully analyzed an account of diaeresis, put into Socrates' mouth by Plato, and in a dialogue of the same period to which the *Sophist* belongs. Indeed, it is agreed that the *Philebus* is later than the *Sophist*. Our analysis has shown us that the account of diaeresis in the *Philebus* does not support the usual interpretation to which it is subjected. It remains to be seen what is the role of diaeresis in the *Sophist*, and whether this role is the same as, or compatible with, Socrates' description of dialectic in the *Philebus*.

Hunting the Sophist

(218b6–219a3)

We are now prepared to return to the *Sophist* and to study the introductory formulation of the central problem. The Stranger has agreed
to tell his hosts what is the Eleatic teaching with respect to the
three distinct human types: sophist, statesman, and philosopher. I
want to emphasize from the outset that we are not simply engaged
in the task of defining a pure form, or even a τέχνη. We are hunts-
men who pursue living quarry. In general, one may say that, whereas
in philosophical treatises persons are represented by types, in a Platonic dialogue types are represented by persons. As Socrates put it
in the *Phaedrus* with respect to the perfect writing, Plato's speeches
are alive (*Phaedrus* 264c2–5). One reason why the contemporary
scholar is inclined to disregard the dialogue form is because he draws
a distinction between philosophy and psychology. This distinction
is rooted in modern science, and even if it is true, it cannot serve as
a guide to understanding Plato. For Plato, an essential dimension of
philosophical pedagogy is the representation of the soul at work.
The point of a drama is to show us the interplay between speech
and deed. The deeds in the *Sophist* are much more subtle than those
in, say, the *Oedipus* trilogy, but it is certainly not a qualification for
the interpretation of Plato that we be obtuse. With respect to the
hunting of the sophist, there is a more specific reason for the drama.
In the *Sophist*, contrary to what is said in other dialogues, the sophist is assigned a τέχνη. I shall have more to say about this after we
have made some progress in our diaereses. Here we need note only
that the sophist's art is extremely ambiguous; it consists in the
manufacture of false images. If we cannot define the nature of images, then regardless of our skill at diaeresis, we shall not succeed
in arriving at a technical definition of the sophist. Whatever their
function, the diaereses must be supplemented by a portrait of the

sophist's work: his cunning and evasiveness. Part of the purpose of
the portrait of the sophist (as opposed to specious definitions) is to
show how he escapes our attempt to hunt him down, even as we
apply our heavy technical machinery to that task. By studying this
portrait, we also learn something about the philosophical nature.

The Stranger informs Theaetetus that their common investigation must begin, "as it seems to me," with the sophist. No reason is
given for accepting the order in which Socrates listed the three human types. Such a reason might be inferred from a remark by the
Stranger in the sequel to the present conversation. In the *Statesman*
(284c6), the Stranger says that it is a bigger job to understand "the
measure" (τὸ μέτριον) of political intelligence than it is to understand non-being. Perhaps the Stranger means something like this.
The proferred analysis of non-being turns upon a technical device
which, in theory, amounts to an effective procedure for determining
the meaning of a negative statement. But the nature of political intelligence, as is emphasized at the end of the *Statesman*, is not technical. There is no technical procedure for deciding in each case what
is the "measured" or sound response to the events. As a small but
not insignificant confirmation of the Stranger's observation, one may
note that there are many more competent technicians than there
are statesmen.

In any event, there is another reason which may be given for beginning with the sophist. Since he assumes all looks, we must first
identify and isolate him, lest we be tricked later into taking him for
a statesman or philosopher. To say this in another way, there is
something comprehensive about the nature of the sophist, who is
sometimes caricatured in Plato as claiming to know everything (as,
for example, in the *Hippias Major* and *Minor*). This claim provides
us with a clue as to why we need to study the soul of the sophist.
For the claim is a sign of a character defect, not of a faulty τέχνη.[1]
The Stranger will provide a good bit of evidence about this relation
of character and art, yet, as we shall see, he does not address it directly. His own account of diaeresis rather serves to obscure the cen-
trality of that relation. There can be no doubt that the Stranger makes
remarks about diaeresis which encourage us to regard it as a quasi-
mathematical procedure of universal competence. But these remarks must be measured against the actual functioning of diaeresis
in the Stranger's hands. Perhaps diaeresis is like the sophist in
claiming, wrongly, to "know" everything.

1. Cf. Aristotle, *Metaphysics* Γ2, 1004b17ff.

To continue, we must make evident in discourse the nature of the sophist (καὶ ἐμφανίζοντι λόγῳ τί ποτ' ἔστι; 218c1). We start with the assumption that the sophist is not just a "who" but a "what." This is the necessary presupposition for the applicability of diaeresis. In the language of the previous excursus, the sophist must be a complex unit consisting of formal elements, each of which may be pinned down by a number. If these elements "wander," or are themselves sophistical, then we cannot count them; each is not merely a one-in-many, but a multiplicity that shifts its number as we seek to establish it. We will see how this develops.

The Stranger goes on to draw an important distinction between speech and thought. More specifically, the distinction is between a name and the thing it names. First, a point about terminology: in the present passage, the Stranger refers to the bearer of the name as an ἔργον, and then as a πρᾶγμα (218c2–4). These words have a primarily active sense, which is brought out by translating them as "deed," "work," or even "event." They express the dynamic interplay of the phenomena of everyday life, as the abstract dynamism of the participle ὄν does not. This dynamic character of phenomena will play a role in the later discussion of being at 247d8ff. Deeds and events are not simply passively perceived; they are not the "sense data" of the epistemologist. They impress themselves upon the senses and intellect, they both shape and are shaped by our cognitive faculties, and this has two different, even conflicting, consequences. The first is that the cognitive faculties take on the shape of the deeds and events, and this is the basis of subsequent knowledge. But second, perceiving and knowing are themselves activities, work, events. What we know, at least with respect to the phenomena of everyday life, is not "neutral" or independent of the activity by which we know it. This interplay of activity and passivity is not transcended by a "definition," which rather confirms, or fixes, the result of that interplay as the publicly acceptable "nature" of the "thing" (as it may now be called) in question. We transcend the interplay of activity and passivity if and only if we have access to the "work," "deed," or "event" as it is in itself, independent of its effect upon us. But how is this possible? Are not "works," "deeds," and "events" *already* the consequence of the interplay between cognition and "things"? The "thing" of a scientific definition is not the "thing in itself," but an abstraction from the "deeds" and "events" of everyday life. There seems to be only one way in which to elude this problem. We must possess some cognitive faculty, a kind of intellectual perception by which the pure form, the true answer to the question "What is it?", is accessible to us, as it is in itself, rather than as it manifests itself within the phenomena.

In the so-called middle dialogues, Socrates explicitly discusses such a cognitive power: he calls it νόησις. It is widely believed that, in the later dialogues, Plato abandoned the doctrine of intellectual perception together with the doctrine of separated forms or ideas. The Stranger makes no reference to such a doctrine of intellectual perception. On the other hand, he never explains how we know pure forms. They are simply cited as though they are directly accessible; and in discussing them, the Stranger continues to use cognitive terms derived primarily from the language of vision. The Stranger's silence about the manner of accessibility of the forms hardly constitutes a theoretical advance over the previous doctrine of νόησις. However, in the present passage, the question is rather this: *Is* there a form of sophistry, let alone of the sophist? Can there be a form of a being whose nature is to be continuously changing his form? Or is the continuously changing nature of the sophist due to the continuously changing ways in which we perceive him? Is sophistry a πρᾶγμα or an ὄν?

To come back to the text, the Stranger says that we share the name for something, thanks to the public nature of language, and this name stands for what each of us "possesses privately" (ἰδίᾳ . . . ἔχομεν; 218c3). He goes on to say that "one must always arrive at agreement concerning the πρᾶγμα itself by way of λόγος, rather than by the name alone without λόγος" (218c4–5). A name is not a λόγος, which could here be translated as a "statement" or a combination of "names" (as Plato designates both nouns and verbs). But this is not the central problem here. What we each "possess privately" can be nothing other than the πρᾶγμα. A πρᾶγμα, however, is not an εἶδος or form. It already incorporates "statements" in that our everyday perceptions of "things" (in all senses of the term) are conditioned by our natural language and, still more fundamentally, by our nature as talking animals. If diaeresis begins with πράγματα, it may very well reach definitions or publicly certified accounts. Definitions, however, are not pure forms. In the middle section of the *Sophist*, we start with pure forms, and we do not arrive at them by diaeresis. This is in no way different from the account in the *Philebus*; we begin with a complex unity and then proceed to number its formal elements. Whereas there is no numbering of the elements of the Stranger's atomic forms, in both cases the initial step is prior to diaeresis.

Our private possession of the "thing"—that is, the sophist or the tribe of sophists—is the basis for the public task of hunting down, or defining, the nature of the sophist. As the Stranger puts it, it is not a simple task to get hold of the nature of the tribe we have in mind (ἐπινοοῦμεν; 218c5–7). The problem, we may say, is two-fold. The first aspect turns upon the nature of what each of us privately possesses but which we cannot communicate to anyone else except by way of public language. If what we privately possess is not already linguistic, how can we talk about it? But, if it is linguistic, how can we arrive at its pure form? The second aspect of the problem is thus the question of how we move from private or intellectual possession to public discourse. We cannot be sure that what we cognize privately is the thing itself. And our attempt to certify this by way of discursive analysis transforms our private possession into a linguistic artifact. This problem, of course, touches our investigation of forms as well as of ἔργα or πράγματα. It is especially pressing in the latter case, since we do not seem to be able to bring in a claim to have perceived intellectually the form of the sophist. Needless to say, none of this prevents us from talking about sophistry, or from arriving at "definitions" of the nature of the sophist. The serious difficulty concerns the status and value of our talk and our definitions. Do these achieve stability and fixity at the price of abstracting from, and indeed disregarding, the continuously changing nature of the sophist himself? If there is no form *sophist*, to what does our definition correspond? Definitions are images; but what is the original, and by what means can we perceive it, so as to determine whether our definition is an icon or a fantasm? As we may infer from the metaphors to be introduced about the need to grasp the sophist with both hands (226a8), or to employ all the holds of the wrestler (231c5–6), discursive thinking is work. The discussion of "things," names, and statements suggests that it is also productive work.[2]

The Stranger makes a suggestion concerning the hard task of capturing the sophist. It has long been agreed by everyone that when we have a difficult piece of work to carry out well, we ought first to practice on smaller and easier things (218c7–d2). It is here that the Stranger introduces the guiding metaphor for diaeresis: the sophist is extremely difficult to hunt down (χαλεπὸν καὶ δυσθήρευτον; 218d2–4). Let us pause to examine this metaphor, in the light of what was

2. One may compare Socrates' reference to ὄνομα as διδασκαλικόν τι ὄργανον (*Cratylus* 388b10–c1). See also Derbolav (1972), pp. 80–87. As David Lachterman points out, however, the use of δήλωμα at *Cratylus* 435b2 (and δηλοῦντα at *Sophist* 261e1) may carry the sense of "revealing" a natural form.

said above about ἔργα and πράγματα. Hunting is a form of work which makes use of technical devices and methods to capture something that is not accessible in itself. Consider briefly the form of hunting which we are about to study in detail: fishing. Nature produces the fish, but the fish is transformed by the art of fishing into a quasi-artifact satisfying a variety of human intentions. We may fish merely for the sport of it. We may wish to display the captured fish in an aquarium for aesthetic reasons, or as a money-making venture. We may dissect the fish in order to satisfy our scientific curiosity. And even if we eat the fish, we transform it by means of fire, cooking implements, sauces, and so on. Finally, our livelihood may depend upon the profit to be gained from marketing fish, which are thus transformed into commodities. The simple art of fishing modifies the fish, but correlatively, it modifies us into sportsmen, scientists, merchants, gourmets, and so on.

There are two main points to this little example. The first is that hunter and hunted are modified by the activity of hunting. The second is that they are modified in various ways. No doubt we may arrive at a "scientific" definition of fishing that would be sufficiently general to cover most or all of the intentions or uses of fishing. But whatever its specific excellence, such a definition would not tell us anything, or certainly not enough, about the concrete variety of intentions for fishing. Why we fish would depend upon the everyday context. We could, of course, draw up a chart containing all the "species" of fishing. Such a chart, however, would leave us with the problem of deciding *what is* fishing. A definition that consists of a list of the species of fishing is quite different from a definition of the "essence" of fishing. And neither an essential definition nor a list of the species of fishing enables us to explain precisely what fishermen are doing in their various acts, guided as they are by different purposes.

One need not reject scientific definitions in noticing that, to the sportsman, hunting is something quite different from what it is to the scientist. It is far from evident that these different views of the process can be encompassed in a single scientific definition. This would not be true in all cases, however, for we can surely "hunt down" processes which are quite amenable to scientific definition. The question is whether sophistry is such a process. Here is a related point. Methods of hunting vary with the nature of our quarry. For example, we hunt for gold quite differently from the way in which we hunt for fish. If the term "hunt" is to be restricted to living quarry, we hunt for fish in a way quite different from the way in which we hunt for viruses or bacteria in a modern scientific laboratory.[3] However, the Stranger immediately takes it for granted that there is a "method" (μέθοδον) common to all kinds of hunting, and so, independent of all of them. It is this assumption that leads him to propose a preparatory exercise (218d4–6). The assumption may be restated as follows: "to be" is to be the member of a tribe, hence to be huntable and capturable.

Theaetetus, having no simpler suggestion to make, accepts the Stranger's proposal that they employ a lesser thing (than the sophist) as a paradigm (παράδειγμα) for the greater (218d7–e1). They will practice by defining the angler, who is both well known and trivial, yet carries a definition (λόγος) no less than do great things.[4] The Stranger says of the angler: "I hope that he has a method and a λόγος for us which are not unsuitable for what we desire" (219a1–2). It remains to be seen whether this hope will be fulfilled.

---

3. Manasse (1937), p. 29, points out the practical motives for recommending diaeresis in the *Phaedrus* and *Philebus*. All the more so is this true in the *Sophist*.
4. Cf. *Phaedrus* 263c and Wiehl (1967), p. 171, n. 10.

SCENE THREE

The Angler

(219a4–221c4)

In order to familiarize Theaetetus with his method, the Stranger will apply it to a simple example. The term in Greek for "example" (παράδειγμα) may also be translated as "model." Since the angler and the sophist are both hunters, it is not impossible that the subject matter of the present example is a model of the sophist. The situation becomes more complicated when we recall that philosophy, and hence diaeresis, is itself a kind of hunting. The paradigm of the angler thus illustrates the ambiguity of the sophist, or the difficulty we face in attempting to distinguish between the original and the image. We need to be as careful in considering the steps of the paradigm as we do in studying the diaeresis of the sophist. Let us also note that the Stranger has not yet introduced the name of his method. This is because Theaetetus does not possess a "private" cognition of the method.

STEP ONE: The angler practices an art, or is a τεχνίτης rather than an untechnical man (ἄτεχνον) with "another power" (ἄλλην δὲ δύναμιν; 219a4–7). This initial statement contains two important points. The first is that, according to the paradigm, sophistry is to be regarded as a τέχνη. I have already discussed some of the difficulties this raises in the prologue. We have an apparent difference here between the doctrine of the Stranger and the usual or explicit doctrine of Socrates. Socrates usually denies that sophistry is a τέχνη. By attributing a technical status to sophistry, the Stranger is obligated to grant a genuine knowledge to sophistry. And yet, he is (to say the least) reluctant to do this. Here is another aspect of the same problem. In the *Statesman* (258a7ff), the Stranger makes arithmetic the paradigm of the gnostic (nonproductive) arts, or in other words of what is usually called ἐπιστήμη in the dialogues. In the same passage, carpentry and handicraft are said to be paradigms of the practical (productive) arts. Sophistry, as a productive art (namely, the production of inaccurate images), is thus separated by the Stranger from arithmetic. Socrates, in what some would call his middle and late periods, represented by the *Republic* (VII, 522a3ff) and *Philebus* (55d10–e3), respectively, identifies arithmetic as the king or ruling element of *all* τέχνη and of ἐπιστήμη. To this we may add Socrates' remark in the *Gorgias* that "no deed without reason" (ἄλογον πρᾶγμα) is a τέχνη (465a5–6).

The passages just cited indicate that there is some disagreement between Socrates and the Stranger on the relation between arithmetic and production. This disagreement is not mitigated by Socrates' subsequent distinction in the *Philebus* (56d4ff) between arithmetic of the many and arithmetic of the philosophers. Vulgar arithmetic counts objects of sense perception; vulgar logistics and metrics consider the relations obtaining amongst objects of sense perception because of their numerical properties. Philosophical arithmetic, as we saw in our excursus on the *Philebus*, counts pure monads or intellectually visible units; philosophical logistics and metrics deal with geometrical forms and "exercises in calculations" (57a1), which latter I take to refer to exercises like those of eidetic counting. Philosophical arithmetic and its associated arts must be related to the "power" (δύναμις) of dialectic, which considers being, genuineness, and that which is by nature always the same (57e6ff). This "power" is the most precise ἐπιστήμη, even more so than is philosophical arithmetic. Philosophical arithmetic is not only not productive, but, as we saw previously, when it approaches dialectic, it is also not "logico-deductive" (I employ this expression to distinguish between counting what one sees and proving mathematical theorems). In other words, Socratic diaeresis is acquisitive, not productive. It is not a demiurgic or manual τέχνη. And it is certainly not rooted in the everyday looks of things like anglers, sophists, and other human types. The Stranger's use of diaeresis is restricted to the articulation of human perspectives on human types, and as such it is from the Socratic standpoint inextricably bound up with sense perception. Thus, even if the Stranger were to associate some kind of arithmetic with the productive arts, this would not alter the fact that diaeresis, since it deals with impure or perceived objects, employs vulgar arithmetic for productive purposes.

Perhaps one could summarize the preceding reflections as follows. If the productive arts are for the Stranger not genuinely "gnostic," then the production of accurate images, as for example in true statements, cannot be, either. This is too paradoxical, not to say self-contradictory. On the other hand, if the productive arts *are* genuinely gnostic, then (putting to one side the division in the *Statesman*) the sophist is not himself a "fantasm" or inaccurate copy of someone possessing genuine knowledge. This dilemma will play a prominent role in what follows. One last comment along these lines: the Stranger's discussion of the "greatest kinds" (μέγιστα γένη), which serves as the basis for his resolution of the problems of non-being and falsehood, shows no trace of the use of diaeresis, and it unmistakably treats our perception of the greatest kinds as "acquisitive" in a sense applicable, on the surface at least, to Socrates' conceptions of dialectic and (somewhat more problematically) philosophical arithmetic in the *Philebus*. Once again, there is a clear difference between the Stranger and Socrates with respect to diaeresis or dialectic.

I turn now to the second point raised in 219a4–7. The primary division is not of τέχνη but of power (δύναμις).[1] This may well have some bearing on the Stranger's assertion (not clearly in his own name, however) at 247d8ff, to the effect that being is power. Coming back to the present distinction, those who lack a technical art are not thereby powerless. We may accomplish something spontaneously or at random, by inspiration, and in other ways that do not follow rules (cf. *Philebus* 28d6ff). It should be noted that in the *Statesman* (258b6) the Stranger says that, in the previous discussion, we divided the sciences (τὰς ἐπιστήμας). This does not, however, cancel out the text at *Sophist* 219a4–7. There is no reason for the Stranger to refer to "powers" in the *Statesman* passage, which shows only that τέχνη and ἐπιστήμη are interchangeable for the Stranger.

STEP TWO: The Stranger now shifts his attention from "powers" to technical powers, and from technicians to the arts themselves. The latter may be divided into two "looks" (εἴδη) or kinds. This terminology is of course reminiscent of the *Philebus* passage, in which the dialectician is said to pick out the formal elements of an initially selected complex unit. In the present case, the complex unit would be either "the arts" or "the powers." Since the word εἶδος is not applied to δύναμις, let us assume that "the arts" is the first step in our division to which diaeresis can be applied. In other words, "power" is not a look, any more than "being" is a predicate. There

---

1. Cf. Zadro (1961), p. 65: "Τέχνη, si è visto, è una certa determinazione di δύναμις, cioè avere la τέχνη, relativemente ad un certo ogetto, è un certo modo di essere *capaci* in relazione a quell'oggetto." [Τέχνη, it is seen, is a certain determination of δύναμις, therefore in truth τέχνη, relative to a certain object, is a certain mode of being *capable* in relation to that object.]

is no visible property called "power" or "being." Powers or beings first become visible as *this* or *that* power or thing.[2] Diaeresis cannot begin with what is not already definite, a unit, and hence distinct from other units. But the arts do possess the desired definiteness, and, according to the Stranger, their "surface structure" consists of two "looks," namely, production and acquisition.

So the two kinds of arts are the productive (ποιητικαί) and the acquisitive (κτητικαί). The angler falls under the acquisitive arts: he shows himself to us (cf. 218c1) as someone who exercises the power of acquiring fish. The productive arts are of three kinds: the care of living beings (plants and animals), the making of tools, and mimesis. These three kinds all bring into being what would not otherwise exist. They also produce something which does not belong to the same family as does the producer. There are two possible exceptions to this. First, mimesis might possibly include human sexual reproduction (although this is not stated). Second, those arts which take care of "the mortal body" may include arts like medicine and midwifery (again, this is not stated). In all three cases, the producer begins with something preexistent; there is no creation *ex nihilo*. The farmer and other tenders of living bodies begin with things of the same kind as those to be produced. The imitator, however, makes a copy of an original which is not of the same kind as the copy (for example, a painting of a human being is not a human being). The toolmaker does something still different. He takes preexisting materials and makes something that is neither of the same kind as those materials nor a copy of the original. If diaeresis is itself a productive art, it looks more like mimesis than like farming or toolmaking. And yet, concepts are tools which are used to acquire knowledge (219a8–c1).

To turn back to the acquisitive arts, these are "the entire εἶδος of the learnable (τὸ μαθηματικόν) and of knowing (τὸ τῆς γνωρίσεως), as well as of moneymaking, contesting, and hunting. These construct (δημιουργεῖ) nothing, but either master or subdue (χειροῦται) things, via words and deeds, which do exist or have existed; or else they prevent others from mastering them" (219c2–c7). We note that the things acquired may conceivably have been produced by some other art; nothing is said to exclude this possibility. Another interesting point: the acquisition of knowledge, money, and victory corresponds to the three ends attributed by Socrates in the *Republic* (IV,

---

2. Cf. *Republic* V, 477c9–d2: δυνάμεως δ'εἰς ἐκεῖνο μόνον βλέπω ἐφ' ᾧ τε ἔστι καὶ ὃ ἀπεργάζεται. In other words, δυνάμεις in themselves are invisible.

440e8ff) to the parts of the soul: the love of knowledge, the love of wealth, and the love of glory. Hunting, however, cannot be fitted into this scheme. Perhaps this is because it is more comprehensive than any of the other three.

The Stranger classifies knowledge under acquisition rather than under production. We may reasonably wonder, however, whether "mastering" does not imply a certain violence, and hence a possible alteration of what one subdues. It is also curious that knowledge is associated with what has existed or exists, but not with what will exist. This should be contrasted with Theaetetus 178a5–8, where Socrates says that there is general agreement that the advantageous is to be classified under the rubric of future things. Finally, it is plain that moneymaking, contesting, and hunting all use tools of various kinds. Even geometry employs the straightedge and a piece of string. The question whether geometry is acquisitive or productive is, of course, much deeper than the level at which such tools are employed. But these tools at least point toward the deeper problem of "mathematical construction." Not quite so plain is the fact that words and deeds are used as tools in the acts of acquiring and blocking acquisition. But where man uses tools, he modifies nature.

Our initial division of the "complex unit" of the arts has not produced a clear act of enumeration. Whereas the surface structure of the arts consists of production and acquisition, these are already compounded, as is evident from the need to give examples. For example, the acquisitive consists of learning, moneymaking, contesting, and hunting. In what clear sense, compatible with their representing attributes of a surface element of acquisition, do these look alike? Has the Stranger not engaged in a diaeresis of acquisition within the same step of diaeresis that is designed solely to isolate acquisition? Has he not generalized sharply distinct looks, looks which, at the level of surface structure, we would inevitably distinguish? Yet diaeresis is supposed to be specification, not generalization. We are supposed to be moving downward to an "uncuttable form." These questions about diaeresis will be multiplied in what follows.

STEP THREE: The Stranger and Theaetetus agree that the practise of the angler falls under the acquisitive arts. In other words, they know in advance where to find him. If the angler is an "uncuttable atom," he will not be located by diaeresis. On the contrary, we can use diaeresis because we already know how to locate the angler. What we have to do now is cut the look of acquisition in half. One of the resultant looks is voluntary exchange by means of gifts, wages, and purchases. The second look "masters" (χειϱούμενον) by deeds or speeches (219d4–8). This is unexpected, since at 219c5 the same Greek verb was used in describing the entire acquisitive family as either "mastering" or "preventing from mastering." If the involuntary part of this family "masters," are we to assume that the voluntary part does not, but merely prevents from mastering? To draw the distinction in this way, however, would exclude the voluntary part from the function of acquiring. Yet there does not seem to be an art of involuntarily preventing others from mastering. So there is a degree of confusion in the formulation of this family. Theaetetus's response may reflect this confusion. Until now, he has given unqualified assent to the Stranger's conclusions. Here he replies, "It appears so from what has been said" (219d8).

We may also ask whether voluntary exchange is invariably for material consideration. Can gifts include, for example, knowledge? The Stranger seems to imply that when exchange takes place freely and without money, it is of the nature of a gift. If mastery or coercion is a defining mark of the entire tribe of acquirers, then gift giving is presumably also a form of mastery. Furthermore, if knowledge is a gift, why is giftgiving distinguished from mastery by deeds or speeches? And would not confusion be avoided by a more careful selection of terms? In sum, the numbers corresponding to the performed steps in the diaeresis by no means correspond to definite element-forms of the initial complex unit.

STEP FOUR: In the previous steps, the Stranger asks Theaetetus to choose the division to which the angler belongs. Now (219d9) he himself advises that they continue with the mastering or dominating art (τὴν χειϱωτικήν). This is again divided into two: contests held in the open (ἀναφανδόν) and secret hunting (219d9–e3). If we think for a moment of the sophist, it seems plain that he might be classified within either branch of the division. Sophists gather at gymnasia and other places of public assembly; but according to Protagoras, they have also hunted secretly, in disguise, a practice which he claims to be the first sophist to reject (*Protagoras* 316d3ff; cf. *Theaetetus* 152c8ff). In the prologue to our own dialogue, Socrates claims that philosophers also don disguises, although he does not there describe them as hunters. They are also to be found in the open, although it is not clear that the wearing of a disguise is incompatible with the public assertion that one is a philosopher.

STEP FIVE: The Stranger again leads the way. "It would be unreasonable not to divide the hunting class in half." There is, then, secret hunting of both souled and unsouled beings (219e4–7). Once again we remind ourselves that the present diaeresis is intended as a paradigm for the definition of the sophist. What about open contests between sophists, or between sophists and philosophers? Are these in fact secret hunts, and if so, what precisely does that mean? But there is a more obvious difficulty. We may assume that all hunting is secret because the hunter must conceal himself from his prey. The prey of the sophist, however, the wealthy youth of Athens, *seeks out the hunter*. This cannot be the same as other kinds of secret hunting. And in what sense is the hunting of unsouled beings conducted in secret? Theaetetus is also puzzled; he questions whether both kinds of hunting exist. The Stranger assures him: "how shall they not exist?" (219e8–220a1).

Ensouled beings have now appeared twice within the diaeresis, once under production and once under acquisition. This is quite natural, since arts of all kinds are practiced for the sake of human beings. In other words, the articulation of the arts is also an articulation of the human soul. But it is far from clear that the forms of the soul may be distinguished even as sharply as are the kinds of arts. If the arts are directed toward the soul, and the forms of the soul blend into one another, then the division of the arts, as a purely technical exercise, becomes of secondary importance.

STEP SIX: The Stranger passes by the nameless and presumably trivial hunting of lifeless things, of which an example is diving. This shows that hunting for definitions may also be classified within our schema. The hunting of living things has a "double look" (διπλοῦν εἶδος). In other words, the complexity of life is evident in its surface structure. The Stranger's analysis in fact leaves out a "look." The first look, he says, the hunting of walking or land animals, has many looks and names of its own. The second look is the hunting of swimming or water animals (220a1–11).[3] This division overlooks flying animals, which will be tacitly assimilated into land animals in the next step. This is misleading, however, since some birds also swim, whereas others do not. The classification of birds is part of a tangled passage in the *Statesman* (261e5ff), in which the central issue is how to divide the family of human beings.[4] Whatever baroque resonances may be contained in the traditional definition of man as the featherless biped, there is a more accessible point here. The Stranger divides the arts, not simply in terms of their functions (such as hunting of living things), but also on the basis of their objects (for

3. Cf. Benardete (1963), pp. 193–95.
4. Cf. Rosen (1979) for a discussion of diaeresis in the *Statesman*.

example, land animals, water animals). These two types of division are not the same. The generality of the function is blurred by the various looks of the objects, each of which requires a specification of the function. If we were giving a number to the element of hunting living things, in accordance with Socrates' instructions in the *Philebus*, how would we choose the appropriate number? A "double look" seems to require two numbers, whereas a single element requires one number.

STEP SEVEN: The Stranger divides the hunting of swimmers into birdcatching and fishing. As was just noted, this overlooks the fact that not all birds can swim. He does not refer to the hunting of land animals, and this causes a slight flaw in the symmetry of the diaeresis (220b1–8).

STEP EIGHT: Some fishing occurs by means of nets or enclosures and some by means of blows. So the hunter uses tools, whether or not he makes them himself. In addition, the tool selected will account for a specific modification of the fish. Whereas it may be a part of the art of fishing that some tools are preferable for one type of fish and other tools for another type, it remains true that we may use different tools to catch the same type, depending upon whether we wish to eat or preserve the fish. Even if there are "natural joints" (*Phaedrus* 266b3–c9) in the diaeresis of fishing, human intention will lead us to disregard these joints. It is far from clear that beings like the angler or the sophist possess "natural joints" that permit a rigorous articulation terminating in a λόγος, because what we mean by "angler" or "sophist" is a function of human intention, not merely of natural forms (220b9–d4).

STEP NINE: If enclosures are like sound definitions that preserve the nature of what we define, perhaps blows are like the persuasive and distorting speeches of sophists. The Stranger directs Theaetetus to look for the angler among those who fish by blows. This kind of fishing, whether with hooks or spears, is divided into night fishing by firelight and fishing by daylight with spears or hooks specially equipped with barbs (220d5–e1).[5] We note that secret hunting may take place by day or by night.

STEP TEN: The angler belongs to those who fish with barbed hooks by daylight. In one kind of barb fishing, he strikes with a trident from above downward, and onto any part of the body. In the other kind, angling, he strikes from below upward, and exclusively on the head and the mouth (220e2–221a6). We see here an amusing in-

5. Consider the distinction between sunlight and firelight in *Republic* VII, 514a7ff.

stance of the inapplicability of Heraclitus's remark, that the way up is the same as the way down, at the level of human activity.

SUMMARY: The summary is accurate, although we may note that it tacitly includes, but does not explicitly mention, the distinction between hunting by firelight and by daylight (221a7–c4). The angler is a practitioner of the mastering kind of acquisitive art called hunting, namely, of hunting water animals of the fish family, and his method is to strike the fish with a barb from below. The summary is certainly less informative than the diaeresis itself; for example, it makes no reference to secrecy and openness, or to daylight and firelight. The summary thus abstracts from the question of the manner of visibility peculiar to hunting for fish, and this is an amusing comment on its own inferiority to the antecedent discussion. A method that concludes with a list of salient characteristics, more or less plausible in themselves but hardly unarguable candidates for necessary or defining properties, is surely something less than scientific. I do not question the fact that the Stranger introduces and illustrates his method with a straight face. The same procedure is followed by many characters in dramatic comedies, as for example Socrates.

Division and Multiplication
of the Sophist

(221c5–226a8)

If the form of an entity is a complex unity consisting of a definite number of elements, each of which may be divided into a definite number of subelements, and so on down to the complete enumeration of the formal constituents of the original complex, then there cannot be more than one diaeresis of that form. Any two enumerations of the same number of elements must be numerically the same. If we can produce different enumerations of the elements in a unique form, then the form cannot present us with a definite look. And if many enumerations, all of the same number, but differing qualitatively, are possible, then the counting operation, whereas perhaps significant, is secondary to the operation of perceiving the multiple sets of countable properties. The Stranger is about to produce a number of diaereses of the sophist. As we shall see, the exact number of these diaereses is not clear; it may be six or seven. The division of the look of the sophist thus leads to a multiplication of "definitions" of the sophist. Since the dialogue concludes, after an unusually long digression, with what purports to be the "definitive" diaeresis of the sophist, one might wish to discount the initial multiplicity as due to inexperience or the process of gradually correcting technical errors in the application of the method. For this hypothesis to be plausible, it must be shown that the initial diaereses are defective, and that the final diaeresis not only rectifies the initial defects, but contains none of its own. In my analysis, I shall present evidence that neither of these conditions is met. Whereas from a quasi-mathematical or arithmetical standpoint, all of the diaereses are defective, in a phenomenological sense, they are all accurate. In this scene, we will study seriatim the first four (or perhaps five; cf. 231c8–e7) diaereses. These descend from the paradigm case and are clearly distinguished from the fifth (or perhaps sixth), which is also the longest and the most important.

We have now constructed the paradigm to be followed in the opening set of efforts to hunt down the sophist (221c5). When the term "paradigm" was introduced at 218d9, I suggested that it refers to the content as well as to the form of the initial exercise. This is now confirmed by the Stranger. The angler is of the same family (ξυγγενῆ) as the sophist: both are hunters. Since we are ourselves hunting, it looks as though we, too, are related to the sophist. At this stage, it would be appropriate for the Stranger to provide us with a diaeresis of hunting that is finer-grained than was the segment of his initial example. He will in fact do this in his opening diaeresis of the sophist. Before we turn to this diaeresis, two brief comments on the text are in order. First, the Stranger seems to be surprised at the relation between the sophist and the hunter, which he expresses with his first oath in the dialogue (221d8–11). I suggest that the real surprise lies more in the unstated fact that the Stranger and Theaetetus, as hunters themselves, are also related to the sophist. This point reminds us of our previous observation on the puzzling attribution of a τέχνη to the sophist. Why could the Stranger not have classified sophistry as an untechnical power? Those who believe that diaeresis begins with the arts are not in a position even to ask this question, although in another sense they are right, since "power" is too "transparent" a term to serve in an initial division. With what would it be contrasted? Lack of power? But this would be to give formal status to "non-being" *qua* nothing. The term δύναμις does not mean "possibility" in the *Sophist*; it refers to an "actuality" which does or suffers something tangible, let us say something countable. In order to divide, we must begin with a definite form. The attempt to capture the sophist by diaeresis thus requires us to begin with something divisible. Nevertheless, it is still not evident that the Stranger had to begin with the arts. By so doing, he necessarily attributes some kind of knowledge to the sophist. This brings me to the second point.

The difficulty in which the Stranger finds himself is shown by his refusal to include the sophist among those who are truly wise (221c8–d2) and by his assertion that the sophist possesses "a sort of art" (221d5). But what sort of art? Both angler and sophist, he says, "seem plainly to me to be some sort of hunter" (θηρευτά τινε καταφαίνεσθον ἄμφω μοι; 221d13). One could say this: since philosophers are also hunters, and granted that philosophical knowledge is a kind of τέχνη, then at least some part of hunting must be a τέχνη. But need all of it be technical? Could the sophist not be an untechnical hunter? However, further thought reveals that this, too, must be excluded. The heart of the dialogue turns upon the difficulty in distinguishing between the sophist and the philosopher. This is a political, and not just a theoretical problem, as we know from the fact that Socrates was widely perceived to be a sophist. The art Socrates practices is no more clear than that of the sophist. Socrates claims to know only the art of love, but this is so ambiguous an assertion as to be relatively useless, both politically and analytically. If the sophist and the philosopher could be distinguished simply by saying that one is an untechnical and the other a technical hunter, then there would scarcely be any need for six or seven diaereses to pin down the sophist. More fundamentally, the problem of the sophist as a false image or fantasm of the philosopher would disappear. Not to have an art can hardly qualify as a fantasm of having an art. If it is objected that the sophist "pretends" to have an art, the answer is straightforward. The pretension is so accomplished that the sophist must possess an art of pretending, and this is indeed the art that is attributed to him. The sophist has the art of making fantasms. This is the essential background to the diaereses, which otherwise seem to be absurd.

Theaetetus still fails to perceive the sense in which the sophist is a hunter. He can hardly be expected to have carried out the necessary reflections on the spot. The Stranger reminds him of the previous diaeresis (step six) in which hunting was divided into the pursuit of swimmers and that of walkers. It is now time to divide further the hunting of walking animals, since it is at this point that the angler and the sophist separate (221e1–222a8). The sophist hunts in the rivers of wealth and youth (222a9–b1); in so doing, he may remind us of Socrates. The series of diaereses of the sophist thus begins, not with an argument or a deduction, but with a metaphorical reference to everyday life. We "know" what a sophist is in advance, and not by diaeresis. What seems to be required is an analytical explanation of the precise nature of the being who is directly visible to us as an ἔργον or πρᾶγμα.

DIAERESIS 1: 222b2–223b8

STEP ONE There are two kinds of land hunting, namely, of tame and of wild animals. In the *Statesman*, "land animal" is a species of "herd animal" (264d1–3), and "herd" is taken as synonymous with "tame" (263e6–264b5). The possibility that human beings may be either tame or wild is there excluded. Here, the Stranger says that there is a hunting of tame animals, "if indeed man is a tame animal" (222b6–7). At least a shadow of a doubt is thus cast upon man's tameness, and this doubt will be confirmed shortly. Meanwhile we note another point. Tame animals appeared under the angler paradigm in the division of productive tending by farmers. The reference there was of course to beasts. Some beasts are tame, and others are wild. Farmers are themselves tame animals but not beasts; they have been "tamed" by political life. However, in discussing the human animal, we are abstracting from this or that political modification. The Stranger gives Theaetetus a choice: is the family of the human animals tame or wild? What is involved in this alternative? The general sense of "tame" in the *Sophist* and *Statesman* is that of "herd animal," as we have just noted. But this in itself is ambiguous. Animals may live in herds and still be wild; as an example, consider wild horses. If a herd animal is understood as a domesticated animal, then the attribute of living in a herd is not natural but imposed by man. Domesticated animals are, by extension, politicized animals. In the case of human beings, the sharpest form of the question is whether man is by nature a political animal. This Aristotelian definition of man never appears in the Platonic dialogues. One could conceivably infer it from the thesis in the *Republic* that the city is the soul writ large. It would take us too far afield to examine the arguments employed to sustain this thesis by Socrates. I will note only two objections to its accuracy. First, when speaking of the individual soul, Socrates attributes no characteristic virtue to the epithymetic or desiring part, which must be kept in check, or "moderated," by the force of thymos or spiritedness. In the city, however, moderation is the characteristic virtue of the worker class, which ostensibly corresponds to the epithymetic part of the individual soul. Second, the city cannot be a philosopher, whereas the individual soul can.[1] In any event, the Stranger is not responsible for Socrates' metaphors. He accepts Theaetetus's "tame" response that humans are tame (222b6–c2). This presumably refers to the fact that man can enter into political life. But it does not commit us to the view that all citizens remain tame, or even that all human beings are essentially defined by their political existence. For the moment, let us leave this question open.

STEP TWO: Tame animals may be hunted in one of two ways: by force, as in piracy, kidnapping, tyranny, and war; or by persuasion (as in the law courts), by public speaking, and in conversation (222c3–

---

1. In *Republic* IV, 430e11–431b3, we are told that the better masters the worse in the human soul that is marked by self-mastery. Cf. *Republic* IV, 442c10–d3: the "worse" is the desiring part of the soul, which has no intrinsic virtue because it is by nature intemperate. Temperance comes to the desiring element from outside itself, and by force.

d2). The first set of examples increases our doubt as to the "tameness" of the human animal. Criminals and tyrants are surely outside the law, and even the *Republic* shows us that cities stand to one another in something very much like what modern political philosophers called the "state of nature."[2] Nevertheless, it might be objected that only a political being can stand "outside" the law, or even that the "unnatural" deviations of scattered individuals do not alter the general rule concerning human nature. However, the question I am pursuing is not whether some human beings can subsist without any political contact. The interesting question is rather that of the various senses of "tame," and the implications of the activity of hunting human beings, whether as philosopher, sophist, or kidnapper. Shortly stated, if the sophist is tame, this has implications for the soundness of his political doctrines. A parallel question holds good for the philosopher. If to be tame is to be a herd animal, what are we to make of Socrates' comprehensive rejection of the laws and customs of the Athenians, as for example in the *Republic*? It would be naive to reply that Socrates always obeyed the laws, to the point of accepting his death sentence. Revolution, and thus treason, begin in speech, not in deed. Besides, beasts are not capable of advocating a shift from one herd to another. The human animal's capacity to do this suggests that he is "wild" in a sense that does not apply to the beasts.

STEP THREE: The Stranger puts to one side hunting by force, and thus draws a veil of silence over questions like those just raised. Instead, we divide persuasion, which is either private or public (222d3–6). In the present instance, these terms are presumably intended to characterize herd speech.

STEP FOUR: The Stranger passes by public persuasion without comment. He divides private persuasion into two kinds of hunting; in one, the hunter accepts a salary, whereas in the other, he gives presents. Theaetetus does not understand this distinction. The Stranger assumes that this is because Theaetetus has paid no attention to erotic hunting and so does not know that, other things aside, lovers also make gifts. I have already commented on the relation between this point and the general disregard of eros in the *Sophist*. Nevertheless, an erotic distinction of sorts is visible in this division.

2. Cf. *Republic* III, 398a1ff. Those poets who are capable of becoming all things and of imitating all things are to be crowned with myrrh and fillets of wool and sent to another city. We will retain only those poets who tell useful tales and imitate no one but the decent man. The resemblance between the poet who is expelled from the just city and the sophist is obvious.

The Stranger suggests tacitly that persuasion for a salary is like prostitution (222d7–e4).

STEP FIVE: Hunting for the purpose of gaining salaries is divided into two parts. The first part is the art by which its practitioners engage in conversation for gratification. Here pleasure is the bait, but the unique purpose is the support or nourishment of the persuader. The other tribe converses, as it claims, for the sake of virtue, but its members accept monetary wages. The tribes are those of flattery and sophistry, respectively (222e5–223a10).[3]

SUMMARY: In presenting the summary, I shall disregard almost entirely the emendations in the manuscript readings of modern scholars. So far as I can see, with the exception of one point, the manuscripts raise no intrinsic problems, whether of a grammatical or substantive kind. The summary is of course peculiar, in the sense that it does not give an accurate account of the preceding diaeresis, but we have to understand this fact, not excise it from the text. (1) In naming the acquisitive art, the summary uses οἰκειωτική in place of κτητική, but then adds κτητική as the next word, thus making it a branch of "the art of making things friendly or one's own." If an explanation is required for this shift in terms, it is easily available. The Stranger indicates to us that human beings make themselves "at home" in their environment through the use of their persuasive powers. This suggestion is reinforced by the next point. (2) Mastery or subduing (χειρωτική, cf. 219d4–8) is omitted from the summary in the best manuscripts. This casts a doubt on the distinction between force and persuasion, and raises anew the question of man's tameness. (3) The summary gives two words for "land animals," and I shall assume that this may be a copyist's error.[4] (4) The summary, unlike the diaeresis, distinguishes between the hunting of tame animals and the hunting of human beings. In the diaeresis, these two were not distinguished (222b7). Man is now made a subset of "tame animals," and so is categorized with greater precision. (5) The summary adds "claiming to educate" as a distinct division and qualifies the expression "wealthy youths" employed in the diaeresis by "of good repute." Again, the summary is more precise. Theaetetus is

3. What if the sophist teaches the identity of virtue and pleasure? Cf. *Protagoras* 358a1–b6.

4. For an ingenious interpretation of this passage, cf. Benardete (1960). Benardete's main point can be substantiated by a more straightforward analysis of the text than he supplies. The point is that "the sophist has imperceptibly slid over into a kind of making" and so that "the rest of the dialogue tries to bring together ἐριστική and δημιουργική, which can only be effected by considering imitation" (p. 139).

not disturbed by these variations, no doubt because he does not expect exactness in nonmathematical investigations.

I pause here to make a brief methodological remark. Some readers will be disturbed by my attempt to find significance in the variations between the summary and the diaeresis, and will accordingly regard the scholarly emendations, noted in Burnet's edition, as justified. Nothing of crucial importance to my interpretation of the *Sophist* has emerged in the remarks about these variations. The reader is thus free to disregard them if he so chooses. But there is a deeper point at stake here. The *Sophist*, like virtually all of the Platonic dialogues, is filled with unexpected turns, most of which cannot be directly explained as errors in the manuscript transmission. Recourse to the unexpected is a fundamental aspect of Plato's literary style. To weed out these "rough" spots in the text is no more permissible than it would be to eliminate all passages from Aeschylus, or for that matter Shakespeare, which are odd or at first glance inconsequent. If we are going to read a Platonic dialogue, then scholarly decency requires us to read it carefully and to think about what we are reading. It is an odd turn of events when one must apologize for the effort to take seriously the text of the author one is interpreting. Those who regard the "literary trimming" as irrelevant to the "arguments" are still obligated to point out exactly what are the arguments, and I see no way to do this except by studying as minutely as possible what Plato wrote. Set-theoretical analyses of "arguments" are worthless in this context if the arguments themselves do not appear in the dialogue. In sum: the variations in the summary are of no great importance in themselves. They are, however, part of a test: Can we read accurately?

DIAERESIS 2: 223c1–224d3

"Let's also look at the matter in this way," says the Stranger. We need a variety of looks because the sophist's art is "many-colored" or "intricate" (ποικίλης). There is no deductive connection between one look and the other. We look around, noticing now one look and now another. Of course, we are not proceeding in a merely haphazard way. Our paradigm continues to give us guidance, but it is not itself a deductive structure. Nothing is said about why we begin from one step in the paradigm rather than another, or about the order in which we consider these steps. Even if we are able to figure out why the Stranger proceeds in the order he chooses, the reasons are not deductions in the mathematical sense. We are moving from one inspection to another of a complex phenomenon in everyday life. For example, the first diaeresis took up hunting because the most obvious oddity to emerge from our paradigm was the relation between sophists and anglers, on the one hand, and philosophers, on the other. There is no formal reason for the Stranger to have begun with hunting. On the contrary, his motive depends for its visibility on our capacity to relate the metaphor of hunting to his oath at 221d8ff. I can easily imagine some readers denying that a motive may be inferred from the evidence cited, but that is precisely my point. If we do not think about what the Stranger is doing, and specifically, about the order in which he carries out his diaereses, his explicit statements will tell us nothing about the underlying order. I want to underline that to think about what is said is not the same as to argue from total silence. The inferring of a quasi-mathematical method from the Stranger's procedures is, however, an excellent example of an argument from silence (223c1–5).

STEP ONE: According to the Stranger, we previously divided the acquisitive art into hunting and exchange (and ἀλλακτικόν here replaces μεταβλητικόν, employed for "exchange" at 219d5). In fact, if we check back, we find that acquisition was divided originally into voluntary and mastering or coercing exchange (219d1ff). So far as I know, no one has suggested that we alter the text at this point to bring it into conformity with the earlier passage, but neither can we simply pass the discrepancy by in silence. Once more, the recommended procedure is to try to understand what Plato has written. First, a general remark: since the sophist is continuously changing his form, the paradigm must vary continuously in order to be an accurate model of the sophist. However, we can be more specific. In the previous diaeresis, mastery (coercion) was distinguished from persuasion within the segment devoted to the hunting of tame animals (221c3ff). Diaeresis 2 thus omits any reference to coercion, as well as to the distinction between open contests and concealed hunting. The summary of the first diaeresis prepared us for this shift by omitting "coercive" from its resume of the main steps of the division. *The "form" of the sophist is itself shifting, even as we attempt to describe him.* This is a beautiful touch on Plato's part, and it is totally obliterated by the textual emenders. The main point now is that the sophist is the hunter whose victim pays him a salary. We begin this time from step three in the angler paradigm, and divide exchange into giving and selling (223c6–11).

STEP TWO: Giving, which was associated previously with eros, is now dropped. Commerce, if it is not to be associated with prostitution, at any rate becomes a substitute for eros. We divide selling into two kinds: of one's own productions and of the work of others (223c12–d4).

STEP THREE: In yet another terminological shift, the Stranger now uses μεταβλητική, originally the word for "exchange" in general, to designate selling the goods of others. This shift in terminology is another aspect of the nonmathematical character of the diaeresis of the sophist. Part of the selling of the goods of others is carried on within the city (καπηλική) and part is carried on between cities (ἐμπορική; 223d5–11).

STEP FOUR: The Stranger takes us directly to merchandising between cities; this is because he knows in advance where the sophist is to be found. Diaeresis, so far as we can tell from its current employment, is no more a method of discovery than is the Aristotelian syllogistic. In both cases, something known previously is presented in a certain format. A more difficult point is that the Stranger also goes from city to city (from Elea to Athens), not to sell, but to give as a present the doctrines of others (as he implies, of the Eleatic school). This is not to suggest that the Stranger is a merchant. It is rather to draw a contrast with Socrates, who goes to no other cities (in his role as philosopher) and makes no presents (since he has no doctrines). Socrates draws an at least rhetorical or public connection between his philosophical and his political activity. He purports to "enlighten" (if that is the right word) only his fellow citizens, whereas the Stranger is indifferent to the question of citizenship.

Merchandising between cities is now divided into the nourishment and service of the body and of the soul (223e1–3). The absence of coercion, and the concomitant emphasis upon utility, contains the implication that commerce plays a critical role in the taming of the human animal.

STEP FIVE: We turn from the body to the less well-known merchandising of the commodities of the soul. Theaetetus did not understand the previous division (223e4–7). He is not familiar with psychic merchandising. The Stranger provides the following examples: music, painting, and conjuring or wonder working (θαυματοποιική). This initially odd grouping presumably contains a reflection, by no means favorable, upon the power of the fine arts. Some of these commodities of the soul are used for relaxation and some for serious purposes. The Stranger then places the merchandising of culture (as we may call it) on the same level as the merchandising of food and drink. To this, Theaetetus strongly assents, whether from an objection to professional artists or because of a lack of interest in the arts is not clear (224a1–8). Soul merchandising is then divided into two equally laughable parts: epideictic or show-off oratory and the selling of knowledge (224b1–8). This division associates the sophist's knowledge with the productions of others. It thus seems to preclude the sophist's having produced his own knowledge, but also precludes his selling knowledge that has been "acquired" rather than produced. Yet we are in the act of dividing "acquisition." Of course, sophistry is an acquisitive art in the sense that it charges a salary, just as the merchant makes a profit.

STEP SIX: Show-off oratory is discarded (cf. 217e2) and its coordinate is divided into the selling of τέχνη and of virtue (ἀρετή). This last is sophistry, as Theaetetus readily notes (224b9–c8). The sellers of art are no doubt the professors or artisans themselves, who train their apprentices. More precisely, the Stranger distinguishes between virtue and "the other arts." So, presumably virtue is also an art, if a peculiar one.

SUMMARY: This division is said to show sophistry as acquisitive, exchanging, selling, and merchandising from city to city the goods of the soul in words and knowledge dealing with virtue (224c9–d3). In fact, the steps were: acquiring, selling, selling the goods of others, merchandising, merchandising the goods of the soul, selling knowledge, selling virtue. Perhaps the main difference here is that the summary drops the distinction between selling one's own productions and those of another. As we shall see, this revision again prepares us for the next diaeresis; the sophist is once more shifting his form.

DIAERESIS 3: 224d4–e5

According to the first diaeresis, the sophist is a hunter who charges a fee for conversations about virtue. Under normal circumstances, the hunter's prey does not pay for the privilege of being caught. In the present case, the oddity must have something to do with the secrecy of hunting or the sophist's disguise. The sophist must not appear to be a hunter; on the contrary, he must be sought out by his clientele. What is the disguise by which the sophist transforms involuntary prey into voluntary customers? There can be only one answer; the sophist is disguised as the philosopher or wise man. He claims to be useful precisely because he teaches the truth about human affairs, or in other words, he claims that the true is the useful.

In the second diaeresis, we shifted our attention from hunting to exchange. Questions of the origin of the product to one side, the central point here is once more utility. Diaeresis 3 is an extension of this concentration upon utility, and it also introduces a modification in the issue of whether the sophist makes his own products. However, this diaeresis is marked by two distinct oddities, one of them of considerable importance for the structure of the diaeresis scene as a whole. The first odd point is less interesting; the Stranger does all the work, with no assistance from Theaetetus, and in two short speeches. Theaetetus does nothing more than assent to the Stranger's statements. The second odd point will not be fully visible until we come to the summary of the diaereses. However, it will be necessary to anticipate that summary. What counts here explicitly as the third diaeresis (224d4) will later be divided into two diaereses (231d8–10).

STEP ONE: I give in full the first of the Stranger's two speeches: "If someone, who was settled down here in the city, would arrange himself so as to gain a living by selling these same kinds of knowledge, buying some and making others himself, you would not call him by any other name than the one which you just used." Theaetetus replies: "How could I?" (224d4–8). In this step, we unite two elements which were both rejected by the previous diaeresis: selling within the city and selling one's own productions. By symmetry with diaeresis 2, we might have expected "selling one's own products from city to city." This should be distinguished from two kinds of selling within the city, namely, of one's own products and of the products of others. Let us see what happens.

STEP TWO: Here is the second of the Stranger's two speeches in this diaeresis: "The part of acquisition which engages in exchange and sale, whether of the goods of others or of one's own, in both cases, so long as it falls under the genus of the seller of knowledge, you will always, it seems, call sophistry." Theaetetus replies: "Necessarily, for one must follow along with the λόγος" (224e1–5). Let us recapitulate. In diaeresis 2, the sophist buys his goods in one place and sells them in another city. In the first paragraph of diaeresis 3, the sophist sells within the city; some of his goods he makes himself, others he purchases. In the second paragraph of diaeresis 3, reference to whether the sophist sells within the city or from city to city is suppressed. These two steps are part of a single diaeresis. We shall see later that, when they recapitulate the definitions, the Stranger and Theaetetus subdivide this third definition into separate definitions. One is of a κάπηλος or seller within the city of learning commodities for the soul. It is not said whether he makes or purchases his products, but we may infer the latter from the sec-

ond definition, with which it is juxtaposed. The "fourth" definition
of the sophist is of one who sells his own productions. The term
used for "seller" is αὐτοπώλης (231d8ff), "seller of one's own," which
tells us nothing about where the selling takes place.

Is there any discernible pattern in this confusing set of circumstances? Up to a point, I think the answer is yes. Let us start with
two remarks. The net result of the shift from the first to the second
step in what is here diaeresis 3 is to cover over the possible case in
which the sophist sells something in his own city. This is also true
of αὐτοπώλης in definition 4 of the final summary. Now I cannot see
that this has any historical significance; we are surely not meant to
assume that the city of Athens produced no sophists of its own, who
sold to their fellow citizens. On the other hand, Socrates is surely
included in the case of those who stay within their own cities, but
who, however we are to describe their activity, do no selling of any
kind. The Stranger, we have already had occasion to note, goes from
city to city, and gives, but does not sell, the products of others. We
know from the *Statesman* (262c10ff) that the Stranger objects to the
division of mankind by cities, or more generally, to the distinction
between Greek and barbarian. He compares this division to an inaccurate division of numbers, thereby underlining his abstraction
from political loyalties. I offer the following suggestion. By Socratic
standards, the Stranger has not successfully avoided the charge of
sophistry. This is primarily because he teaches a positive doctrine,
which is open to misunderstanding and misuse. By the Stranger's
standards, however, Socrates is the sophist, because he has accommodated his philosophical practice to the Athenians, yet without
teaching any positive doctrine of his own. In this sense, Socrates is
guilty of corrupting the young; he turns them into skeptics and dog-
matists, to allude here to an actual consequence of the decay of the
Platonic school. The Stranger might reply to Socrates' charge that,
since his own teaching is theoretical rather than practical, it has
nnothing to do with politics, and is thus free of sophistry. But this
implies that there is no such thing as "political philosophy" (or as
τέχνη πολιτική). More sharply stated, the Stranger now seems to make
philosophy abandon politics, which is thus left to the mercy of the
sophists.

The student of the Platonic dialogue is often called upon to make
conjectures, whether with respect to the state of the manuscripts or
in attempting to establish the sense of an obscure and disputed passage. In order for the conjecture to be plausible, it must be supported
by textual evidence. The kind of textual evidence required will de-

pend upon the nature of the conjecture. In some cases, the issue can be resolved by a careful grasp of a few lines. In others, however, the conjecture gains credence only when considered in the light of our understanding of the dialogue as a whole. The problem I am here discussing is a mixture of these two cases. We are faced with an unmistakable problem in the structure of the diaereses, which is called to our attention by a discrepancy between the number of diaereses and the number of definitions in the summary. I am suggesting that this discrepancy points us in at least two directions. The first has to do with the adequacy of diaeresis to pin down the nature of the sophist. The applications of the method shift their forms, and even their "numbers," just as does the nature of the sophist. What would be inconsistencies from a "formalist" standpoint thus become appropriate qualities of a "metaphorical" representation. The diaeresis is from this standpoint an accurate image of the sophist; as an example of a universal method for establishing the eidetic structure of a complex unit, it is a fantasm. The second direction takes us to a consideration of the difference between Socrates and the Eleatic Stranger. On this point, my conjecture makes sense only in the light of the dialogue as a whole. That is, there can be no doubt of the difference between Socrates and the Stranger, but a reasonable doubt exists as to whether the diaereses illustrate, or refer to, that difference. The reader must decide whether the conjecture illuminates the point. But there can hardly be any doubt that we are being asked by Plato to consider the sense in which the Stranger has come to "judge" Socrates, or that this has a bearing on the impending trial of Socrates in an Athenian court.

DIAERESIS 4: 224e6–226a8

So much for the peaceful arts of acquisition; the Stranger turns next to contests. Up to a point, the shift is from utility to honor; I say "up to a point," because the sophist will continue to charge fees. The Stranger does not mention here that contests are a branch of domination or coercion. At 219e1, contests were called "open" and distinguished from "secret" hunting. The distinction between openness and secrecy is also passed over. We should also notice that, whereas the sophist's prey wishes to be captured, participants in a contest do not wish to lose. The point of a contest is to win, and one may win honor, money, or both. In general, the pleasure that comes from winning cannot be entirely explained as due to the money gained, even where money is involved. We need only imagine a contest in which the financial prizes would be awarded to losers; surely this would reduce the amount of pleasure felt by the recipient of the prize. There is, fortunately, a more direct route to the relevance of honor. We need only think of the portraits of the great sophists and orators in the Platonic dialogues, and especially of Protagoras's retinue at the convention which is described in the dialogue bearing his name. The sophist's fees depend upon his reputation as an effective speaker (224e6–225a3).

STEP ONE: Contests are divided into peaceful and warlike rivalries (225a4–7). At 226c6, war appeared as a branch of the secret hunting of tame walking animals. The distinction between war and peace is present in both branches of "grasping" or domination, but it is not mentioned in the discussion of exchange.

STEP TWO: It is proper to divide warlike rivalries into two types of contest: bodily or violent, and verbal or argumentative (225a8–b2). Peaceful contests are therefore discarded. It is of some interest that the Stranger contrasts the body with λόγος rather than with "soul" (ψυχή).

STEP THREE: Next we cut in half the contest of words with words. When lengthy speech is set against lengthy speech, in public, and concerning justice and injustice, the result is judicial disputation. When speeches are cut up into questions and answers and delivered in private, we call it contradicting disputation (ἀντιλογικόν; 225b3–11). I note that private disputation and the coercive hunting of walking animals appear in parallel positions within the branches emanating from coercion or dominance. This suggests a natural relation between privacy and secrecy. We should also note that Socrates uses contradicting disputation regularly, whereas the Stranger does not. It is also odd that the Stranger assimilates all private examples of question and answer under the rubric of disputation. I regard it as conceivable that he is here distinguishing between his own procedure, which is much more like a long speech, and that of Socrates. If this is right, then we have another bit of evidence for the conjecture that the Stranger is here to judge Socrates.[5]

STEP FOUR: One type of private disputation takes place "at random and artlessly" (εἰκῇ δὲ καὶ ἀτέχνως). It deals with business contracts, has no name, and is unworthy of our attention. Nevertheless, we may wonder how an activity lacking in art can fall under a diaeresis of the arts. The other segment of private disputation is technical

5. A small piece of evidence for my conjecture: the verb κατακερματίζω has a tendency to appear in ambiguous contexts. See Scene 15, n. 16.

dispute "about the just things themselves, unjust things, and about the other things generally" (225b12–c10).

STEP FIVE: Disputation (eristics) is of two kinds. The first, "youthful chatter" (ἀδολεσχικός), leads a man to neglect his property and to waste money for the pleasure of talking. However, the style of this talk causes no pleasure to the majority of its auditors. The second kind makes money, no doubt because it causes pleasure in its audience, and is correctly identified by Theaetetus as that of the sophist (225d1–e5). The reader should note carefully Theaetetus's response: "What else could one say without making a mistake except that the marvellous being whom we have been pursuing closely has arrived once more for the fourth time: the sophist." Theaetetus here emphasizes the need to count correctly and says that 224d4–e5 is to count as number three in our series of definitions. The reference to "youthful chatter" has often been taken as a dig at Socrates, and I agree with this view.[6]

SUMMARY: This summary is unique among those of the present scene. It names the same steps as are negotiated in the diaeresis, but in the reverse order. Are we to assume, amusing though it seems, that in this case the way up *is* the same as the way down? In other words, is this not a sign that it makes no difference whether we start our division with the sophist or with the arts, since the results are in either case arbitrary? Whether or not this is right, there can be no doubt that the Stranger allows himself considerable latitude in his summaries for variations of a suggestive sort. A standard enumeration is inappropriate to the task of understanding so intricate a creature as the sophist, who, the Stranger says, cannot be caught with one hand. "Then we must use two hands," Theaetetus replies (226a1–8; cf. 223c2). The metaphor is from wrestling. It tells us not merely that force is required, but that we need to use "all the tricks of our trade," in the contemporary expression. Counting alone will not do the trick. In one last formulation, we need to use both branches of our diaeresis, and not merely the right-hand side, which according to the Stranger is the usual procedure (264e1). One last but extremely important point: the Stranger calls the sophist a wild animal (θηρίον). This admittedly metaphorical expression nevertheless bears upon the question of the tameness of the human family.

---

6. Cornford (1935), p. 176, denies the reference to Socrates, but quotes passages from Eupolis and Aristophanes which in fact support such a reference.

Nature and Work

(226b1–231b8)

We come now to the last, longest, and most interesting of the initial set of diaereses. There will be a final division of the terrain at the end of the dialogue. The major stretch of the dialogue from 231b9 to 264b9 is thus a digression from the diaeretic exercise. However, the digression is needed, according to the Stranger, because of the inadequacy of diaeresis, which cannot grasp the sophist by itself. A similar situation arises in the *Statesman* at 268b4ff. The Stranger says there that he must shift from diaeresis to myth because of the failure of the former to distinguish the statesman from those who also lay claim to the title, such as merchants, farmers, grain workers, gymnasts, and physicians. These claimants "look like" the statesman in some salient respect, just as the sophist "looks like" the philosopher in a confusing way. Diaeresis does not seem to be able to distinguish between originals and images, at least in these cases. If I am not mistaken, the reason for this is that sophists, merchants, and so on, are not forms, but neither are philosophers or statesmen. There may well be a formal structure underlying any true definite statement we are able to make about these human types, but it does not follow from this that there is a definite formal structure underlying each of the types. We note in passing that grain workers, gymnasts, and physicians play a role in the diaeresis we are about to inspect.

The Stranger agrees with Theaetetus that both hands are needed in order to capture the sophist (226b1; cf. 231c5–6). He then starts off abruptly on a new scent, one which is entirely independent both of the angler paradigm and of the first four definitions of the sophist. The Stranger does not call attention to this fact, nor does he explain why such a shift is necessary. We must therefore try to think it out for ourselves. Let us take our bearings by the principal defect of the paradigm and its consequences. These did not provide a satisfactory analysis of the main distinction between production and acquisition. We have seen at various stages of the argument that knowledge about human beings is not the same as knowledge of pure formal structure. Let us assume for the moment that the latter kind of knowledge is acquired rather than produced. The same cannot be said about our knowledge of human beings or (more generally) everyday experience, since this seems to be a consequence of our linguistic and cognitive perspectives. We cannot "translate" the privately possessed πρᾶγμα into publicly certifiable knowledge except through the mediation of the "tools" of language. Even if there should be pure forms corresponding to the elements of language, it hardly follows that there are pure forms corresponding to the empirical "things" and events which we describe by weaving together the elements of our language. We have already discovered that the sophist presents us with many looks, and that some of these are inconsistent with one another. The inconsistency is not a formal contradiction; but that is irrelevant, as we are not in the domain of formal logic. To take the case in point, the sophist is said both to produce and to acquire. But this places him within both branches of the bifurcation of τέχνη. Someone might object to this that, in both cases, he acquires a salary. However, this objection backfires, because it is a moral rather than a technical one. What difference could it possibly make to the genuineness of the sophist's knowledge that he charges a fee for teaching it to his pupils? In itself, this consideration is as irrelevant to the genuineness of the knowledge as is the moral character of a philosopher to the validity of his arguments.

If charging a fee is the decisive mark of the sophist, then the entire technical analysis seems to be superfluous, or at the least, vastly overextended. But fees to one side, there is indeed a technical question at play in our pursuit of sophistry. What precisely do we mean by specious, or nongenuine, knowledge? In what sense could the sophist be said to claim to, but not in fact, know? The line taken by the Stranger is that the sophist makes false copies of knowledge. This is obviously a much deeper analysis of sophistry than is contained in the charge that he takes a fee. It is deeper, but it is by no means clear that the deeper charge can be sustained. The charge is now that the sophist produces rather than acquires his knowledge. However, as we have seen in part, and as will be confirmed by the Stranger's analysis of discourse, true knowledge, to the extent that it is discursive (and to what extent is it *not* discursive?), *is also produced*. A true statement is said to be an icon or accurate image. In order to distinguish between the sophist and the philosopher, or more broadly, between the sophist and the genuine knower, we need to present a satisfactory analysis of cognitive or epistemic production. Speaking very broadly, this analysis will turn upon a doctrine of the prediscursive apprehension of pure forms. If these forms are also discursively produced, then obviously there is no hope of a solution to the Stranger's problem. At this level of our analysis, we can disregard the question whether forms are or are not predicates. For even if they are predicates, they will not be any the less pure forms and, as such, will be distinguished from the linguistic entities we call "predicates," and with which we construct our linguistic statements. In other words, the linguistic predicates will still need to be backed up by prediscursively accessible, hence nonproduced, forms. But this is still not enough. Even granting the doctrine of the acquisition of pure forms, we still need to distinguish between genuine and specious production; that is, we need an account of images, and so of the difference between accurate and inaccurate images. Nothing accomplished by the diaeresis to this point has shed any positive light on this cluster of essential questions. We have been dividing, and hence multiplying, the images of the sophist. But this division and multiplication tells us nothing about the nature of what we are dividing and multiplying. I summarize the cluster of questions just noted as posing various aspects of the problem of the relation between nature and human work.

The Stranger poses a question that puzzles Theaetetus, but which our preliminary reflection makes quite pertinent. Do we give names to some tasks performed by servants? As is usual in Plato, we are about to explore a very deep problem by means of everyday examples. I will not press the point, but there seems to be a difference between the Stranger's examples and those favored by Socrates. Socrates often if not invariably starts with examples taken from the everyday arts like shoemaking, carpentry, navigation, gymnastics, and medicine. The Stranger begins his investigation of human work with a very specific set of examples: the household tasks. The relation between servant and master is central here. We do not need to attempt to tie this up with modern accounts of the master-servant relation, such as that in Hegel's *Phenomenology*. The same distinction exists in Plato's own *Republic*, namely, in the distinction between the guardians and rulers on the one hand and the workers on the other. In the *Republic*, the artisans do not practice philosophy, which is described in largely mathematical terms and hence as a kind of pure acquisition. In the present diaeresis, however, the explicit theme is division, in a sense which obviously includes diaeresis. Diaeresis is a linguistic production of definitions. What we want to know is whether this production is a modification of acquired natural forms. Whereas in the *Statesman* the Stranger explicitly compares diaeresis to the homely art of weaving, in the *Sophist*, he implicitly (or almost explicitly) compares diaeresis to bread and clothes making. In both these arts, natural products are modified in accord with human need; the result is in each case an artifact, but one directed toward a natural end, the preservation and care of the living body. Finally, it is the servants, not the masters, who produce these artifacts. If there is an analogy here between such artifacts and knowledge like that of the nature of the sophist, then the analogy tells us that this knowledge is not mathematical. Mathematics, as it were, is the activity of the masters. It is accessible to us only with respect to pure forms. Where there are no pure forms, the work of the servants is required. We turn now to the task of confirming or refuting this general thesis by a close inspection of the details of diaeresis 5.

DIAERESIS 5: 226b1–231b8

As was noted above, we shall be engaged in the study of dividing or sorting. The Stranger begins with a list of examples, all of which, he says, are "somehow diaeretic" (διαιρετικά που; 226c3–4). They include tasks like straining, sifting, winnowing, and separating (or even judging: διακρίνειν), but also those like carding, combing, and closing the web (226b5–10). These tasks take raw material (grain, wool) from nature and produce goods to satisfy basic bodily needs. This is a different form of caring for the living body than was cited at 219a10ff.

Theaetetus, to repeat, is puzzled by this shifting of tracks. It is, so to speak, highly unmathematical to jettison one's paradigm in midstream. What, he asks, does the Stranger want to make plain by these (new) examples (παραδείγματα; 226c1–2. Cf. 226b4)? The Stranger replies that the aforementioned "diaeretic mark" of the household tasks enables us to collect them into the art of διακριτική, which may be variously translated as separating, discriminating, deciding, or judging (226c5–9). It is interesting to note that this is the first diaeresis which begins with a collection of examples into the type to be divided.

STEP ONE: The Stranger asks whether they are able to see two forms of διακριτική, which in its general use I shall translate as "separating." To this, Theaetetus replies with a complaint: "You require a quick look for one like me" (226c10–12). The Stranger divides separating into the separation of worse from better (straining, sifting, winnowing) and the separation of like from like (carding, combing, closing the web). He has no name for the second kind, but the first is called "a sort of purification" (καθαρμός τις; 226d1–11). We shall soon see that the Stranger thinks of diaeresis as a separation of like from like.

STEP TWO: The Stranger now discards the anonymous branch of separation and turns to purification. He divides this into the purification of bodies, alive or not, and of souls (226e1–227c9). This step in the division is developed at some length and contains a crucial methodological excursus. The Stranger begins by discussing two subsegments of bodily purification before he turns to purification of the soul. A lengthy treatment of a section that is about to be discarded is found nowhere else, and it must therefore present a special problem to the Stranger.

We begin with living bodies. Their purification takes place from within, as by gymnastics and medicine, and from without, as by the art of the bathkeeper (226e8–227a2). Work like that of the bathkeeper is paltry or vulgar to mention (227a1). In saying this, the Stranger evidently employs the criterion of better and worse. Let us be careful here. We are engaged in an exercise of diaeresis which, as the Stranger is about to tell us, must disregard questions of better and worse. And we are applying this "neutral" method to the study of that kind of separation which does turn upon the distinction between better and worse. The Stranger is presently warning us that, as masters of diaeresis, we must disregard our normal disdain for the paltry or vulgar. He is thus explicitly commenting upon his own method. There are also paltry arts of caring for inanimate bodies, with many trivial and laughable names (227a2–6).[1] We must, however, suppress our perception of the trivial, the laughable, and the ugly, and concentrate upon likeness and unlikeness. We must do this even (perhaps especially) in those cases which would otherwise require our condemnation or scorn.[2]

1. Cf. *Parmenides* 130e1–3. However, Parmenides says that Socrates will be a philosopher when he does not dishonor low things (οὐδὲν αὐτῶν ἀτιμάσεις). This is not the same as to disregard the honorable altogether. See also Socrates' advice to Theaetetus at *Theaetetus* 184c1ff. Avoidance of linguistic precision τὰ μὲν πολλὰ οὐκ ἀγεννές, ἀλλὰ μᾶλλον τὸ τούτου ἐναντίον ἀνελεύθερον, ἔστι δὲ ὅτε ἀναγκαῖον. Once again, occasional deviation from the noble is one thing; complete abstraction is another.

2. Sayre (1969) has interesting things to say about this diaeresis. He takes it to be an articulation of a τέχνη as distinct from an ἐπιστήμη like philosophy. But see *States-*

The Stranger makes precisely this point in a lengthy remark
(227a7–c6). The method of the λόγος pays no more attention to
medicine than to sponging, nor does it regard the question of which
of these is most serviceable for human beings. Utility is not at issue
here. We want to understand which of the arts are related and which
are not (τὸ ξυγγενὲς καὶ τὸ μὴ ξυγγενὲς κατανοεῖν), and we want this
simply in order to think or know (ἕνεκα νοῦν). The principle of relatedness is thus likeness, and this shows us why diaeresis cannot
in itself resolve the difference between originals and images. Images
not only look like originals, but they also look like each other, when
they are images of the same thing. Even worse, fantasms look like
icons, and in certain cases (as will be made clear later by the Stranger), they "look" more like the original than do icons. So long as we
are dividing by look, we cannot possibly distinguish between original and image. It is all very well to claim that diaeresis is the division of forms, and hence of originals par excellence. But how does
diaeresis establish the "originality" of what it is dividing? In the
case of "logical" analysis, the method of diaeresis actually encourages us to disregard the "ontological" distinction between a pure
form and its copies, since the pure form is visible within the copy
as a definite "look"; thus visible, the pure form is indistinguishable
from, and can render superfluous any reference to, an original. The
method of diaeresis in fact encourages us to adopt nominalism, or
to invoke Ockham's razor and dispense with superfluous theoretical entities. Or so it seems.

The Stranger does not say that there are no relations of better and
worse among the arts. On the contrary, his allusion to paltry and
vulgar arts shows that such relations manifestly exist. His point is
that, as diaereticians, we are to disregard these relations of better
and worse. He thus strongly implies that the "look" of an art can be
distinguished from our estimate of its human worth. The Stranger's
methodological point thus reminds us of the distinction between
"facts" and "values," popular among empiricists until a decade or
so ago, but now widely recognized as an ambiguous, if not illegitimate, distinction. What we must decide is whether it is possible to
perceive, and hence to define, a sophist, purely on the basis of his
look, and with no regard for his worth. It is already obvious that this

---

man 258b6, which shows that the Stranger draws no sharp distinction between τέχνη
and ἐπιστήμη in the Sophist.See also Sayre's discussion (pp. 152ff) of the function of
this diaeresis as a criticism of Socrates' lack of positive dialectic, or of a method for
pursuing the common form revealed by elenchus. I accept the first half of this interpretation. The second half seems intrinsically implausible and is not supported by
any contrasting division of a common form (in the pure sense of the term) by the
Stranger.

will be very difficult, not to say impossible. To characterize a sophist as one who takes a salary for teaching wisdom is to condemn
him implicitly on moral grounds, as I have already observed. Strictly
speaking, it is not even enough to place the sophist in a category
distinct from that of the knower merely on the ground that he teaches
"false" wisdom, since fantasms of knowledge look like knowledge.
But this aside, what we clearly require is a definite and technical
distinction between "true" and "false" knowledge (to say nothing
of "true" and "false" wisdom). We can thus see that this stage in the
argument already points ahead to the problem of false statement,
but that is a problem of the distinction between accurate and inaccurate images.

It is fair to observe that the decision to disregard purification in
favor of the distinction between like and like is itself an application
of the distinction between better and worse. Whereas the method
of diaeresis honors all the arts equally, those who choose this method
honor it more highly than they do the method of purification. This
point is not blunted, but rather sharpened, by the objection that diaeresis is more appropriate to the enterprise of pure theory. "More
appropriate" means "better than." Nor is this a merely "technical"
sense of "better than," since it embodies the decision that diaereti-
cal knowledge is better than everyday, or (let us say) political, art. It
embodies the fundamental decision that the philosopher is *better
than* the sophist, and not simply "of a different look." Who could be
said to understand the sophist, and so the philosopher, if he were
unable to see which look is better than the other? To say this is of
course in no way to denigrate the "neutral" discrimination of like
from like, where such discrimination is in fact "better than" the
distinction between better and worse. Let me add a general remark
here: I have not said that the Stranger is aware of the ambiguity of
the distinction between the two methods. Thus far I have been merely
pointing out that ambiguity. It will shortly be entirely clear, however, that the Stranger recognizes the failure of diaeresis to capture
the art of image making. Finally, whereas it may not be *entirely*
clear, I regard it as reasonably obvious that the present diaeresis is a
commentary by the Stranger on his own method. I must leave it to
the reader to decide whether the Stranger is aware of the fact that,
from the human or everyday standpoint, a method that classifies
louse catchers with generals is not simply laughable, but untrue to
the phenomena.[3]

3. In the *Gorgias* (464b2ff), gymnastic and medicine are also assigned to the care
of the body, in contrast to law giving and justice, which care for the soul.

STEP THREE: When Theaetetus agrees to divide purification, the Stranger praises him for the first time since 218b5, and for the first time within the diaeresis section: "Most excellent." Theaetetus agrees that he will try to assist the Stranger in the next cut. Apparently he has made a rapid adjustment to the pace of the "looking" or discussion (227c10–d3). The first distinction to be drawn is between evil or defectiveness (πονηρία) and virtue or excellence (ἀρετή) of the soul. We are then reminded that purification is the removal of evil from the soul (227d4–12). The ground is thus cleared for a more substantial point. The Stranger distinguishes two forms of evil in the soul and two associated kinds of purification. One form of evil is like bodily sickness (νόσος), whereas the other is like bodily ugliness or deformity (αἶσχος). Theaetetus does not understand (227d13–228a3). It is just possible that he is disturbed by the shift from πονηρία at 227d4 to κακία at 227d9. He may have understood illness and deformity to be defects, but not to resemble moral evil. In itself, the shift from one term to the other would be insignificant, since they are often used synonymously. We need to follow the discussion in order to determine whether the Stranger makes a distinction in his use of these two terms. There does seem to be a distinction between two kinds of "unnaturalness," sickness and deformity. This distinction, incidentally, rests upon the tacit assumption of the distinction between "better by nature" and "worse by nature." In other words, the diaeretician must make that tacit distinction in order to separate like from like in dividing the purificatory arts. And whereas both sickness and deformity are unnatural, and in that sense "evils" qua defects, there is surely a distinction between moral viciousness and physical ugliness, which seems to be echoed in the Stranger's terminology without being explicitly drawn.

To Theaetetus's continued perplexity, the Stranger next identifies disease with sedition or discord (στάσις). Sedition or discord is the corruption through disagreement of what is by nature related.[4] Ugliness or deformity, however, is disproportion rather than discord (228a4–b1). Although the Stranger does not say explicitly that proportion is also the agreement of what is by nature related, he presumably intends this. For ugliness and deformity are no more unnatural than is sedition; conversely, political agreement is not more natural than well-proportionedness. Both political agreement and a well-proportioned body come about through exercise or the improvement of nature by art. On the other hand, a naturally graceful

4. I follow MSS B and T here.

body acquires the perfection of beautiful proportions by exercise whereas, to enjoy good health, a body has only to retain its natural constitution. It may possibly be more difficult to be well-proportioned than to be healthy, but I do not believe the matter is clear enough to allow of a positive decision. There is another, more visible difference between disease and disproportion. Disease requires internal treatment by the ingestion of medicine, whereas disproportion is more a defect of the body's exterior and is treated by gymnastics. In this sense, gymnastics is related to the art of the sponger or bathkeeper.

There is one other point that needs to be mentioned here. The Stranger associates ugliness with "disproportion" (ἀμετρία), and hence by implication, beauty with "proportion" (συμμετρία). Later, he will speak of the συμμετρία of accurate images, and hence will imply that inaccurate images are marked by ἀμετρία. Whatever the mathematical resonances of "symmetry," beauty in the human body cannot be defined purely by arithmetical proportions. We thus see here an at least partially nonarithmetical prototype for the sense of λόγος as *ratio*.

Our task is now to identify the two arts of psychic purification. The Stranger begins with disease or discord, which he illustrates as follows. In the souls of worthless persons (τῶν φλαυρῶς ἐχόντων), opinions (δόξας) are opposed to desires (ἐπιθυμίαις), and spiritedness (θυμόν) is opposed to pleasures; reason (λόγος) is opposed to pains, and so on (228b2–5). This terminology reminds us of Socrates' discussion of the soul in the *Republic*, but there is no exact parallel. In the *Republic*, for example, reason is said to govern desire through the instrumentality of spiritedness. This suggests an affiliation between spiritedness and opinion as well as between desire and pleasure. So far, there is a general correspondence between the two passages, but the opposition between reason and pain has no exact analogue in the Socratic analysis. In any case, I do not believe that comparisons of this sort are our primary task. The main point is that πονηρία is now identified as the disease of the soul, or in other words, moral viciousness, and compared to sedition. Therefore if bodily ugliness or disproportion is a κακία, that term must be distinguished from moral evil (228b6–10).

The Stranger turns next to disproportion (ἀμετρία), or the constant failure of some moving thing to hit the mark at which it aims (228c1–6). At 228a4–b1, the Stranger did not say explicitly that proportion is natural, but I took him to imply this, for reasons just given. Now, however, doubt arises, for aiming at the mark is often a general metaphor for intending or willing. The Stranger, however, gives just one example of such a missing of the mark, ignorance. He calls ignorance an involuntary (ἄκουσαν) "passing by" (παραφρο-σύνη) in which the understanding misses its mark (228c7–d3). The ignorant man intends to hit the mark, but does not. Yet if this were in no way connected with freedom of the will, then the ignorant man could never be educated or persuaded to change those ways which cause him to miss the mark, however involuntarily. In general, I cannot aim at a target without intending to aim at that target. I may involuntarily be aiming at the wrong target, or holding the bow incorrectly, and so on, but that does not alter the main point. On the other hand, the movement of the body toward health is involuntary or a dimension of its natural growth. The body both aims at health, and misses it, involuntarily. At least this is the general case, prior to complications arising from the human will. In sum, if we take "involuntary missing of the mark" to refer to bodily dispro-portion, and so not to refer to intentionality at all, then how are we to understand the example of knowing? The failure to hit the mark is said to be constant (καθ᾽ ἑκάστην ὁρμήν). But it does not seem reasonable to hold that ignorant men always miss the mark; no one is completely ignorant. The least that can be said is that the Stran-ger's intention is far from lucid at this point. He presumably means to say that nothing, whether a body or an intelligent being, ever voluntarily misses the mark. But this seems to be much too sweep-ing a claim, apart from the fact that it attributes "intentionality" *qua* ends to physical indulgence. What about the man who know-ingly damages his bodily proportions by physical indulgence? Can this be explained as an involuntary missing of the mark?

Unfortunately, a further difficulty is about to arise. If ignorance is a kind of deformity, then the genuine teacher, among whom we may include the philosopher, must be like the gymnast rather than the physician. This is puzzling, since it goes against the usual tendency in Plato, and of common sense, to rank the physician higher than the gymnast and to draw an analogy between philosophy and med-icine. The likeness between the teacher and gymnast can be sup-ported to some degree by the fact that medicine is downgraded in the *Republic*, whereas the education of the guardians consists ini-tially of music and gymnastics. Here is a second consideration. In the *Gorgias*, Socrates distinguishes between the removal of ugliness by gymnastics and its disguise by cosmetics. One consequence of this distinction is that someone may be both ugly and well propor-tioned, since we normally refer to the face as "ugly" and the rest of the body as "well proportioned." However, the Stranger ignores this distinction and combines the two by calling the foolish (ἀνόητον) soul "ugly and ill proportioned" (αἰσχρὰν καὶ ἄμετρον; 228d4). Of the two evils (κακῶν) hitherto distinguished, says the Stranger, one is called "wickedness" (πονηρία) by the many, and is plainly a disease. The other is called "ignorance" (ἄγνοια) by the many, who, however, refuse to call it an evil (κακία) of the soul.

The Stranger began by using πονηρία as the generic term for psychic defect (227d4ff), but since then has employed κακία generically and πονηρία in the sense of wickedness or moral viciousness, in contrast to ugliness or ignorance. As I noted previously, this shift in terminology may well have caused some initial confusion for Theaetetus, but it does not seem to play a substantive role in the development of the distinctions. A more important fact is that the Stranger distinguishes his view from that of the many. The many do not dispute the involuntary nature of ignorance, but only that it is an evil. If it is not an evil, then it does not need to be avoided or eradicated. Second and quite interesting, the Stranger accepts the Socratic thesis that ignorance is involuntary. He distinguishes, however, between ignorance and vice, which latter is compared to a disease. This is not simply a matter of terms. The point is that, for the Stranger, moral virtue is the product of medicine, not of teaching (or gymnastics). Despite being involuntary, then, vice is not ignorance (228d5–11). It therefore looks as though virtue, rather than being an art, as was implied at 224b9–c8, is the consequence of an art. We are about to learn that this art involves punishment. Let us not forget that the Stranger is, so to speak, a "punishing" or refuting god.

Theaetetus agrees with the Stranger, after having previously been on both sides of the point (or wandering with the many), that cowardice, intemperance, and injustice are diseases (228e1–5). After this difficult preparation, we come at last to the actual division. In the case of the body, gymnastic treats ugliness whereas medicine treats disease (228e6–229a2). The Stranger then asks, "In the case of hybris, injustice, and cowardice, is not the punishing art the one naturally most fitting for righteousness?"[5] I note in passing that hybris here replaces intemperance. The main point is that we have arrived at the art of punishment, of which two kinds are gymnastic and medicine. Righteousness is thus a kind of punitive medicine, di-

5. Reading Δίκη with Cobet. However, δίκη (B and T) does not change the sense of the passage.

rected against the vices or diseases of the soul. Theaetetus gives a qualified assent: "It is likely, according to human opinion" (229a3–7). Theaetetus is not certain about the analogy between medicine and righteousness. The Stranger had said that what the many call wickedness is in fact a disease. As Theaetetus suggests, the many also agree that righteousness treats wickedness, but he himself seems to doubt that righteousness is the treatment for disease.

The art that corresponds to all forms of ignorance is teaching (δι-δασκαλική; 229a8–10). Theaetetus entirely agrees. At last, not without difficulty, we have our division of psychic purification into punishment (κολαστική), the art most akin by nature to righteousness, and the art of teaching. Punishment, therefore, is like medicine,[6] but the Stranger does not explain in what sense teaching is like gymnastic. Perhaps the Stranger wishes to indicate that consultation of the gymnast is voluntary, whereas consultation of the physician is not. If so, this supports the view that ignorance is involuntary, whereas the desire to learn cannot be. However, it leaves unanswered why, if disease is involuntary, we should be punished for it. The answer may be found in the view that punishment is required by justice, in the sense that human political life depends upon our taking responsibility for our acts. However we look at it, the Stranger's diaereses illustrate the tangled and unmathematical nature of human experience. By this very quality, they bring out something accurate about the nature of sophistry. The appeal of the sophist is rooted in the persuasiveness of his doctrine, and this does not arise simply from human baseness. The sophist's doctrine is persuasive (if not convincing) because human life is indeed a sequence of continuously shifting perspectives, rather than a mathematical structure whose "natural joints" are accessible to diaeresis.

I turn now to consider a point that retains its stability in the flow of the Stranger's distinctions. There is no doubt that, rightly or wrongly, the Stranger associates the punishment of vice with medicine and the removal of ignorance with gymnastic. It seems fair to say that medicine goes deeper than gymnastic in the following sense. A well-proportioned body may be suffering from a fatal disease or a deformed organ, just as a badly proportioned body may be entirely healthy. Disease kills, or can do so in itself, whereas ugliness cannot. If teaching is like gymnastic, it would thus seem to be more superficial than punitive medicine or righteousness. We can take two different attitudes toward this. We may assume that the Stran-

6. Cf. *Gorgias* 464b.

ger is simply muddled. Or else we may assume that he knows what
he is doing. If the latter is correct (and certainly we have a better
chance of making sense out of the *Sophist* if we do not dismiss as
muddle every passage that initially looks odd to us), then the Stranger is saying that ignorance is a more superficial deformity of the
soul than wickedness.

This inference will strike many readers as altogether too specu-
lative. I do not assert it as an obvious consequence of the text. I say
merely that it follows naturally from the text, and that it makes
sense in connection with the description by Socrates of the Stranger
at the beginning of the dialogue. If the inference is wrong, the reader
will reject my conjecture as it bears upon the relation between the
Stranger and Socrates. To do this will in no way affect my analyses
of the "technical" discussion. In the case of the diaereses, numerous
points have emerged that are in no way conjectures. One such point
is that diaeresis is not a proceeding like the counting of eidetic elements. Another is that the Stranger's view on punishment and medicine is different from Socrates' view on vice as ignorance. We can
hardly be said to have understood the *Sophist* if we have no explanation at all for the bearing of the diaereses upon the main themes
under discussion. I am giving two kinds of explanation. One is
"technical" in the narrower sense of the term; the other is dramatic
or "technical" in the broader sense of the term. The short summary
of the narrower explanation is that diaeresis cannot account for the
distinction between production and acquisition, or in other words
between original and image. The broader explanation is that the
diaereses bring out something crucial about the Stranger's attitude
toward Socrates. These explanations are independent of one another.

With this in mind, I ask the reader to consider my suggestion that
the Stranger means to charge Socrates with the "crime" of not advocating a positive teaching. Socrates is indeed guilty of corrupting
the young, whatever may be the case with the charge of bringing in
new gods. He is guilty because he dissolves their allegiance to the
laws of Athens and puts nothing in the place of this allegiance, except a kind of technical cleverness which soon degenerates into dog-
matism and skepticism.

STEP FOUR: The Stranger next establishes that there are many kinds
of teaching, of which two are the most important. However, the
Stranger says, in view of the many kinds of teaching, it will be much
quicker to proceed by cutting ignorance in half. This is another obscure passage. We will presumably save time because we are accus-

tomed to giving names to many different kinds of teaching, but not to the kinds of ignorance (229b1–10). The Stranger arouses our suspicions by expressing a wish to save time (cf. 226c10–12). If there is no common name for the kinds of ignorance, then how can they form a single family? Theaetetus is also puzzled as to how we are to cut ignorance in half. The Stranger is somewhat more confident, but he too expresses himself rather obliquely: "I believe myself to see a large and troublesome form of ignorance that weighs as much as all the other parts combined." The reference is to the belief that one knows what one in fact does not know. This, says the Stranger, is the cause of all discursive error, and Theaetetus agrees (229b11–c7). The bulkiness of this form of ignorance guides the Stranger to the right place for his division. He asks which form of teaching removes "absence of knowledge" (ἀμαθία), the bulky kind of ignorance. Theaetetus replies: "The other teaching is called demiurgy; this one is called education (παιδεία) here at Athens through our usage" (229c8–d3). Theaetetus has apparently overcome his puzzlement; he gives more than the Stranger asked for, and also shows his patriotism. Note that this last distinction implies that παιδεία is nonproductive.

STEP FIVE: The Stranger corrects this unscientific display: nearly all Hellenes speak of παιδεία (cf. *Statesman* 262c10ff). We now divide παιδεία. "Of teaching by discussion [τοῖς λόγοις], one road seems to be rougher and the other part smoother" (229d4–e2). The Stranger passes silently by education by deed. The rough road is the traditional admonishing of sons by their fathers. Sometimes fathers respond to the errors of their sons by harshness and sometimes by softness (229e3–230a3). Roughness thus contains both harshness and softness as subkinds. There is a difference between softness and smoothness. Perhaps this is because softness has rough consequences in the form of spoiled children. The smooth road is taken by those who "seem to have talked themselves into believing that all ignorance is involuntary." They regard admonition as useless in the case of those who believe themselves to be wise. Theaetetus agrees (229e3–230a10). One of those who follow the smooth road is Socrates. But what of the Stranger himself? At 228c7ff, he defined ignorance as an involuntary missing of the mark. The Stranger presumably means that, whereas ignorance is involuntary in the sense that men naturally aim at knowledge, the task of education is nevertheless to attempt to correct the aim, and so change the "intention" or will, of the ignorant. The Stranger's discussion of ignorance and education shows that he distinguishes between intellectual and moral purification in a way reminiscent of Rousseau. We can "enlighten" mankind intellectually by presenting them with a positive doctrine (as Socrates does not). In the case of evil, however, we must administer the medicine of punishment.

The Stranger explains the smooth road at some length. Those who take it employ contradiction by leading the ostensibly wise man to utter conflicting speeches on the same topics. The man is thus shown that his words "wander." Having been chastized in this way, he becomes harsh toward himself and gentle toward others (230b1–9). Therefore, the smooth road has an internal division parallel to that of the rough road. The division, however, is now made in terms of the student, whereas the division of the rough road was made in terms of the master. Smooth teaching is thus the same in its treatment of all students. One should compare this passage with Socrates' discussion of philosophical rhetoric in the *Phaedrus*. Socrates first associates philosophical rhetoric with dialectic (or diaeresis), and then says that dialectic is like the art of medicine (270bff), since both analyze natures. A consequence of this analysis is that the philosophical rhetorician will speak differently to men of differing natures. For the Stranger, we recall, education is a kind of gymnastic. But, we may object, even the gymnast must vary his exercises in accord with the bodies of his students.[7] The Stranger's analysis of education thus confirms our inference from his preliminary remarks about interlocutors and speeches. He does not take into account, as does Socrates, the variations in human type when formulating his pedagogical speeches. This abstraction from philosophical rhetoric in the Socratic sense seems to be required by the intention to present a positive teaching.

Those who listen to education by contradiction receive the greatest pleasure from it, and those who undergo it become most stable or reliable (βεβαιότατα). Their words cease to wander (230c1–3; cf. Theaetetus 150a8ff). The Stranger does not say that the recipients, too, receive pleasure from this process of education. Examination by refutation, or elenctic (cf. 230d1 and 230d7), must be distinguished from the segment of eristic that was called "youthful chatter" at 225d10. This last causes no pleasure to its audience. We recall that at 216a6–b6 Socrates asks whether the Stranger is an elenctic god. At the beginning of the *Statesman* (257a1–2), Socrates says that he has been gratified by his acquaintance with the Stranger. Socrates is

7. Cf. *Statesman* 294d7–e3. If the Stranger's account of the general nature of gymnastic instruction is sound, it accentuates the inappropriateness of the comparison in the *Sophist* between gymnastics and education.

thus pleased by the sight of Theaetetus under interrogation; he evidently does not believe himself to have been interrogated in a refutatory way by this sight.

The Stranger concludes this long speech by comparing elenctic to the purging of the body by the physician (230c8ff). Since elenctic is a kind of teaching, this contradicts the previous analogy between teaching and gymnastic. The contradiction occurs within the discussion of teaching by contradiction. In elenctic, it is the student rather than the teacher who is contradicted. One ought, if only in passing, to consider the possibility that the Stranger (or perhaps Plato) is here testing us. Let us take a moment to examine this point. What might the Stranger be attempting to teach us? The two main difficulties we have encountered in this section are the distinction between medicine and gymnastic, and the distinction between voluntary and involuntary. According to Socrates, teaching is like medicine and ignorance is involuntary. The most obvious implication of Socrates' view, from the Stranger's standpoint, is that a link may be established between education and a rhetoric that accommodates itself to human types. On the other hand, it could also be said that if education is like medicine, and specifically like purging, it must address itself to a certain generality in human nature. Whereas purging is not used for all illnesses, it is used for a general type of illness that attacks human beings regardless of differences in their "spiritual" natures. Another way to bring out the possible criticism of Socrates in this passage is to note that, according to the Stranger, purging is *prior* to teaching or the actual administration of a positive medicine (230c8ff). Once we have purged the patient by refutation or contradiction, it is necessary to give him a medicine to treat his illness more positively. And this, Socrates does not do.

Theaetetus praises the purified disposition as best and most temperate. The Stranger agrees with his temperate interlocutor, while emphasizing that elenctic is the greatest and most authoritative of purifications. Whoever has not undergone it, even if he be the great king himself, is uneducated and ugly in those qualities which should be the purest and most beautiful in the truly blessed man (230d5–e4). By speaking of ugliness and beauty, the Stranger continues the process of erasing his own distinction between medicine and gymnastic, and so between punishment and teaching. Who is the practitioner of this authoritative art of refutation? The Stranger is afraid to honor the sophist too highly by associating him with this art (an interesting reference to better and worse), but Theaetetus thinks that the description resembles the sophist. We note that it is impos-

sible to regard only the distinction between like and like when attempting to define the sophist: "the wolf also looks like the dog,
the wildest like the tamest" (230e5–231a6).

In order to distinguish between the "wolf" and the "dog," we must
consider something more than formal looks. In certain cases, the
Stranger suggests, the wolf looks too much like a dog for us to tell
them apart on this basis alone. We thus turn to the distinction between "tame" and "wild." In the present context, however, this refers to philosophers and sophists, or to the difference between the
original and the copy. Incidentally, if the sophist is a wolf, then the
human race cannot be entirely tame. But how do we know that the
philosopher is not the wolf? In the *Republic* (II, 376a5), Socrates says
that the dog is the most philosophical of animals because he barks
at strangers and is gentle to friends. That this assertion is ironical is
easily seen. In the first place, it illustrates Polemarchus's definition
of justice, not that of Socrates. But second, it is absurd to draw inferences about human nature from the behavior of beasts. Finally,
dogs are the paradigm of soldiers, not of rulers; they exhibit spiritedness, not reason. One must be excessively tame to consider the
question of the difference between dogs and wolves as settled or
trivial.

The distinction between the dog and the wolf is no doubt a metaphor or "likeness." For this very reason, it is appropriate as the antecedent to the Stranger's next remark: "The man who goes se-
curely must always be especially on guard against likenesses [τὰς
ὁμοιότητας]; this family is the slipperiest" (231a6–8). This is essential advice for the reader of the *Sophist*, and especially for those
readers who hope to avoid slipping by disregarding metaphors in
favor of arguments. The Stranger agrees to call the refuters sophists,
but his closing words in this diaeresis are that we must be sufficiently on guard (231a8–b2).

SUMMARY: This summary follows the diaeresis, but with one important addition. It tells us that "we have defined nothing other than
the species of noble sophistic" (ἡ γένει γενναῖα σοφιστική). Thus the
criterion of better and worse enters into the diaeresis of diaeresis,
and more specifically, of purification, which itself proceeds by way
of the criterion of better and worse. For the first time, there is no
mention of charging a fee (231b3–8). This qualification is hence not
a necessary property of the sophistical nature, as I pointed out above.
The consequence, however, is the breakdown of diaeresis. Instead of
producing a definition of the sophist, we have arrived at a hybrid of
the sophist and the philosopher.

Summary of the Diaereses

(231b9–e7)

Theaetetus agrees to the summary of the fifth diaeresis, but complains to the Stranger about the results of their investigation thus far. The sophist "has made so many appearances" (διὰ τὸ πολλὰ πεφάνθαι) or shown himself to possess so many different looks, that Theaetetus is at a loss as to how to say anything true about him. The Stranger grants that the aporia is reasonable (εἰκότως), or in other words that the diaeresis has not proceeded like a mathematical demonstration, but like an icon (or, as I believe, a fantasm). We must hope that the sophist is also in aporia as to how he can continue to escape the λόγος, for the saying is accurate that it is not easy to escape all the wrestler's grips. "Now we must really set ourselves to the attack" (231b9–c7). This last remark implies that we have not yet brought our serious "grips" into play.

Let us pause for a general observation about the diaereses. Theaetetus attributes the aporia to the multiplicity of the definitions, not to their inconsistency or separate unreasonableness. Why is multiplicity a problem here? Consider an analogy from mathematics. There are frequently several different proofs of the same theorem, but it is always the same theorem that is proved. If not, we do not call the multiplicity of proofs proofs of the *same* theorem. One of the great oddities of Wittgenstein's later philosophy of mathematics, for example, is his contention that theorems change once they are proved. The proved theorem no longer has the same meaning as the unproved theorem. It therefore seems reasonable to extend this doctrine, and to say that the same theorem *cannot* be proved in many ways; each distinct proof leads us necessarily to a distinct theorem. In the Wittgensteinian doctrine, mathematical structures change their looks, if not continuously, then as a function of the changes in the ways that we look at them. This is very much like what has hap-

pened in our diaereses. Theaetetus, however, is no more a late Wittgensteinian than is the Stranger. Both, if I may put it in this way,
are "platonists." For both, a mathematical structure is stable and
self-identical, as well as independent of the process by which we
prove that it possesses such-and-such properties. In this sense, proof
is for the "platonist" a process of discovery rather than of construction or invention. *It is acquisition rather than production.*

If the method of diaeresis, as practiced by the Stranger, is a type
of quasi-mathematical dissection of formal structure, then the complex unity from which the dissection begins must be, like the object
of pure mathematics, stable, self-identical, and independent of the
process by which we prove that it possesses such-and-such properties. At this point, however, if we accept Socrates' account of diaeresis in the *Philebus*, the analogy with mathematical proof breaks
down. Whereas there may be more than one way to prove the same
theorem, there cannot be more than one "count" of the formal properties, at each "level" of analysis, of the complex unity with which
we begin. But there are many different ways in which to analyze the
complex look of the sophist. One might object that this is because
the method has not yet been accurately applied, as it will be in the
final diaeresis. There are two things to be said in reply. First, assume
that the objection is sound. In this case, the Stranger is employing a
complex rhetorical presentation of the teaching he claims to have
learned thoroughly in Elea. We can hardly be said to have understood the dialogue until we are able to explain the Stranger's pedagogical method. The objection is not sound, however, and this brings
me to the second reply. There is a fundamental sense in which the
method is indeed being applied accurately: it is producing accurate
results. The sophist does in fact look like each of the definitions at
which we have arrived. Neither Theaetetus nor the Stranger disavows the accuracy of any of the definitions; on the contrary, they
regularly agree that each definition is accurate. The diareses are thus
both accurate and inaccurate; taken collectively, they are both an
icon and a fantasm.

The fundamental soundness of the method in the sense just noted
is not invalidated by the inconsistencies within each diaeresis. It is
not invalidated by the fact that the sophist turns up in all the major
branches of the paradigm. The definitions, to be sure, are inconsistent with one another in this formal sense: the avowed purpose of
diaeresis is to sort out the sophist from all other practitioners of a
technical power. The purpose is to isolate him within a single branch,
a single subbranch, and so on to the end of our process of division.

Incidentally, how could we know that we had in fact reached the end of our task of definition? In the case of the diaeresis of pure forms, we are done when there is nothing more to count. But in the case of a human type, and above all of the sophist, there is always something more to count. To return to the question of consistency, it is precisely the art of the sophist, according to the Stranger, that he can look like anything at all; that is, he can look like the practitioner of any art at all. By showing him as visible within each branch, subbranch, and so on, we have painted an accurate portrait of the sophist, at least as far as we have gone. We could have gone even further; if the Stranger is right in holding that the sophist can assume all looks, then it would have made no difference *how* we conducted our diaereses. We would always have discovered the sophist within each family.

The diaereses regularly violate the principle of noncontradiction, and thus produce a series of inconsistent definitions. The sophist does and does not take fees. He does and does not produce his own goods. He is both a producer (of knowledge or pseudoknowledge) and an acquirer (of wages, but also of other men's knowledge via exchange). He is both tame and wild, and so on. I repeat: the sophist can look like a member of any family. Therefore, we cannot discover his true family (assuming he has one) until we are able to distinguish between "being" a member of a family and "looking like" a member of a family. We have to distinguish between "being" and "looking like," or between original and image, and diaeresis is totally incapable of providing us with this knowledge. I add once more that mathematical proof is incapable of producing this knowledge with respect to mathematical objects. This is why Kurt Gödel, the greatest "platonist" of the twentieth century, was a proponent of mathematical intuition.[1] Of course, what we can prove, or what we count as a proof, will be affected by what we claim to intuit, but the intuition is not itself validated by the proof. There cannot be a doctrine of "platonist" form, whether in the Gödelian or in the Stranger's sense, without a doctrine of the intuition of pure form. If I am not mistaken, this is why those who cannot discern a doctrine of the intuition of form in the *Sophist* often feel themselves justified in demoting the Stranger's forms to the status of linguistic entities. This in turn encourages them to overlook the difference between the pure forms of the eidetic alphabet and the "predicates" in the

---

1. K. Gödel (1964), pp. 262, 271–72. Gödel is primarily, but not necessarily exclusively, concerned with the intellectual intuition of transfinite sets.

discussion of true and false statement. However, there is no textual basis whatsoever for taking the eidetic alphabet as a linguistic entity. The letters in this alphabet are pure forms. They are not arrived at by diaeresis, a process to which the Stranger never alludes when he introduces these forms into the discussion (although there is subsequently a brief and extremely obscure account of "dialectic," which we shall consider in the proper place). Even if some pure forms could be discriminated from others through the assistance of diaeresis, this would be merely a classificatory procedure, applied to the results of intellectual intuition. In other words, the applicability or nonapplicability of diaeresis to the counting of elements in formal structure is irrelevant to the question of the ontological status of formal structure. Since the Stranger's forms are not linguistic entities, they must have been perceived by intellectual intuition, regardless of whether he alludes explicitly to such a doctrine.

To come back to the diaeresis section, there is another way in which to bring out the shortcomings of diaeresis as a method for defining the sophist. This method is presumably based solely upon the distinction of like from like; in other words, it disregards the distinction of better from worse. In fact, as we have already seen, the Stranger employs both distinctions in carrying out his divisions. The fact is that some things cannot be sorted out into complementary looks except by the application of the "better-worse" distinction. If we are sorting formal looks, as distinct from what people call the phenomena we are sorting, then we cannot distinguish between, let us say, a tyrant and a monarch, without passing judgment on these two looks. In general, and certainly in any sense by which the term could be applied to human lives, Plato's forms are hierarchically ordered. The dialogues contain numerous "rankings" of humans lives. The philosopher's life is invariably at the top of this ranking, and the sophist's life is invariably at or near the bottom. What is the basis for this radical difference in the rankings of the two lives? It certainly cannot be the fact that the sophist charges fees whereas the philosopher does not. After all, Socrates was presumably supported by his wealthy friends. In general, no one can philosophize without money. A more reasonable distinction would be this: the philosopher takes enough money to support himself and his family, whereas the sophist tries to make as much money as possible. However, I do not find even this criterion very convincing. Plato, after all, was an extremely wealthy man, and this wealth made it possible for him to found his school in the Academy, not to mention contributing to the support of Socrates.

We come much closer to the heart of the matter by observing that sophists sell their wisdom to anyone who can pay a fee, whereas philosophers are highly selective in choosing their students. However, we still have to answer a further question. Why is it better to be selective in choosing one's students? And here the answer surely turns upon the nature of one's doctrine. For example, in a contemporary university, it is true that certain standards of merit are used in selecting the student body. It is nevertheless true, especially at the undergraduate level, that the professor of philosophy sells his wisdom to those who can pay the fee and who wish to do so. I believe that most contemporary professors of philosophy would object to being called sophists. They would probably justify themselves in a variety of ways, but one would surely be political: the Platonic distinction between the few and the many is no longer acceptable in an egalitarian society. Furthermore, as residents of the modern Enlightenment, we normally believe that it is both just and desirable to spread the fruits of knowledge as widely as possible. In sum, the difference between us and Plato is not simply one of historical epochs and changed economic conditions. It is a difference of doctrine, and hence of what is meant by philosophy. Those who call themselves "Platonists" (as distinct from "platonists") would do well to ponder this point.

The Stranger is far from forthright in the manner of his presentation of the nature of sophistry. We are frequently given the impression that the sophist is a false copy of this or that technician, say a shoemaker or a carpenter. But this is of course nonsense. The fundamental distinction to be drawn is between the sophist and the philosopher. Especially in the *Sophist*, but generally in Plato, sophistry is presented as an alternative to philosophy. It is very important to notice that the Stranger (to restrict ourselves to the *Sophist*) does not hold to the modern notion of a variety of philosophical "positions" or "conceptions" of philosophy. This will emerge in part from his comprehensive criticism of his predecessors (including Parmenides). There is philosophy; there are no "philosophies." Philosophy is the love, but also the teaching, of the truth, and the life of the truly free man. There is not a variety of versions of the truth and of the free life. Instead, there are false copies of the truth and of freedom; in other words, there is sophistry. The reader might wish to protest that there is a distinction of character or motive between mistaken philosophers and sophists. I agree. But please note that in making such a distinction, we shift the difference between the philosopher and the sophist from the "technical" to the moral level.

We apply the criterion of better and worse. And this cannot be done by the application of diaeresis alone.

If we penetrate to the heart of the Stranger's presentation of sophistry, we see an ambiguous relationship between the technical and the ethical differences involved in defining the philosopher and the sophist. Let us here restrict our attention to the technical problem. Sophistry is not just an alternative to, but an enemy of, philosophy. This is because the sophist denies the distinction between original and image. He therefore denies the existence of falsehood. Let us be careful here. The sophist does not claim that it is impossible to make a mistake, or to utter a mistaken assertion. What he claims is that the true is the useful and the false is the useless. It is therefore of no interest to him whether a statement does or does not accurately mirror the formal relations connecting the objects of which he speaks. The sophist would no doubt deny the "existence" of forms, but he is more properly described as indifferent to them. A statement is true if it is useful. Whether it is true in any other sense is irrelevant. The usual Socratic procedure of demonstrating a hierarchy of uses is not itself useful in refuting sophistry, because it begs the question. It assumes that we have noble souls, or that we perceive the worth of the philosophical hierarchy. It would take me too far afield to pursue this question in all its intricacies. Suffice it to say that one may be a moderate sophist as well as a moderate philosopher. Socratic virtue is useful even to the sophist, so long as one is "moderately" virtuous. In other words, what counts here is *what* we regard as useful. But what we regard as useful depends upon our natures, upon whether, so to speak, we are by nature philosophers or sophists. The "ethical" analysis of sophistry will therefore persuade only those who are by nature philosophers.

This last result gives us another basis for understanding the Stranger's criticism of Socrates. We need a technical analysis of sophistry, not an ethical one. In the *Theaetetus*, Socrates attempted to develop a technical refutation of sophistry. The attempt failed, however, because Socrates could not establish the nature of knowledge; hence, he was unable to establish the difference between genuine and specious arts. We cannot analyze the arguments in the *Theaetetus* here. I want to make only one very general remark. The sophist's claim that the object of perception is modified by the act of perception is in fact confirmed by the diaereses in the *Sophist*. This claim can be refuted only on the basis of a distinction between stable, self-identical, and independent forms on the one hand, and unstable, changing copies on the other. We might start our refutation of the sophist as follows.

In order to distinguish between the useful and the harmful, we must accept that there is such a thing as nature. Something is useful for me because I am of such-and-such a constitution. If human beings vary continuously, whether in themselves or in comparison with each other, then it will be impossible to pursue the useful on the basis of any kind of teaching, including that of the sophist. Furthermore, to say that something is useful is to say that it will continue to be useful, while I am pursuing it and after I have acquired it. In short, there must be a certain regularity of nature. The sophist could reply that such a regularity exists, with respect to men as a family and nature as a whole, but that there is no stability in what men will regard as useful from one city to another or one historical period to another. This variation is even visible among citizens of the same city. So the regularity of nature is such that, once we decide what is useful, we can get it if we are clever enough (cf. *Theaetetus* 172a1–c1). There is, however, no way to say that this or that is more desirable than something else, with a single exception: the art of persuasion.

In other words, Socrates' analysis of perception in the *Theaetetus* does not meet the sophist's actual claim. The sophist does not claim that things are whatever we take them to be. He claims that they have no intrinsic worth, but only the worth which we invest in them. Given his admission of the regularity of nature, the sophist might be brought to admit some doctrine of forms. But he could not be brought to admit that there is a natural hierarchy of forms, or that one form is by nature, intrinsically, worth more than another. Socrates might object that the sophist, by placing the highest value on the art of persuasion, in effect contradicts himself, or places sophistry at the top of the hierarchy of lives. The sophist's reply to this is that *he* so values sophistry and enforces this evaluation by virtue of his cleverness; the same cannot be said for other human beings. Does this reply in fact meet Socrates' objection? Has not the sophist just claimed that the art of persuasion is intrinsically, and thus by nature, the highest because most useful art? Before replying to this, let me emphasize that the sophist does not claim to be able to persuade us that a tree is actually a human being, or that he himself, who cannot make shoes, is actually a shoemaker. This will be of considerable importance later. The sophist claims to be able to teach us how to persuade others to do what we desire. He does not claim to teach us the art of sophistry. Up to a point, this is like claiming to teach others how to make shoes without teaching them the knowledge of shoemaking. But there is a perceptible difference. There is, to say nothing else, a difference between knowing how to construct a persuasive speech and knowing how to teach others to construct a persuasive speech.

Let us now return to the sophist's praise of his own art. There is a sense in which the sophist has contradicted himself. But this is of no interest to the sophist. *It is Socrates, or the philosopher, not the sophist, who values consistency.* When it comes to persuasion, inconsistency is far more powerful than consistency. The empirical proof of this is the great reputation of the sophists. So far as we can tell from the Platonic dialogues, the only persons who are impressed by Socrates' many acts of reducing the sophists to self-contradiction are his own students and friends. My point, incidentally, is not that the sophists are ignorant of "formal logic" whereas Socrates is a master of this art. Strictly speaking, there was no art of "formal logic" prior to Aristotle, but this is irrelevant. I do not doubt that Socrates was a much cleverer constructor of arguments than the sophists; in this sense, let us allow that he was also a more subtle "logician." Yet, the degree of logical subtlety needed to argue coherently on everyday issues of human desire is not great. And even if the sophists were as prone to elementary fallacies as Plato makes them out to be in his various portraits, they could still *consistently* maintain that consistency is of secondary importance in the art of persuasion.

In other words, sophistry is not defined as defective knowledge of formal logic or sound argumentation. There is no intrinsic reason why sophists could not be masters of mathematical logic and *still* intentionally contradict themselves, in exactly the way that we noted a moment ago. The value of mathematical logic does not lie in its powers of persuasion, except with respect to other mathematical logicians. If nonlogicians place great value upon logic and mathematics, it is not because of the consistency of mathematics (which, incidentally, has never been demonstrated), but because either or both are useful in obtaining what they desire. And what they desire is not formal consistency. It is not very difficult to imagine a great mathematical logician who values his art, not for itself, but because of the academic power it obtains for him. Would we not call such a man a sophist?

What Socrates, or the philosopher, must do, then, is not merely show the sophist that he has contradicted himself. Contradictions are often useful tools in the art of persuasion. It is not even necessary for the philosopher to get the sophist to agree that the art of persuasion is the highest of the arts. The philosopher must prove that the high estimation bestowed by the sophist on the art of persuasion is already a sign of the superiority of philosophy to sophistry. And even this is not enough. He must also be able to prove, not just to the sophist, but to the neutral observer who is neither a philosopher nor a sophist, that the sophist's art of persuasion is *useless.* In my opinion, this last task is impossible, and for a very simple reason. The sophist's art of persuasion *is* useful, regardless of any logical inconsistencies it may embody. We are more likely to succeed if we try to demonstrate to the nonphilosopher that philosophy is *more* useful than sophistry. Current quarrels in the philosophy of science concerning the methodology of scientific discovery show that even this demonstration is not a trivial one. But the fact of the matter is that, to the extent that the philosopher addresses his refutations of sophistry to the nonphilosopher, he himself employs rhetoric, inconsistency, and even, to quote Socrates in an exactly parallel situation, "noble lies." As I noted above, appeals to consistency and the exposing of logical fallacies are of interest only to other philosophers. If then we define sophistry as the pseudoart of persuasion by inconsistency and logical fallacy, there is nothing more for us as philosophers to do. We have refuted sophistry by definition, or at least by our avowed preference for consistency and the avoidance of logical fallacy.

This is not the procedure followed by the Eleatic Stranger. There is a philosophical problem at stake. The crucial point is that, up until the present conversation, no philosopher, including Socrates, has successfully explained the nature of false statement. No one has ever explained how we can say "the thing that is not" (to quote the Houyhnynms); no one has ever resolved the problem of non-being, and so, of the pure nothing or (to employ another later phrase) the *nihil absolutum.* What this means is much more radical than that sophistry has not yet been refuted. Strictly speaking, it means that, thus far, there has been nothing but sophistry. Prior to the Eleatic Stranger, *there have been no genuine philosophers, but only fantasms of philosophers.* The Stranger will make this as explicit as one might desire when, in a later passage, he rejects the views of all of his predecessors.

Let me recapitulate. The difference between the philosopher and the sophist is either ethical or technical. In order to perceive the first, we must ourselves possess noble souls. But if "noble" means "highest," and the highest soul is the philosophical soul, then we cannot perceive the ethical difference between the philosopher and the sophist without perceiving the technical difference. Prior to the

Stranger, no one has perceived this difference: no one has explained it properly. In other words, without the knowledge of the technical difference, our virtuous rejection of sophistry is not secure. We may be persuaded that we are wrong, or that we do not understand the virtue of sophistry. We may be persuaded that sophistry *is* virtue, as for example in the formulation given to this point by Nietzsche, when he says that "art is worth more than the truth." This statement means that persuasion is more useful than truth, which is itself a modality of persuasion. Nietzsche's statement is no doubt a self-contradiction. To this charge, Nietzsche might reply by citing Walt Whitman: "Do I contradict myself? Very well, then, I contradict myself. I contain multitudes." If virtue, as Socrates claims, is knowledge, then those who, like Socrates, cannot produce knowledge are vicious. They are sophists. And this is the implicit charge leveled against Socrates by the Eleatic Stranger.

What may have seemed to some readers as a digression was in fact not a digression at all, but a necessary reflection on the sense of the diaereses we have just studied. The title of our dialogue is *Sophist*. The announced purpose of the conversation within the dialogue is to define the sophist. The method of diaeresis was introduced by the Stranger as just the right tool to employ for the purpose. Yet it is a failure, despite its success in arriving at a variety of accurate descriptions of the sophist. Why does it fail? Why was it chosen by the Stranger? I have now answered the first of these two central questions. We are not yet in a satisfactory position to answer the second question, because we have not yet finished our study of the dialogue. Nevertheless, a preliminary response suggests itself on the basis of what has been accomplished thus far. The use of diaeresis has nothing to do with the Stranger's serious analysis of sophistry which, for better or worse, will follow in the ostensible "digression" from the process of diaeresis.[2] The Stranger is using diaeresis for a pedagogical purpose that is subordinate to the serious analysis of sophistry. Part of that purpose must be to show the limitations of diaeresis, and specifically, the inappropriateness of attempting to define someone like the sophist by means of diaeresis. In my opinion, this inference is obvious. Nevertheless, I know very well that it will strike many readers as forced, and even as outrageous. What is their evidence for this judgment? Once we put aside imaginary reconstructions of diaeresis as a quasi-mathematical technique for artic-

2. I repeat that I regard the discussion in the digression as serious, even though I have no doubt that Plato did not consider it to have successfully refuted sophistry. See the remark in the text at the end of Scene 16.

ulating pure formal structure, and study carefully the Stranger's actual procedures, what is the upshot? Either the Stranger is a bungler, or he is educating Theaetetus (and us) by indirection.

We may now return to the Stranger. He advises us to stand still, catch our breath, and count up the appearances of the sophist thus far. Since we are omitting the paradigm case of the angler, there should be five definitions of the sophist (231c8–d2). Here are the definitions as agreed to by Theaetetus and the Stranger in the present summary:

1. A hunter of rich youths who takes wages (231d2–4). If we compare this with the first diaeresis, we see that the Stranger here omits the earlier reference to "the teaching of opinion" (δοξοπαιδευτικῆς; 223b1–7).

2. A kind of merchant who goes from city to city and deals with learning of the soul (231d5–7). If we look at diaeresis 2 (224c9–d2), we see that this summary omits reference to merchandising speeches and virtue.

3. A merchant within the city, again of psychic learning. The Stranger asks Theaetetus whether this is not the third appearance of the sophist. Theaetetus says "yes" and adds, "fourthly," thereby introducing the next definition.

4. A merchant of his own productions of learning (231d8–e10). I have already noted the discrepancy between the enumeration in the diaereses themselves and the present summary. At 224d4–e5, the seller of psychic goods produced either by himself or another is a single class. This case was clearly labeled the "third" by Theaetetus at 224d4. What was originally diaeresis 3, then, the shortest of the series, is now divided into two. Originally, we passed over the distinction between selling one's own productions and selling the productions of another. This question is far from being a triviality: it raises the issue of whether sophistry is (to use a slightly anachronistic expression) an "original theory," or whether the sophists are merely selling the views of other thinkers. In either case, the problem of imagemaking is present. The confusion in the number of diaereses suggests an ambiguity in the problem of the origin of the sophistic teaching. It also illustrates dramatically the confusing fluidity of the appearances of the sophist, and the inapplicability of diaeretic "counting" to the task of defining him. Even a brilliant mathematician like Theaetetus makes a simple arithmetical error in attempting to enumerate the appearances of the sophist. And the Stranger himself confirms Theaetetus's inaccurate enumeration: "You

have remembered correctly. I will try to remember the fifth"
(231b11–e1).

What are we to make of the Stranger's error? It is, after all, his
doctrine, and he should know its stages. Did he not claim to have
remembered it perfectly? Either the Stranger does not himself remember the previous count or he is purposely agreeing with Theaetetus's new division. Whichever of these is the correct response, the
practical consequences, as outlined above, are the same. Thus, if the
Stranger intentionally accepts the new division, then he is tacitly
admitting that his initial presentation was erroneous or incomplete.
The great fuss that is made about the numbering process in the original diaeresis, as well as the interchange here concerning the accuracy of Theaetetus's memory, constitutes an assurance that Plato at
least intends us to notice the discrepancy.

5. An athlete of discursive contests who takes as his own the eristic art (231e1–2). The Stranger's memory is faulty here. In the
original diaeresis, the money-making art falls under the eristic segment of contradiction (226a1–4). Here the Stranger forgets (or intentionally suppresses) money making, or the difference between
childish chatter and sophistry. In this case the fee is unimportant;
what counts is the content of the teaching.

6. This case, the Stranger says, was open to dispute. He is referring
to the problem of the nobility of this kind of sophist, one who pur-
ifies beliefs that prevent the soul from learning (231e4–7). The
Stranger here omits the previous distinction between rough and
smooth teaching (231b3–8).

It is entirely possible that so careful a writer as Plato intends to
make subtle substantive points by each of the variations between
the final and the preliminary summaries. However, I shall not attempt to argue this, as it would take us too far into speculation.
What is self-evident is that the variations, in both the diaereses and
the summary, reflect the intricate, and indeed fluid, nature of the
sophist. He appears wherever we look for him. *Nothing will be said
in subsequent sections of the dialogue to annul this result.* But let
us not anticipate later developments. Thus far, the attempt to pin
down the sophist within a single family has been a comedy.

ACT TWO

IMAGES

The Problem of Images

(232a1–235c7)

We are about to turn to the Stranger's analysis of the art of image making. As we shall see, the Stranger introduces a new paradigm to guide us in the next section of the analysis. Our two previous paradigms were the angler and the household servant; the third will be the portrait sketcher. It will be helpful, before we become immersed in details, to state the most general characteristics of this model and the questions it raises. To begin with, the portraitist may produce accurate or inaccurate sketches of his subject, whom we may call the original of the image. In the subsequent discussion, as I shall argue, an accurate sketch, or icon, corresponds to a true statement by someone who possesses genuine knowledge. The inaccurate sketch corresponds to a false statement and is called a fantasm. It is not entirely clear whether the inaccurate sketch misleads intentionally or because of the incompetence of the portraitist (cf. 234b5–10, 235e3–236a2). The Stranger will refer to the "portraitist" *qua* sophist as trickster and juggler, which suggests that he intentionally deceives us. On the other hand, the Stranger will also attribute a theoretical doctrine to the sophist, namely, that there are no originals, or rather, that there are nothing but originals, which is to say that human beings "produce" their knowledge. If this is the sophist's doctrine, then it seems unfair to accuse him of deceit. What the Stranger calls an "inaccurate" image is from the sophist's standpoint an original. In other words, on the basis of the doctrine attributed to the sophist, the paradigm of the portrait sketcher itself inaccurately represents the art of the sophist as he himself understands and would justify it. The paradigm of the portrait sketcher thus rests on the assumption that the Stranger's interpretation of the sophist is accurate, but the issue of intention versus ignorance is not resolved.

When considering the paradigm, we can determine whether the sketch is accurate or inaccurate by looking away from the sketch to the original. This conveys two points: that the doctrine of truth represented by the paradigm is what we would today call a "correspondence doctrine" and that the basis for deciding whether the sketch (or statement) corresponds to the original is intrinsically visual or perceptual. Let us distinguish two cases, which I shall call formal and empirical for the sake of convenience. An example of the empirical case is the statement "snow is white." The Stranger seems to hold to the thesis that the statement "snow is white" is true if and only if snow is white. According to the paradigm, we determine whether snow is white by looking at snow. The snow is accessible to us independently of the statement which purports to describe it truly. An example of the formal case is the statement "*change* is *other* than *rest*" (where, as usual, the italicized words are the names of pure forms). Once again, that statement is true if and only if *change* is *other* than *rest*. Again, we determine this by looking at the forms, which are accessible to us independently of the statement which purports to say something true about them.

If the original were not accessible to us independently of its sketch or image, we could never know whether a given image is an icon or a fantasm. On the other hand, the Stranger's paradigm does not commit us to a purely visual or perceptual doctrine of truth (and falsehood). Truth and falsehood remain properties of statements, which is to say that knowledge is discursive. For example, in the empirical case, it is not enough to look at snow. I must be able to say that "snow is white" in order to possess knowledge about snow. Conversely, I must be able to look at snow, and see its color, in order to confirm that my statement is true. Obviously enough, something can go wrong at both ends of the transaction. Snow can seem grey to me, or I may make some error in formulating my statement about the color of snow, whether through an imperfect command of the language I am speaking, carelessness, or for some other reason. An analogous situation obtains with respect to pure forms. I may very well be assisted in the process of coming to see a pure form by the analysis of several statements concerning what I do not know in advance to be pure forms in the Stranger's sense. There is, however, a crucial difference between the empirical and the formal cases. In looking at snow, it is indeed true that I see snow, a perceptible, extended, colored stuff. I do not literally see the nature or definition of snow, nor does the statement "snow is white" flash across my intellect in large, easy-to-read letters. To the extent that the color of snow is part of its (phenomenal) nature, however, I am able to arrive at my statement, and to confirm it, by the fact that I can see snow itself.

In the case of pure forms, things are different. There is no sensuous or literally visible thing or event, analogous to white snow, that corresponds to the form *being*. There are things which derive their "being," whether directly or indirectly, by combination with the form *being*. We may call these things "beings," but they are not sketches, accurate or inaccurate, of *being*. It is therefore extremely difficult to grasp the application of the Stranger's paradigm to the case of pure forms. Some of us will be inclined to think of a certain statement about a pure form as the embodiment of that form. I mean by this the view that the form, say *being*, has no independent subsistence apart from the statements we use to define what we mean by the term "being." Others will agree in part with this, but contend that, since the statements in question can be repeated, we must distinguish between the "concept" of being which is described in each appropriate statement and the statements themselves. If a concept is not just another statement, or in other words if the statement which defines the concept is taken to refer to an independent entity, we come closer to the Stranger's doctrine. What counts here is the nature attributed to the independent entity. Is it an abstraction "produced" by the human intellect? This of course is not what the Stranger means by a pure form. But even if the concept is understood to be an eternal and independently subsisting entity, it is normally something which we can describe by specifying its properties. However, the Stranger's pure forms have no properties; if they did, they would no longer be pure or atomic. They enter into various concatenations, to be sure; but each in itself is exactly what it is, *being, change, rest*, and not another thing.

This peculiarity remains true of the pure forms even if we wish to think of them as predicates. In this case, they are pure formal predicates, or in more accurate terms, they are pure forms to which certain peculiar predicates correspond. We may then predicate a form of some "thing" which is not itself a form. But, for reasons which I have already given, we cannot predicate one form of another form. Strictly speaking, a statement describing some concatenation of pure forms is not a predicative statement. A concatenative statement, if I may call it such, is distinguished from all other statements in that it, and it alone, is an icon or accurate image of the original formal concatenation. But statements like those in which I am now describing the Stranger's doctrine of forms are not concatenative in the pure or strict sense. These statements, nevertheless, are finally confirmed or disconfirmed by our perception of the pure forms themselves. In that sense, any statement, whether concatenative or indirect, about pure forms is analogous to a statement like "snow is white." We must have direct access to the original, independent of our statements about it, in order to confirm or disconfirm these statements. A form is not a person or an event, but it is as distinct from statements about it as are persons or events from statements about them.

These preliminary and very general reflections must now be supplemented by a more circumstantial resume of the theme of images in the *Sophist*. The Stranger develops this theme in a way that is both fundamental to his argument and excessively cryptic. We shall have to dissect the stages of his discussion and how the central issue has been understood by others in considerable detail, here as in later scenes. The following summary analysis is intended to provide a synoptic view of what will subsequently be studied in smaller segments. In this synopsis, I shall disregard almost completely the related but distinguishable problem of the combination of forms, and so too the question of the senses of "is" in the Stranger's account of being and non-being. Apart from its synoptic or orienting function, the following summary analysis is intended to establish the previously mentioned association of true statements with accurate images as the required coordinate to the explicit if ambiguous association of false statements with inaccurate images. My contention will be that the Stranger continues to employ the Socratic paradigm of original and image in his account of meaningful discourse, but in such a way as to rob that distinction of its inner coherence. What follows directly is the first step in support of this contention, which will be argued at greater length in Scene Ten.

The distinction between accurate and inaccurate images (icons and fantasms) is introduced at 235c8ff as a consequence of the antecedent conclusion that the sophist belongs to the family of wonder workers or makers of tricks (τῶν θαυματοποιῶν; 235b5–6). These in turn are a kind of juggler, or "imitator of beings" (μιμητὴς ὢν τῶν ὄντων; 235a1. Cf. 264d3–5). The question is then initially whether the sophist, as such an imitator, produces accurate or inaccurate copies of beings (or of things as they are). However, the investigation is compromised by the following difficulty. An image in general (and so an icon as well as a fantasm) has the property of appearing and seeming, but not being (that which it copies; τὸ γὰρ φαίνεσθαι τοῦτο καὶ τὸ δοκεῖν, εἶναι δὲ μή). In order to establish the existence of images (or the manner of their being), and hence to define the art of the sophist, we must demonstrate that it is possible to speak and think falsehoods without contradicting ourselves (236e1–5). We note that the Stranger here commits himself to the view that *all* images contain falsehood. To be false is not to be true; a falsehood is thus apparently a self-contradictory combination of being and non-being. This puzzle will in turn require us to demonstrate the sense in which "non-being is" (τὸ μὴ ὂν εἶναι; 237a1–2).

After outlining the paradoxes which such an attempted demonstration must face, the Stranger asserts that we cannot define the sophist until these paradoxes are resolved. This is because the sophist will otherwise take advantage of our perplexity by denying the existence of images (239c6–d4). In other words, the sophist will appeal to Parmenides' injunction against stating (or thinking discursively) that "non-being is," and thereby deny that falsehood exists. Again we note that the sophist is here denying the existence (or being) of *all* images. Here as elsewhere, the initial distinction between icons and fantasms is blurred at crucial points. Nevertheless, it is not jettisoned, and the Stranger returns to it explicitly in his final diaeresis. To continue, the sophist next forces us to shift from visual images to the many senses of "image" (εἴδωλον) that follow from our discourse (ἐκ τῶν λόγων; 239e5–240a6). Once again it is established that all images, although genuinely images, are not genuinely their originals (240a9–b13). Hence they are and are not, and so we are once more faced with the need to explain how non-being can combine with being.

If we say that the sophist deceives us, then we say that his art leads us to judge falsely (ψευδῆ δοξάζειν; 240d1–4). We say that he leads us to think "the things that are not" (τὰ μὴ ὄντα) as "in some sense being" (Εἶναί πως τὰ μὴ ὄντα δεῖ γε; 240e3). This commits us to the thesis that falsehood, a version of non-being, "exists" in judgments and statements (241a8–b1). Once again, the Stranger, in formulating the problem, associates falsehood with images, icons, imitations, and fantasms (241e1–5). Since an accurate image cannot falsify the proportions of its original, its falsehood must be due to the fact that it is like but not the original. The relevant issue here is proportionality; to oversimplify slightly, an accurate image contains the same proportions as its original. It thus looks *exactly* like the original in the relevant respect; and yet, it is other than that original. As I shall contend, this is the case with respect to the relation between a true statement and that which the statement "reports" or portrays. Unfortunately, the Stranger never explains how we are to distinguish between the original proportion and its accurate image. (Note that the medium in which the proportion is realized is not directly relevant to the question of the being of the proportion itself.)

We can now skip ahead to 260c6ff, where the topic of images surfaces again. The Stranger argues as follows. If falsehood "exists," so too does deceit. And if deceit exists, all things are full of images, icons, and fantasms (260c8–9). The Stranger does not explain why the existence of falsehood guarantees the existence of deceit; he will, however, recognize that falsehood is a larger family than deceit. First he reminds us of the sophist's earlier claim: if non-being can be neither discursively thought nor spoken (as Parmenides held), then there can be no falsehood at all (260c11–d3), and of course, no images. But (in the intervening section, which I am not summarizing here) we have now resolved the problem of non-being. Therefore, we are now able to place the sophist among those who practice the art of "image making and fantasm making" (260d8–9). This phrase seems to anticipate what needs to be proved, namely, in which family of image making the sophist belongs. However, the sophist can still protest that discourse (λόγος) and judgment (δόξα) do not share in non-being, and so, that falsehood cannot be (260e1–3). We must therefore go on to show that discourse, judgment, and fancy do combine with non-being, and thus that falsehood exists (260e3–261a1).

This is the background for the discussion of false statement. I draw the following general conclusions from our resume thus far:

1. Images in general "are and are not," and are thus *all* associated with non-being and falsehood. Nevertheless, an accurate image is not false in the same sense as an inaccurate image. The latter deceives, whereas the former does not, concerning the proportions of the original.

2. Sophistry is a version of deceit, hence of falsehood associated with inaccurate images. But falsehood is broader than sophistry; not all false statements are sophistical, because not all are spoken dissemblingly or deceitfully (cf. 268a5–7). Incidentally, this point shows that sophistry is at bottom a matter of character.

3. False statement in general is for the Stranger the production of an image, that is, a statement in which the words are so related as to copy inaccurately some original. The "relations" of the words (compare the early Wittgenstein's doctrine of logical form) are a kind of inaccurate representation of the proportions of the original. (This will lead to the same problem later recognized by Wittgenstein: how any statement can be false, or falsely exhibit logical form.)

4. By denying images altogether, the sophist denies falsehood altogether; that is, he asserts, or wishes to assert, that all statements, including his own, are true.

5. Hence the sophist also implicitly denies that true statements are accurate images of some original.

6. The fact that the Stranger associates all images with falsehood does not rule out the thesis that true statements are accurate images of originals. This is because of the previously noted fact that an accurate image is "false" only in the sense that it is not the same as what it looks like.

7. It is precisely the characteristic of not being the same as what it describes that enables, and perhaps requires, us to identify true statements as accurate images. One might wish to argue that the Stranger implies a separation between images on the one hand (among which false statements are included) and true statements on the other. However, this leads to insuperable difficulties. If true statements are not images, then they must be "originals" in some sense. But in what sense? Either they are themselves the originals of which they speak, in which case there is no distinction between being and discourse. This contention is made by no one, not even by those who see a doctrine of predication in the Stranger's explication of formal structure. Or else, true statements are some *other* original, in which case they are either like or unlike the original of which they speak. However, this is to say that they are accurate or inaccurate images.

I turn now to the discussion of false statement. The points which interest us here are the following. We are given one example of a true statement, namely, "Theaetetus sits," and one example of a false statement, namely, "Theaetetus, with whom I am now speaking, flies" (263a2–b1). The true statement states "things as they are about you" (τὰ ὄντα ὡς ἔστι περὶ σοῦ), whereas the false statement states "the things that are not as being" (or less clumsily, "as obtaining"; τὰ μὴ ὄντ' ἄρα ὡς ὄντα λέγει; 263b4–9). We know from the previous discussion that the false statement is an inaccurate image of Theaetetus's condition. This will be reconfirmed shortly. First, however, the Stranger distinguishes between affirmation and negation, and speaks briefly of the relation between false speech and the faculties of discursive thought, judgment, sense perception, and fancy (263d1–264a7). In this passage, genuinely false speech (ὄντως τε καὶ ἀληθῶς . . . λόγος ψευδῆς) is described substantially as at 263b4–9: namely, as a combination (σύνθεσις) of verbs and nouns by which "things are said about you," but things which are other (that is, other than those characterizing you) are said as the same (that is, as those character-

izing you), and the things that are not are said as being or obtaining
(καὶ μὴ ὄντα ὡς ὄντα).

The Stranger does not describe false λόγος here as an image, although we know that this is his view. He in fact goes on to say that
some λόγος, and therefore some διάνοια and δόξα, is false (264a8–b3).
This in turn leads him to reinstitute the earlier distinction between
eikastics and fantastics (264b9–c6). He then contradicts the sophist's previous assertion that neither an icon, an image (εἴδωλον), nor
a fantasm exists at all, since (as the sophist contends) there is no
such thing as falsehood (264c10–d1). However, since false λόγος and
false δόξα have been shown to exist (πέφανται δ᾽οὖσα), "it is possible for imitations of beings to exist" (ἐγχωρεῖ δὴ μιμήματα τῶν ὄντων
εἶναι), and hence for there to be an art of deception (264d3–5). In
sum, a false λόγος is an imitation of beings, or in other words an
image, based either upon the ignorance of the speaker or upon his
intention to deceive (267b7–9, 267d4–e2). The intention of the
speaker has no bearing upon the fact that falsehood is apparently to
be found throughout the image-making family (266d8–e1), but certainly and unequivocally in the art of making fantasms. The Stranger is imprecise on this point to the end. Once more, certain conclusions may be drawn from this summary.

1. If icons (or nonfantastic εἴδωλα) also contain falsehood, they
must (as we have seen) do so in a way different from fantasms, whether
these last are intentional or not. The false λόγος in the proper sense
of the term is one which says what is not as what is. It must be an
inaccurate image, or more precisely, an inaccurate verbal representation of the proportions of the original. The "proportions" are in
turn the connections of forms and instances of forms (the logical
form) of activities or conditions of the subject of the λόγος.

2. The Stranger says even less about true λόγος than he does about
false λόγος, since it is the latter with which he is primarily concerned. He never explicitly connects true λόγος with icons or accurate images, except in the metalinguistic sense that true analyses of
false statements depend upon the ability to identify the false images
embedded in the latter, and hence upon the ability to distinguish
accurate from inaccurate images. It seems to follow necessarily that
a true analysis of a false statement itself "contains" (or "is") an accurate image of the original in question. However, the entirely general connection between true statements and accurate images may
be inferred by parity of reasoning from the Stranger's analysis of false
statements.

3. It may also be inferred by a *reductio* argument, based upon the denial that true λόγος is an image (see the seventh of the previous set of conclusions). To *say* what is, or what is not, is to copy what is, accurately or inaccurately, not in the literal sense of "painting" or "photographing" it, but in the sense of representing by the words and syntax of natural language (or attempting so to represent) the "proportions" or "ratios" (the logical form) of the intelligible or structural elements of what is (τὰ ὄντα).

4. The distinction between discourse and intelligible structure follows from the Stranger's analysis of the sense in which non-being "is." A false statement is about something that "is" or "obtains," not about something that "is not" or "does not obtain." If there were no distinction between discourse and intelligible "ratios," it would be impossible to err regarding the latter: the λόγος *qua* statement would be the same as the λόγος *qua* "proportion" or "ratio." A true statement must therefore "exhibit" or "reveal" (cf. 261e1; δηλοῦντά τι) the "proportion" or "ratio" of the original, without in fact being that proportion or ratio. And this is to say that a true statement must be an accurate image or an icon of the original. As we shall see, this distinction between true λόγος and original structure cannot be maintained. Perhaps this is one reason why some scholars were led to argue that there is no doctrine of original and image in the later dialogues, and hence no such doctrine in the *Sophist*. One can certainly deny that the Stranger explicitly identifies a true statement as an accurate image, but one cannot deny that he identifies a false statement as an inaccurate image. I have now presented my reasons for concluding that we are justified in inferring the coordinate thesis that true statements are images as well. Those who deny this thesis are faced with the difficulty of explaining the relation between a true statement and what true statements are about. The suppression of the doctrine of images thus leads directly to the view that true statements are predications or accurate identity statements. But this leaves unexplained the forms or "properties" corresponding to the predicates, on the one hand, and also, on the other, the ways in which true predications differ from false predications. Why is the former less an image than the latter?

In this preliminary sketch, I want to underline one other problem that arises from the Stranger's paradigm of sketching. The problem turns upon the ostensibly defective nature of images. The Stranger distinguishes between accurate and inaccurate images, which correspond to, among other things, true and false statements. We should note that any deficiency accruing to images as such will apply to true as well as false statements. To take the case in point, the Stranger holds that an image, since it "looks like" but is not an original, is what I shall call "ontologically defective." Now it is easy to see that a statement about snow, or the pure form *being*, is neither snow nor the pure form *being*. One could also say that if pure forms are the ultimate constituents of the cosmos, the eidetic "letters" out of which everything else is "spelled," then perhaps it makes sense to think of everything other than these eidetic letters as ontologically defective. Or we could extend the point from eidetic letters to "Platonic" forms in a wider sense, and say that these forms are the originals, whereas everything else—that is, their instances—are defective copies. However, even if we grant this, why should we also say that a true statement about snow is ontologically inferior to snow? Does this not amount to a depreciation of λόγος and ἐπιστήμη, or of knowledge in general as contrasted with the (nondiscursive) things about which we possess knowledge?

There is another aspect to this problem. Whereas the Stranger's doctrine requires that icons (accurate images) at least resemble their originals, can we also say that originals resemble their icons? If the relation of resemblance is not symmetrical, then what does it mean to say that something "looks like" its original, which, however, does not look like what resembles it? If the function of the icon is to elicit or "present" the original directly, and so if we are seeing the original, rather than its likeness, what sense is there in referring to the icon as looking like the original? And how then will we be able to distinguish between the original and the icon? In thinking about this problem, we soon note that the crucial case is what I called above the formal rather than the empirical. Snow looks nothing like a statement about snow, any more than Theaetetus looks like a statement about Theaetetus. If the paradigm of sketching has any pertinence, it must be because icons or true statements about empirical things or events capture or exhibit the formal structures intrinsic to the things or events themselves. In both the empirical and the formal cases, the form must "shine through" the statement. If the statement is too defective a version of the form, then it will be at best an inaccurate copy, a fantasm or false rather than a true statement. If it is sufficiently accurate to let the form shine through, then the picture or image presents the form itself, and the form is *present in* the statement. But persons who sit for portraits are not themselves *present in* their portraits. In other words, the presumed independent subsistence of the form does not in itself explain the

manner of subsistence of the form within the icon or true statement. And granted that the form *does* subsist within the statement,
it is no longer clear why the statement is deficient. We could say
that the statement is more than the form, since it includes linguistic material, but this seems irrelevant to the point. *Qua* accurate
image, the statement presents, or contains, and hence *is*, the form.

The question of the mode of subsistence of the form in the image
can be expressed in one last way. An inaccurate image of form F, as
I put the point earlier, must still be an image of F. An inaccurate
portrait of Napoleon cannot in fact be a portrait of Alexander the
Great. In the Stranger's paradigm, this point is developed very con-
fusingly by the account of fantasms. As he puts it, a fantasm distorts
the proportions of an original in order to accommodate the laws of
perspective. The result, however, is that inaccurate images provide
us with accurate images of the original! It is obvious that this account of inaccurate images cannot cover all cases. We shall have to
see whether the Stranger expands his paradigm in a technically satisfactory manner.

So much then for our preliminary sketch of the problems we shall
face in the second act of our philosophical drama. Let us now return
to the text. Immediately following the summary of what are now
six definitions of the sophist, the Stranger makes what seems to be
a flat condemnation of their use of diaeresis thus far. He explicitly
compares it to a "fantasm" which is unhealthy because it makes
the sophist appear to be a man who knows many things. Whoever
suffers from this disease "concerning any art is unable to perceive
the point toward which all the types of knowledge look." Something
like this, Theaetetus acknowledges, is why we call such a person by
many names rather than by one (232a1–7).[1] The metaphor of disease reminds us of the ambiguity in diaeresis 5 between medicine
and gymnastics. But whether we need a physician or a gymnast, it
is plain that the diaereses have failed in the task of pinning down
the sophist's art. On the other hand, as we noticed before, they do
not seem to say anything mistaken about the sophist; hence they
are presumably "healthy" when taken as a partial, phenomenological description of sophistry.

Why is it unhealthy to attribute many names to the sophist? The
reason seems to be that the scientific function of diaeresis is to determine the essential "name" or definition of the sophist. Apart from
the powers of the method, this can be done if and only if the sophist

---

1. Cf. Cornford (1935), p. 189, concerning κατιδεῖν at 232a4.

has an essential art. Thus far his capacity to assume various forms has made it impossible for us to determine exactly what that art might be. At the same time our failure itself, or the reason for the failure, suggests a candidate: maker of disguises or false images. We may note that the Stranger never denies that it is possible for one man to possess many arts. Instead he says that, in such cases, there is a single focus of the various arts, something to which all look. This must be the end or purpose to which the polymath addresses his multiple skills. The statement leaves room for interpretation; the Stranger does not tell us whether this single focus (as I am calling it) is one of the many arts or an end in the practical sense. Let us consider the case of the philosopher, who may know many arts, such as geometry, harmonics, astronomy, poetry, and so on. Why does the title "philosopher" take precedence over names like "geometer," "astronomer," and so on, which might also be applied to the person in question? The superficial reason is that the philosopher does not earn his living by teaching, say, geometry; he is not a "professional" geometer. A deeper reason is that the philosopher does not normally make important discoveries or advances in the various arts he knows. In some cases, however, he does (think of Descartes and Leibniz as examples). In the Platonic dialogues at least, the answer to our question is, I think, that the philosopher engages in other arts for the sake of philosophy. But what is the exact distinction between philosophy and the other arts?

Socrates answers our question in political terms in the *Republic* (IV, 428a11ff), when he says that wisdom (σοφία) is distinct from art (τέχνη) because the end of the former is the welfare of the whole city.[2] We can generalize this answer by saying that philosophy is concerned with the whole, and not simply with this or that art. This way of putting the point coincides with the Stranger's identification of dialectic (that is, diaeresis) as the philosopher's art, and with his identification of that art as capable of capturing anything at all. On the other hand, we have no evidence as yet that diaeresis is in fact capable of fulfilling the Stranger's claims. Furthermore, it is plain that for both Socrates and the Stranger, philosophy is a moral or practical as well as a theoretical activity: it is a way of life. But diaeresis, taken as division and collection according to kind, by distinguishing like from like, is itself a strictly "technical" or theoretical method. Since it abstracts from better and worse, it cannot encompass the full range of philosophical activity.

2. Contrast Socrates' remark in the *Theaetetus*, 145d11–e6.

This preliminary reflection shows us that we do not know how to define the philosopher, any more than we know how to define the sophist. But just as, in the case of the philosopher, it is not the multiplicity of arts that confuses us, so too, one may suggest, in the case of the sophist. The problem is not the multiplicity, but the unity. I can bring this out in a slightly different way. The sophist may also know geometry, harmonics, astronomy, poetry, and so on. But his knowing these things does not prevent us from calling him a sophist. We call someone a sophist because of the end toward which he directs his comprehensive energies. In other words, whereas geometry and the other arts do seem to have something specific to do with the comprehensive art of philosophy, they do not seem to have anything essential to do with the comprehensive art of sophistry. The comprehensive or "focal" art of the sophist is analogous to the comprehensive or "focal" art of the philosopher to this extent; we call someone a philosopher or a sophist if he possesses the appropriate "focal" art. Until such time as we are able to define this "focal" art, however, our identifications of philosopher and sophist may be mistaken. If a sophist is a man who believes himself to know what he does not know, then the ostensible philosopher may be the sophist, and the ostensible sophist the philosopher, depending upon which one knows the truth. The truth at stake is not that of geometry, astronomy, and so on. What kind of truth is it? The greater relevance of the other arts to the "focal" art of philosophy is impressive only to someone who agrees with what the philosopher claims to know about the connection between the arts and wisdom. But the sophist may be wiser than the philosopher, in the sense that his account of the whole may be truer than the philosopher's account. This remains to be seen. The sophist can triumph over the philosopher without challenging the integrity of geometry, astronomy, and the rest of the arts precisely because he distinguishes sharply between his "focal" art and the others, whereas the philosopher does not.

We are today inclined to describe the difference between the philosopher and the sophist concerning the whole as one of philosophical positions. This would not be acceptable to the Stranger. Philosophy is for the Stranger that way of life, suitable to a free man, in which he sees the pure forms and establishes their concatenations as the basis for all subsequent knowledge. For the sophist, there are no forms, and hence what the Stranger calls the life of the free man would undoubtedly be styled by the sophist as the life of a slave. It remains to be seen whether this theoretical disagreement can be resolved to the vindication of philosophy. But what of the practical difference between the philosopher and the sophist? If the philosopher is right to claim that virtue is knowledge, how can we decide whether he is virtuous until we determine whether his knowledge is genuine or specious? If we do not know that the sophist's characteristic knowledge, that which is embodied in his "focal" art, is specious, then we are in no position to say that his appearance in all the branches and subbranches of our diaeresis is a mark of the defectiveness of sophistry. It may not, in other words, be the mark of the "sickness" of diaeresis, except in the sense that the sophist's capacity to show up in every family is (on this hypothesis) the mark of his genuine wisdom. However we look at the question, we are not in a position to say that the possession of many kinds of knowledge makes a man a sophist. But neither are we in a position to say that the sophist's ability to *look like* many kinds of technicians is a defect.

At this point, the Stranger disregards the multiplicity of results and chooses a single property to characterize the sophist, namely, contradiction or disputation (ἀντιλογικόν; 232b1–7), a segment of verbal warlike contests (see diaeresis 4). There was nothing in the diaereses to distinguish this attribute as decisive for a definition of the sophist. By making the art of disputation crucial, the Stranger implies his agreement with the Socratic thesis that sophistry is very close to, or the same as, oratory.[3] In the *Republic* (VI, 493a6ff), Socrates says that the sophists teach public opinion. They are regarded as rivals in art by private wage earners, and they gather together what they have learned about the opinions of the public beast and "call it wisdom, having organized it as an art" (ὡς τέχνην συστησάμενος).

This is a very interesting passage. According to Socrates, as we saw above, wisdom is concerned with the welfare of the whole city, unlike art. Sophistry is thus a rival to philosophy because it claims to deal with the welfare of the whole city. This claim is based upon the sophist's putting opinion in the place of knowledge. In other words, the crucial thesis of sophistry is that opinion is higher than knowledge. The sophist does not deny that there is technical knowledge, whether of shoemaking or geometry. His point is rather that there is no technical knowledge of opinions about the good; instead, there is technical knowledge of how to persuade others to accept our opinion of the good. The sophist is a rival to the private wage

3. See *Gorgias* 520a6 and *Eth. Nic.* X, 9, 1181a12–17.

earner, not because he pretends to be a shoemaker, a carpenter, or some other artisan, but because he, too, sells his "art," which he claims to be more important than theirs. Socrates casts doubt on the "wisdom" of the sophist by saying that it is opinion organized *as though* it were an art, but this raises a problem for philosophy as well as for sophistry. Whereas Socrates regularly uses the arts as the basis for his approach to knowledge, and sometimes (as in the above-cited passage from the *Theaetetus*) identifies wisdom as knowledge, he also sometimes (as in the above-cited passage from the *Republic*) distinguishes wisdom from art.

The latter distinction implies that some knowledge is not technical, and this is consonant with the fact that the Stranger initially divides, not τέχνη, but δύναμις. The crux of Socrates' criticism of sophistry seems to be this. The sophist does not possess genuine wisdom, but rather the ability to persuade the public about the common good, on the basis of publicly held opinions about the common good. Socrates thus claims that the philosopher possesses knowledge about the common good. This knowledge is not "technical" in the sense that it is not "mathematical" or derived from the division of like from like. Instead, it is knowledge of human nature, and in the last instance, of the nature of the soul. Socrates claims on behalf of philosophy the knowledge of which life is best for man, namely, the philosophical life. He further claims to be able to order the remaining human lives, and thus to define the public good, on the basis of the superiority of the philosophical life. However, even if we grant the thesis that we must possess knowledge in order to obtain whatever we desire, it does not follow that we ought to desire what the philosopher tells us is good. Socrates denies the validity of public opinion about the desirable or good. The sophist accepts this opinion. It is important to see that the issue cannot be settled by diaeresis or technical knowledge. The philosopher must still persuade the general public that his "perception"of the good (whether as an idea or in some other sense) is right, and that the public perception is not.

How will the philosopher persuade the public to accept his wisdom rather than that of the sophist? He cannot appeal to diaeresis, which is both irrelevant and unintelligible to the general public. It is all very well to say that the philosopher will present his arguments, but this requires him to employ rhetoric or oratory, since he is not dealing with other philosophers, and even if he were, he is not discussing technical issues. In the *Republic*, Socrates uses force and comprehensive rhetoric to enforce the philosopher's opinion concerning the public good. All other considerations to one side, this shows that the nonphilosophical public will not voluntarily accept the philosopher's opinions instead of their own (as modified by the sophist). If we are not inclined ourselves to accept the motives of the philosopher, we would be tempted to say that the public quarrel between philosophy and sophistry is fought with the weapons of the sophist. This is not quite the same as to say that the sophist therefore wins the quarrel by default. But it is enough to show that the philosopher must either appeal to the moral perceptions of the private person, or explain to the public how his wisdom is knowledge whereas the wisdom of the sophist is not.

In sum, Socrates regularly emphasizes the practical or political nature of sophistry, even when he discusses an ostensibly technical subject like the Protagorean doctrine that man is the measure of all things. Socrates transforms this into a doctrine of sense perception in the *Theaetetus* in order to show that it leads to incoherence, and so, to a dissolution of the public world. The consequence of Protagoras's doctrine is thus that no one is wiser than anyone else and that this is specifically true in the domain of politics or legislation (*Theaetetus* 179a–b). Let us now return to the Stranger, and see how he treats the sophistical art of disputation.

The Stranger chooses five topics on which the sophist teaches others to dispute (232b8–12):

1. The sophists are said to teach disputation about divine things which are invisible to the many (232b12–c3). The language implies that these things are not invisible to the few. In other words, the sophists *publicize* discussion of the divine things.
2. They also treat the visible things of heaven and earth (232c4– 6). In a later terminology, the distinction between the invisible and the visible divine things corresponds to the distinction between metaphysics and physics.
3. Next, the Stranger mentions "conversations in private" about genesis and being in general (οὐσία; 232c7–11). Since the sophists deny the eternity of the heavenly beings, or accept change as the principle of all things, topics 2 and 3 seem to concern the same subject. Perhaps the difference is that these private conversations are about the principles of things, which would not be of interest to the general public.
4. The Stranger then asks whether the sophists undertake to teach people how to dispute about laws and the entire political sphere (συμπάντων τῶν πολιτικῶν). Theaetetus replies that no one, so to

speak, would converse with them if they did not make this promise (232d1–4). The Stranger does not demur. Nevertheless, his own analysis of sophistry is much more theoretical than practical. As I have suggested previously, this is because, if knowledge is virtue, we need to assess the sophist's claim to know the truth about opinion before we can decide whether he is virtuous or vicious.

5. The sophist writes down for all to read what the master craftsman should reply to each person with respect to the arts, both individually and collectively (232d5–e2). The sophist thus engages in what we may call "technological enlightenment."

In sum, sophistry seems to be "a kind of power" (τις δύναμις) for disputing about everything (cf. 219a6). Theaetetus agrees that not much seems to have been left out (232e2–5). The Stranger's analysis suggests the following inference. Sophistry imitates philosophy by its concern with the whole, but the sophist's concern is subordinated to politics. The Stranger is thus more or less in agreement with Socrates' account of sophistry, although he tries to take the analysis of the sophist's "power" down to a deeper level. "By the gods!" the Stranger swears. How is it possible for a mortal to know all these things? The Stranger suggests to Theaetetus that the sharper sight of the young can discern what is inaccessible to the duller sight of old men. This does not prove to be true; Theaetetus requires a restatement of the question. He then says that ours would be a blessed race if comprehensive knowledge were possible (232e6–233a4).

The Stranger then asks another question: Since no one can know everything, how is it possible for the sophist to say "anything healthy" (ὑγιές τι) when arguing with someone who knows (233a5–7)? In this passage, the Stranger seems to assume that, if the sophist does not know everything, then he knows nothing. This is an illegitimate inference, and it colors with ambiguity the subsequent reference to "the marvellous power of the sophist" (233a8–9). Surely no one else knows all things, either. If the sophist is arguing with someone who knows, and knowledge is relevant to the argument, then they must be arguing about something specific. But the Stranger goes on to a further question: How is the sophist able to make and furnish young men with the opinion that he is the wisest of all men in all things? (233a10–b2). This question tacitly contradicts the Stranger's previous assertion that the young have keener eyes than the old when it comes to perceiving the sophist. The Stranger restates the problem and gets Theaetetus to agree that young men seek out the sophist on the assumption that he knows all things. Thus young men are now presented as wishing to be able to dispute about all things, not merely about politics (233b3–8).

The sophists appear to their students to be wise about all things, and their students wish to be wise about all things. However, the appearance is false and the wish is for the impossible (233b9–c11). The Stranger does not say so, but the pursuit of wisdom here makes it plain that the sophist's rival is the philosopher. At the same time, the philosopher cannot know everything any more than can the sophist. If wisdom is the knowledge of all things, then the philosopher is on that point no better off than the sophist. One could object that the more one knows, the closer one is to wisdom. But we have already seen that the sophist can know the individual arts just as well as the philosopher. What counts here is not shoemaking or geometry, but the "focal" art, what Socrates calls in the *Republic* the "synoptic" vision of the whole (VII, 536c2), and so "wisdom" in a sense that goes beyond, if it is not entirely distinct from, technical knowledge. We have also seen that the question of the relation between the individual arts and the focal art is answered only when we have identified the focal art itself. Even worse, our brief inspection of the difference between technical knowledge and the good, which is reinforced by the Stranger's own definition of philosophical diaeresis, seems to support the sophistical thesis that there is no essential connection between the individual arts and the focal art. The Stranger, therefore, does not refute the sophist's pretensions by identifying his knowledge as based upon opinion.

Theaetetus says that the claim of the Stranger concerning the sophist's pretension to know everything may be the most accurate statement they have made so far. The Stranger, however, thinks that more clarity is needed. He suggests that they take up "a clearer paradigm" of supposed or doxastic knowledge. Despite its ostensible clarity, the paradigm must contain some difficulties, or so one would assume from the Stranger's warning to Theaetetus to "try to be especially attentive and to answer carefully" (231d1–8). The Stranger then asks: What if someone should claim to know how to make and do, rather than to assert or deny, all things by a single art? For the first time in their conversation, Theaetetus interrupts the Stranger in mid-sentence. "What do you mean by 'all'?" (233d3–e1). Theaetetus had no trouble with this word earlier in the dialogue. The reason for his present perplexity may be the shift from talking about everything to making and doing everything.[4]

4. Cf. *Theaetetus* 204a1ff.

The Stranger says that the failure to understand "all things" shows that Theaetetus has not understood "the beginning of what was said." He explains: "I refer to you and me among all things, and besides us the other animals and plants" (233e2–6). The Stranger's examples are not of all things, but of a subclass, namely, the class of living things. Theaetetus still does not understand. The Stranger reformulates the point: "If someone would claim to make me, you, and the other living things—" For the second time, Theaetetus interrupts: "What is meant by 'making'?" This is obviously much more difficult than it would have been if the Stranger had referred, for example, to counting all things. Theaetetus doubts that the Stranger could be referring to the farmer, who was identified in the initial diaeresis as a "maker" of animals (233e7–234a2). The Stranger asserts that he does include the making of animals, but also of "sea, earth, the heavens, gods, and all other things together" (234a3–4); this maker also works very quickly and sells his productions for very little money. "What you say is a kind of joke," Theaetetus responds (234a4–6).

The Stranger is about to introduce the paradigm of sketching. To "make" everything is to copy or sketch everything. If we take the model literally, the sophist will pretend to be the master of each art that he "sketches" in an appropriate set of speeches. In fact, this is not what the sophist does at all. The false image produced by the sophist is not an inaccurate copy of a pair of shoes or a geometrical proof; it is a speech about the ends or political utility of the makings and doings of the various artists. Even this is done in an indirect way, since the primary theme of sophistical speeches is the law, written and unwritten, of the city. If the sophist pretended to be a shoemaker or geometer, but was unable to do the work of these arts, we could easily expose him as a maker of false images, and we could do this with no knowledge of the "ontological" nature of images, whether false or accurate. By presenting a pictorial model of sophistry, the Stranger conceals, whether intentionally or not, the nature of the sophist as disputer.

The purpose of the "focal" art of sophistry is to enable us to persuade others to satisfy our desires. This in turn points toward an understanding of the good life. If a sophistical speech is a "picture" of anything, then, it must be of a conception of the good life. In this case, however, the distinction between an accurate and an inaccurate picture cannot be made where there is no agreement as to the nature of the good. And this agreement, as I noted above, cannot be acquired by purely technical means. One might, of course, catch the sophist in a contradiction. The sophist claims both that his "focal" art is independent of τέχνη, or that there is no technical definition of *the* good, and that he genuinely knows the art of persuasion, which he can teach to others, and so is himself a technician. However, this contradiction dissolves upon closer inspection. That there is no technical definition of the good does not preclude the possibility of possessing technical knowledge of how to satisfy one's desires. This aside, contradictions are impressive only to philosophers, not to sophists or to their prospective customers. The fact is that human beings can be persuaded to do as we wish. The only serious question, from the standpoint of the sophist and his clientele, is whether or not the sophist can teach others to be persuasive. In sum, the sophist can be shown to produce inaccurate images only if we are able to demonstrate what it is to produce an accurate image, and with respect to the pertinent original. If this cannot be done, then the joke is on the philosopher.

Theaetetus, to continue, has just accused the Stranger of joking. To this, the Stranger responds, "Is there any more technical (τεχνικώτερον) or more charming joke than the mimetic kind?" This is a double-edged question, because if sophistry is the production of inaccurate images, then philosophy is presumably the production of accurate images. The same conclusion follows from the Stranger's analysis of discourse, even granting the irony of the present question. Theaetetus replies affirmatively to the Stranger's question. The Stranger is right about mimesis, and he has "collected into one look" (or form) "an all" (πάντα), namely an everywhere-occurring and most intricate form of joke (234b1–4). This exchange implies that sophistry and mimesis are, if not coextensive, then certainly in the same family. It also implies, however, that the philosopher, or more broadly, the man of genuine knowledge, is not in that family. This conflicts with the basic distinction about to be drawn between accurate and inaccurate images.

The art of drawing, the Stranger now explains, enables one person to imitate all things and, by showing these drawings at a distance, to deceive unintelligent youths into taking copies for originals (234b5–c1). The Stranger then explicitly makes his comparison between drawing and an art that enchants the young with words or spoken images (εἴδωλα) of all things. This art is not said to be restricted in its "power" to the unintelligent. It affects the young because of their inexperience; they are still at a distance from the "affairs of truth" (234c2–7). The eyes of the young are not in fact sharper than those of the old with respect to sophistry (cf. 232e6ff). More

important, however, is the misleading nature of the analogy between drawing and sophistical rhetoric. I have already insisted upon
this point, but it is sufficiently important to bear repeating. The
sophist does not pretend to be, say, a philosopher by copying inaccurately the speeches of the philosopher. Instead, he gives different
speeches, namely, his own. What both the philosopher and the sophist are "copying" (if that is in fact the right expression) is, according
to the philosopher, the good life. According to the sophist, even this
is true only in an attenuated sense. The good life is that of pleasure,
which comes from the satisfaction of our desires. Each of us, however, furnishes to himself his own desires. What we acquire from
the sophist is the art of persuasion, which is thus "neutral," like
any other art, with respect to the ends toward which it is directed.
Once again there is a contradiction here from the philosopher's
standpoint. The sophist says both that there is no single good life,
and that the good is the pleasant. This contradiction can be dissolved as follows. The sophist has only to reply to the philosopher
that the philosopher pursues knowledge, with the attendant sense
of virtue, because he finds it pleasant. If the philosopher objects that
even the sophist must grant that some pleasures are not good, the
reply is again simple. "Good" means "as pleasant as possible." We
thus pass by those pleasures which are "contradictory" in the sense
of being counterproductive. There are no doubt practical problems
in carrying out this program, but they are no greater, and perhaps
less, than the obstacles to the acquisition of knowledge.

According to the Stranger, as the young mature, the majority come
closer to things. They are focused by the modifying effects of life to
grasp things as they are, openly or plainly, rather than as they look
in their verbal copies (234d2–6). Those who do so will have their
youthful opinions transformed. What was previously thought to be
great will now appear small, and what was easy will now seem difficult. In sum, the formerly persuasive verbal fantasies will be over-
turned by things as they are experienced (ὑπὸ τῶν ἐν ταῖς πράξεσιν
ἔργων; 234d6–e2). As the Stranger's terminology makes evident, it
is the business of life, affairs (πρᾶξις), and practical encounters with
things (ἔργα), rather than abstract speeches, that cure us of sophistry. This remark of the Stranger, while sound, is thus inconsistent
with the methodological context of the discussion.

So far as Theaetetus can see from his present youthful distance
from things, the Stranger is right (234e3–4). The Stranger adds that
all the present elders will try to bring Theaetetus as close to things
as it is possible to come "without experience" (ἄνευ τῶν παθημάτων).

The implication here is that the Stranger's philosophical methods will function like those of mathematics to enable young men to see genuine originals. In other words, he claims to possess technical methods for exposing the sophist as a kind of trickster or juggler who is an imitator of things. Theaetetus agrees at once that the sophist does not know the things about which he disputes, and that he belongs to the family of jokesters (234e5–235a4).

Having put diaeresis to one side, the Stranger now feels free to employ rhetoric and the distinction of better from worse in his pursuit of the sophist. The least one could say is that these are not superfluous tools in the task of educating Theaetetus, and more broadly, in the presentation of the Stranger's comprehensive teaching. The sophist, as a juggler and imitator (235a8–9), hence as a kind of jokester or game player, is manifestly assimilated into a low class of person: a paid entertainer. The sophist provides us with a low *pleasure*. Our job (ἔργον) now is not to let the beast escape. "We have almost got him surrounded in a kind of net made up of discursive tools, so that he will not now escape what comes next" (235a10–b4).

This remark brings out the role production has played in pursuing the definition of sophistry. It also introduces another description of the sophist's own mode of production; he belongs to the class of wonder workers (235b4–7). This was anticipated at 233a8. Perhaps wonder workers constitute the genus of which joking mimetic jugglers are a species. Instead of taking up the cluster of names introduced in connection with the sophist, the Stranger begins a rather long speech by ordering that they divide the image-making art as quickly as possible (235b8–9). Why this unseemly need for haste (cf. 229b1ff)? It seems to be connected to the shift from diaeresis to the new model of sophistry with its attendant reliance upon abusive rhetoric and the distinction of better from worse. In the same vein, the Stranger introduces a political metaphor: "Should the sophist stand his ground against us at first, we will seize him by the orders of λόγος, our king, to whom we will deliver the sophist and display the booty. But if he tries to sink away into any of the parts of mimesis we will follow him, always dividing the part that has received him, until he is captured. For certainly neither this nor any other family will ever boast of having escaped from those who are able to pursue, in each and all points, the method" (235b9–c6).

The Stranger is about to start a final diaeresis which, as we shall see, will founder very quickly. No doubt the Stranger is attempting to encourage Theaetetus after the discouraging multiplicity of definitions produced by the previous applications of the method. If it is true that the method cannot fail when it is correctly employed, then obviously the Stranger, by his own lights, has not yet employed it correctly. This, of course, is true only if we accept the Stranger's thesis that a single technical definition is required.

Diaeresis Once More

(235c8–236c7)

The Stranger has determined, without any evident assistance from diaeresis, that the sophist is a mimetic jokester or wonder worker. Diaeresis cannot tell us what to divide. For that matter, on the basis of the immediately preceding discussion, it is not clear whether we ought to divide mimesis, joking, or wonder working. The Stranger opts for mimesis and returns to diaeresis, although in a much more tentative manner than initially. "I seem to see two forms of mimesis, but I do not think I am yet able to discern in which one of these the look we are searching for happens to be" (235c8–d3). The Greek word rendered here as "look" is ἰδέαν, which makes its first appearance in the dialogue, but which, like εἶδος before it, does not carry its later technical sense as a pure form. The Stranger is having trouble distinguishing the looks of mimesis because no pure forms are involved.

The Stranger offers the following explanation to Theaetetus of the two looks in question. The first art he notices is that of eikastics. This art makes its copy in accord with the proportions of the original (τὰς τοῦ παραδείγματος συμμετρίας) in length, breadth, and depth. It also gives the proper colors to each copy. Theaetetus asks whether it is not true that all imitators try to carry out these tasks. The Stranger replies that those who make large paintings or sculptures do not obey the proportions of the original (and there is no further allusion to color). In these cases, a proportionally accurate copy of beautiful things would make the upper parts seem smaller and the lower parts larger than they ought to be (cf. 234d6–e2). The Stranger says, "The true proportions of the beautiful things cannot be perceived by means of accurate copies" (235e5–236a3). This statement, together with what follows, identifies the makers of inaccurate copies as artisans concerned with the representation of the beautiful.

These craftsmen, as Theaetetus agrees, "say goodby to truth" and construct their copies, "not in the actual proportions of the original" but "in those which seem to be beautiful" (236a4–7). So, beautiful images, contrary to what we were told at 228a4–b1, can be marked by dissymmetry. Nothing is said here to suggest that symmetrical images are beautiful.

The images which are "other . . . but like" (ἕτερον . . . εἰκός γε ὄν) are justly called by the name "icons," and the mimetic art which produces them is called "eikastics." The constrasting mimetic art produces images "appearing to look like the beautiful because not seen from a beautiful vantage point, but which, if it were possible for someone to perceive the originals adequately, would not look like what they claim to resemble." This art is correctly called "fantastics," since its productions are "fantasms" (236a8–c4). In general, the contrast is between those mimetic arts which aim to produce a beautiful image and those which aim to produce a "true" image, in the sense of one that accurately reproduces the "proportions" of the original. Once again, the underlying paradigm employs visual objects. If we think of the implicit reference to sophistry, the Stranger seems to be saying something like this. The sophist is concerned primarily if not exclusively with sense perception, and his speeches are an accommodation of the object to the perspective of his audience. This point is quite close to the interpretation by Socrates in the *Theaetetus* of the Protagorean doctrine of perception. But the Stranger adds that the sophist's audience is more pleased by beauty than by truth, or, as one could also put this, by rhetoric than by λόγος. We should note once more a difficulty in the Stranger's account. Fantasms correct a natural defect in human perception. In the present context, the Stranger associates this correction with the aim of producing beautiful views, and thereby expresses the same criticism of the "creative" arts (as we now call them) that we find elsewhere in the dialogues. Yet, it is easy to think of circumstances in which the production of fantasms would serve a useful function with respect to the pursuit of truth. One has only to recall that Socrates, in the *Republic*, recommended various noble or useful lies, which he classified under the rubric of medicines.[1] The Stranger is silent on this and related points.

The Stranger's formulation brings out another interesting point.

1. Cf. *Republic* II, 376d9ff, and especially 381e8–383c7, with IV, 459c2–d2. Lies are required for the foundation of the just city, with respect to various aspects of the education of the guardians, and especially in order to regulate sexual intercourse. In all these cases, lies are classified as medicines.

Sophists do not merely repeat public opinion, as Socrates implies in the previously quoted passage from the *Republic* (VI, 493a6ff). They "alter the proportions" of these opinions in order to make them beautiful. In other words, the sophists provide a theoretical justification of what the majority of human beings desire by nature, but which the laws condemn as shameful. Sophistry makes the shameful look beautiful. The "large copy" produced by the sophist is thus an interpretation of the good life, according to which the good is the pleasant, and the pleasant is what we desire. On the other hand, it is not clear from this interpretation how the philosopher is able to produce a large image that is both accurate and "beautiful," in the sense of politically efficacious. Even further, the Stranger's example seems to exclude the possibility of producing accurate copies of large "bodies" (which I am here reading as "large" *qua* comprehensive interpretations of human political life). The distinction between beauty and proportional accuracy thus assumes major importance in the new paradigm. If the sophist simply corrected for human perspective in his representation of large bodies, there would be no reason to condemn his art, since its result would be useful: an image that looks like the original. At the same time, the distinction between beauty and truth leaves the producer of accurate images in the awkward position of *misleading* his audience with copies that do *not* look like the original (given the laws of perception), and hence are not beautiful.

The fantasm does not look like the original because it alters the original proportions, but it does look like the original to the audience. Gilles Deleuze comments on this passage: "For, in Plato, an obscure debate is carried out in the depth of things, between that which submits to the action of the Idea and that which escapes this action (copies and simulacra)." [2] There is no explicit reference to ideas in the text we are studying, but one may take the Stranger's reference to a "beautiful vantage point," from which we would see that the beautiful-seeming copies are inaccurate, as an allusion to the perception of originals as they truly or genuinely are, independent of distortions imposed by sense perception. This makes the same point as does Deleuze's reference to "the action of the Idea." However, Deleuze oversimplifies in saying that "the copy is an image endowed with resemblance; the simulacrum is an image without resemblance." [3] An image that does not resemble X cannot be an

2. Deleuze (1969), p. 15.
3. Ibid., p. 352.

image of X. Despite its "dissymmetry," the fantasm looks like the original to the viewer.

The description of icons as "other but like" plainly anticipates the problem of non-being. But the description of fantasms is, if anything, even more puzzling. The fantasm appears to look like the beautiful because of the "place" from which we view it. If we could see the original directly, we would also see that the fantasm does not look like it. It is easy enough to conceive of a device which, while not itself resembling what it copies, produces a copy of the original that does resemble it. A verbal expression is such a device. A statement about a tree conveys to us an "image" of the tree, even though the statement does not itself look like a tree. But this is true of both true and false statements. One must therefore distinguish between the "embodiment" of the image and the image itself as perceived look. On this point, the Stranger's paradigm is inconsistent. On the one hand, the perceived look (conveyed by the embodiment of the fantasm) does resemble the beautiful original. To repeat, "the true proportions of the beautiful things cannot be perceived by means of accurate copies." A large painting altered to accommodate the facts of perspective *does* convey a resemblance of the original.

On the other hand, the Stranger says that the fantasm "appears to look like" but in fact does not resemble the original. What could this possibly mean? One might distinguish between the physical embodiment of the image, such as the painted canvas or carved stone, and the image as a perceived look. It is true that human beings do not look like painted canvases or carved chunks of stone, but on the basis of this distinction it is hard to see how *any* image, including a statement, could fail to qualify as a fantasm. After all, human beings do not look like words or sentences, either. The Stranger must be fundamentally concerned here with the image as perceived look. If in some cases an alteration of the proportions is necessary to provide a correct perceived look, then fantasms perform a veridical task. But if the alteration of the proportions is enough to suppress the likeness between copy and original, how do we receive the impression that we are seeing the original? If it is not the original that we see (in the sense of receiving a look that resembles it), then how can a fantasm of a given original be an image of that original? Must it not be an image of something else? This is exactly the problem involved in the Stranger's subsequent analysis of false statements.

Let us summarize by translating the Stranger's paradigm into the language of the good life. He implies that a reliance upon fantasms gives us the impression that we are living a good life, whereas we are actually not doing so. This implication rests upon the further assumption that there is a genuinely good life, of which an accurate copy is accessible, presumably in the speeches of philosophers. If the genuinely good life is beautiful, then according to part of the Stranger's paradigm, it is *not* accessible in icons or accurate copies. In this case, philosophers will also have to make use of fantasms, as does Socrates in the *Republic*, in order to teach the good life to the nonphilosophers. But how do the philosophers themselves acquire an accurate perception of the truly good life? What is the original of which their true statements are accurate images? It cannot be another statement or set of statements, since these are copies. Hence too the philosopher cannot perceive the good life merely by talking about it. He must have access to the original from "a beautiful vantage point" which is not itself primarily or fundamentally discursive. Even if we grant this, however, it is still not plain what the philosopher would "see" from that beautiful vantage point. Surely the good life is not a form or a formal structure, especially since these are presumably accessible via diaeresis, which looks away from better and worse. The visual paradigm leads us to look for forms, and so too for copies, whether by the sophist or the philosopher, that are like paintings or photographs. It is fair to call this a tendency toward the *reification* of the good. This tendency, however, interferes with our understanding of the good life, and so too of the nature of the sophist.[4]

4. The Stranger's teaching in the *Statesman* (285e4ff) is quite different.

The Problem of Non-Being

(236c8–239d5)

The initial set of diaereses failed to pin down the sophist in a unique family. The Stranger has now suggested that this is because the sophist is an imitator. He can therefore look like, without actually resembling, all kinds of technicians. This assertion, apart from the fact that it is supported by an ambiguous paradigm, does not in itself terminate our pursuit of the sophist. We cannot, in other words, define him as an imitator, because there are various kinds of imitation. The Stranger therefore begins a new diaeresis of imitation, which he tacitly understands to be the art of producing images. The Stranger has just concluded the first step in that diaeresis, namely, the division of the art of eikastics and the art of fantastics. Instead of continuing, however, he admits that, now as before, he is not sure in which segment of mimesis the sophist belongs. Whereas the Stranger's power to see the sophist clearly is impaired, the case is otherwise with the "marvellous man's" ability to slip away into an "aporetic look" or place where he will be extremely hard to track down. Theaetetus agrees that "it looks this way," and the Stranger in turn asks whether the agreement is based upon a grasping of the point, or habitual quick assent (236c9–d7).

If Theaetetus is hurrying, the Stranger must bear part of the blame, since he himself instructed the young man to divide image making as quickly as possible (235b8). However, it is necessary to go slowly at this point in the investigation. "For appearing and seeming, but not being, and saying things, but not true ones, all this has always in the past been full of puzzles and is so now. How one is to say or think that falsehood possesses genuine being [ὄντως εἶναι] without uttering a contradiction: that is extremely difficult" (236e3–237a2). Several points in this passage require comment; perhaps the most comprehensive is the connection between seeming to be and speaking (or thinking) false statements. Least germane to the technical discussion, but of dramatic interest, is the question whether the continuous puzzlement to which the Stranger refers is itself part of the "Eleatic" doctrine which he is ostensibly reporting to his audience.

In the case of the sophist, the connection between seeming to be and false statement is plain. The art of the sophist is discursive; from the Stranger's standpoint, the sophist claims to know, but in fact does not. His statements thus copy the truth, or "look like" true statements. On the other hand, they do not pretend to be, but actually are, statements. In terms of the previous discussion, they are images, and further, inaccurate images. The most obvious level of the problem to which the Stranger refers is then that of the ontological status of images. We have seen before that this problem exists for true statements or accurate images as well, but the Stranger formulates his aporia in terms of false statements or inaccurate images only. This is perhaps natural, given the fact that he is investigating the sophist. Nevertheless, it is a point which the reader must keep in mind.

It is worth noticing that the Stranger refers to the sophist as a trickster, or, as will be made explicit in the final stages of his concluding diaeresis, an ironical or dissembling speaker. The sophist's false statements are thus intentional. This is important because it means that the sophist can see enough of the "original" or intrinsically true situation to know that his claims to knowledge are false. In other words, we do not call a statement "false" unless we have independent access to what the statement is about. Therefore, we can make at least the true statement that the statement we are inspecting is false. The sophist, however, as will emerge in due course, denies the distinction between originals and images, which is to say that he denies, with respect to his "focal" art, the distinction between true and false statements. The sophist claims that all statements about the good life are true. Does this involve him in contradiction? He will attempt to avoid the force of this charge by saying that the good for each person is whatever he believes it to be. Further, human nature is such as to lead us to assert as good what pleases us. The implicit claim of the sophist is that the general statement "the good is the pleasant" is true, but that the pleasant is relative to the individual person. In slightly different terms, even if human beings tend to agree on a finite number of candidates for *the* good, or are in general pleased by much the same things, it remains the case that the goodness of these things arises from the fact that the individual person finds them pleasant, and not from their intrinsic excellence.

I do not suggest that the foregoing sketch of the sophist's defense enables him to avoid contradiction. One can, however, say this: to the extent that the sophist takes seriously the charge of self-contradiction, he raises a serious problem for the Stranger. In a contradiction, one statement is true and the other is false. According to the Stranger, statements are images. He must therefore answer the question: Of *what* is a false statement an image? As the Stranger puts the point: "The λόγος has dared to postulate that non-being is [τὸ μὴ ὂν εἶναι]; for otherwise, falsehood could not come to be [οὐκ ἂν ἄλλως ἐγίγνετο ὄν]" (237a3–4). It is too soon to make a precise analysis of the Stranger's words; we cannot do this until we have heard his technical doctrine. We can observe that he distinguishes between the ostensible "being" of non-being and the "coming-to-be" or "existence" of falsehood. Crudely but not misleadingly put, a false statement is an image of non-being. In a way, the Stranger is suggesting that all false statements refer to the same "abstract object" (my term), which the λόγος dares to suppose is *non-being*. Whereas a true statement refers indirectly to *being*, it refers directly to the situation it describes. But a false statement cannot refer directly to the situation it describes, since, as false, it fails to describe the situation on which it attempts to report. It distorts the proportions, and thus does not exhibit the formal structure, of the original.

It is worth reminding the reader at this point that the expression "proportions" must be used metaphorically with respect to verbal copies of formal combinations, whether these latter are pure or embedded within sensuous particulars. To some extent, the metaphor is backed up by the συμμετρία attributed to accurate images. But the attempt to take literally the notion of "accurate proportion" in such cases (and hence to preserve the Stranger's original distinction between icons and fantasms in a discursive context), leads us away from the forms as looks to the "formalizable" relations of the forms, in the sense that "formalizable" is employed in modern mathematics. One step along this path is taken by those who regard the "deep structure" (my expression) of the forms as arithmetical. I see no evidence in the dialogues to support this "neopythagoreanism," as one might call it. Even in the *Philebus*, as we have already seen at length, the "counting" of monadic units in complex formal structures serves to focus our attention upon the "perceived" or "phenomenological" forms. It does not "explain" these perceived forms as being in fact quasi-numerical structures or ratios of magnitudes. For further discussion of this point, see the prologue, section 5. Here I add only that the Stranger will turn eventually to the metaphors of spelling and weaving, in an attempt to explicate the original "proportions" exhibited in discursive icons. But neither of these metaphors explains with epistemic precision the perceived facts of ontological combination.

Coming back to false statement, a fantasm exists *qua* fantasm, and so possesses being. But *qua* fantasm—*qua* perceived look and not *qua* verbal or material embodiment of that look—it exists as not that which it shows itself to be. Therefore it cannot refer directly to what it shows itself to be or derive its existence solely from that and hence indirectly from (the pure form) *being*. So it looks as if the fantasm refers to, and derives its existence from,(a pure form) *non-being*. If, however, *non-being* is a pure form, then it too derives its being from combination with the pure form *being*.

If non-being is indeed a pure form, then "non-being is" in the sense just explicated. This statement contains a self-contradiction because it can be unpacked into the two statements: "'non-being' means 'complete absence of being'" and "'non-being' means 'presence of being'" or something of the sort. Actually, the problem is even worse than this, because to deny that non-being possesses being is by the Stranger's analysis meaningful if and only if the expression "non-being" refers to something. We can make this point sharply, if not in the Stranger's own terms, by saying that, for him, "non" or "not" cannot be explained entirely as a syntactical particle or function.

This leads to another preliminary remark that I think worth making here. We should not assume that it is self-evident what the Stranger means by a "contradiction" (ἐναντιολογία). I want to bring this out by making use of an unpublished paper by Richard Routley. Routley distinguishes three kinds or senses of "contradiction." (1) One statement may cancel another. In this case, the result of "*A* and not-*A*" is silence or nothing. (2) The collision of the statements "*A*" and "not-*A*" results in what Routley calls the "explosion" of "*A*" into every statement whatsoever. In other words, from a contradiction everything follows. (3) The statement "not-*A*" constrains but does not totally control "*A*." Routley is thinking here of relevance logic, in which the choice between "*A*" and "not-*A*" can be sensibly raised if and only if "*A*" and "not-*A*" are each the opposite of the other. The semantical rule for evaluating relevant negation is then: "not-*A*" holds in a world *a* if and only if "*A*" holds in world a^*, the reverse of *a*. Following this third case, "not-*A*" is the reverse of "*A*," and reversal is the relevance-restricted version of "otherthanness," or what looks like the Stranger's eventual explanation of non-being. In sum: within relevance logic, there must be a substantive connection between "*A*" and "not-*A*" for *any* meaningful (and hence truth-functional) connection to hold between them. To the extent that this applies to the Stranger's doctrines, we may take the connection to be semantic; since the Stranger has no doctrine of possible worlds, the connection between "*A*" and "not-*A*" must hold in this world. However, this world has two different aspects. Some statements refer directly to pure forms. Other statements, like "Theaetetus flies," do not. So "Theaetetus flies" and "Theaetetus sits" are contradictory, if and only if there is someone we know named Theaetetus who is either flying or sitting.

To this extent, then, the Stranger may be called a relevance logician. The Stranger is not reduced to silence by the assertions "non-being is" and "non-being is not." At least, this is not his intention, as his subsequent analysis makes plain. Similarly, the Stranger cannot accept the "explosion" interpretation of contradiction. For within this interpretation, the statement "non-being is" would continue to hold, side-by-side with "non-being is not." Differently stated, the Stranger's fundamental interest is ontological, not "formal," in the sense used in contemporary logical calculi. If the Stranger's interests were merely formal, he could easily avoid a contradiction by stipulation. This is of course an anachronistic way of looking at the actual situation, but that is precisely my point. One comes closer to the truth by saying that the Stranger is investigating the semantical basis of logical rules, and that for him "semantics" is in the last analysis a doctrine of ontological or pure forms.

For this reason, it is already misleading to analyze the Stranger's proclivities toward a relevance logic in terms of "*A*" and "not-*A*." This can be seen by considering Routley's description of the connection of relevance as the case in which "*A*" and "not-*A*" have at least one variable in common. However, the two expressions with which we are concerned are "being" and "non-being." What variable could these two expressions have in common? Since the *being* to which "being" refers is an atomic form, it is evident that the two expressions can have nothing in common but the expression "being" with the designated reference. But this amounts to nothing more than stating the problem; it provides no analysis, let alone resolution, of that problem. Furthermore, whereas the Stranger does explain "non-being" as "otherthanness," we are very far from understanding what this expression means. So far as we can tell at the moment, "otherthanness" is just a disguised way of saying "not being so-and-so."

To come back to the text, the Stranger counters the daring λόγος

with the authority of the great Parmenides. As befits a member of
the Eleatic school, the Stranger has been raised from childhood to
obey the command recorded in Parmenides' poem: "Never let this
tame you, that non-beings are [εἶναι μὴ ἐόντα], but exclude your
thought from this path of inquiry" (237a4–9).[1] According to the
Stranger, a moderately detailed analysis of this command would make
Parmenides' intention entirely clear. However, he does not himself
initiate such an analysis. Instead, he suggests that, if it is all the
same to Theaetetus, they "look at" (θεασώμεθα) another point first.
The youth is entirely agreeable: "Take me where you like, looking
only to what is best for continuing the discussion" (237b1–6). This
polite exchange shows that we are about to enter a new stage of the
discussion. It also brings out the fact that, in order to conduct a
relevant analysis, we have to see which direction to take.

The Stranger begins the discussion by asking whether we are bold
enough to use the expression "the altogether not," as I shall translate τὸ μηδαμῶς ὄν. The Greek word μηδαμῶς means "in no way
whatsoever." Plato uses τὸ ὄν to mean either "being" (as, for example, the pure form being) or "the thing" in the sense of an existing individual item. Taken in itself, then, τὸ μηδαμῶς ὄν could mean
either the nihil absolutum or a definite instance of something which
has no existence at all. The Stranger employs the expression in a
way that is not identical with either sense, but which combines
elements of each. Let us see how he indicates this.

First he distinguishes between eristics and joking, on the one hand,
and serious cognitive consideration (συννοήσαντά τινα), on the other.
When asked seriously to what we must apply the name "non-being,"
the student must answer "to what thing and what kind of thing"
(εἰς τί καὶ ἐπὶ ποῖον) he applies the term (237b7–c4). A name is the
name of something; it has a reference. This principle was introduced as long ago as 218c1–5. In the present passage, the Stranger
also indicates that "things" are not general but of such-and-such a
kind; to be a thing is to be some definite thing. Finally, in the present passage, the Stranger takes his bearings by how we talk. It would
be going altogether too far to say that the ontological attributes are
for the Stranger inferred from the linguistic rules governing how we
talk about an entity. But the Stranger unmistakably believes that
the way in which we talk about things provides essential clues to

1. David Lachterman points out that the Stranger twice quotes what is printed as
Diels-Kranz, fragment 7, here and at 258d2–3, in which μὴ ἐόντα is unmistakably
plural. The Stranger never quotes a passage (such as Diels-Kranz, fragment 2) in which
Parmenides employs the singular τὸ μὴ ἐόν. I shall address this point in the text.

the natures of these things. Rightly or wrongly, he believes that our talking shows "non-being" to refer somehow to a *thing*. In other words, it cannot be the *nihil absolutum* to which we refer by "non-being," because the latter expression has a sense if and only if it refers to *some thing or other*. It is hard to state the point in a consistent manner (as the Stranger will himself point out) because language is "thing-oriented." But the Stranger means something like this: we cannot even deny that "non-being" names a form or an existing thing, unless "non-being" *does* name some definite, and hence (in an extended sense) existing thing. This will be developed in the sequel.

Theaetetus says that the question posed by the Stranger is entirely too difficult for him to answer. The Stranger therefore leads the way. It is plain, he says, that non-being (τὸ μὴ ὄν) does not apply to any of the beings (τῶν ὄντων ἐπί ⟨τι⟩), and so, that it cannot apply to "something" (τὸ τì). For the word "something" is always said of a being or thing (ἐπ' ὄντι). It is impossible to speak of something "by itself" as naked or stripped of all beings (237c5–d5). If this were possible, "non-being" would mean "not-to-be-a-thing." Such a name, as it were, asserts of itself that it has no reference, and so, that it is not a name. Hence someone who attempts to say "non-being" has not succeeded in speaking at all. Theaetetus finds all this to be the height of perplexity (237d6–e7).

Let me interject a brief comment. To the contemporary reader, the expression "not-to-be-a-thing" is unproblematical. Problems arise if and only if we attempt to apply this expression as the name, not of a concept, but of a thing. The Stranger however, does not distinguish between a concept and a thing. Even a form, which is not, incidentally, a concept, is a "thing" or a definite entity. But suppose that we do allow concept-talk, or, what comes to the same thing, suppose that we distinguish between two predicates, "—— is a thing" and "—— is not a thing." The set defined by the predicate "—— is not a thing" is itself not a thing, and so belongs to itself. This raises the question of the "being" of sets or predicates. What is the status of "things" that are "non-things"? This boils down to one question: What is the sense of "non"? A non-thing cannot in all cases be a *nihil absolutum*. It must have some kind of being, which we are therefore required to distinguish from the mode of being appropriate to "things." However we look at this problem (and I do not wish to pursue it here), we return to the difficulties raised by the Stranger. We cannot avoid asking about the meaning of "non" simply by calling "non" a syntactic function. This is because syntactic functions

are themselves "things," or something rather than nothing. In formulating a rule governing the use of "non" or "negation," we are already employing the "concept" of "non"or "negation." What is the ontological status of that concept?

To continue, the first aporia concerning non-being is that its ostensible name, "non-being," does not refer. To say that it refers to a concept is merely to move the puzzle about "non" up one level. Theaetetus, as we saw above, regards this as the greatest of puzzles. "Don't talk big," the Stranger warns him; "the greatest and first aporia remains." This aporia affects the very beginning of the inquiry, so presumably it is more fundamental than the referential aporia (238a1–3). The Stranger has captured Theaetetus's attention completely. "Don't hesitate to speak," the youth implores him. He then accepts the following argument. The Stranger claims that we can add some being (τι τῶν ὄντων) to a distinct being, whereas we cannot add anything to what is not (238a4–9). In other words, if we start with nothing and then pose something, the something that we pose is not a property of nothing, but stands as the starting point of subsequent speech. Theaetetus underlines the Stranger's assertion that all of number is to be included among the beings (238a10–b1). The Stranger then makes the following point at some length. To say "non-being" or "non-beings" is to apply unity or plurality (that is, numbers) to non-being in the sense of "nothing to count." It is to try to count the uncountable, and so once more to apply being to non-being, and is therefore neither right nor correct. "You speak most truly," the young mathematician confirms (238a4–c7). Let us call this the aporia of enumerability.

If it was not sufficiently evident hitherto, this aporia makes it unmistakable that, in the Stranger's eyes, paradoxes arise when we attempt to consider the reference of "non-being" as a thing or determinate being (and in the overall context of the discussion, as a form). The name "non-being," or (if there is one) the concept to which that name refers, can be counted, at least if we allow that "one" is a number. What was perhaps not so evident is that the Stranger deviates from the way in which Parmenides formulates the problem. Parmenides forbade us to be tamed by thinking "non-being to be" (εἶναι μὴ ἐόντα). It is true that the Stranger quotes a passage in which Parmenides employs the plural ἐόντα. It is also true that in other fragments, not quoted by the Stranger, Parmenides uses the definite article (for example, τό γε μὴ ἐὸν; Diels-Kranz, fragment 2). However, Parmenides calls no attention to what we would call referential puzzles that are ostensibly induced by definite articles and the syntactic necessity of employing the singular or the plural. I take Parmenides' own variations in terminology to be entirely compatible with an indifference to grammar, and hence with the interpretation that he is forbidding us to think nothingness, or the *nihil absolutum*. He might or might not agree with the Stranger on one point, namely, that language supports the impossibility of such a thought. But he could hardly agree with the Stranger's underlying principle with respect to the statement of the aporias: that non-being, were it to be, would be a thing. For Parmenides, non-being cannot be, and so of course it cannot be a thing. *But this does not solve the problem of what we mean by "non-being" or "nothingness."* I am not implying that there is a solution to this problem, if by "solution" we mean a discursive account. The Stranger's puzzles bring out reasonably well that no such account is possible. But at the same time, they transform the deeper problem into a more limited and hence accessible difficulty. Pure nothingness is never considered in the Stranger's analysis. The Stranger is "thing oriented" from the outset, as is plain in his shift to τὸ μηδαμῶς ὄν, which, despite its grammatical form, *could* mean "pure nothingness," but is instead treated by the Stranger as a pseudothing.

The Stranger does not proceed directly to the third aporia, but interposes a general conclusion. "Do you understand [συννοεῖς] that it is not possible to pronounce, speak, or think discursively [διανοηθῆναι] in a correct manner [ὀρθῶς] non-being taken apart by itself [τὸ μὴ ὄν αὐτὸ καθ' αὑτό], but that it is discursively unthinkable, inexpressible, unpronounceable, and without λόγος?" "Altogether so," Theaetetus replies (238c8–11). We see here plainly how the Stranger excludes pure nothingness from consideration. Let us put to one side for a moment the paradoxical aspects of his own formulation and try to grasp his main point. Non-being "in itself" (αὐτὸ καθ' αὑτό) or regarded as a pseudoform, is entirely inaccessible to discursive thinking. But we can understand or mentally perceive (συννοεῖν) that this is the case. Discursive thinking functions with countable elements; in this sense it is exactly like mathematics. At a certain point in its "calculations," discursive thinking stumbles onto the problem of nothingness. This problem, if I may speak somewhat metaphorically, is "presented" to calculative thinking by "understanding" or a kind of precalculative perception. If this did not arise, there would never be any problem about the sense of "not" or "nothing." Calculative thinking insists that what I am here calling "understanding" has misunderstood the problem, that is, has not calculated "correctly" (ὀρθῶς) or has made a "mathematical" error. Like a good analytical philosopher, calculative thinking restates the problem and then proceeds to devise a technical solution. The original problem is left untouched. And this is what happens in the *Sophist*.

We are now ready for the third aporia. Initially, this aporia seems to take cognizance of the deeper problem of nothingness. As we shall see, however, the problem is concealed. The key to the concealment lies in the Stranger's previous attribution of the expression αὐτὸ καθ' αὐτό to "non-being." In attempting to mention pure nothingness, the Stranger takes it for granted that he can succeed only if he is able to refer to something definite, like an idea or pure form. The Stranger now asks Theaetetus to "consider" (ἐννοεῖς) the puzzle once more. It was a mistake to see the question of counting as the greatest aporia. Even greater than this is the aporia that the attempt to "refute" non-being (that is, to prohibit use of the pseudoname "non-being") forces us to contradict ourselves (238d1–7).

Theaetetus requests greater clarity of speech from the Stranger, who declares that he is incapable of it. As evidence of his incapacity, he presents the aporia of self-contradiction in the form of a resume of the first two aporias. Initially he said that non-being could share in neither the one nor the many. Yet then and now he has called it "one" by saying "the" or "that" which is not (τὸ μὴ ὄν; 238d8–e4). Furthermore, in saying that it was unpronounceable, inexpressible, and without λόγος, the Stranger attached the verb "to be" to non-being, thereby speaking of it as one (that is, as an element that has no being; 238e5–239a12). In other words, the contradiction amounts to a simultaneous attribution and denial of unity. The Stranger has in effect said "non-being is one and not one." Contradiction is a defect of discursive or calculative thinking. It is the error of taking back what one grants in the same step. To put it cautiously, it is by no means clear that one commits a contradiction in thinking pure nothingness, *so long as one makes no attempt to provide a discursive analysis.* Given a contradiction, we may attempt to resolve it by suppressing either one or the other of its elements. The way is open to the Stranger to assert either that non-being is one or that it is not one. However, as he presents the situation, to assert that "it" is not one is already to have contradicted oneself, since the reference of "it" must be "one," a thing.

The Stranger berates himself for having been shown to be, now as before, defeated in the attempt to refute non-being. "We must not look to me for correct speech [ὀρθολογία] about non-being; but come, let us look to you, instead" (239b1–5). I remind the reader of the dramatic puzzle. Surely this cannot be part of the ostensible teaching of the Eleatic school, memorized by the Stranger. It is all very well to say that the Stranger is in fact Plato, but why then did Plato present himself at the outset as a convinced Eleatic? This apart, the present appeal to Theaetetus is justified by another reference to his youth, which will enable him to strain very hard to say something correct (κατὰ τὸ ὀρθόν) about non-being without attributing to it either being, unity, or plurality of number (μήτε οὐσίαν μήτε τὸ ἓν μήτε πλῆθος ἀριθμοῦ; 239b6–10). Throughout this passage, there is an emphasis upon the need for "correct" thinking, that is, for a correct calculation of the kind performed by mathematicians. Obviously enough, if correctness is a property of calculative discourse, which works with nameable and countable units, then neither Theaetetus nor anyone else will be able to fulfil the Stranger's request. The deeper problem of nothingness is, so to speak, visible here, but it is addressed by the wrong questions, questions which conceal rather than illuminate the problem, questions which force us, if we take them seriously, to look for a solution to a different problem. Calculative thinking treats puzzles as challenges to find solutions. This is the "mathematical" heritage of the Stranger, and so of this aspect of Platonism. In this deep sense, it is accurate to refer to the Stranger as an "analytical" philosopher.

Theaetetus fairly replies that it would require an excess of zeal on his part to attempt to solve the puzzle, especially when he has seen the Stranger's suffering (239b6–10). The Stranger excuses him: "Let us say goodby to you and me." But until we can find someone who is able to speak correctly about non-being, we must admit that the sophist has crept into an inaccessible place. If we try to pin him down as a practitioner of the art of fantastics, he will twist our words against us and give them an inverted meaning. In other words, if we call him an image maker, he will ask us what we mean by "image" (εἴδωλον). This, of course, is because an image contains non-being, or rather, because we cannot explain what we mean by "image" without explaining what we mean by "non-being." I note in passing that this is true of *all* images, not just of fantasms. Once again the Stranger asks Theaetetus to look for some reply to "the young man's" question (239c4–d5). This odd way of referring to the sophist is presumably a comment on his character, although the Stranger's meaning is impossible to determine exactly. Whatever it means, the Stranger's language on one point tells us that, when we reach an aporia, we have to *look around* for a solution. The problem is that the Stranger seems to leave us with nothing to look at.

Another Look at Images

(239d6–241c6)

An icon is a copy that preserves the exact proportions of the original. Our attempt to describe non-being exactly has thus been an attempt to construct a discursive icon. However, we cannot construct an icon of something unless we can first see the original. The puzzles introduced by the Stranger apparently establish that we cannot see non-being "in itself" because it has no "self" or thinghood. Actually, what the Stranger has shown is that we cannot give a correct discursive analysis of non-being, namely, an analysis which obeys the rules of reference, enumeration, and noncontradiction. It has *not* been established that we have no intellectual apprehension of pure nothingness, nor is it plain how this could be established. Consequently, it has not been shown that icons are necessarily discursive in the sense just defined.

There is a second preliminary point that bears upon the apprehension of pure nothingness and the perception of pure forms. We need to distinguish between two questions about "looks." The first question asks: "What does X look like?" The second question asks: "What is the look of X?" This distinction is not a case of mere hair splitting. If I ask what X looks like, then I obviously assume that it resembles something antecedently seen by myself and the person to whom I address the question. It follows that the antecedently perceived look itself looks like X. But if I ask "What is the look of X?" I am allowing for cases in which X does not look like anything else. Of course, the question cannot be answered unless expressions are available for conveying the look in question, but this does not entail resemblance between X and a distinct Y. The look in question may be unique and at the same time pervasive or common, as well as more or less directly visible. It is at least arguable that pure nothingness is such a "look." Whether in an existential or a logical sense,

186

many if not all persons grasp directly the "sense" of the expression "pure nothingness," which can easily be paraphrased as the complete absence of all determinations whatsoever. However, if we accept this claim, it is nevertheless true that pure nothingness does not "look like" anything else.

A similar point holds in the case of pure forms or Platonic ideas. How can we understand a form which does not look like its instances, but which its instances resemble? One might suggest a rather simple answer to this question. Form X does not "look like" its instance x because it is just X that we see when we grasp what x is.[1] This answer, although simple in itself, raises other problems. If it is the form X which we see, in what sense does x "look like" X? One might reply along these lines: the instance "resembles" its form as an object of ordinary perception or cognition. We thus see the original initially as a "look" which guides us toward (enables us to "recollect") the nature (the form) of x. I do not believe that this reply resolves all difficulties. On the contrary, I am in the process of arguing that it is impossible to provide an exact or "correct" analysis of the nature of images, and hence of the relation between originals and images. If the previous general suggestion is useful, it can only be as a way to think about the original-image distinction without engendering logical antinomies. These antinomies arise as soon as we press what are obviously metaphorical explanations or try to fit them into the machinery of formal analysis. The reasonableness of the Platonic doctrine of forms, pure or complex, can be established, if at all, not by logical analysis, but by attempting to explain formal structure on the assumption that the Platonic doctrine is false. In other words, what we have to do is think about the phenomenon of logic, not translate the Stranger's (or Socrates') remarks into the first-order predicate calculus. The problem is already visible in the calculus itself. Are the symbols of the calculus mere artifacts, even "marks on paper," or do they exhibit, in the stability and generality of their connectability, a formal structure independent of our contingent symbolization?

So much by way of background. If pure forms are points of illumination, then pure nothingness may simply be the intervals between these points. (Needless to say, I am not referring here to points on a line, but to the necessarily finite "alphabet" of formal elements from which the visible world is "spelled" or composed.) However, the Stranger is about to take quite a different approach to the prob-

1. See the two valuable articles by A. Kosman: (1973), p. 390; and (1976), p. 67.

lem of non-being. In the previous scene, the "young man" (presumably the sophist) parried our effort to define him as an image maker with the question "What is an image?" He was able to do this because images, on the Stranger's own account, "are and are not," and we have not yet been able to explain what it means "not to be."

We must now have another look at images, and thus try to answer the sophist's question. Theaetetus responds to the Stranger, as he did yesterday to Socrates, by giving examples. It is plain, he says, that by "image" we mean images in water and in mirrors, as well as drawings, sculpture, and so on (239d6–8). We note that the Stranger and Theaetetus are discussing images (εἴδωλα) in general, not just fantasms. Furthermore, the Stranger does not rebuke Theaetetus, as Socrates did yesterday, for giving examples when asked for a definition. Instead, he reminds Theaetetus of his inexperience: "It is plain that you have never seen a sophist." This is, of course, an ironical remark, since the preceding conversation makes it clear that Theaetetus has encountered sophists. But Theaetetus has not understood the nature of the sophist. More precisely, the Stranger is about to deny that visual imagery is relevant to the identification of the sophist's nature. The sophist, he goes on to say, will seem to Theaetetus to have his eyes shut, or to have no eyes at all, because he will laugh at talk about mirrors or modellings (πλάσμασι). He will deny that he recognizes anything connected with sight, and will question Theaetetus exclusively about the consequences of the young man's words (239e1–240a3).

This is a puzzling turn of events. It was the Stranger, not Theaetetus, who introduced the visual model of sophistry, namely, image making as illustrated by painting or sketching and sculpting. Granted that the sophist produces speeches rather than pictures, the model is appropriate in that we cannot distinguish between icons and fantasms unless we can perceive the original independently of our statements about it. On the other hand, the model is misleading because there are no pictures or visual images of the originals to which the sophist, according to the Stranger, refers. To this we should add that there are no pictures of pure forms like *being*, and certainly none of *non-being*. Let us try to make as much use of the model as we can. By closing his eyes, the sophist in effect denies the distinction between originals and images. More specifically, the sophist implies that discourse produces "originals." One may wonder how the sophist will be able to distinguish between true and false statements. To some extent, we have already indicated his line on this point. The sophist, *qua* sophist, produces speeches on the good life (that is to say, on those aspects of the good life that can be implemented politically). And whatever we say about the good life, whatever opinions we hold, are therefore true. So there can, on this defense, be no false speeches about the good life. In fact, the Stranger does not raise this defense for the sophist; it follows indirectly, however, from his subsequent characterization of philosophy (which the sophist imitates) as the life of the free man.

According to the Stranger, sophistry is the art of disputation. The sophist's disputations are designed to persuade us *regardless of what things look like.* Another way to say this is that the sophist does not "imitate" things, but advocates an interpretation of the human significance of things. The sophist does not try to persuade us that he does the characteristic work of the scientist, poet, or artisan. Sophistical persuasion is directed instead toward the end or purpose to which we apply this characteristic work. We are not persuaded by sophistry that a false pair of shoes is actually a pair of shoes. Instead, we might be persuaded that shoes play such-and-such a role in the good life, or no role at all. One of the problems in the attempt to define the sophist is that we must distinguish between his art and its theoretical justification. As an art, sophistry is concerned solely with persuasion. But as a theory, sophistry justifies its art, and thereby offers a doctrine of human nature. The Stranger does not keep these two aspects of sophistry clearly distinct; for the most part, he is concerned with the art, and so with the logical and ontological questions raised by that art. But, just as we cannot understand philosophy merely by definitions of diaeresis or dialectic, neither can we understand sophistry merely by definitions of disputation. By closing his eyes, the sophist takes a stand on logical and ontological issues. However, these issues are inseparable from the question of better and worse kinds of life.

The Stranger directs Theaetetus's attention away from how we perceive images to how we talk about them. By way of anticipation, let us note that, whereas this encourages us to shift from an original-image model to a model of logical predication, it is not, as developed by the Stranger, a justification of such a shift. Whatever the problems with respect to the nature of images, statements about formal combinations, facts, or events remain images, either icons or fantasms, of their originals. On the other hand, as we shall see, those who claim that Plato rejects the original-image model in such dialogues as the *Sophist* are not entirely wrong. More precisely, Plato does not reject this model, but he reformulates it in such a way as to deprive it of inner coherence. One aspect of the incoherence is that the model suppresses the role of the image which it purports to explain.

The pivotal discussion in the *Sophist* of the nature of an image runs from 239e5 to 240b11. This passage has been subjected to extensive commentary. Our first step is to see as exactly as possible what is said there. We shall then develop our results by an inspection of representatives from the secondary literature. The passage begins with a request from the Stranger to Theaetetus, made on behalf of the sophist. Theaetetus is asked to produce a verbal or discursive (ἐϰ τῶν λόγων; 240a1–2) unity from the many examples of things bearing the name "image." By applying the same name (εἴδωλον) to all these things, Theaetetus referred to them "as being one" (ὡς ἓν ὄν; 240a4–6). In other words, Theaetetus attributed both unity and being to the family of images. It is therefore not enough to say that the Stranger is asking Theaetetus to define (and in that way to unify the manifold of instances of) the name "image." One can define what does not exist. As will become directly evident, the Stranger is challenging the being of images. This distinction between the definability or intelligibility of what it means to be an image and the being or mode of existence of images plays a considerable role in the subsequent discussion, as well as in the secondary literature. Unfortunately, as we shall see, it is a very confusing distinction.

Theaetetus replies: "What, Stranger, can we say an image is except another such thing that is made like the true thing?" (τὸ πϱὸς τἀληϑινὸν ἀφωμοιωμένον ἕτεϱον τοιοῦτον; 240a7–8). In this quasi-definition, τἀληϑινόν, "true" in the sense of "genuine," refers to the original. The ἕτεϱον τοιοῦτον, "another such," the image, lacks this truth or genuineness. However we analyze the sense of "another such," it is plain that this sense depends upon the original. To be "such" (whether in Greek or in English) means normally to be an instance of a given kind. Since the "kind" in question is the original, one would assume that the original and the "other" are both of the same kind. But this analysis gives rise directly to a deeper problem of interpretation. Does the "otherness" of the copy derive from its being the same kind as the original? In this case, the kind is a second form standing above both original and copy, and we seem to be on the way toward an infinite regress. Or is the "otherness" due to a distinction between the kind (or "look"), which is the same in original and copy, and the medium in which the image is displayed? In this second case, I shall try to show at length, the danger of an infinite regress is averted, but at the price of destroying the essential distinction between original and image.

Let us withhold judgment on this question for the time being. This much, I believe, is clear. As a semblance of what is truly an original, the image lacks truth or genuineness. It is not truly an original. However, as Theaetetus is about to say, it is truly (ἀληθῶς) an image (or lacks truth "except in the sense that it is genuinely an image": πλήν γ' εἰκὼν ὄντως). In saying this, Theaetetus corrects an objection by the Stranger that runs as follows. "Another such" is "certainly not true"; it is not the original, "but like it" (οὐδαμῶς ἀληθινόν γε, ἀλλ' ἐοικὸς μέν). However, Theaetetus also agrees that "the true" (τὸ ἀληθινὸν) is genuine (ὄντως ὄν), whereas "the non-true" (τὸ μὴ ἀληθινὸν) is the opposite of "true" (ἀληθοῦς). Therefore, Theaetetus is saying that the likeness (τὸ ἐοικός) is not genuine (οὐκ ὄντως ὄν).

The Stranger plays upon the ambiguous relation between τἀληθινόν and ὄντως ὄν, on the one hand, and ὄν or εἶναι, on the other, but Theaetetus sees at least partway through this ambiguity. An image is not nothing at all (it is not τὸ μηδαμῶς ὄν, as we might say). Qua image, it has an ontological status: truly (ἀληθῶς) to be an image (or an icon; note the shift from εἴδωλον to εἰκών). Even though something cannot be an image except thanks to an original, "to be an image" is a unique look, a defining mark of a family of instances, and in this substantial sense it possesses ontological independence. There are various ways in which one thing may be dependent upon another, as for example in the relation of causality, which is distinct from the dependence involved in the relation of likeness. Only one of these ways is the way of likeness or imaging, and the way of imaging is not reducible to the "matter" in which the image is realized. We arrive at the following puzzling result. An (accurate) image of a given original "is and is not" the original, and *in the same respect*, not in two different respects. An accurate copy of a certain look is the same look. And yet, precisely as the copy (not, in other words, as a distinct material realization of the copy look), it is not and cannot be the same as the original. In sum: if it is the same, it is not a copy. If it is a copy, it is not the same. If you and I both have the same look on our faces, the look on my face is not a copy of the look on your face, just because your face is not my face; and this is true even if you were the first to have the look on your face. We each have the same look, which does not have any existence, "genuine" or otherwise, except on our respective faces. This is of crucial importance. It follows from what has been said that no sharp distinction can be drawn between the "ontological" and the "epistemological" statuses of the image. The image is epistemically reliable (or unreliable) precisely because it is genuinely an image. Its being is "truly" to be an image, and to be an image is to be and not to be the original, in the same respect.

In order to understand the ambiguity of the nature of the image, it is essential not to confuse the image *qua* likeness with the medium in which the image is realized. The fact that the medium, say the surface of a mirror, a painted canvas, or some flesh-and-blood creature, is not the same as the original (whether a spatio-temporal thing or a "separate" form) is irrelevant to the intrinsic ambiguity in the nature of the image. As an image, the likeness is obviously, one might say intuitively, not the original look (again, I am disregarding the realization or medium of the respective looks). But as an icon or accurate representation of an original look, it must be the same look. In the case of "picture images," the degree of sameness is of course limited *because* of the difference in the medium of representation. A painted man cannot be an accurate duplication of the look of a real man, because the look of a real man is a flesh-and-blood look. However, in shifting from a picture model to a discursive model, the Stranger renders null and void this relativity to the medium. This is plain in his definition of an icon as an accurate presentation of the proportions of the original; in other words, of a ratio, not a picture. The significance of this emphasis upon proportion, however, is concealed in the first stage of the discussion by the example of painting. A discursive image is thus a λόγος in two senses: it is a verbal expression of a ratio or, as we would perhaps put it today, of a formal structure. The re-presentation of the original ratio must therefore be a presentation of the original ratio. If it deviates from the original, it is no longer accurate, hence not an icon, but a fantasm. However, a fantasm, considered as a picture, is no longer an image of the original ratio. It is now an image, if of anything, then of some other ratio, which it consequently mirrors exactly.

The shift from a picture model to a discursive model is intrinsically a rejection of the likeness thesis in favor of what one might call a "duplication thesis." A duplicate of a ratio, however, is not an image of that ratio, nor is it in any way, ontologically or epistemologically, inferior to that ratio. The ratio is the same in both (or in innumerable) cases. *The Stranger's shift thus amounts to a departure from what we may call "classical Platonism" to Aristotelianism.* I will come back to this point below. Here we must note that the Stranger gives no signal of a doctrinal change of this sort. He continues to use the language of originals and images throughout the dialogue. One other remark: when I speak of an intrinsic shift to Aristotelianism, I do not mean to say that the Stranger adopts a doctrine of logical predication with respect to pure formal structure. His proto-Aristotelianism amounts to having committed himself, presumably without realizing it, to a distinction between "form" and "matter" in which the form of a given species or family of instances is the same in all its realizations, none of which can then correctly be called "images."

So much for 240a4–b11. The next section, 240b12–13, presents some problems in the manuscript readings, but the general sense is clear enough. We have said of the icon that it is and is not "genuinely" (ὄντως). This seems to weave together being and non-being in an odd way (240c1ff). The stage is thus set for a transition to the analysis of non-being; but, we are not ready to leave the topic of images. It is time to look at the secondary literature that has grown up on the passage just studied. Let me give one last summary of the main point. What is genuinely an image is not genuinely an original. But what is genuinely an image is genuinely like the original. If we are careful not to replace "is like" with "duplicates" or "is the same as," but wish to preserve the distinction between original and image, then (I claim) the closest we can come to analyzing "is like" is to say that the image, *qua* likeness, is and is not the original. If we are not careful to preserve the distinction between original and image, and replace "is like" with "is the same as," then the same look is displayed throughout every family of look-alikes. The "look" in question has no separate existence, *except* in the sense that we "abstract" it from its manifestations by thinking or speaking about it. This is Aristotelianism, not Platonism.

In what follows, I shall restrict myself as usual to discussion of representative alternative interpretations of the problem of imagery. I have tried to select representatives of the two dominant views which have exercised great influence upon current scholarship. The views to which I refer are these: that there is no rejection by Plato, in his "later" period, of the paradigm-resemblance model; and that the "later" Plato rejects the paradigm-resemblance model in favor of a kind of logical or linguistic analysis very much like that of contemporary analytical philosophy, if at a much cruder level. According to this second view, then, the paradigm-resemblance model is not to be found at all in the *Sophist*.

It may be helpful to make some preliminary remarks about two topics which Plato scholars regularly associate with the nature of images. The first topic is the distinction between identity and predication. In addition to what has already been said in the Prologue, I shall be dealing at a later juncture with this topic, and can be rather brief here. The distinction between identity and predication has nothing to do with the problem of the nature of likeness. An image is a copy, whether pictorial or verbal, of an original; neither is predicated of the other. The person who sits for a portrait is not a predicate of that portrait. But even if Platonic forms are taken to be logical predicates, an instance of a formal structure does not take that structure as a set of predicates. As an instance (or an image) of that structure, *it is the same structure.*

The second topic is that of "gradational ontology." As we saw above with respect to terms like ὄντως ὄν and τἀληθινόν, the Platonic characters seem to distinguish degrees of being. In fact, there are two problems blended together into one at this point. If we distinguish between "being" and "existence," and reserve the former term for pure forms while applying the latter to spatio-temporal instances, we do not commit the absurdity of holding that there are degrees of existence. In "Degrees of Reality in Plato," [2] Gregory Vlastos rightly points out, "As we commonly use the word 'existence,' degrees of it (as distinct from degrees of perfection of things in existence) make no sense whatever; the idea of one individual existing more, or less, than another would be a rank absurdity" (p. 65). However, Vlastos's subsequent analysis shows that he does not himself distinguish between the being of the form of the bed and the existence of individual beds (to take his own example from Book X of the *Republic*): "It would take strong, unambiguous evidence to establish that Plato had any such thought in mind when he spoke of some things as being more, or less, real than others." Interestingly enough, Vlastos does not consider the doctrine of forms itself as such evidence. It seems to me that Vlastos produces his own problem by translating ὄντως ὄν as "real." Whatever the correct English equivalent of the Greek expression, it is surely associated by Plato with forms, so as to make an ontological distinction between forms and their instances. To anticipate slightly, I would certainly not deny Vlastos's later point that forms are intended to be more reliable epistemically than spatio-temporal instances. But this reliability is a consequence of the ontological distinction, which must not be suppressed and cannot be suppressed without suppressing the epistemological distinction as well. The next two sentences from the same passage in Vlastos's paper are: "And there is no such evidence. Would anyone seriously suggest that Plato wants to undermine our faith in the existence of the beds we sleep on, buy and sell, etc., when he

2. Vlastos (1965).

compares their 'being' unfavorably with that of their Form" in *Republic*, Book X? (p. 65). The answer to this question is no. Yet, the unfavorable comparison between the "being" of the existing beds and the "being" of the form is exactly the kind of evidence Vlastos demands. He has furnished it himself without noticing it, perhaps because he accepts the modern, post-Fregean suppression of a distinction between being and existence.

This apart, Vlastos's distinction between reality and existence (which in fact is a distinction between being and existence) does not serve as well in the *Sophist* for reasons that have already been made plain. Theaetetus and the Stranger both accept that originals *and* images are ὄντως ὄν. In Vlastos's terminology, an image "really" is an image in the same sense that an original "really" is an original. The application of terms like ὄντως ὄν or τἀληθινόν in our passage thus seem to carry senses differing from those invoked in passages in *Republic* X. Similarly, at *Sophist* 236e7–237a2, the problem set by the Stranger, ostensibly to be resolved in subsequent sections of the dialogue, is this: How can we say that falsehood ὄντως εἶναι without contradicting ourselves? What is unreliable from an epistemic standpoint, contrary to Vlastos, can be "real" or "genuine" in no discernibly different way from what is epistemically altogether reliable (cf. Vlastos, 1965, p. 69). Finally, in Vlastos's analysis, the grounds for denying epistemic reliability, hence the highest stage of reality (ὄντως ὄν), or for saying that something is "*F and not-F*" all involve comparisons of distinct aspects of the same thing or of different relations between one thing and several others (p. 67). But an image "is and is not" the original in the same respect (namely, as displaying the same ratio).

I turn now to the two views that predominate among contemporary scholars with respect to the problem of imagery. In an essay first published in 1953, G. E. L. Owen claims in effect that Plato's primary concern was always to explain predication.[3] In his early period (as Owen tells the tale), Plato made use of the paradigm-resemblance model for that purpose. Owen sees the *Parmenides* as Plato's official rejection of that model. He thus regards the *Timaeus*, in which the model plays a pivotal if obscure role, as an early dialogue. "In fact, Plato does not again introduce such παραδείγματα to explain predication" (p. 322). Against Harold Cherniss in particular, Owen argues that the criticism of participation in *Parmenides* 132c12–133a7 is valid, and that it signals Plato's rejection of ὁμοι-

3. Owen (1953).

ὤματα and παραδείγματα. Since the relation of resemblance is symmetrical, an infinite regress ensues: "If participation in some character *A* is to be construed as resemblance to some παράδειγμα in respect of *A*, then, since resemblance is symmetrical, both παράδειγμα and ὁμοίωμα must exhibit *A* and hence *ex hypothesi* resemble a further παράδειγμα in that respect" (pp. 318ff).

Owen concludes his essay with these words: "It is time, I am sure, to be quit of such ancestral puzzles as that of inserting the Paradigms into the more sophisticated metaphysic of the *Philebus*, and to leave the profoundly important late dialogues to their own devices" (p. 338).[4] Whatever may be the case with Plato, there is a straight line connecting the early and the late Owen, culminating in the 1971 essay on not-being in the *Sophist*, which we will study in a subsequent scene. Plato's "metaphysics" is a gradually ripening episode in the ancestral saga of Fregean analysis.

The early Owen's assertion that the paradigm-copy model does not appear in Plato's "later" dialogues, or in fact after the "early" *Timaeus*, is in my opinion indefensible and has been thoroughly refuted by Harold Cherniss.[5] However, Owen's contention that the relation of resemblance is symmetrical is not only defensible but irrefutable. The serious question is the role played by symmetry in Plato's thought and, specifically, in the *Sophist*. In other words, the question is whether Plato uses a straightforward sense of likeness throughout, in which case he is certainly in danger of generating infinite regresses as the old Parmenides pointed out, or whether he shifts from a "likeness" to a "duplication" conception of images and back again, without calling these shifts to Theaetetus's (or the reader's) attention.

I have already shown that I accept the second of these two alternatives. We are thus faced with the following curious situation. The Stranger calls images likenesses, whether he is speaking of pictures or statements. But this makes sense only when the originals are spatio-temporal things (like the sitter for a portrait). It makes no

4. Cherniss (1957) responds to these lines as follows: "These phrases of Owen's have their own interest for anyone who has followed the fascinating and perplexing history of Platonic interpretation, which has been so largely a series of insistently charitable efforts on the part of western philosophers and their acolytes, each to baptize Plato in his particular faith—having shriven him first, of course, by interpreting the heresies out of his works. Now, the Analysts of Oxford have succeeded to their own satisfaction in reading the dialogues that they call 'critical' as primitive essays in their own philosophical method" (p. 347). Cf. Lafrance (1979), pp. 33–34, for a similar point.

5. Cherniss (1957). Brandwood (1976), pp. xvi–xvii, confirms Cherniss on stylistic grounds.

sense at all in the case of pure forms (like *being* or *sameness*), facts
(like the whiteness of snow, even though an accurate picture of snow
would color it white), or events (like Theaetetus's flying, walking,
or sitting). And even when it does make sense, there is no noncir-
cular discursive analysis of "likeness." It follows that there is no
epistemically reliable refutation of the sophist. Either we see that
one thing is like another, or we do not. If we do not, we shall never
be able to demonstrate the resemblance of the two things by means
of λόγοι. To put this in one more way, Theaetetus insists upon attributing an independent ontological status to the image *qua* image,
and the Stranger agrees. An image is truly or genuinely an image; it
is not, however, truly or genuinely the original. But neither Theaetetus nor the Stranger can preserve this distinction, since truly or
genuinely to be an image of ratio *A* is truly or genuinely to be ratio
A. The Stranger's λόγος does not "save," but makes nonsense out of
our direct, intuitive experience of the difference between originals
and copies. The analysis seems to show that the content of the intuition is self-contradictory, because it blends together what must
be kept distinct, namely, *sameness* and *otherness*.

Owen's thesis was initially refuted by Harold Cherniss, whose
own interpretation of images was continued and developed by E. N.
Lee. We will now look at two of their papers. Cherniss makes the
following criticism of Owen's account of *Parmenides* 132d1–4:
"Socrates had suggested only that the relation of things *other than
ideas* (i.e., phenomenal particulars) to ideas is that of images or likenesses to their original; and, even if an idea does resemble the phenomenon that resembles it, it still does not follow from his hypothesis that both are likenesses of a single original, for they are not *both*
'other than ideas', and by hypothesis one is itself the original of
which the other is a likeness."[6] Cherniss adds that, whereas Parmenides assumes "that *any* two things which are similar to each
other must participate in one and the same thing," it is nevertheless
true, as shown in Alexander's report from Aristotle's *De Ideis*, that
"the inference that similar things are likenesses of a single original
depends for its validity upon exclusion of the possibility that any of
them is itself the original of which the others are likenesses" (1957,
p. 365).

Cherniss goes on to restate his defense of Plato in terms designed
to prevent an infinite regress (pp. 366ff), but the main point is al-

6. Vlastos makes the same point in his original (1954) version of "The Third Man
Argument in the *Parmenides*" (in Allen 1967), p. 260.

ready clear. The entire paper is thus a development of the point made initially by Cherniss in *Aristotle's Criticism of Plato and the Academy*.[7] The relation between original and image is not "reciprocal"; it is asymmetrical.[8] Cherniss makes this claim about *Timaeus* 52c, but also about *Sophist* 240a–b. In his earlier work, Cherniss infers his view from the difference in being between original and image, but also on the grounds (repeated in the *Timaeus* paper) that "the idea *is* that which the particular *has* as an attribute" (p. 298). In the *Timaeus* paper, Cherniss argues similarly, and yet not identically, against Vlastos's "third man" paper: Vlastos explicitly accepts "that the ideas are *themselves* attributes or properties of particulars; but this is a complete misapprehension." As Aristotle points out in *Metaphysics* 1079b3–11, ὃ ἔστι attached to terms designating ideas makes it impossible for them to be attributes. So "what appears 'dispersed,' as the *Timaeus* puts it, in particularisation as a property is in reality an unparticularised entity, indivisible and identical with itself, and so not a property of anything" (1957, p. 373).

If we compare the earlier and later texts, it looks as though Cherniss has shifted from the view that an idea is an attribute to the view that an idea is not an attribute. However, I do not believe that this is the case. What Cherniss means in the earlier text (as I understand him) is that there is a distinction between the "phenomenal" structure of the attributes of particulars, as expressed in ordinary language, and the role of the ideas in the metaphysical structure of that particular. At the metaphysical level, for Cherniss, there is no doctrine of predication in Plato.

However this may be, Cherniss does not seem to have noticed that his argument is composed of two incompatible elements. If the relation between original and image is asymmetrical, the idea cannot *be* that which the particular *has* as an attribute. Cherniss might reply that the asymmetry lies in the "being" of the original with respect to the lack of "real existence"[9] by the likeness. But as I have already shown, and as Cherniss's own argument requires, the likeness is genuinely a likeness: it is not "really" the original, but it "really is" like the original. It does have "real existence," and of a sort which requires us to understand "likeness" as *both* sameness and otherness. Cherniss separates the sameness and otherness of the image in such a way as to make the dilemma invisible. He also overlooks the "real existence" of the image *qua* image, as well as of

7. Cherniss (1962), pp. 297–99.
8. Ibid., p. 297. Cf. p. 283, n. 191.
9. Cherniss (1962), p. 298.

the implications of that existence. Once again, the problem is not that of an infinite regress, but rather of the step taken by Cherniss (or rather Plato) to block such a regress. The sameness of idea and particular makes any distinction between them impossible; it destroys the paradigm-resemblance model. But Cherniss is right, as against Owen, that the model is still present in the *Sophist*.

In his paper on the *Timaeus*, E. N. Lee develops Cherniss's interpretation in a subtle manner, but without removing the difficulties to which Cherniss's account is subject.[10] Lee is concerned primarily with *Timaeus* 48e–52d. He too claims that this (late) passage resolves the difficulties raised against the metaphor of imaging at *Parmenides* 132d–133a. Lee begins with a distinction between two kinds of image. A substantial image "can survive the destruction of the original it represents." An insubstantial image depends for its existence "on a continuing relation with [its] original, and if that original is removed or destroyed, the image must also disappear" (1966, p. 353). According to Lee, *Timaeus* 48e–52d is restricted to the insubstantial image, an "in-between nature" (50d3–4) "in mutual opposition to" forms and receptacle (p. 346). More specifically, it is a mirror image "resultant from the interaction" of the original and the mirror, which is Lee's metaphor for Plato's own metaphor of the receptacle. Lee says, "Strictly speaking, nothing at all can be said here of the 'image itself'" (p. 356). And again, of the phenomenal particular, "Strictly speaking, it does not have a 'nature' of its own at all" (p. 349), whereas form and receptacle do.

Lee thus follows Cherniss in denying "real existence" to the insubstantial image. "In the case of a 'substantial image', the relatedness of the image to its original is, so to say, extrinsic to its simply *being*. Insofar as an imaging object possesses ontological status quite apart from any form or original, it may with propriety be viewed as being 'just what we see'" (p. 360). Thus Lee, like Cherniss, in effect accepts the distinction drawn by Vlastos between existence (being) and reality (genuineness or truth). We have seen that this is a mistake, and that it is due to an inadequate perception of Plato's own ontological distinctions. As a result, none of the three can explain how an image can lack "real existence" without ceasing to exist altogether. In effect, all three accept the notion of grades of existence, willingly or not.[11] None sees that the genuineness of the image *qua* image produces the dilemma of the self-contradictory na-

10. E. N. Lee (1966).
11. Cf. Leszl (1970), pp. 278–79.

ture of "likeness," regardless of the fact that the image is not genuinely the original. In particular, Lee does not see that if an image has no nature of its own at all, then it cannot have the nature of an image. The result is that the distinction between ontology and epistemology falls to the ground. He also overlooks the fact that mirror images can be painted or photographed, and so his way of distinguishing between substantial and insubstantial images is inadequate.

This leads us to the heart of the matter. According to Lee, the *Timaeus* passage explicated with the help of the mirror metaphor (an image of an image of an image) resolves the problem posed by the *Parmenides*. "To revert to our analogy, the situation is like looking from a mirror-image of a thing to the thing itself: it is not a matter of looking at two different things (at 'both' of them, whether separately or together), but two different ways of looking at the same thing" (p. 362). Lee certainly does not mean that the mirror image, *qua* "reflection" in the mirror, is the original. On the contrary, the reflection "is" in itself nothing at all, according to his own interpretation. Nevertheless, it is a look, and the same look as its original. This being so, the material realization, or the mirror itself, is irrelevant to the problem of the nature of the look.

In his important study *Logic and Metaphysics in Aristotle*,[12] Walter Leszl objects to Lee's thesis as follows: "On this account things in this world are not talked about at all" (p. 489).[13] Leszl means that if the look is the same, what we talk about is the look or original. It is, however, equally possible that what we talk about is the "image," for if the resemblance between original and image is in fact an identity, then there are no images but only originals. There are no separate paradigms at all. This is the position of the sophist. In sum, the attempt to save the doctrine of likenesses from infinite regression terminates in the impossibility of making a rational distinction between philosophy (in the Stranger's or Plato's sense) and sophistry.

This brings us directly back to the text of the *Sophist*. The question before us is therefore one of language: "How can we define the sophist's art in such a way that we speak in harmony with ourselves?" Language mediates between the cosmos and the soul of the speaker. In reply to a further question from Theaetetus, the Stranger says that the sophist makes fantasms and thereby deceives us. If we therefore assert that the sophist's art leads the soul to entertain false opinion, we admit that the result is to think "the things that are

12. Leszl (1970).
13. Cf. also pp. 464–66 for a summary statement.

not" (τὰ μὴ ὄντα δοξάζειν; 240c7–d10). The Stranger shifts here from
the previous singular expression (240c1–6) to the plural "non-beings."
I noted above (p. 182) that Parmenides speaks of both "non-beings"
(μὴ ἐόντα) and "non-being" (τὸ μὴ ἐόν), in apparent indifference to
the possible ontological and linguistic implications of the distinction. The Stranger quotes only the lines in which Parmenides speaks
of "non-beings." He makes no comment on Parmenides' shifting
terminology, which (with respect both to the Stranger's silence and
the shift itself) is at least compatible with my suggestion that the
shift is irrelevant to Parmenides' thesis. On the other hand, the
Stranger does employ the distinction between singular and plural
when he develops in his own name the puzzles concerning speech
about non-being. The present terminological shift (240c7–d10), which
goes without comment, may perhaps be explained by the context.
Both δόξα and the art of the sophist, as rooted in τὰ φαινόμενα rather
than in ontology or meontology, result in a *multiplication* of non-
being. Interestingly enough, this amounts to the same reification of
non-being that is performed by the Stranger.

In any event, Theaetetus agrees that the situation is necessarily
as follows. The soul thinks that the things that are in no way at all,
"some how are" or possess being (πῶς εἶναι). The present discussion
already anticipates the later explicit reference to *being* as an ontological unit. Language is able to multiply this unit but not to produce it. However, if there is no corresponding ontological unit named
"non-being," then it must be the case that this name is produced by
language. "Non-being" will be interpreted in this case as a pseudoname, having no reference of a direct sort, and thus having a sense
that must be derived from other, genuine forms. Briefly stated, "non-
being" will be analyzed to mean "not-this-being" and thus "some
other thing."

The Stranger then takes Theaetetus through the kinds of false
opinion. In general, false opinion believes the opposite (τἀναντία) of
"the beings" or "things which are" (τοῖς οὖσι). After he has completed his analysis of the problem of non-being, the Stranger will
conclude that "non-being" is not the opposite (ἐναντίον) of "being"
(257a8–b5). In other words, there is no form *non-being*. To believe
the opposite of what is, is not to believe something that is ultimately grounded in *non-being*. It must therefore be a belief in what
"somehow" is, in what is also ultimately grounded in the form *being*.
The Stranger will accordingly explain falsehood as the belief that
things are "other" than they are. The net result of his analysis is
that we commit a falsehood by taking one thing for another, or some

things for other things. In both cases, however, we are dealing with things or beings. Strictly speaking, then, we cannot think "the things which are not." This is not the place to go into the deficiencies of such an explanation. It will, however, be helpful to bear in mind the ultimate conclusion as we work our way through the intricacies of the intervening argument.

The general point is restated by the Stranger and accepted by Theaetetus. False opinion thinks "the things which are not" (τὰ μὴ ὄντα). However, this has to be qualified. False opinion thinks that "the things which are altogether not, somehow are" (πῶς εἶναι τὰ μηδαμῶς ὄντα). Second, it thinks that the things which entirely are, are not at all (μηδαμῶς εἶναι τὰ πάντως ὄντα; 240e1–241a1). The Stranger says nothing here about true negative statements. He concentrates upon falsehood because he is intent upon capturing the sophist. False statements are statements; in other words, they possess a sense or truth value and are not mere noises. They must therefore share in being in two senses, first, as images (albeit fantasms), and second, with respect to their "look," however distorted. A false statement is neither "nothing" nor about "nothing." To take it as either of these is to suffer from a linguistic confusion, that is, from a failure to understand the correct analysis of how we speak. But we must not ourselves be misled by this point. The problem of what we may call the hypostasizing of non-being is a linguistic problem. The problem of being, however, is not merely a linguistic problem. We commit no "grammatical" error in talking about *being* (or, as we shall see later, about οὐσία in the sense of "the whole").

These are "virtually" all the ways in which falsehood may occur. The sophist, however, will not agree with us, nor could any reasonable person, the Stranger adds, in view of our previous conclusion that expressions of non-being are "unpronounceable, inexpressible, without λόγος, and discursively unthinkable" (241a2–7).[14] Theaetetus expands upon the sophist's refusal to admit falsehood. Our contradiction turns upon the assertion that falsehood exists in thoughts and speeches. We are thus committed to the attribution of being to non-being, despite our previous admission that this is impossible (241a8–b3). This is an interesting remark, since it seems to anticipate the subsequent conclusion that non-being is to be explained on the basis of discourse, or discursive thinking. The Stranger accepts Theaetetus's summary, and adds that it is now necessary to decide what must be done about the sophist. We are once more at a transi-

14. Disregard Madvig's emendation.

tion point in the dialogue. We have apparently still not succeeded in getting any kind of firm grip on our quarry (241b4–c6). The trouble, again, is that we have tried to assign him to the art of false workers and jugglers, and this is an unending family. In other words, diaeresis will never be able to finish its assigned task. We need additional tools, and specifically, we need an explanation of non-being.

SCENE ELEVEN

Precise and Imprecise Myths

(241c7–245e5)

The sophist has been tentatively identified as one who disputes about everything, and in so doing, produces false images. It is far from clear that this identification rests upon the antecedent use of diaeresis. What is clear, however, is that diaeresis cannot distinguish between true and false images. The shift from diaeresis to the discussion of this distinction has brought us to the problem of non-being, and therefore, to the problem of being. The Stranger is about to make yet another detour in his attempt to define the sophist. This detour was occasioned by the need to come to terms with Parmenides' ambiguous injunction against discussing "the altogether not." In doing so, the Stranger will criticize, not merely his old teacher, but the entire Greek philosophical tradition. To anticipate, the Stranger will claim that he is the first person to speak correctly about non-being. It is important to notice the "metalinguistic" nature of the Stranger's criticism of his predecessors, but at the same time, to preserve the Stranger's distinction between being and discourse about being.

The Stranger has three requests to make of Theaetetus. First, he asks to be forgiven for withdrawing a short distance from the sophist's powerful accusation that we have attributed being to non-being. The second request is even more emphatic. Theaetetus must not suppose that the Stranger is turning into a kind of parricide. He does not assert that he is about to commit parricide. This is important; as we shall see, the Stranger's criticism of Parmenides is not a refutation of his teacher so much as a new doctrine. In order to ward off the parries of the sophist, it will be necessary to interrogate by torture (βασανίζειν) the saying of Parmenides. We shall have to constrain non-being in a way to be, and being in a way not to be (βιάζεσθαι τό τε μὴ ὂν ὡς ἔστι κατά τι καὶ τὸ ὂν αὖ πάλιν ὡς οὐκ ἔστι πῃ; 241c7–d7).

Theaetetus agrees that some such battle of words is needed. As the Stranger asserts, even a blind man must see this. In other words, just as the sophist closes his eyes and challenges the consequences of our words, so too we must close our eyes to visual images and meet that challenge. For otherwise, we shall be laughed at for having fallen into self-contradiction (241d8–e5). That is, the sophist will laugh at us for having violated one of our own principles. We must therefore be brave enough (cf. 237a3 and 241a9) to attack the "paternal" λόγος or, if some hesitation prevents this, to give up the entire investigation (242a2–4). The recurrent reference to bravery shows that the guiding metaphor of the discussion is shifting from hunting to war. The Stranger is about to declare war on *all* of his predecessors.

The third request follows, and quite a small one, according to the Stranger. He fears that the youth will think him mad (μανικός) because he has reversed himself about non-being. It is for Theaetetus's sake that he is going to attempt to refute the assertion of Parmenides (242a5–b2). Theaetetus encourages him to continue bravely, and to present a refutation and proof (242b3–5). The Stranger said nothing about a proof (ἀπόδειξιν); Theaetetus makes a "mathematical" correction of the Stranger's proposed itinerary.

In keeping with the invocation to bravery, the Stranger says that we need a beginning that is appropriate to this daring verbal escapade (242b6–9). However, the first step is rather cautious: "Let's have another look" at what seems to be clear so far, in order to check against erroneous agreement. Theaetetus wants this stated more clearly, perhaps because he is not sure what they have agreed to (242b10–c3), but the Stranger does not supply a review of the discussion. Instead, he turns abruptly to a sharp criticism of his predecessors. Parmenides, and whoever set out "critically" (ἐπὶ κρίσιν) to define the kinds and numbers of beings, "have all conversed rather carelessly with us." This is not quite an act of parricide. Even if Parmenides has spoken "carelessly" (εὐκόλως) by the Stranger's principles, he may have said something irrefutable (242c4–7).

The first group of thinkers to be attacked are called "critical," because they attempt to speak precisely by defining and counting the kinds of beings. Yet "each of them seems to me to have told us a kind of myth [μῦθόν τινα], as though we were children" (242c8–9). Myth as such cannot be objectionable, since the Stranger is himself about to tell us the story of the "battle of the giants" and will tell the myth of the reversed cosmos in the *Statesman*. The criticism may be directed against their inept use of defining and counting the elements.

This at least is the principle by which the Stranger distinguishes three kinds of storyteller, which he will later contrast with a fourth type. The first storyteller says that there are three kinds of beings (τρία τὰ ὄντα). Sometimes these kinds are at war, but sometimes they become friends, marry, and beget and raise children (242c9–d2). The second storyteller distinguishes two kinds of beings, wet and dry or cold and hot, with each pair again living in matrimony (242d2–4). The myths of these two storytellers are Ionian, although they are not explicitly identified as such. The storytellers of the Eleatic tribe, starting even before Xenophanes, tell a tale that all things, so called, are one (242d4–6).

Next, the Stranger unites an Ionian myth and a Sicilian myth (Heraclitean and Empedoclean) into a single class, which is then divided into two. The united thinkers share the attribute of considering (συννοεῖν) it safest to "weave together" (συμπλέκειν) the two tales that beings are many and that they are one. In other words, the many are united by both enmity and friendship (242d6–e2). The Stranger refers to these mythtellers as "Muses." Of these, the "stricter" or more intense (αἱ συντονώτεραι) say that being "is always at odds and in agreement with itself" (that is, continuously self-differentiating and reuniting; 242e2–3). But the "softer" (αἱ δὲ μαλακώτεραι) Muses "loosen" the web of the strict doctrine by suppressing perpetual war (or self-differentiation). For these Muses, the all (τὸ πᾶν) is sometimes one and friendly, thanks to Aphrodite, but sometimes, thanks to a kind of strife, it is many and at war (242e4–243a2).

In this summary of "critical" myths, being is said to be one, two, three, and many as well as one. Where multiplicity is allowed, the numbers refer to kinds, not to individual things. In this sense, the pluralists approach a doctrine of forms, although their kinds are dynamic and animated rather than static and mathematical. In the case of monism, it is hard to say whether "one" refers to a kind or an entity, or to both. This will shortly be the basis for an antinomy. Where multiplicity is involved, the metaphor of weaving expresses very well the conception of order. There cannot be an ordering of one element (in a nontrivial sense); hence, it is inappropriate to speak of a "cosmos" with respect to monism. Despite the Stranger's avowed Eleaticism, then, he adopts the two points of multiplicity and weaving from the pluralists. This is brought out in another way. All the myths except the Eleatic refer to sexual reproduction. But what comes into being passes away. The Stranger will transform the dynamic and animated "kinds" into a doctrine of logical or ontological forms. However, he will not entirely suppress the life or soul of the cosmos. His ontology has, as we shall see, two levels.

It would be harsh and improper to accuse such famous and ancient men of lying. But whether or not they said anything truly in all these myths, the Stranger can properly say that they had little esteem for the many "like us." Each looked down upon us as he pursued his idiosyncratic discourse to its completion, whether we could follow him or not (243a2–b2; cf. 216c6–7). Like a contemporary analytical philosopher, the Stranger chastizes traditional thinkers for their obscure language. Like the analyst, he wonders whether it is possible to understand what these myths say. When he himself was younger, the Stranger supposed himself to understand "precisely" (ἀκριβῶς) what now perplexes us, namely, non-being. Perhaps, then, our souls are in the same condition with respect to being (243b3–c1).

The paramount task, as Theaetetus himself sees, is thus to study being in order to determine what is revealed (δηλοῦν) by those who speak about it (τὸ ὄν; 243c2–d5). The best way to do this is to question those directly who use this term, as though they were present. We thus begin a dialogue within the dialogue. This rhetorical device makes the discussion more vivid than it would otherwise be. The Stranger begins by addressing the dualists: "Come, those of you who say that the all [τὰ πάντ'] is hot and cold or any two such, what is it that you pronounce about both when you say that both and each are? What are we to understand by this 'being' [τὸ εἶναι] of yours?" (243d6–e1). Is it a third in addition to the two (such as hot and cold)? If you call one of these two "being" (ὄν), do you mean that both are? In this case, are not the two actually one (243e1–6)?

These questions require clarification. The attempt to classify existing things under two kinds, like "hot" and "cold," is not successful, because "being" is a third kind. Or so the Stranger claims. It is not obvious that the dualists would agree with him. They might claim that "being" is a blend of "hot" and "cold," which are, of course, principles, not things. The Stranger's criticism makes it plain that, for him, "being" cannot be reduced to a name for the copula. By the same token, it cannot be assimilated into two predicate forms corresponding to the dualist principles: "____ is a hot thing" and "____ is a cold thing." This is not to suggest that "being" is a predicate. On the contrary, none of "being," "hot," and "cold" is understood by the Stranger as a predicate. We can already see the Stranger's own doctrine of forms at work here. In the statement "x is hot," both "is" and "hot" are the names of ontological forms, and "x" stands for the name of an instance of the combination of these two forms.

Theaetetus is not sure whether we reduce "hot" and "cold" to unity by linking both to "being" (243e7–9). He quickly acquiesces, however, in the Stranger's charge that this reduces two to one (244a1–3). Let us refer to this as a version of the familiar aporia of enumeration.[1] This aporia applies to everyone who claims that the all (τὸ πᾶν) is more than one (244a4–b5). If we fail to list "being" as one of our principles, then we cannot say that these "are" principles. Again, this is because the Stranger excludes from the outset a purely syntactical analysis of "being." His criticism of the dualists is not clearly stated, but amounts to this: even though "being" is not listed as a distinct principle, the dualists say that each principle "is," and this makes each principle an instance of "being." The criticism does not merely assume that "is" stands for the principle "being." It also assumes that two distinct principles, when combined with "being," become indistinguishable from "being." Needless to say, the Stranger does not in fact believe this, as will be made plain by his doctrine of atomic forms. The Stranger's implicit criticism of the dualists is that they have no account of "is" or "being" that will rescue them from incoherence. They are not in a position to make a precise count of their principles. To this we can add that the dualists' failure to develop a doctrine of language, and so of the copula, leaves them open to the otherwise farfetched charge that, by saying "hot is" and "cold is," they contradict themselves, or say that two (and perhaps even three) are one.

The Stranger now turns to the monists, or rather to Theaetetus, who plays their role. "Do you say that one only is?" (ἕν πού φατε μόνον εἶναι;). They affirm that they do. The Stranger then raises a problem. The Eleatics apply the word "being" (ὄν) to something (τι), and use it as a name or referring expression. It looks, then, as though they use two names for the same thing (244b6–c3). Why is this a problem? Are there not many things with two names? For example, "Cicero" and "Tully" name the same person, as do "Joe Louis" and "the brown bomber." The Stranger evidently rules out all such examples. They are relevant only for those who allow multiplicity, or differently stated, for whom names do not count as "things." If we pose nothing except unity (ἕν), then, according to the Stranger, it is laughable to say that there "are" (εἶναι) two names (244c4–10). It might be objected to the Stranger that, by "unity," the Eleatics are referring to a principle, not to an individual thing. But the Stranger can easily reply that "unity" and "being" are distinct principles, and

---

1. Cf. Klein (1977), pp. 60–64, on the significance of ἄμφω here and throughout the dialogue.

so, that monism is in fact dualism. The Stranger's point is fallacious
if he is taken to be referring solely to a plurality of names. It becomes valid when the names are taken as referring to distinct principles. Throughout this criticism of monism (which continues at
244c11–d13), the Stranger equivocates in what must be for the reader
an annoying manner between "being" as a principle and "a being,"
such as a name or something named. However, underlying this
equivocation, we discern his conviction that names like "being" and
"unity" refer to distinct logical (and so ontological) elements.

This brings us to the following point: the dualists have multiplicity
but no unity or stability, and thus, no names or numbers. As a result,
it makes no sense to refer to them as "dualists." The monists, on the
other hand, have a specious unity with two names, each referring to
a distinct principle. They are (at least) dualists. In both cases, the
problem, which one may refer to as internal dissolution, arises from a
failure to treat "being" as the name of a distinct principle. The monists attempt to do this, but as soon as they try to state their doctrine
("being is one"), they contradict themselves.

Hitherto the Stranger has been discussing countable elements or
principles. He therefore employed the term "the all" in contrast to
"the one." Now he shifts for the first time from "the all" to "the
whole" (τὸ ὅλον). He does so by constructing a dilemma which purports to show that Eleaticism is self-contradictory, regardless of which
horn of the dilemma it chooses to grasp. The Eleatics must say that
the whole is the same as "the one that is" (τοῦ ὄντος ἑνός; 244d14–e1).
But if we are to take Parmenides at his word when he describes the
whole as a sphere with weight, a middle, and extremities, then it
must have parts (244e2–8). Here it may seem that the Stranger is
unfairly combining elements from two different levels of the Parmenidean teaching. The Stranger can defend himself against this
charge by noting that a dualism of unity and illusion is still a dualism. Underlying the Stranger's dilemma is something like the following argument. "Being" names either an ontological principle (like
the form *being*) or the totality of things constituting the cosmos:
the all. The poem of Parmenides apparently gives us a basis for holding both views. It speaks at least indirectly of being as both "all"
and "whole."[2] The Eleatic being is therefore ontologically "double."

2. David Lachterman has furnished me with the following note. "If Simplicius's
reading is accepted, οὖλον in fragment 8.4 (DK) is the only occurrence we have for
'whole,' and may be metrically required. Everywhere else, πᾶς and its derivatives are
used. There does not seem to be any semantic distinction at work here, comparable
to the Platonic differentiation of τὸ πᾶν and τὸ ὅλον." My point in the text is that the
Stranger is caught in a dilemma by the application of his own distinction to the
interpretation of Parmenides.

It possesses two formal properties which are ostensibly the same. Therefore it cannot be "unity itself" (τὸ ἓν αὐτό; 245a1–10).

The monist faces the following dilemma. Either being (τὸ ὄν) is marked by unity, and so is one and whole, or we must entirely deny that being is a unitary whole (245b1–5). By the first horn of the dilemma, the monist enunciates three principles: being, unity, and wholeness. On either horn, monism dissolves into multiplicity. Either unity is hypothetical whereas pluralism is actual, or else "wholeness itself" (αὐτὸ τὸ ὅλον) subsists independently of being, and therefore lacks something of itself or is not a whole (245b7–c4).

Just as in the case of the dualists, so too here; the Stranger's criticism of monism presupposes his own doctrine of form. What we might be inclined to call "predicates" of the whole are for him distinct ontological elements. However, the monists do not have access to the doctrine of pure forms; as a result, they can say nothing about being without contradicting themselves. On the other hand, to deny that being has a distinct property is to make it less than itself. To that extent, "being will not be" (245c5–7). But as a collection of distinct properties, the "all" is a multiple that cannot be reduced to unity (245c8–10). The Stranger's criticism of monism is less arbitrary than his criticism of the dualists, because monism is the more extreme of the two doctrines. Whether one speaks of formal elements or predicates, a unity of principles is not the same as the assertion of a unique principle. Furthermore, the monists (or at least the Eleatics) do refer to "being" as the one, whereas the dualists (at least those referred to by the Stranger) do not. Hence the monist cannot defend himself by interpreting "being" as the copula.

The Stranger first considered the paradoxical result of taking the whole as a unity apart from being. On this assumption, the whole itself possesses being, which latter property is thus doubled. But disaster follows for monism even if there is no sense in which the whole "is" or possesses being. For if there is no whole, then there cannot be unity. Consequently, being will not be (οὐκ ὄν).[3] Even worse, since what is, is wholly what it is, in the absence of the whole, there

---

3. The use of οὐκ here instead of μή or μηδαμῶς is noteworthy; cf. Cornford (1935), p. 225. I take the Stranger to be implying that to be is to be a unit, a definite entity, and that this principle is applicable to the "whole." One could object to the Stranger here that, if this is his meaning, he has reified the "whole" and thus blurred if not dissolved the distinction between τὸ ὅλον qua οὐσία and ὄν qua existing particular.

is neither being nor becoming. And the same argument can be extended to cover quantity. These and countless other aporias will face anyone who says either that being is some given two, or that being is only one (245c11–e5).

The Stranger's analysis of monism and dualism leads to the conclusion that, among his predecessors, precision was actually imprecision. It does not follow that one can in fact accurately count the principles or formal elements of the whole. At no time in the presentation of his own doctrine does the Stranger state the exact number of pure forms. Furthermore, he introduces his doctrine of forms by way of a simile: the alphabet. If this is not exactly a myth, it is very far from being a mathematical λόγος. The main point of this section is that precision is not a matter of arriving at an exact count of the kinds of beings, but rather of having definite, and so countable, formal principles. As a corollary to this, the Stranger silently excludes the possibility of taking "being" as a copula or nonfunctioning particle in a predicative expression.

The Battle of the Giants

(245e6–249d8)

The Stranger introduced the discussion of his predecessors by calling them all "popular" or "careless" speakers (242c4). We have just examined the views of those who speak "accurately" (διαχριβολογουμένους) about being and non-being (245e6–7). They are marked, in other words, by careless (or specious) accuracy. We must now have a look at "those who speak in another way," in order to complete our investigation (245e7–246a3). These will not have recourse to a specious accuracy; they will not attempt to count up the principles. Their carelessness is of another kind.

The Stranger introduces the new speakers as follows: "There seems to be something like a battle of giants among them, because of their disagreement concerning being" (τῆς οὐσίας; 246a4–6). The simile refers to the struggle between the Olympian gods and a race of giants who attempted to storm Olympus and become its masters.[1] We seem to be shifting from a quasi-mathematical to a theological ontology. Even more important, the Stranger employs the term οὐσία to name the topic of the battle. This name occurred only once during the investigation of the "accurate" speakers, at 245d4, where it was contrasted with γένεσις. Henceforth, I shall transliterate οὐσία as ousia, but will not italicize it, in order to avoid confusion with the elements of the atomic or formal alphabet. Plato often uses ousia to convey a more general notion than τὸ ὄν. For example, in the *Republic* (VI, 509b6–10), Socrates tells Glaucon that the good is responsible for the presence of τὸ εἶναί τε καὶ τὴν οὐσίαν. He adds that the good is ἐπέκεινα τῆς οὐσίας, or beyond "being" in a sense equivalent to "the whole" rather than to the formal principle *being*.

If ousia is the whole, can it be counted? This depends upon whether

---

1. Compare Aristophanes' use of this myth in the *Symposium*.

"one" is a number, of course. But perhaps more fundamentally, ousia is a differentiated unity rather than a pure monad. The accurate thinkers, as represented by the Stranger, did not attempt to count ousia, although the Stranger does count "the whole" as a single principle when constructing his dilemma for monism. The evidence, to say the least, is ambiguous. The one clear point is that the Stranger shifts from τὸ ὄν to οὐσία in his account of the battle of the giants.

The giants drag down everything from heaven, and thus bring the invisible down to earth, or make the invisible visible. They state confidently that ousia is body, or what can be struck and touched, and they scorn those who disagree with them (246a7–b3). The giants, instead of trying to count the uncountable, *define it*. Their definition, "ousia is body," is not posed as a web of three formal elements. Nevertheless, this should not render them immune to a subsequent demand for semantic analysis. Meanwhile, their view is familiar to Theaetetus, who has encountered many of these "terrible" men (246b4–5).

The opponents of the materialists defend themselves "very cautiously" by means of "certain noetic and incorporeal forms" (νοητὰ ἄττα καὶ ἀσώματα εἴδη) from the invisible domain. Their caution does not preclude their forcible assertion (βιαζόμενοι) that these forms are the true being or ousia (τὴν ἀληθινὴν οὐσίαν). The gods are cautious with respect to bodies, rather than with respect to the views of the giants. They do not handle bodies directly, but employ formal intermediaries. They break the bodies of their opponents into small pieces with λόγος, and speak of the result as a sort of moving genesis rather than as ousia (246b6–c2). These two camps are always at war. This implies that the dispute cannot be settled by argument. Something much deeper than the perception of logical cogency is at work here; hence the use of theological imagery.

Who are these "gods"? To begin with, they are not "Idealists" in the modern sense. They accept matter, as we may call it, or "moving genesis." To use λόγος to dissolve bodies is not the same as to use forms to "produce" bodies. Second, the Stranger never identifies himself as one of the "gods." On the contrary, he introduces them as a camp of predecessors, all of whom he is rejecting. There is then no *prima facie* reason to identify the Stranger's forms with those of the "gods."[2] I suggest that we avoid speculations on the identity of the "gods" until we have more reliable evidence.

2. Cf. Wiehl (1967), p. 189, nn. 74, 75.

The Stranger asks that we obtain a statement from each "family" (ἀμφοῖν τοῖν γενοῖν) on what they mean by ousia. We can easily do so in the case of the "gentle" family of gods. However, it may be impossible to succeed with those who forcibly drag everything down to the level of body (246c5–d1). This suggests that the giants are unaccustomed to employ the term "ousia," and so, that the Stranger has formulated a definition on their behalf. As the Stranger says explicitly, we ought to make the materialists "better in deed" than they are; if this is impossible, let us at least make them better in (our) speech, by assuming that they are more amenable to the customs of civilized discourse than is the case (246d4–7). The Stranger then enunciates an important principle of interpretation: "What is agreed to by better men is more authoritative [κυριώτερον] than what is agreed to by worse men" (246d7–8). We are not interested in these men as historical personages, but in the truth. "Quite correct," Theaetetus agrees (2468d–e1).

If we wish to understand a philosophical thesis, we ought to formulate it in the best or strongest possible way. We gain nothing from refuting a weak or inaccurate version of a doctrine we dislike. However, in order to consider the strongest version of our opponents' views, we must be just. The issue is not simply one of technical proficiency, but of excellence of character as well. The Stranger's assertion gives rise to an interesting question, which I shall merely mention here. Is it possible to combine one's own statement of a philosophical doctrine with a fair account of the views of one's opponents or predecessors? Has the Stranger himself fairly represented the views of the monists and dualists? Questions like these point to an awkward possibility. It may be that to pronounce one's views is already to engage in a kind of violence or injustice. Perfect fairness seems to require that we respect everyone's views as equal to our own. Yet this is tantamount to the negation of all views. We are given another indication of this difficulty when the Stranger instructs Theaetetus to "command" the improved materialists to speak. Theaetetus is to "interpret" (ἀφερμήνυε) what they say (246e2–4). By making the materialists "better," we also impose our version of their doctrine and, additionally, assume that we are right in thinking our version "better" than theirs. In the case of the Stranger's analysis of monism and dualism, the assumption amounts to a refutation of the predecessors on the basis of the preferred doctrine.

The interpretation of the materialists falls into two parts. The first part runs from 246e5 to 247c8. In this part, the materialists are made to agree that there is such a thing as a mortal animal or ensouled body. By so doing, they include soul among "the beings" (τῶν ὄντων; 246e5–247a1). In itself, this statement need not (for us) refute materialism. Soul might be a "breath," and hence corporeal. But the next admission is considerably more damaging. The materialists are made to grant that there are just and unjust, as well as intelligent and unintelligent, souls. Worse yet, they are made to accept the assertion that souls become just "by the possession and presence" (ἕξει καὶ παρουσίᾳ) of justice, and that they become the opposite via the possession and presence of the opposite (247a2–7). We note that παρουσία means here the presence of justice in the soul, but that it attributes ousia to justice itself. In fact, the Stranger explicitly attributes to the materialists the view that justice "is" (οὔσης), which is enough to raise the question whether or not it is a body. The materialists further admit that the virtues and vices in addition to justice and intelligence are able to present and absent themselves (παραγίγνεσθαι καὶ ἀπογίγνεσθαι), as a consequence of which they must "be something" (εἶναί τι; 247a9–b1). They also grant that "hardly any of these is visible" (247b5).

This passage raises a number of difficulties. Why do the materialists make such damaging admissions? Theaetetus will suggest below that they are moved by shame. If this is a fair explanation, it supports my previous inference that their dispute cannot be settled by dispassionate argument. But this does nothing to resolve the question whether materialists need feel shame. Differently stated, the Stranger makes them "better" in a moral sense, or at least in his own moral sense, but he does not necessarily intend to strengthen their argument. It looks suspiciously as though the Stranger gets the better of the materialists by weakening their argument.

We must also say something about the use of "presence" and "absence." I note first that the Stranger speaks initially of a παρουσία of justice and its opposite, but then generalizes by using the terms παραγίγνεσθαι and ἀπογίγνεσθαι. The first expression seems to attribute incorporeal status to justice and its opposite, whereas the second pair of expressions does not. It is therefore not at all clear what kinds of "beings" are being referred to here. Furthermore, if justice is an ousia, can injustice be an ousia as well? Do the improved materialists believe in negative ousiai?

The Stranger continues the interrogation. We learn through Theaetetus that justice, intelligence, and the rest of virtue as well as of the opposites of the virtues, are largely invisible. But they make a more complex reply to the further question whether these invisible beings possess body, or whether there are bodies which cannot be struck or touched. They believe that the soul possesses a kind of body. In the case of intelligence and the rest, they are ashamed either to dare to exclude them from existing things (τῶν ὄντων) or to assert that they are all bodies (247b7–c2). This is quite interesting. Why is it more shameful to deny the being or corporeality of justice than of the soul? It is hard to avoid the inference that political considerations influence the materialists on this point. Once we grant that justice is a "being," it becomes impossible to treat it as a body, whereas the same is not true of the soul.

Since shame is not the same as theoretical conviction, it is possible that under other circumstances the materialists would not accept the Stranger's "improvement" of their position. However, he does not raise this possibility. "It is plain that our gentlemen have become better." They are thus promoted from giants to ἄνδρες. This political term is also reinforced by the next observation. The Stranger compares the improved materialists with the aboriginal earthborn warriors or genuinely fierce materialists, who would not agree to this self-refuting modification of their thesis, because they feel no shame (247c3–8). This is undoubtedly because they are sprung from the earth rather than from a polis. But the Stranger does not pause to examine the arguments of these earth-born materialists. Perhaps they have neither shame nor arguments, but only a fierce conviction which it is impossible to refute.

The second part of the interpretation of materialism runs from 247c9 to 248a3. In this part, Theaetetus is no longer the interpreter. The Stranger answers his own questions. Those who admit both corporeal and incorporeal beings (τῶν ὄντων) must state what is "connatural" (συμφυὲς) to them. It is to this that the materialists look in stating that both the corporeal and the incorporeal "exist" or "are" (εἶναι; 247c9–d4). The connatural element is the sought-for ousia. This suggests the following problem. If ousia is common to corporeal and incorporeal beings, it cannot be merely the one or the other. But if it is a mixture, then it cannot be the connatural element from which the being of each follows. The way in which the Stranger formulates his question here suggests, I believe, that he is already thinking of a sense of "ousia" as superordinate to both visible and invisible beings. "Ousia" in this sense cannot name a "thing" and does not stand for a reified conception of being. We come closer to this sense of "ousia" with the expression "the whole." In other words, "ousia" is here synonymous with τὸ ὅλον. This point will resurface a little later in the discussion.

Apparently some of the improved materialists remain close to their aboriginal counterparts; we must therefore question them again (247c4–9). "It will be enough if they are willing to admit any incorporeal being, however small. They will then have to tell us what is connatural to the incorporeal as well as to the corporeal things, looking toward which, they say that both kinds are [or exist]" (εἶναι; 247c9–d4).

I have just urged the point that what is connatural to the corporeal and the incorporeal must be distinguishable from the corporeal *qua* corporeal and the incorporeal *qua* incorporeal *thing*. In other words, both the corporeal and the incorporeal, as ὄντα, are defined as genuine beings (ὄντως ὄντα) by virtue of their connatural element or principle: ousia. If the term "incorporeal" is to apply to ousia, then, it must be in a sense different from that in which "incorporeal" applies to "beings" or ὄντα. However, this is not a point which the Stranger makes on behalf of the improved materialists. Thus far, I alone am responsible for the inference. It remains to be seen whether the Stranger will explicitly confirm it. My point is that he must confirm it, in order to render consistent his analysis of materialism and "formalism" in the present discussion.

We are now ready to see whether the improved materialists will agree that "being is of the following kind" (τοιόνδ' εἶναι τὸ ὄν). This may be a reversion to τὸ ὄν instead of (what I take to be the required) οὐσία. It could also be meant to ask whether having met the following definition of one's principle (οὐσία) is required, to qualify as a "being" (τὸ ὄν). Here is the Stranger's suggestion for that definition: "I say that whatever possesses any sort of power (δύναμιν) either to alter any nature whatsoever, or to be affected in the smallest degree from the most trifling thing, and even if only once, all this is genuine being (ὄντως εἶναι). For I fix as the boundary of the beings that it is nothing other than power" (τίθεμαι γὰρ ὅρον ὁρίζειν τὰ ὄντα, ὡς ἔστιν οὐκ ἄλλο τι πλὴν δύναμις; 247d8–e4). I will consider the details of this definition in a moment. Let us first ask whether the Stranger speaks here merely on behalf of the improved materialists, or for himself as well.

The Stranger never dissociates himself from this definition in what follows. Indeed, he will say shortly that "the friends of the forms" reject this definition of "ousia," which he will defend as if it were his own. If he does accept the definition, then of course the Stranger cannot be a "friend of the forms." One could plausibly argue that the emphasis throughout the discussion of power prepares us for the present definition of ousia. There is no reference to this definition in the subsequent discussion of forms, but we may be intended to

think of combination and separation as manifestations of the intrinsically dynamic nature of the whole. However, the Stranger will say
nothing to resolve this problem for us. When Theaetetus accepts the
definition on behalf of the materialists, the Stranger replies, "Perhaps something else will present itself to us and to them. For the
time being, let this be agreed upon between us" (247e5–248a3).

Let us now see what we can learn from a closer look at the details
of the definition. To begin with, the term "ousia" appears nowhere
in the definition. One might suggest that "genuine being" (ὄντως
εἶναι) is intended in a synonymous sense, but this is not certain. We
come somewhat closer to the Stranger's explicit words in taking
ὅρον ὁρίζειν to refer back to 246b1, where the Stranger says that the
materialists "define 'ousia'" (οὐσίαν ὁριζόμενοι).[3] On this reading,
the "mark" of ousia is δύναμις. But what exactly does the Stranger
mean by "power"? It cannot be the same as the Aristotelian δύναμις,
except perhaps in the sense that "actual" things have a capacity to
do or suffer. But forms are themselves "actual," not potential. On
the other hand, instances of forms cannot be understood as Aristotelian "actualities," and these too must be marked by a capacity to
do or suffer. Neither do we gain much by shifting to the terms "active" and "passive," which tell us nothing that is not more directly
conveyed by "doing" and "suffering."

It is also interesting to observe that the conception of power seems
to fit better with τὸ ὄν, which contains in the participle a notion of
dynamism, than it does with the abstract noun οὐσία. However, I
do not think that we can draw any certain inferences from grammatical considerations; philosophers are always free to coin technical terms as they see fit. A more fruitful observation is that of the
difference between a form and a power. Powers must inhere in forms,
given the present definition, but they cannot themselves be identical with forms qua looks, shapes, or patterns. A formal look is
something definite, whereas a power is capable of altering. To take
the active case first, a look does not change its intrinsic ratio or
proportion when it affects us. For example, when we speak of "looks
that kill," we distinguish between the look itself and its effect upon
us. The same look may "kill" one person but not another. More
generally, the same form must "do" different things under different
circumstances. If there were no distinction between the look and
the power, there would be no definite look. Much the same can be
said with respect to suffering. A look is not seen by everyone; when

3. Cf. Owen (1971), p. 230, n. 14.

one person is looking at a form, or thinking it, someone else may be undergoing a different effect from the same form, even though he is not thinking it. Looks must therefore preserve their nature even while they are suffering as well as doing.

Nevertheless, the definition of ousia as power goes a long way toward what one may call a "process" ontology. Even if my attempt to distinguish between a look and its power points in the right direction, the forms can no longer be conceived as static or entirely unchanging. The very capacity to do or suffer differently under differing circumstances introduces a dimension of *transformation* and thus of interaction. Consider the alphabet of pure forms which the Stranger will introduce shortly. The Stranger clearly intends each letter in this alphabet to be understood as independent of the others with respect to its intrinsic nature. And yet, each element derives its being from the form *being*, its sameness from the form *sameness*, and so on (with the massive exception that no form can *derive* its own power from itself, since it cannot combine with itself). This is not the place to examine the difficulties inherent in the Stranger's doctrine. My point here is solely that each form possesses a power to "do" (to donate its power to other forms) and to "suffer" (to receive the power of other forms). Are these instances of "transformation?" In one sense, clearly not, since no form can turn into some other form. On the other hand, no form can be what it is apart from the interaction of the forms. If a form is not "transformed" by this interaction, surely it is *formed* by it. But this is only a step away from conceiving of the "formation process" as a self-differentiating "power," capable of assuming the various "looks" of the ontological alphabet.

I am certainly not attributing such a "process ontology" to the Stranger. I am merely exploring the consequences of an effort to connect the definition of "ousia" as power with the Stranger's own doctrine of form. If the power is the same as the form, then what purported to be a phenomenological "look" is transformed into an activity: the look *qua* actual is transformed into the possibility of the look, and "official" Platonism is transformed into modern philosophy. If the power is not the same as the form, then either it "belongs" to the form, which thus seems to lose its intrinsically simple, "elemental" nature, or else "power" is a synonym for "combination." In fact, as we shall see, the Stranger never refers to a power of *being*, *sameness*, and the like, but only to the "power of combination" (as has been pointed out to me by David Lachterman). Might we infer from this that, whereas *being* is a static form, ousia is the dynamic power of formal combination? I do not think so; to say nothing else, this does not square with the identification of ousia as the divine whole. But even if we were somehow persuaded to draw the inference just mentioned, the result would be to subordinate the static atomic letters to the dynamic process of spelling itself. I suggest that this amounts to a transformation of Platonism into neo-Platonism, itself a way station on the road to Hegel.[4]

We may now turn to the interrogation of "the friends of the forms" (τοὺς τῶν εἰδῶν φίλους). Once again, Theaetetus will be asked to serve as interpreter.[5] The formalists separate genesis from ousia and take each apart from the other. This reminds us of the materialist distinction between visible and invisible things. However, the invisible things are not the same as ousia, which was said to be connate to the visible and the invisible alike. The formalists hold further that we "share in" (κοινωεῖν) genesis via bodily perception, whereas we share in "genuine being" (τὴν ὄντως οὐσίαν) via the calculative thinking (διὰ λογισμοῦ) of the soul. This distinction does not occur in the materialist doctrine, which refers merely to "looking at" the invisible and visible beings (εἰς ὃ βλέποντες; 247d3). According to the formalists, genuine being or ousia is always the same (hence not dynamic). Genesis, on the contrary, is continuously "othering" or changing (ἄλλοτε ἄλλως; 248a7–b1).

According to the materialists, being (presumably ousia) is a power of any kind, whether to change something else or "to suffer" (τὸ παθεῖν), in however slight a degree. In a subsequent passage, the Stranger will explain "being known," according to the materialist hypothesis, as "being changed through suffering" (κινεῖσθαι διὰ τὸ πάσχειν; 248d10–e5). The materialist thus contends that to be "looked at" is to be changed; in other words, this "change" occurs even though there is no direct contact between the knower and the known, as is indicated by the metaphor of vision. The formalists, on the other hand, claim to "share in" genuine ousia thanks to the calculative intelligence, and so to know it without changing it. However, they were said to break up bodies into small pieces with their speeches or reasonings (246b6–c2). This no doubt refers to cognitive analysis or the activity of knowing, but there is some difference in their cog-

4. In the *Republic*, V, 477c1ff, Socrates asks us to consider δυνάμεις as "a certain form of beings" (γένος τι τῶν ὄντων).

5. This interrogation consists of twenty-one interchanges from 248a7 to 249d5, the eleventh of which begins with an oath (248e6), the Stranger's fourth oath thus far. There will be a fifth oath at 253c7. The relative infrequency of oaths is appropriate to the abstract nature of the subject matter, and adds significance to those oaths which in fact occur.

nitive relation to ousia and to genesis. The "looks" of genesis are not directly accessible via the perception of bodies, which perception must be "broken up" into smaller pieces; that is, into the flux of genesis itself, which is accessible to thinking, but not to sense perception. Nothing is said of an analogous "breaking up" of the domain of ousia. Yet since ousia is known via calculation, the soul must be able to pick out distinct elements in the structure of ousia. Ousia is not resolved into some homogeneous flux, but rather it is seen more sharply, in finer detail.

The Stranger now presses the formalists on the sense of "sharing," which they attribute to both body and soul. (I note in passing that the perception of bodies is not the same as the cognitive breaking down of bodies into genesis.) He wants to know whether it is not the previously mentioned "passive and active condition of a certain power that arises from the coming-together of distinct elements" (248b2–9). In other words, the Stranger is raising the question whether "sharing" does not entail "changing." The Stranger replies to his own question, since Theaetetus may not be familiar with the views of the formalists (as he evidently was with the views of the materialists). "We," that is, the Stranger together with the materialists, "set up as a satisfactory definition of the beings [τὰ ὄντα] the power to suffer or act even to the smallest degree." The formalists reply to us that whereas genesis "shares" (μέτεστι) in the power of suffering and doing, neither of these belongs to ousia (248c1–10). The Stranger uses different verbs to refer to the sharing of the body in genesis via sense perception and the sharing of genesis in the power of suffering and doing. His point seems to be this: sense perception, although attributed to the body, is an activity of a living organism, and in human beings at least, it is inseparable from other powers of the soul, such as cognition. Genesis, the intrinsic process of bodies, is not solely the activity of a living organism, but that which is common to all bodies, animate or inanimate. This process both affects the perceiver and is affected by him (or it). Since the perceiving body is itself "part" of genesis, it too must be modified in the process of perception. So the sharing of the body in genesis is also a sharing in the doing and suffering of genesis. But the same cannot be said of the soul.

Theaetetus is impressed with the reply of the formalists and wonders whether it may not contain some truth. The Stranger rightly points out that we still need to determine more plainly whether the formalists agree that the soul perceives (γιγνώσκειν) and ousia is perceived (γιγνώσκεσθαι; 248c10–d3). The Stranger is here making a grammatical point reminiscent of his earlier distinction between the singular and the plural as applied to non-being. If "to know" is to do something, then "to be known" entails "suffering" (πάσχειν) the cognitive act. Since ousia is "known by knowing" (γιγνωσκο-μένην ὑπὸ τῆς γνώσεως), "to the extent that it is known, it is changed through suffering, which we say cannot occur in the case of what is at rest" (248d10–e5).

We have to pause and ask ourselves whether the Stranger's point is persuasive. If the Stranger had distinguished between "being changed" and assuming the passive relation of "being known," perhaps we could agree with him. Then too, some things may change through being known. For example, a murderer is placed in jeopardy by being known to the authorities as the perpetrator of a fatal crime. Subatomic particles may be changed by the interference of the light waves or the instruments with which we seek to perceive them. But if I perceive someone across the street who neither recognizes nor even notices me, how is that person changed by my act of perception? A negative reply to this question should raise our suspicions about previous inferences from Greek syntax. The fact that a Greek uses the definite neuter article in employing the expression "non-being" is in no way evidence that he intends to reify nothingness. Greek is not the only language with expressions that employ words that do no cognitive work in those expressions. Furthermore, a passive expression can invariably be transformed into an equivalent active expression. There is no cognitive difference between "he is perceived by me" and "I perceive him." The expression "to be perceived" thus, taken in itself, implies nothing about the object of perception. Conversely, if the object *is* affected by perception, this is entirely compatible with suppression of the passive voice. The point is a scientific or philosophical one, and has nothing to do with grammar.

It is impossible to say with certitude whether the Stranger poses these puzzles ironically or seriously. The fact is that Theaetetus takes them seriously. They serve some pedagogical function, but they play no role in the Stranger's own doctrine of form or in his resolution of the problems of non-being and falsehood. At this point in the dialogue, there is another peripety, this time one with fundamental consequences for the entire discussion. The Stranger suddenly swears: "But by Zeus! Shall we be easily persuaded that change, life, soul, and intelligence are truly not present to what altogether is [τῷ παντελῶς ὄντι μὴ παρεῖναι], that it neither lives nor thinks but, awesome and holy, lacking intellect, is unchanging and fixed?" (248e6–249a3). Theaetetus replies: "We would be agreeing to a terrible assertion." This passage has to be considered in the light of both what precedes and what follows. In the first instance, the passage sharply separates the Stranger from the friends of the forms, and accordingly strengthens the link between him and the improved materialists. Furthermore, the passage confirms my earlier remark that the shift from precise to imprecise myth culminates in a theological ontology, or in what Heidegger and his followers call an "ontotheology." This last point holds regardless of whether the Stranger is speaking for himself or in an accommodated fashion. Under either hypothesis, the flow of the discussion is the same. Nor can there be any doubt that the Stranger is much more sympathetic to the imprecise than to the precise mythtellers.

With respect to what follows, it is plain that the present conception of ousia as divine has nothing to do with the subsequent doctrine of *being* as an element in the eidetic alphabet. *There are two distinct ontologies at work in the Sophist.* The Stranger not only does nothing to reconcile these two ontologies; he never refers to the fact that he has introduced two distinct conceptions of being. But this silence on his part does not excuse the interpreter for overlooking the obvious. There are then two critical passages in the Stranger's discussion of his predecessors. The first is the definition of being as power, offered on behalf of the materialists, and the second is the statement of being as comprehensive and divine, made in objection to the doctrines of the friends of the forms. In general, it is fair to say that both passages refer to "being" understood as οὐσία rather than as τὸ ὄν, although the substantive point is independent of terminological variations. When the Stranger turns to the doctrine of *being* as a letter in the eidetic alphabet, he will again shift to τὸ ὄν as the characteristic term. The doctrine of forms, so to speak, is the Stranger's version of a precise speech about being. The doctrine of the divine ousia is his version of imprecise speech. We should have learned by now that, in questions of ontology, precision is not necessarily more suitable or fitting than imprecision.

We began the discussion of imprecise speech by investigating definitions of "being" understood as "the all" or "what is altogether" (τὸ παντελῶς ὄν), of "ousia" or "genuine being" (τὴν ὄντως οὐσίαν; 248a11). The variations in terminology, appropriate to imprecise speech, do not conceal the fact that "being" is taken throughout as totality, not as a formal element of intelligible structure. In this sense, being is alive and even divine. The Stranger goes on to investigate the properties of divine ousia. Since it has intellect, it must possess a soul. Therefore, it cannot be unchangeable (as this is out of the question for a soul), and we must agree that the changed, together with change, "are" or are ingredient in comprehensive being (249a4–b4). This leaves room for the acceptance of the definition of being as power, although change and power are not identified. I note in passing that a changing deity is not the same as a formal element *change*. Nor can the deity be an "instance" of what changes by sharing in that form, since, as totality, it must include that form along with all the others (and give them their being). But even if the formal properties of divine being are to be derived from the eidetic alphabet, this does nothing to suppress the difference between the two ontologies.

The Stranger now introduces a puzzle. It is true that intellect must change, since to cognize is to act and suffer and thus, by the earlier definition, to be or to possess power. If we extend this doctrine to everything (πάντα), however, then we shall exclude intellect itself from the beings (τῶν ὄντων; 249b5–11). Theaetetus does not understand. The Stranger's point, which is obscurely expressed, is as follows. What we may call stability and self-identity (in the Stranger's terms, "sameness, in the same way, and with respect to the same") cannot come into existence apart from rest. Sameness is absence of alteration or change of any kind. Thus each entity, including the intellect, in order to "be" itself, must be the same as itself. Yet thinking is changing (249b11–c5). It is forbidden to make knowledge, intelligence, or intellect "invisible" (that is, nonexistent). We must consequently deny that the intellect is either pure change or pure rest (249c6–9). The Stranger puts the conclusion in more general terms. The philosopher, who pays the highest honor to knowledge, intelligence, and intellect, must deny that "the all" (τὸ πᾶν), whether as one or as many forms, is entirely at rest. But neither may he listen to those who say that being is comprehensive change (τῶν τε αὖ πανταχῇ τὸ ὂν κινούντων). The philosopher, as the child's wish puts it, must ask that all things, hence "being and the all" (τὸ ὂν τε καὶ τὸ πᾶν), be both changing and changeless (249c10–d5).[6] Like the child, the philosopher must have it both ways.

---

6. Klein (1977), p. 47, claims that this new definition replaces the definition of being as power. However, Sayre (1969), p. 168, takes the opposite view: "The Stranger's suggestion that δύναμις is the mark of the Real is never refuted in the dialogue." With the Stranger's remarks from 248e6ff, cf. *Timaeus* 30c5ff. Timaeus identifies the cosmos produced by the demiurge as a "single visible living thing" modelled after the living thing "of which all other living things, individually and by family, are parts. For it embraces all intelligible living things (νοητὰ ζῷα) in it, just as this cosmos contains us and all visible constructed animals." The original is described as τῷ παντελεῖ ζῷῳ at 31b1, and the model again as τῷ δὲ τὰ πάντα ἐν αὑτῷ ζῷα at 33b2. So *both* are alive.

The Stranger does not say explicitly that we must deny that the intellect is pure change or pure rest. This follows from the nature of his dilemma: thinking is change, but that which thinks, in order to be, must be the same as itself, hence (in that sense) resting. His formulation of the general problem prepares us for the subsequent need to distinguish change and rest as elements in the all. It must be the case that both the intellect and its objects of thought are in one sense changing, in another, resting; the same, of course, must be true of divine ousia. If then *change* and *rest* were predicates, or rather properties named by the predicates "change" and "rest," they would be properties of the all, of divine ousia, not of changing and resting things within the all.

Let us not fail to observe the important reference to philosophical honor in the previous passage. Philosophy cannot be equivalent to the application of dialectic understood as diaeresis, which disregards honor and shame, or better and worse, and looks only for like and like. Philosophy is the life of the truly free man, and such a life is unthinkable apart from honor.

It now looks to Theaetetus as though we have reached a satisfactory account of being (249d6–8). This is a signal that we are about to turn to a new stage in the analysis (249d6–8). The main theme of the Stranger's criticism of his predecessors may be summarized as follows. Careless speech is not the same as imprecise speech, if by "imprecise" we mean "not employing numbers." Second, despite his ostensible Eleaticism, the Stranger is far from unsympathetic to the materialists, at least in their "improved" version. The notions of power and change are indispensable to an adequate ontology. Third, these notions are in themselves not sufficient, any more than is the notion of unchanging formal structure. They must be supplemented by life, and specifically by the divine life of the cosmos.

ACT THREE

FORMS

SCENE THIRTEEN

Identity, Predication, and Existence

(249d9–252e8)

The following sections of the *Sophist* are at once the most obscure
and the most widely discussed. The difficulty, perhaps even the impossibility, of establishing a noncontroversial sense for the text has
led to conflicting interpretations of the Stranger's doctrine of formal
combination. It seems to be quite clear that the Stranger introduces
forms into the discussion at this point. There is also no doubt that
these forms are explained by means of two paradigms, spelling and
music. We shall examine these paradigms closely at the appropriate
moment. This much needs to be said now about the paradigms. Both
spelling and music are the concatenating of simple, indivisible, or
monoeidetic elements into compounds. Neither has anything to do
with, or is anything like, the grammatical operation of predication.
It is true that the Stranger does not regularly make explicit distinctions between forms, on the one hand, and names as well as instances, on the other. It is also true that he regularly illustrates how
forms do and do not combine by reference to how we talk about
forms. But he never compromises the integrity of his paradigms. He
never shifts (from 249 to 261) from the primacy of forms over language. The Stranger is explicit about this, even when he expresses
his intentions with respect to language: the object of this stretch of
the conversation has been to show "that discourse is for us one of
the kinds of beings" (260a5–6).

The Stranger never so much as hints at the possibility that "being"
is one of the kinds of discourse. Nowhere in his discussion of the
kinds of beings or μέγιστα γένη does he allude to a doctrine of predication. Strictly speaking, there is no such allusion even in the subsequent discussion of the combinations of nouns and verbs, or names.
But even if there were, predication is a grammatical combination,
not a συμπλοκὴ εἰδῶν. The "rules" governing the combination of

nouns and verbs in discourse about forms are not the same as the "rules" governing the combination of forms themselves. That the elements combined cannot be the same is (or should be) dramatically plain from the central case of being. As we shall see in detail, those who assume that the Stranger is discussing predication are led to obliterate the form *being* by assimilating it into the syntactic functions of identity and predication. On this analysis, "being" remains only as the copula of predication. This in itself is enough to rule out even the suggestion that, by introducing the language of predication into our analysis of Plato's text, we bring out his intentions and make order out of apparent confusion.

In this and the following section, I want to contrast in some detail my own analysis with the results of two distinguished scholars, M. Frede (*Prädikation und Existenzaussage*, 1967) and G. E. L. Owen ("Plato on Not-Being," 1971). If I am not mistaken, theirs are the most influential versions of the view that the Stranger is attempting primarily to distinguish the senses of the verb "is." This view takes it for granted that what I call formal combination is in fact grammatical predication. Since this assumption governs the textual analyses by which the Stranger's ostensible distinctions are established, a consideration of the aforementioned view must proceed simultaneously on two different levels. One cannot sort out the uses of "is" until one is quite clear about the distinction between forms and discourse about forms. Differently stated, one cannot start from the assumption that "combination" (as we shall see, the Stranger employs a variety of verbs and nouns to express this crucial notion) is predication. On the thesis of the predicationalists, the Stranger's distinction between forms and the combining of forms disappears. As I put it in the Prologue, this leads inevitably to the "discovery" of a linguistic ontology in Plato, namely, that being is language, or more narrowly yet, grammar.

Let me begin with some preliminary and general remarks. We have now seen that the *Sophist* does not provide us with a "unitary concept" of being. This expression is taken from the study by Owen, where it plays a small but important role.[1] Owen assumes that being remains for the Stranger a unitary concept in large part because he does not concern himself with the dialogue as a whole. He therefore

---

1. Owen (1971), p. 258. Owen holds that for the Stranger, "is" is employed either in identity statements or as the copula of predication. Since "identity" is Owen's term for what I call *sameness*, it follows that his "concept of being" must be the copula of predication. As I will show in the text, the net result is to eliminate the form *being*.

overlooks the patent difference between "being" (if that is the best translation) as οὐσία or the divine whole and *being* as a pure formal element in the eidetic alphabet of "greatest" or "most important kinds." The definition of being as power (δύναμις), offered by the Stranger in ostensible agreement with the improved materialists, may or may not be a common link between those two senses. Since the Stranger never again alludes to this definition, it is arguable that we must count it as a third sense of "being." It is certainly not self-evident that "power" is synonymous with "the whole" (or with "divinity"), nor that it stands for the nature of the form *being* in a way that does not obtain for the other forms. Finally, we must not forget the peculiar nature of images, which "are and are not," and the special problem of the fantasm, which is not the original, but seems to look like it without genuinely doing so. An image lacks "genuine" (ὄντως) or "true" (ἀληθινόν) being; this may be a fourth kind of being.

Second, despite the ambiguities in the details of his account, the Stranger makes a fundamental distinction between the forms he calls the "greatest kinds" and their names, or what we say about them. Both Frede and Owen acknowledge this uncontroversial point; yet they do so almost in passing, and concentrate their attention on what they call "predicates," but what the Stranger calls "names."[2] In general, accounts of rational speech in the Platonic dialogues are of the combinations of names, or of nouns and verbs, and the *Sophist* is no exception. The language of subjects and predicates is post-Aristotelian, not Platonic; and the language of one-place or two-place predicates like "___ changes" or "___ is ___" is of course not Aristotelian but Fregean. The issue here is not which of these doctrines is preferable, but only which is to be found in the *Sophist*. In order to see exactly what is at stake, let us ask ourselves this: What is the fundamental difference between combination and predication? When we combine two elements, we need not blend them or transform one into a constituent of the other. When we predicate, however, we say that one element is contained in another, either accidentally or essentially. That is, we distinguish between accidental and essential predication if we are Aristotelians. In Fregean predication, however, we are two steps removed from combination of the Platonic variety. There is no distinction between "essential" and "accidental" in Fregean predication. In the case of Aristotelian predication, one could at least say that an essential predicate corresponds to a necessary combination between two forms. But even

2. E.g., Frede (1967), p. 15; Owen (1971), p. 237.

this, as I have previously emphasized, is misleading. A necessary predicate is one which inheres essentially within the nature of the indicated subject. But forms do not become essential elements within each other's structures by combining. *Being* does not become *change* or *rest* simply because *rest* necessarily combines with *being*, and so on.

For this reason, "predication" is a fundamentally wrong term to use in discussing statements about forms. It misleads us in a variety of ways. Let me turn to another crucial way in which this occurs. The attempt to reconstruct the Stranger's doctrine as one of predication leads naturally to transform the problem of being into the problem of existence. In the first-order predicate logic or its extension, we may make identity statements or statements of predication, with or without quantifiers. It is, however, impossible to make an existence statement without the use of an existential quantifier or its defined equivalent. In modern logic, "existence" is normally understood as a quantifier. One could restate this in the traditional Kantian thesis that existence is not a predicate. But if forms are themselves predicates, or at least the referents of predicates, then obviously there is no form *existence*. Not all those who find a doctrine of predication in the *Sophist* make explicit or extended use of the language of modern predicate logic, but the underlying conceptual machinery of modern logic is plainly at work in these interpretations. This, I suspect, is why those who argue that Plato distinguishes the existential use of the verb "is" are so hard pressed to defend their thesis against the newer school, of which Frede and Owen are perhaps the most prominent representatives.

From the contemporary standpoint, efforts to distinguish between "being" and "existence" may seem like terminological hair splitting. However, the distinction is essential for a proper understanding of the *Sophist*. In fact, the serious question is not at all whether Plato ever uses "is" in such a way that the normal English translation is "exists." Owen says this explicitly, but in conjunction with an illustration from contemporary logic.[3] He claims that Plato's analysis is preliminary to a consideration of the difficult problem of existence. This may be so, but only because the Stranger is not concerned with existence, or certainly not primarily, but rather with being. To exist, in contemporary logic, is normally to be the value of a bound variable within a definite interpretation. In Platonic language, it is to be an instance of a definite formal structure. Forms

3. Owen (1971), p. 248.

do not exist for Plato any more than they do in first-order predicate logic. For Plato if not for the logician, forms alone possess being. In the Stranger's doctrine, they do so by combination with the form *being*.

This is an indispensable preface to asking whether there is a "complete" or "existential" sense of "is" in the Stranger's analysis of form. One other point has to be made here, although I cannot profitably develop it until a later section of my study. The "predicationalist" and "existentialist" readers of the *Sophist* make no distinction between the discussion of the pure forms of the eidetic alphabet and the names of verbs like "flies" and "sits" which are introduced in the subsequent section of false statements. I admit at once that this is a difficult point in any interpretation. I shall, however, be arguing in considerable detail that the best understanding of the text, the one which is most faithful to the Stranger's words and which gives him as coherent a doctrine as possible, requires us to distinguish between statements like "change is other than rest" and "Theaetetus sits." More on this later.

To return to the question of existence, I am presently concerned exclusively with the discussion of forms, prior to the introduction of the problem of falsehood. In this passage, the question of whether "existence statements" occur is, if not irrelevant, certainly of secondary interest. The crucial point is this: the Stranger attributes being to each of the remaining "greatest kinds" by way of their combination with the form *being*. Hence, to say "motion exists," for example, is entirely permissible from the Stranger's standpoint, provided that we take "exists" to be the English version of "possesses being," since it is intolerable to say in English "motion be's."

Now I want to consider the opening arguments of Frede's very influential study, in which he ostensibly shows by textual analysis of 255c12–d7 that the passage normally cited to establish an existential use of "is" in the *Sophist* fails to do so and, rather, points in quite another direction. This preliminary part of Frede's study is the basis for his reading of other crucial passages in the *Sophist*, and hence for his overall doctrine of the two senses of "is" in Plato. It goes without saying that Frede's later arguments must also be considered, and that he says much of value. But if I can show that his orienting refutation of the "existentialist" thesis is wrong, and wrong in such a way as to invalidate his own "predicationalist" approach, this will surely be an important result in its own right. I believe it is necessary to do this here, rather than in footnotes, because of the dominance among Plato scholars today of the "predicationalist" approach. I shall be as brief as possible, but I do suggest that my criticism of Frede is not of merely "scholarly" significance. It bears directly and centrally upon my own interpretation of the *Sophist*.

Frede states in advance that he is concerned only with the middle section of the *Sophist* ranging from 241c through 249b (1967, p. 9). This is somewhat misleading, as he often cites passages from the last section of the dialogue, in keeping with the aforementioned tendency not to distinguish between the doctrine of forms and the doctrine of falsehood. His main concern is to determine whether Plato introduces the distinction between various senses of "is" and "is not." The three senses Frede has in mind are the identifying sense; the copulative sense, used in various ways but primarily (as it seems from Frede's study) in predication; and the existential sense. In each case we ask ourselves: What must we find in the text in order to persuade ourselves that Plato is consciously using this or that sense? We will not be helped by Plato's explicit language on this point. Whereas he (Frede does not distinguish between Plato and the Eleatic Stranger) distinguishes explicitly between two senses of "other" (243e4–5) and of "same" (256a11–12), he never makes an analogous distinction in the case of "is" (pp. 10–11).

According to the "existentialists," such a distinction is ostensibly to be found at 255c12–13. Frede proposes to study this passage closely, in order to show that no existential use of "is" in fact occurs there, and by extension, that it occurs nowhere in the *Sophist*. Let me make a preliminary point that bears upon Frede's study as a whole. Frede takes forms to be concepts or *Begriffe* (for example, "von dem Begriff der Verschiedenheit die Rede ist"; p. 13). By using the modern notion of "concept," Frede makes the transition to "predicates" in what seems from the contemporary standpoint a natural way. Concepts define predicates. But Frede presents no arguments for the assumption that the Stranger's "greatest kinds" are concepts. The term "concept" is not a straightforward one; it requires further analysis. Some concepts are manmade; others (as in Frege's use) are eternal, whether in a "platonist" or a "Kantian" sense. Even the modern "platonist" concepts may be subject to analysis and definition. It is far from evident that the same can be said of the "greatest kinds." There is no doubt that we can talk about them, but what we say seems to presuppose their intelligibility or visibility as atomic constituents of all rational discourse. They seem to be antecedent to analysis and definition in any but an indirect or finally circular manner. We can name them: but names are not predicates.

I turn now to a survey of the main arguments in Frede's refutation of "existentialism" that begins at 255c12. We start with his discussion of 255d4–6. This is connected by Frede with 255d1. The question is how to understand the sharp separation made by the Stranger between τὸ ὄν and τὸ θάτερον. Whereas he has not yet explicitly introduced the doctrine of forms, the Stranger is plainly referring to *being* and *sameness*, and this is how Frede also understands the point (although he speaks of Begriffe as well as of forms). Frede calls our attention to a shift, common in Plato, from talk of forms to talk of predicates. Since Frede is primarily concerned with talk of predicates, it is worth looking closely at his treatment of this shift. We should do this in any case, since his ostensible refutation of "existentialism" is at issue here. In 255c12–13, the Stranger says that some beings are spoken of αὐτὰ καθ᾽ αὐτά and some are spoken of πρὸς ἄλλα. We are not yet prepared to consider the sense of the Greek expressions. I cite the lines because they contain the verb λέγεσθαι. In 255d1, The Stranger then says, τὸ δὲ γ᾽ ἕτερον ἀεὶ πρὸς ἕτερον. Frede infers a λέγεσθαι from c12–13 and considers various translations of this line, all of them dealing with what is said about either the form "das Verschiedene" or the predicate "verschieden."

This brings us to 255d4–6. According to Frede, although we are not yet able to translate 255d1, we can say the following about "das Verschiedene," or "the different," not the form but instances of the form (pp. 13–14):

1. If it is truly said of an object *a* that it is different, then the following condition is always fulfilled: there is an object *b* of such a kind that, with respect to it, it is said of *a* that *a* is different, and *b* is an object different from *a*. Frede infers this from 255d4–6, which he takes to say that the different existing thing ("das Seiende" *a* considered as different from "das Seiende" *b*) shares in just one of the two forms there mentioned (that is, in *otherness* but not in *being*). I paraphrase this as follows: *a* is other by virtue of sharing in *otherness*; its otherness is not derived from the form *being*. Frede continues: the same passage tells us that "das Seiende" (a being or existing thing) also shares in (what I call) *otherness*, but that there is a distinction between the existent and the different. If not, "is different from" would sometimes be used falsely to express the true statement "*a* is."

2. If it is truly said of an object *a*, that it is, then in some cases the following condition is fulfilled: there is an object *b* of such a kind that it is said of *a* that it is, relative to *b*, and *b* is a different object from *a*. How does Frede arrive at this condition? He does so on the

basis of the reasonable assumption that a cannot "be" or "exist" unless it also is "different from" each other existing object; that is, unless it also shares in *otherness*. This assumption is reasonable in itself, but we must not be misled by it. Whereas existing objects share in both *being* and *otherness*, the "being" of the existing object comes exclusively from the form *being*, exactly as, in item 1 above, the "difference" of a comes exclusively from *otherness* (which thus makes a different from b). Frede fails to make this distinction because he does not draw the antecedent and crucial distinction between being and existence. To anticipate: the fact that an existing a is necessarily different from an existing b in no way transforms "being" into a two-place predicate (to use Frede's terminology). Of course, even if we use the term "existence" instead of "being," the existential difference between a and b again does not transform "exists" into a two-place predicate. It is easier, though, to avoid the confusion between "existence" and "difference" if we make explicit the difference between "exists" and "possesses being."

3. If it is truly said of an object a that it is, then in some cases the following condition is not fulfilled: there is an object b of such a kind that it is said of a that it is relative to b, and b is a different object from a.

These are the three inferences from the Stranger's distinction between *being* and *otherness*. Frede turns next to the question of the sense of "is" in inference 3 (pp. 14ff). The standard or "existentialist" interpretation on this point, he tells us, is that "is" is a one-place predicate in the sense of "exists." Frede rejects the standard interpretation on the basis of his own wording of the condition; he claims that the text distinguishes between a and b here, too (in the ostensible "existential" use), but with the possibility still open that a and b are the same object. This assumption is crucial to Frede's case, since he will transform "existential" appearances of "is" into instances of identity statements ("'is' is applied to things with respect to themselves"; p. 29). The assumption thus underlies his translation of 255c12–13 in such a way as to eliminate existence statements and to leave a separation between identity statements and difference statements. As we shall soon see, this requires him to interpret the form *being* in an illegitimate manner.

First, we must reply to Frede's rejection of "existentialism" by saying that, as I have already argued with respect to inference 2, his reading of 255d4–6 is mistaken. I grant that the Stranger's formulation is cryptic. I suggest that the key to the passage is the total separation between τὸ ὄν and τὸ θάτερον. Since they are totally separate, they cannot be predicates, because the predicates "is" (whether taken as "exists" or as "is self-identical") and "is different from" can and must be applied to the same objects. It might be objected that the forms *being* and *otherness*, in my account, combine with one another. This is correct, but they do so without sacrificing their separateness. The predicate "is" is, as a predicate, an existing thing, and thus different from all other predicates: in itself, it both exists and is different. The same cannot be said of forms. However difficult it may be to express the point with exactness, "*being* itself" and "*otherness* itself" (cf. 256b6, αὐτὴ κίνησις) each has in itself no other nature but its own. In sum, we can make a logical or ontological distinction between the "being" and the "difference" of each existing thing, including predicates. But *qua* existing, the thing is indissoluble, a unity of being and difference, until it perishes.

The section 255d4–6 thus distinguishes the following cases: (1) with respect to *being*, we can say (because it is true) that "*a* is" and "*b* is"; (2) with respect to *otherness*, we can say "*a* is other than (or different from) *b*"; and (3) with respect to the combination of *being* and *otherness*, we can say "*a* is, *b* is, and *a* is other than *b*." However, this is not all that can be said against Frede's analysis. Frede then considers whether his "condition" (which I have just analyzed) can be reworded in such a way as to allow "*a* is" an existential sense (p. 14). He then denies that condition; in other words, he assumes that inference 3 concludes with the following clause: in some cases, the following condition is not fulfilled; there is an object *b* of such a kind that it is said of *a* that it is, relative to *b*. Frede then claims that this is unsatisfactory, as is shown for example by 250a–b. In Frede's interpretation, 250a–b tells us that "predicates of distinct significance are connected to distinct forms." However, 250a–b tells us only that *change, rest* and *being* are distinct from one another. It says nothing whatsoever about predicates, nor does it refer to how we talk about these distinct forms. One could object that the passage does not speak of forms, either, but this would hardly help Frede's case. However, at 250c, the Stranger refers to τὴν αὐτοῦ φύσιν, or to *being*'s own nature, which makes reasonably clear that he is talking about forms.

Frede's point is thus not supported by the passage he cites. It is also intrinsically unlikely, since there are various predicates which might be used to refer to instances of *change*, such as "alteration," "locomotion," "genesis," and "decay." But there is a much more serious flaw in Frede's analysis. According to Frede, if there were two

senses of "is," they would have to be "exists" and "＿＿ shares in
＿＿" understood as the copulative sense (p. 15). By "copulative,"
Frede means the predicative sense: "＿＿ shares in ＿＿" is to be filled
out as "object *a* has predicate *b*." But this means in turn that Frede
interprets the "sharing," "communing," "participating," or in my
expression, "combining" of forms as predication. The Stranger's form
being is thus identified with the relation obtaining amongst the forms
(including, incidentally, separation via *otherness*). *Being* is thus silently replaced from the outset by identity and predication. On this
basis, it is no trick for Frede to arrive at his conclusions; indeed, the
balance of his analysis is superfluous.

I think that there is a real problem in the Stranger's doctrine concerning the "self-identity" or "intrinsic nature" of individual forms
like *being*, which must, however, be kept distinct from his intention to distinguish between *being* and *sameness*. This distinction is
blurred by those who take "identity" instead of "sameness" as the
name of the form *sameness*. According to the Stranger, the sameness of the form *being* does not follow from its "intrinsic nature"
(τὴν αὐτοῦ φύσιν) or "itself" (its "identity" as *being*), but from its
combining with the form *sameness*. In Frede's analysis, the two distinctions between *being* and *sameness* on the one hand, and between *being* and formal combination on the other, both disappear.

I can summarize this part of the discussion by putting my objection to Frede's study in a way that applies to Owen's essay as well.
Owen also claims that there is no distinct use of "is" by the Stranger
in an existential sense. Owen too regularly interprets the Stranger's
"is" to be that of identity or the copula of predication. Despite variations in the argument, then, his fundamental thesis is exactly the
same as Frede's.[4] If this thesis is sound, then there is no way to say
that form *F* combines with the form *being*. Consider the following
example. It is immediately false to say that *change* is identical with
(the same as) *being*. Now suppose that we wish to predicate "being"
of *change*. From the Frede-Owen standpoint, this is impossible. We
have just ruled out the identifying sense of "is." This leaves us with
the sense of "is" as in "is predicated of." But we cannot predicate
"is predicated of" of *change*. The natural question arises: *What* is
predicated of *change*, or of *what* is *change* predicated? "Is predicated
of" can be predicated of *change* only in the sense that something
else is predicated of change. Strictly speaking, "is predicated of"

---

4. Frede acknowledges the assistance of Owen in his *Vorwart*; cf. Owen (1971), p.
223, n. 1.

cannot be predicated of *change* or for that matter of anything else. This is because the expression serves to unite something other than itself with something else that is other than itself. In this way, the form *being* disappears. There is a variation of this argument that leads to a still more absurd result. Suppose that "is" takes the sense of the copula in "___ is ___," where we fill in the blanks with the names of forms to obtain a complete expression. Since we are trying to predicate "being" of *change*, let us fill in the lefthand blank with *change*, which may stand for the name of the form as well as for the form itself. Now, with what do we fill the righthand blank? The only possibility seems to be "is," which cannot be italicized because it is not a form and not the name of a form. We then have "*change* is is." And this makes no sense at all.

The Frede-Owen approach sets out to determine the senses of "is" in the passage on the forms. By beginning with the distinction between identity and predication on the one hand, and the conviction that they are actually studying a doctrine of predication on the other, Frede and Owen end up by dissolving the form *being* altogether. For this they have not the slightest textual justification; on the contrary, their reading flatly contradicts the text, with all of the latter's obscurity. Owen's starting point is different from Frede's, but takes him to the same destination. He begins by positing what he calls the "parity assumption" (PA), according to which "any light thrown on either being or not-being will equally illuminate the other." This assumption is inferred from 250e5–251a1 (pp. 229–30). Since the Stranger, according to Owen, "sets himself to justify expressions of the form 'A is not' only when they can be completed into 'A is not B,' it is an incomplete use of the verb that we can expect to find vindicated in positive constructions too" (p. 230). However, "A is not," where "A" stands for a form, cannot be left without a "B," where that is the name of another form, for a very simple reason. Every form "is," as we have seen, and contrary to Owen's assumption, by virtue of its combination with *being*. Exactly contrary to Owen's contention, then, "A is" in the sense of "form A possesses being" cannot be negated. Owen's description of what the Stranger sets out to do is therefore mistaken, as we have already seen from our inspection of Frede's argument to the same effect. "Existential" statements referring to instances of forms, to *a*'s and *b*'s but not to A's and B's, can of course be negated. But that is neither here nor there, so far as the Stranger's main thesis is concerned. "A is not B" is not the negation of a statement that A possesses being. It is the negation of an identity statement, as Owen sees (p. 260). But since, like Frede, he takes the only other use of "is" to be copulative, he is entirely unable to explain expressions like μετέχειν τοῦ ὄντος. Owen is forced to take this expression about *change* at 256a1 as either fragmentary for "change is different from rest" or elliptical for "change is with respect to something." Again, there is no textual justification for his proposal.

To return to Frede, he cites *Parmenides* 144c4–6 and 155d3–e2 to show that it is self-evident for Plato that "*a* is" is always to be expanded to "*a* is *b*." In fact, this passage shows at most that such a view is attributed by Plato to Parmenides. It has no bearing on the Stranger's doctrine of pure forms, since he has developed this doctrine as an innovation with respect to Parmenides' teaching. However, provided that we distinguish between A and B, on the one hand, and *a* and *b*, on the other, we may assume that Parmenides and the Stranger agree that to be some existing thing is to be some thing or other. An existent *a* necessarily has properties, not merely *b* but *n* others as well. However, whereas form A may combine with form B, what the Stranger is arguing at 255 is that the being of *a* comes exclusively from the form *being*, and not that *a* has no other properties.

So much then for our introductory inspection of the Frede-Owen thesis. It derives from the misapplication, without argument, of an Aristotelian-Fregean conceptual framework onto the Platonic text. The argument, often of an extremely complex kind, is in fact a forced retranslating of the text into the terms of the theoretical presupposition. This is not to say that all points in their respective studies are wrong. It is, however, to say that what is right in these studies is independent of the main assumptions and procedures which Frede and Owen employ.

Nothing I have said thus far is intended to suggest that the meaning of the passages we are about to study is self-evident or beyond controversy. It is one thing to reject the "predicationalist" reading of the forms, but something else again to provide a sound interpretation of one's own. At least we have been warned against taking a first step that can only lead to disaster.

We are now ready to turn back to the text. When we last heard from him, the Stranger was telling Theaetetus that we must be like children in our insistence upon having it both ways, namely, that being and the all are both unchanging and changing. However, this in itself will not free our inquiry of puzzlement. Theaetetus does not understand, and the Stranger offers the following explanation. Theaetetus agrees that change and rest are "complete opposites" (ἐναντιώτατα). And yet, he also admits that both and each of these "exist"; that is, they "are" in the sense explicated previously. Whereas I have not italicized the critical names, it will shortly be evident that the Stranger is already thinking of forms or "greatest kinds." We may think of them instead as aspects of "being and the all," corresponding to the forms of the same name. The Stranger goes on to say that Theaetetus does not intend to grant, by his previous admissions, that change and rest, as both "existing," are both changing or both resting. Theaetetus agrees that this is not his intention. The point is that "being" or "existing" does not unite the two distinct properties or forms, change and rest; instead, each "exists" as an independent entity. This is a plain use of the "existential" sense of "is" (in the sense defined previously as "possesses being"). In the Stranger's ambiguous expression, Theaetetus presumably regards being as "some third thing besides these in the soul" (249e7–250b10). The probable sense of this expression is that Theaetetus discerns or thinks the independence of the three properties just named. As Theaetetus puts it, we have "divined" that they are three (ἀπομαντεύεσθαι; 250c1–2). The distinction, although expressed discursively, is not reached by argument, but is visible as soon as we consider the properties themselves. In slightly different terms, the diaeresis is virtually immediate.[5]

The visibility of change, rest, and being "in the soul" does not mean that these properties are constituted by a Platonic anticipation of the transcendental ego. Kant's forms are concepts and are defined by a "rule" or discursive formula. The Stranger makes no reference to defining rules; statements about forms are images of, and so posterior to, forms. The Stranger begins directly with change, rest, and being, because these are directly visible in the "looks" of things. To say that "looks" are actually something else (for example, concepts or predicates) is phenomenologically absurd. Commentators place entirely too little emphasis upon the fact that the Stranger offers no justification whatsoever for his introduction of the "greatest kinds." Attempts to justify or to define these atomic forms presuppose their accessibility to what can only be called intellectual perception.[6]

5. Cf. 248a10–b1, where the formalists are said to hold that the soul communes with οὐσία via λογισμός. Here, "divination" replaces calculative thinking. With ἐν τῇ ψυχῇ, cf. Theaetetus 186a2ff.

6. Owen (1971), pp. 229–30, n. 14, cites the definition of οὐσία as δύναμις, against those who say that the Stranger wants to prove "existence" (i.e., being) to be indefinable. But this disregards the question of the difference between οὐσία and τὸ ὄν, as well as whether the Stranger accepts that definition himself.

The capacity to perceive formal elements, however, is not a substitute for, but the basis of, philosophical explanation. Being has "its own nature" (τὴν αὐτοῦ φύσιν), according to which it is neither at rest nor changing (250c3–8). And yet, if something is not changing, how could it not rest, and vice versa? In other words, being seems to be divided into changing and resting things. Yet, being is a third element distinct from change and rest (250c9–d4). The contemporary reader is tempted at this point to resolve the puzzle by asserting that being is not identical with either change or rest, but that each of the latter two may be "predicated" of it. Even if this were the best way to deal with the Stranger's problem, it would depend upon the preservation of being as an element independent of identity and predication. The Stranger's explicit wording of the puzzle shows that the referent of "being" cannot be analyzed away without remainder into identity and predication. Owen's "parity assumption" is therefore wrong to the extent that, when the Stranger says that a little light shed on being will also illuminate non-being (250d5–251a1), the "being" to which he refers is certainly not a "two-place predicate" or an incomplete use of "is." [7] It seems intrinsically implausible that Theaetetus and the Stranger should have confused identity and predication, whatever may be true of duller wits. If predication were at issue here, then the Stranger would have to be understood to be pointing out to Theaetetus the *difference* between the two. Neither is in any doubt about the fact that, although beings both change and rest, being is identical with neither the one nor the other. *And yet the puzzle remains.* This is because the explanation must be sought elsewhere.

If we can see neither being nor non-being by whatever illumination is available, or if there is no light to be found, then we must "push our λόγος through both at once, in as auspicious a manner as possible" (251a1–4). One could almost imagine that the Stranger is alluding to the need to turn to linguistic distinctions in the absence of an intellectual perception of being and non-being. In part, at least, this is exactly what will happen, since there cannot be an intellectual perception of non-being that corresponds to the perception of being. There is, to be sure, a problem about how to talk about being, or so it is claimed by youths and those who come late to learning. The latter are puzzled by how we can call the same thing by many

---

7. In addition to what has already been said, cf. Owen (1971), p. 230, n. 16, and p. 261: the aporia at 250e1–2, it is generally agreed, "depends on confusing identity-statements with predications." This may be true in a sense of someone like Antisthenes, who is apparently alluded to but not named by the Stranger.

names, thus treating the same thing—for example, man—as both one and many (251a5–c7). In Aristotelian terminology, this is the problem of the difference between identity and predication. The Stranger, however, does not speak of predication, but of "naming" (ἐπονομάζοντες). When speaking of man, we attach to his (specific) name many additional names. The analogy with the problem of being is plain. When speaking of being, we attach to its name such additional names as "change" and "rest." If these were predicates, then being *would no longer be one* in the sense of a pure form. The analogy is faulty because man is *not* "one" in the same sense as being is one. If there is a form *man*, it cannot be intellectually perceived except as an internally articulated unity of properties (animal, good, and so on). Man is a one and a many that provides a basis for the subsequent development of the doctrine of predication. That the Stranger has nothing like this in mind with respect to being, change, and rest is obvious from his forthcoming introduction of the doctrine of greatest kinds.[8]

Since being (or *being*) has no internal articulation, we must distinguish the nature of man from the procedure of combining names. It is this procedure that actually plays a role in the following discussion. The Stranger says nothing more about man, but he takes up the theme of combination. We must now address certain questions to all those who have ever spoken about ousia (περὶ οὐσίας). The shift from τὸ ὄν to οὐσία is presumably explained by the fact that this was the operative term in the battle of the giants. When the Stranger comes to the "greatest kinds" or alphabet of eidetic letters, he will shift back again to τὸ ὄν in referring to the form *being*. Nevertheless, it must be noted that the use of οὐσία here tends to weaken the distinction between references to "the whole" and to the formal element. It cannot erase that distinction, but it is a sign of how Plato's fluctuating terminology makes it next to impossible to arrive at noncontroversial accounts of the stages in the Stranger's presentation.

Here are the questions. Shall we "concatenate" or "combine" (προσάπτωμεν) ousia with neither change nor rest, nor anything with anything at all, but assume in our discussions that they are all nonmingling (ἄμεικτα) and incapable of sharing (μεταλαμβάνειν) with one another? Shall we gather all things together (συναγάγωμεν) on the assumption that they can all communicate with (ἐπικοινωνεῖν) each other? Or finally, can some things communicate, and others

8. Cf. Lafrance (1979), p. 33.

not? (251c8–e1). Two remarks about the wording of these questions are in order. First, whereas the Stranger alludes to our λόγοι about these combinations, what we are discussing is the combinations themselves, not how we speak about those combinations. We are not discussing predicates, and not even names, but what will shortly be identified as "greatest kinds." Second, the Stranger uses several verbs to express the notion of concatenation or combination. He does not define this notion, and the multiplicity of verbs reflects its primitive status in his presentation. Entirely out of the question is the view that "combining" or "having a share in" replaces being as an independent property. Being is one of the properties that combines or shares in change and rest, yet without losing its independent and unarticulated unity. If there is no combination at all, then it is certainly true that change and rest will have no share in ousia (οὐδαμῇ μεθέξετον οὐσίας; 251e7–10).

If there is no combination at all, then all ontologies are overthrown at once. In other words, one cannot say that "things" (τὰ ὄντα) are changing, or that they are at rest, because such claims attribute to being (τὸ γε εἶναι) a combinatory role with respect to change and rest themselves, not just to the names "change," "rest," and "is." Remember that, for the Stranger, names are themselves things (252a1–d1). As is plain enough throughout this passage, the denial of combination cannot be rejected solely on linguistic grounds, but the suppression of discourse can be attributed to the suppression of communion in things themselves.

Two possibilities remain. Suppose that all things have the power to combine with each other. Theaetetus is able to refute this supposition; it would allow change itself (κίνησίς γε αὐτὴ) and rest itself (στάσις . . . αὐτή) to be, respectively, altogether at rest and altogether changing, "if these two could come together with each other," as is impossible "by the greatest necessities" (252d2–11). Again, Theaetetus's terminology makes plain that he is referring, not to predicates, but to what the Stranger will shortly call forms. This leaves only the third possibility. Some things will mingle (συμμείγνυσθηι) and others will not (252e1–8). We will consider this more closely in the next scene.

The Eidetic Alphabet

(252e9–255c7)

The Stranger is about to present the critical stage in his doctrine of formal combination. I have argued that we cannot understand his doctrine if we approach it with contemporary solutions to what seem to be analogous problems. The fact is that what is for us problematic is the Stranger's starting point. Without in any sense denying the ambiguity of experience, the Stranger nevertheless takes his bearings by the looks of things. With all due caution, we may suggest that the Stranger is an "empiricist" in a sense that is no longer possible for the post-Kantian epoch. For us, the prescientific, everyday world is already a paradox. On the one hand, it is this world that science is intended to explain; on the other, the everyday world is regarded as already a theoretical construction. The Stranger, to be sure, has among his theoretical possessions what might be called today a scientific ontology, but this ontology is rooted in the phenomena: in what shows itself as it is. It is not simply an affectation of archaism to insist that what we call "forms" are for the Stranger looks. One could object that a "look" is visible only to a looker, and so that the term expresses the implicit perspectivism of Plato's "phenomenology." But this objection misses the point. In the doctrine of forms, the human perspective is defined by the looks of things. Form is the shape of visibility, not the consequence of a rule or an analytical procedure. Forms cannot be "interpreted" to be other than as they show themselves, because they are the presuppositions and the elementary constituents of all interpretations. We can, then, speak of a "theory" of forms only if we use the word "theory" in its classical sense of "gazing upon" or "looking at." The elaborate theoretical (in the modern sense of the term) reconstructions of "Plato's theory of ideas" or forms, to be found in the secondary literature, have no counterpart in the Platonic text. Their diversity and complexity are responses to the admitted silence of the text; they are too frequently signs of exasperation and a will to resolve what was for Plato not a problem by means which apply, if at all, only to the consequences of our initial perception of the looks of things.

The Stranger never raises a problem in connection with the visibility of the "greatest kinds." On the contrary: he turns to them, with no protest from Theaetetus, as the basis for resolving the problem of non-being, and hence of the sophist. Non-being and the sophist are problems precisely because they have no forms. I mean by this that there is a discrepancy between what they look like initially and what we see upon closer inspection. They are images, and worse yet, fantasms. In slightly different terms, they are images of invisible originals. This should be plain enough in the case of non-being, but it is also true of the sophist. The sophist is a fantasm, not merely of the philosopher, but of the wise man. In order to define the sophist, we must know the nature of philosophy; and this requires us to be wise.

I suggest that, for the Stranger, there are two "roots" of human wisdom: the "looks" or formal elements of the self-differentiating unity of phenomena, and the perceptible distinction between freedom and nobility, on the one hand, and slavery and baseness, on the other. The sophist attempts to deny both of these roots. This denial is not itself rooted in the claim to be a genuine practitioner of some art or science about which the sophist is in fact ignorant. Neither does the sophist claim to teach the art of persuading us that what seems (correctly) to be changing is "actually" resting. The thrust of the sophistical claim to wisdom is with respect to the very point for which the Stranger praises philosophy most highly: freedom. The sophist claims to teach the art that sets us free, not of change and rest, but of other men's interpretations of the significance of changing and resting things. In this sense, the sophist is concerned, not with the division of like from like, but of better from worse. The Stranger gives an extreme formulation to the sophist's disinterest in the classification of like and like: he claims that the sophist denies the distinction between originals and images. On this count, the sophist accepts the fundamental axiom of modern philosophy, as formulated by Fichte: freedom is higher than being. The sophist, of course, is no Fichtean. Freedom is for him the satisfaction of desire and the possession of the good things of this world. It is primarily political, and it equates itself with mastery. Nevertheless, the sophist denies the relevance, if not the existence, of all ostensibly objective formal structures that interfere with the satisfaction of desire by means of persuasion.

Whatever may be the defects of sophistry, this should not blind us to the strategy of the Stranger's attempt to trap it in the net of his pejorative definition. The Stranger intends to establish the "being" of ontological originals. To some extent, of course, he will do so by inspection of how we talk. But linguistic analysis is everywhere subordinate to the apprehension of the forms that make discourse possible. In slightly different terms, to the extent that the Stranger is a philosopher of language, his interest is primarily semantics, not syntax. If the forms are to be described in terms borrowed from the philosophy of language, they are meanings, not predicates, intensional and not extensional entities.[1] With respect to the task of refuting the sophist, there is a fundamental defect in the Stranger's strategy. Even if he should succeed in "persuading" us of the truth of his doctrine of forms, he would remain open to the charge that he is himself the most powerful of sophists. Forms are not deduced from prior and better-known premises. They are themselves, so to speak, the "premises" of all the Stranger's deductions. If there is in any sense a "proof" for the truth of the doctrine of forms, it can only be in the comprehensive account of human life that this doctrine makes possible. But we compare accounts of human life, not with respect to the distinction of like from like, and hence not with respect to forms like the "greatest kinds," but with respect to the distinction between better and worse. And there is no directly accessible original or form of the good life.

This, I believe, is the background against which to understand the otherwise puzzling nature of the Stranger's route toward the elusive sophist. In oversimplified terminology, it is in the Stranger's interest to treat sophistry as a logical or ontological rather than as a moral or political problem. I would not deny that sophistical teachings give rise to logical and ontological problems. My point is that the ultimate quarrel between philosophy and sophistry, as both these activities are presented throughout the Platonic dialogues, lies elsewhere, namely, at the level of the distinction between the better and the worse. At this level, however, there is no technical refutation of sophistry. If it were not for the pejorative connotations that have attached themselves to the term, I would say that there is only a rhetorical refutation of sophistry, because the only persons who stand in need of such a refutation are those who cannot perceive the better and the worse in the looks of things.

The preceding remarks were intended to reestablish the continuity between the themes of the first half of the dialogue and those

---

1. Cf. Kahn (1973), p. 173: "Form is the sense of a predicate adjective."

of the scenes we are now studying. Non-being is deeply puzzling because it "shows" itself, like the sophist, in a variety of looks, and indeed, everywhere. It is a radical oversimplification of the puzzle to present it as one of pure forms and their combinations. Yet showing that no form corresponds to non-being (except in a derivative sense rooted in syntax) does nothing to explain the power of non-being, or if the reader prefers, of nothing, in the interstices of the looks of everyday life. Even at the logical level, it could be shown that the difference between one look and another cannot be accounted for on the basis of a formal explanation of negation. Nor does such an explanation cast any light on the peculiar "being" of icons and fantasms. Finally and comprehensively, one does not diminish the status of logic in any way, but arrives at an elementary degree of clarity, when one says that the problem of life is not a logical problem. However fastidious we may be in our obedience to the laws of logic, human life remains suffused with, and continues to be dissolved by, nothingness. This is not an appeal to pathos or melodrama, but a request for thinking. What good is life, or what does it mean to distinguish between a good and a bad life, if each life is an "original" because there are no images in the absence of *the* original?

To come back to the text, the Stranger has just established, with Theaetetus's assent, that if things do not combine at all, then there can be no discourse, sophistical or otherwise. The same result follows from the thesis that all things combine. We are left with the necessary truth of the third possibility: some things combine, and some do not. It is at this stage that the Stranger introduces the paradigm of the alphabet, of which some letters combine and others do not. A preliminary reflection on the nature of an alphabet is now in order. An alphabet is a finite set of sounds, represented more or less arbitrarily by symbols called "letters," sufficient in number and nature to permit us to construct names for the discernible looks of our experience. An immediate peculiarity of the Stranger's paradigm comes to view. Alphabets, and hence letters, are in one sense natural, and in another, conventional. They are natural in the sense that speech is a human faculty, but they are conventional in the sense that human beings articulate the sound continuum in different ways. The Stranger does not make this point in so many words, but it is clear that he wishes to make use of the natural aspect of alphabets, not their conventional aspect. Variations in the names of letters attributed to the same sound (for example, "ell," "lambda," "lamed") or in the exact phonetic quality of the letters so named, if they figure at all in the unstated background of the Stranger's paradigm, must correspond to contingent and readily distinguishable variations in the manner of presentation of formal elements to different individuals or groups of human beings.

In other words, the analogy between the forms and the letters presupposes that there are natural sounds or letters underlying their conventional or contingent representation in this or that alphabet. Second, it presupposes that the relation of the letters to one another within the alphabet is analogous to that of the forms within the visible cosmos or whole. But this is not true. Forms are always and everywhere "actual" (to use an Aristotelian term), whereas the letters must in fact be spoken or written or thought in order to actualize. An alphabet is a power to produce letters, not the produced letters. And even more important, to produce the letters is not to relate them in a way that spells words; the forms, on the contrary, are actual *as* visible in their combinations and separations. The rules governing the combination of letters into words cannot be derived from the alphabet alone; without those rules, there are no words, but (at most) only letters. In the whole, however, the "letters" (that is, the forms) are present *as* combined into words, and indeed, into every possible word, regardless of whether anyone is looking at it.

These simple observations are enough to put us on our guard against the deceptive aspects of the alphabet paradigm. Instead of pursuing this point, let us rather ask ourselves: Why does the Stranger make use of such a paradigm? In what way is it illuminating at the present juncture? I think that the answer to this question is straightforward. Letters are the simplest elements of intelligible language. Once we have combined letters into words, we can then construct sentences with which to describe the properties of the letters themselves. But these properties depend upon the antecedent simplicity and accessibility of the letters. The words and sentences which describe the letters are themselves composed of those letters. Furthermore, words are formed by the "concatenation" or combination of letters, and *not* by "predicating" one letter of another. The combination of "a" with "n" to produce the English word "an" does not change the atomic nature of "a" or "n," whatever modifications are produced in the sounds as voiced by human beings. Besides, such modifications are again not like predication, but rather like blending. If they are to play a role in the Stranger's analogy, then the integrity of the letters is compromised by their participation within "words" or intelligible, and nameable, structures. The model of predication is wrong here because the predicated property becomes a constituent within the structure of the subject. The suggestion of blending is either also wrong or else destructive of the Stranger's point, because elements that blend together undergo a partial or total dissolution. In the case of predication, the defect is complexity of structure. In the case of blending, the defect is dissolution of identity.

These considerations suggest that the relevant feature of the alphabet paradigm is thus spelling, a procedure in which letters combine to produce intelligible structure without either dissolving or impinging upon the integrity of their fellows. Thus, when the Stranger says, after noting that some letters fit together and others do not, that the vowels run through the others like a bond, he should be taken rather literally. A bond joins things together but does not enter into their internal natures or forms. Without a vowel, it is impossible for the other letters to fit together with each other to form syllables and words (252e9–253a7). But the vowel does not become a "predicate" of the letter with which it joins in order to form a syllable or word. We assume that being, sameness, and otherness at least are vowels, and this assumption illuminates another defect of the alphabet paradigm. Every syllable (and hence every word) must have at least one vowel, and it can have no more than one vowel in some cases. In the case of the cosmos or whole, however, the "vowels" being, sameness, and otherness must be present in every syllable and word.

I have already mentioned that the ontological "words" are all written out or "actual" within the cosmos. How then do we pick out in each case exactly those combinations and separations which are pertinent to our analysis of a given "word"? The inner complexity of the formal "code" is one thing; its phenomenological visibility is something else again. Let me take an example from the contemporary domain. The process known as "Gödel numbering" is an exact, well-defined method for moving from a string of symbols to a string of numbers, and vice versa. But this method proceeds by means of mathematical functions that must be applied in a step-by-step manner. The Gödel number of a well-formed formula does not exhibit that formula immediately to the eye of the mathematical logician. In the case of the pertinent combinations of formal letters, however, the connections must be finally accessible to direct inspection. The analysis of statements is not analogous to the operation with mathematical functions in order to retrieve a formula from a numerical code. Discursive analysis as practiced by the Stranger rather exemplifies, and is in turn carried out with an eye to, how the forms combine, as visible to the "mind's eye." The Stranger says that the art of grammar is required in order to know which letters combine and which do not (253a8–12), but he never says that an art is required in order to discern the letters themselves. There is thus a gap between the theory of spelling and the perception of already spelled words. We cannot apply the rules of spelling to completed words until we *see* or *hear* how the word is spelled. The paradigm of spelling, like that of music, to which we are about to turn, thus exhibits this dependence of discursive knowledge upon perception, whether sensuous or intellectual.

The Stranger's language throughout, then, sustains the thesis that we "see" or perceive intellectually the forms and their combinations. *This is the natural basis for the subsequent discovery of the rules by which elements are combined.* If there were no such perception, there would be no ἐπιστήμη, but only νόμος. In the words of an earlier passage, recourse to an exclusively linguistic analysis is recourse to "force" and is recommended only if "we are unable to see" being and non-being (ἐὰν αὖ μηδέτερον ἰδεῖν δυνώμεθα; 251a1). When the Stranger assumes that Theaetetus regards being as some third thing besides change and rest "in the soul" (ἐν τῇ ψυχῇ τιθείς; 250b7), it is to intellectual perception that he refers. This can be confirmed by reference to a parallel passage in the *Theaetetus*. Socrates and Theaetetus establish a distinction between what the soul perceives (αἰσθάνομαι) by way of bodily organs and what it views (ἐπισκοπεῖν) entirely by itself (αὐτὴ δι' αὐτῆς). Theaetetus assigns being (τὴν οὐσίαν), likeness and unlikeness, sameness and otherness, beautiful, ugly, good, and bad to the class of things "the ousia of which the soul views" (σκοπεῖσθαι τὴν οὐσίαν) by itself (185c4–e2). This passage, incidentally, shows us that Socrates' "opinions" are not totally different from those of the Stranger. Nevertheless, Socrates does not develop his opinions into a positive doctrine purporting to be λόγος in the sense of ἐπιστήμη. This apart, in the *Theaetetus* (to which I shall return shortly) as in the *Sophist*, the primary elements of things must be "viewed" (or heard) because they possess no internal structure to be exhibited in discursive imagery. Where there is nothing to be viewed, then we must shift to linguistic analysis. And even in this case, the Stranger attempts to explain "nothing" by way of the "not" of *otherness*, which is itself directly visible.

The paradigm of the alphabet is followed by that of music (253b1ff). In the case of high and low sounds, says the Stranger, it is the art of music that tells us which may be "mingled together" (τοὺς συγκεραννυμένους) and which may not. The verb used here could convey the notion of "blending together" liquids like wine and water, rather than discrete and stable elements. Whereas this slight difference between the spelling paradigm and that of music cannot be entirely overlooked, I do not believe that it illuminates the Stranger's intent. In order to show this, I must look first at the entire text from this point to 262, and then at some passages from other dialogues which illustrate the role of music in Plato. I will then return briefly to the question of "flowing together" suggested by music.

A study of the verbs employed by the Stranger throughout his discussion of the "greatest" or "most important kinds" shows that he makes no explicit distinction between "harmonizing" and "combining," on the one hand, and "mingling" and "sharing," on the other. What gives a unified sense to these verbs is the paradigmatic operation, illustrated by the models of spelling and music, and captured in the ultimate expression συμπλοκὴ εἰδῶν. To begin with a marginal, but not irrelevant consideration, the Stranger uses "mingle" (κεράσῃ) at 262c5 to refer to the combining of nouns and verbs. The Stranger certainly does not mean to say that nouns and verbs "blend together" like water and wine. But he might conceivably have in mind a uniting of the linguistic elements of a statement in something like the sense captured by the concept of predication. Whether or not this is so is debatable. The Stranger refers throughout this subsequent discussion to the combining of names (nouns and verbs), not to predication. In that combination, the names retain their integrity.

The main point, however, is this. The general theme of the discussion from 252b1 to 261c10 is that of the combinations and separations of the elements (στοιχεῖα; 252b3) or forms of the intelligible world. This "ontological" structure is the condition for the possibility of intelligible discourse. The Stranger makes it quite clear that he is not primarily concerned with discourse from 252 to 261. At 261d–3 he says: "Come then, just as we spoke about forms and letters" (περὶ τῶν εἰδῶν καὶ τῶν γραμμάτων), "let us in turn investigate names in the same way" (περὶ τῶν ὀνομάτων πάλιν ὡσαύτως ἐπισκεψώμεθα). By linking forms with letters here, the Stranger indicates that he makes no fundamental distinction between γράμματα and musical sounds (τοὺς φθόγγους; 253b1). Both fulfil the same paradigmatic role. As we shall see in a moment, this is in accord with general Greek practice, as well as with Plato's procedure elsewhere.

Toward the end of the discussion we are now studying, the Stranger can summarize his thesis as follows: "The attempt to separate everything from everything is above all out of tune and in every way the mark of someone who is unmusical and unphilosophical" (ἄλλως τε οὐκ ἐμμελὲς καὶ δὴ καὶ παντάπασιν ἀμούσου τινὸς καὶ ἀφιλοσόφου; 259d9–e2). This musical idiom thus resumes the series of equivalences from 252 between verbs like συμφωνεῖν (253b11) and συμμείγνυσθαι (253c2); κοινωνεῖν (254b8–d2) and μείγνυμι (254d7–255a2); and μετέχειν and κοινωνεῖν (255b1–256b9). Μέθεξις and κοινωνία are interchanged in 256a10–b9; the Stranger returns to μετέχειν at 256d8 and e3 and summarizes with κοινωνία at 257a9. There is also an equivalence between συμμείγνυσθαι (259a4), μετέχειν (259a6–8), and μεταλαμβάνειν (259b1); and finally between the noun συμπλοκή (259e6) and the verb μείγνυσθαι (260a3).

Let me repeat the general point. The paradigms of spelling and music are intended to illustrate a single process by which formal elements (στοιχεῖα) combine in intelligible structures. Despite the use of a variety of verbs with differing senses in ordinary language, there is *one* process here, not several. This process is not, and cannot be, the grammatical function of predication. To the contrary, predication is possible only because of formal combination and separation. As the Stranger puts it in the previously cited passage at 260a5, this is why λόγος is one of the kinds of beings (τῶν ὄντων ἕν τι γενῶν). Our object has been to show this, and not that being is one of the kinds of discourse. The failure to keep this in mind leads to efforts to distinguish the senses of "is" in this stretch of the text, on the unexamined assumption that the Stranger is developing a linguistic doctrine of predication.

To come back more directly to the "elements" or (to use the Stranger's regular terms) kinds or forms, I have argued that the main purpose of the spelling paradigm is to show the pure or "atomic" nature of the "letter" in the formal alphabet. Exactly the same result follows from the paradigm of music. Plato, like the Greeks in general, regularly associates the arts of music and letters.[2] In the *Theaetetus*, 205a4ff, Socrates and Theaetetus are discussing the indivisibility and hence the discursive inaccessibility of primitive elements (τῶν πρώτων οὐκ εἴη λόγος ἐξ ὧν τἆλλα σύγκειται, διότι αὐτὸ καθ' αὑτὸ ἕκαστον εἴη ἀσύνθετον; 205c5–7. The word for "elements" throughout the passage is στοιχεῖα; see 205b10, 205b12, 205d7, 205e3, 205e7, and passim). Letters provide us with the initial

2. Cf. the quotation from Bekker, Anecdota III, p. 1168, cited by Koller (1955), p. 171: ὅτι δὲ ποιητικοῦ τινὸς ἀνδρὸς καὶ μουσικοῦ ἡ τῶν στοιχείων εὕρεσις ἦν, σημεῖον τὸ πάλαι τοὺς αὐτούς εἶναι διδασκάλους καὶ μουσικῆς καὶ γραμματικῆς. I want to acknowledge here the assistance of David Lachterman, who criticized an earlier treatment of the music paradigm and pointed me in the right direction.

example of elements which are "single in form and indivisible" (μονοειδές τε καὶ ἀμέριστον; 205d1–2). Socrates shifts smoothly from letters to music (206a10), and he makes the same point about its elements (στοιχεῖα; 206b2): in this case, the notes or musical sounds (τῷ φθόγγῳ ἑκάστῳ; 206b1).

Socrates argues that the elements are known more clearly than the compounds (πολὺ τὸ τῶν στοιχείων γένος ἐναργεστέραν τε τὴν γνῶσιν ἔχειν φήσομεν καὶ κυριωτέραν τῆς συλλαβῆς; 206b5–8). This prepares the way for a definition of λόγος as a "description of" or "passage through" each thing by way of its elements (207c6–7), which is in turn exchanged for another: the ability to express the mark by which a thing differs from everything else (208c7–8). This definition, in turn, also fails.

For our present purposes, the failure of the definition via elements is, as it were, a success. Spelling and music illustrate the *perception* of indivisible elements, which elements provide the basis for, but are not themselves amenable to, discursive analysis. To this we can add a further point. Music provides us with an even better paradigm for formal combination than does spelling. For, on the Greek view, obviously shared by Plato, whereas music is rooted in the perception of distinct ("pure" or "monoeidetic") sounds, the intervals, and so the distinctions between and combinations of musical sounds into scales, are mathematically regulated by nature. This can be illustrated by comparing *Philebus* 17c4–e6 with Aristoxenus's *Elements of Harmony* (Ἁρμονικὰ Στοιχεῖα), as well as with the views on music attributed to Adrastus, a fifth-century peripatician, by Theon Smyrnaeus.[3]

In the Greek view, music originates in the natural sounds emitted by the human voice.[4] Thus too Aristoxenus: "Each of the scales when sung is positioned in a certain region of the voice (I.7.10). The ratios of the sounds or tones are fixed by nature, not by chance (φυσικὴν γὰρ δή τινά φαμεν ἡμεῖς τὴν φωνὴν κίνησιν κινεῖσθαι καὶ οὐχ ὡς ἔτυχε διάστημα τιθέναι; II.32.15ff). So the dependence of the musician upon precision of hearing, whereas it distinguishes him from the geometer (II.33.15), does not alter the indivisibility and stability of his elements. In singing, the voice moves from one stationary point to an-

---

3. For Aristoxenus, see Macran (1902); for Theon, Koller (1955).
4. The Stranger refers to the voice as a ῥεῦμα through the lips at *Sophist* 263e7–8, as does Socrates (using ῥοή) at *Theaetetus* 206d3–4; cf. *Philebus* 17a6, 17b3–4. This helps to explain συγκεραννυμένους at *Sophist* 253b2. The flow is articulated into elements which are then "blended" into a συμφωνία within which each preserves its individual nature.

other (thus establishing intervals between fixed notes; I.9.12ff). "The more we make each of the sounds one, stable, and the same, so much the more does the melody appear to be correct to perception" (I.10.2ff). As has been shown in detail in studies by H. Koller (1955) and J. Lohmann (1970), the Greeks linked tones, letters, and numbers together as indivisible elements.[5] Thus, for example, in the views attributed by Theon to Adrastus, letters (γράμματα) and musical tones (φθόγγαι) are both called φωναί ... πρῶται καὶ ἀδιαίρετοι καὶ στοιχειώδεις.[6] The basis in hearing is thus evidently taken as analogous to the basis of pure colors in sight. But the musical relations of sounds are not only natural; they are also mathematical.

Despite the distinction in the *Philebus* (56c4ff) between the musical, or less accurate, and the arithmetical arts, and despite Socrates' criticism of the acoustically oriented Pythagorean musicians in the *Republic* (VII, 530d6ff), Plato is obviously aware of, and relies upon, the mathematical nature of empirical music. In an earlier passage in the *Philebus*, Socrates emphasizes that one cannot be a technically competent musician simply by being able to distinguish (acoustically) the high, low, and intermediate sounds. One must go on to grasp the intervals and their combinations in scales, which were "seen" (intellectually, κατιδόντες) or discovered and taught to us by our predecessors. One must also grasp the corresponding bodily rhythms which are measured by numbers (δι' ἀριθμῶν μετρηθέντα). Socrates thus seems to be exaggerating somewhat in Republic VII when he condemns those Pythagoreans who measure "heard harmonies and tones" (τὰς γὰρ ἀκουομένας αὖ συμφωνίας καὶ φθόγγους; 531a1–2). A fairer way to put the point is that, whereas "theoretical" music is always mathematical, there is a firm basis in heard music for the ascent to the pure harmonies of numbers, as Socrates' own words indicate at 531c1–4.[7] So too in the *Sophist*, dialectic, the ἐπιστήμη of free men (253e7ff), is like γραμματική and μουσική in that it perceives the combination and separation of pure, indivisible, monoeidetic elements.

On the basis of the evidence which has been summarized in the

5. Koller (1955), pp. 161–62, 166–67 (where rhythm is associated with letters and tones); Lohmann (1970), p. 10. Lohmann gives an elaborate arithmetical account of the "circle" of scales constituting Greek musical theory. Burkert (1959) denies Koller's thesis that στοιχεῖον is derived from music, and argues that it was originally a mathematical term. However, this point in no way affects the sense of στοιχεῖον in Plato, or its use in the musical paradigm. As to the difference between the paradigms of music and spelling, I address this point in the text.

6. Koller (1955), p. 167.

7. On this point, cf. Barker (1978), pp. 337, 341.

preceding paragraphs, and which could easily be extended (as for example by an analysis of *Timaeus* 36a1ff), I feel confident in supporting the view that the paradigm of music in the *Sophist*, although stated with extreme brevity, is intended by the Stranger to fulfil the same function as the paradigm of the alphabet. In fact, given the conventional character of spelling, music provides, if anything, an even better paradigm of the combination of atomic elements. However, whereas this is the major conclusion of the present discussion of music, it is not the last word. I turn now to the qualification, not of the Stranger's intention, but of the theoretical implications of his paradigm of musical "blending," which arise from the difference between empirical or heard and theoretical music. So far as the sources and the testimony of the experts go, the situation is extremely complex. I shall be as brief as possible.

To begin with, there can be no reasonable doubt that Plato, in a wide range of passages, is fundamentally concerned with theoretical as opposed to heard (or "unphilosophical" and inexact) music. The previous results concerning the indivisible formal elements are therefore secure. But what of heard music? Is there not a blending together of notes which, if not quite like the mingling of water and wine, nevertheless renders it either difficult or impossible for the auditor to distinguish aurally the individual notes? On this point, so far as I have been able to determine, the evidence is ambiguous. I shall restrict myself to citing three specialists on Greek music. Speaking of Greek melody, J. Lohmann says that the tones are inserted into the melody "in an abstract combination of functions," which establishes διαφωνία or difference between one tone and another. This, says Lohmann, is the contrasting concept to sameness of tone (ὁμότονον). One should not follow the Latin translators in rendering "difference" as "dissonance": "The contrasting concept σύμφωνον expresses that these differences come together once more into unities in definite situations."[8] Our second specialist is H. S. Macran, editor and translator of Aristoxenus. In commenting on a fragment from Gaudentius that deals with concords (σύμφωνοι) and discords (διάφωνοι), Macran says: "The language is certainly not happy; but I think the sense is clear enough. If two sounds are discordant, when they are sounded together, the particular character of each will stand out unreconciled against the other; that is, the relation of the higher to the lower or of the lower to the higher will not be one of identity in which differences are sunk. On the other

8. Lohmann (1970), p. 21.

hand, when concordant sounds are heard together, the resulting impression is that of the reconciliation of differences, the merging of particular natures in an identical whole."[9] Substantially the same point is made by A. Barker in a recent (1981) article on passages from Aristotle dealing with the perception of musical ratios.[10]

Is the unity of the concord acoustically perceived as a single note "repeated at different heights of pitch," in Macran's phrase? Or does the quotation from Theo of Smyrna cited by Macran on page 236, in which a definition of Adrastus is reported, support a different interpretation? "Notes are in concord with one another when upon the one being struck upon a stringed instrument, the other sounds along with it by affinity and sympathy [καὶ ὁ λοιπὸς κατά τινα οἰκειότητα καὶ συμπάθειαν συνηχῆ]; and when the two being struck simultaneously one hears, in consequence of the blending [ἐκ τῆς κράσεως], a smooth and sweet sound." For my purposes, the following cautious inference will suffice. As is apparent from Aristotle's *De Sensu*, 7, 448a9ff, as well as from the definition attributed to Adrastus, musical concord arises from the simultaneous striking of more than one note. The ensuing unity is thus a "blending" of a sort that, so far as the ear is concerned, dissolves the differences between the constituent tones. It thus renders indistinguishable to the ear their individual "forms," or sounds. But even if we restrict ourselves to melodies consisting of individual notes struck successively, the ear must be able to perceive that, say, the voice of the singer is striking the same note as is being played by the instrumental accompanist. And so too with the notes sung by individual members of a chorus: these must also be "blended" into one.

In all of these senses, "blending" takes us a step away, albeit acoustically rather than theoretically, from a dialectic of mono-eidetic elements toward a dialectic in which, as in modern music, we can no longer readily perceive the distinctness of the elements within chords. To this extent, and when considered in themselves rather than in the context of the Stranger's (and Plato's) intentions, there is a slight difference between the paradigms of spelling and of music. Again, without attributing this thesis to the Stranger, we are entitled to wonder whether, whereas *being* does not "blend" with *change* and *rest*, if there is a form corresponding to, say, human being, it does not blend with the form corresponding to, say, animal. In other words, whatever may be true of the eidetic letters of the pres-

9. Macran (1902), pp. 235f.
10. Barker (1981), p. 260.

ent section, the term "form" (or "idea") is used in a variety of senses in the Platonic dialogues. There is no reason to assume that all of these senses are of indivisible elements, elements which cannot "participate" within one another's structure. I want to emphasize that to grant this possibility is one thing; to find an explanation in Plato of intereidetic participation is something else again. Furthermore, whereas we require knowledge of the rules in order to know how to combine, to blend, or even to predicate, no rules are required in order to be pleased or pained by various combinations of sound. Even, then, if it were true, as the Stranger holds, that the role of art is the same in all cases (253b5–7), the relationship between art and nature cannot be held static by an insistence upon the naturalness of a given set of technical rules. Plato's main characters in general attempt to block technical progress, or at least change, by an appeal to nature. But the nature of art is not amenable to this attempt: hence the conflict between acquisition and production.

What then are we to say about the knowledge required to show which kinds (or pure forms) will combine and which will not? One thing we shall not say, or so I will argue, is that this knowledge is diaeresis, in the sense illustrated by the definitions of the angler and the sophist. Does this science proceed διὰ τῶν λόγων (253b10)? We can answer provisionally that it is possible to state discursively which of the forms "harmonize" (συμφωνεῖ; 253b11) with which, once we have perceived these harmonies. The same holds good for the separations among the forms (253c1–3). Theaetetus agrees that knowledge of combination and separation must be a science, and perhaps the greatest of sciences. The Stranger responds: "What shall we call it, Theaetetus? Or by Zeus! Have we stumbled unwittingly upon the science of free men and, although we were looking for the sophist, happened first to have found the philosopher?" Theaetetus does not understand (253c6–10). The Stranger explains: "Shall we not say that division in accordance with kinds [τὸ κατὰ γένη διαιρεῖσθαι], and never taking the same form to be another, nor another to be the same, is part of the science of dialectic [τῆς διαλεκτικῆς . . . ἐπιστήμης]?" Theaetetus agrees (253d1–4).

The question naturally arises whether the science of dialectic is the same as the method of diaeresis. There is reason to doubt this identification.[11] In the first place, the Stranger never identifies the two procedures. The surprise with which he notes their unexpected discovery could be taken as a sign that dialectic is a distinct enter-

11. For a different route to the same conclusion, cf. Gomez-Lobo (1977).

prise. Second, diaeresis was called a method of hunting at 218d2ff and 235c4ff, but not a science. Third, the various divisions of the sophist violate the principle just stated of not taking the same form as another. Perhaps the use of the partitive genitive in the passage defining dialectic is intended to suggest that the method of diaeresis, when applied to appropriate subject matter, is a part of dialectic. However, even if we are intended to identify the two methods, two further points must be kept in mind. First, the application of the method depends upon the antecedent perception of the kinds by which one divides and collects. Second, we have apparently stumbled upon the science of the *free man*. The Stranger does not discuss the connection between dialectic and freedom. To give only one example of the issues this connection would raise, if virtue is knowledge, in what sense is being virtuous an epistemic activity? In terms of the present discussion, knowledge of the "look" of the sophist, as obtained by diaeresis, cannot be the same as the rejection of the sophistical life, or the judgment that it is worse than the life of philosophy. If dialectic is the comprehensive science of the free man, then it must combine the criteria of like and like and of better and worse.

There follows an extremely difficult passage which has been subjected to much scrutiny and has given rise to conflicting interpretations.[12] The reason for this is plain; the Stranger is describing the science of dialectic, and one wishes to understand him on this crucial point as exactly as possible. Here, however, as in the case of Socrates' accounts of the ideas, one runs the risk of overinterpretation. It can hardly be an accident that Plato, who writes with such lucidity and in such detail on lesser issues, expresses himself as obscurely as possible on the two crucial issues of the ideas and the nature of dialectic. But even if it is an accident, the fact remains. The Stranger apparently distinguishes four aspects to the science of dialectic. I shall consider them in order.

1. Whoever is able to engage in dialectic perceives adequately as extended everywhere throughout many (πάντῃ διατεταμένην ἱκανῶς διαισθάνεται) one form through many (μίαν ἰδέαν διὰ πολλῶν), each of which lies apart (ἑνὸς ἑκάστου κειμένου χωρίς); that is, each form is an independent letter in the eidetic alphabet (253d5–7). We note once more that the dialectician *perceives* these forms; nothing is said here of a procedure of linguistic analysis, not, perhaps, because none takes place, but because it is altogether secondary to noetic

12. Cf. Meinhardt (1968), pp. 37–88, and Wiehl (1967), p. 196, n. 98.

perception.[13] Second, the statement implies that what the dialectician sees is a single form combining with many other single forms.
His attention is directed toward what is presumably a "vowel" like
being, sameness, or *otherness.*

2. The dialectician also perceives adequately "many forms differing from each other, and surrounded by one from outside" (253d7–
8). Here the attention is directed toward the many distinct forms
which are united by a single form, again presumably a "vowel" (in
the somewhat inaccurate sense of the analogy with the alphabet).
The phrase "from outside" (ἔξωθεν) I take to mean that the "surrounding" or "uniting" form retains its independent identity. It does
not enter into the natures of the forms with which it combines, as
would be the case with properties designated by predicates.

3. Again, the dialectician perceives adequately "one joined together through many wholes into unity" (253d8–9). This apparently
refers to the combining of many unified multiplicities into a larger
whole, that is, the combining of multiplicities described in aspect 2.

4. Finally, the dialectician perceives adequately "many forms apart
and altogether separate" (πολλὰς χωρὶς πάντη διωρισμένης; 253d9).
Here, individual forms are perceived as individuals, hence not as
entering into some combination or other.

What can be said of an indisputable nature by way of summarizing
these four aspects? Dialectic is the *perception* of combining forms
(vowels), of distinct forms combined into a unity, of combinations
of such unities, and of individual forms as separate or distinct "letters." On the basis of 253b8ff, we can say that the dialectician proceeds "by reasoning" (διὰ τῶν λόγων). It is not explicitly stated,
however, that this "reasoning," whatever it is, precedes, and is the
condition for, the perception of forms as distinct and combined. No
doubt the two procedures are themselves combined. One cannot divide and collect without a standard, and this standard cannot itself
be acquired solely by dividing and collecting. Conversely, it is not
enough to perceive the standard; one must also "show correctly"
(ὀρθῶς . . . δείξειν) the perceived combinations and separations. And
this "showing" takes place through discourse or λόγος. The Stranger
does not tell us what he means by λόγος. Strictly speaking, then, he
does not describe the method of dialectic, but only what it does, its
results.

This reticence leaves considerable room for the speculations of

13. Cf. Manasse (1937), p. 48; Marten (1965), pp. 41. n. 39; 43–44; 220.

the interpreter. I prefer not to read my speculations into the text, because I see no secure basis for a detailed positive account of what is here meant by "dialectic." It is anything but plain that dialectic is the same as the method of diaeresis. Our study of the *Philebus* shows us that Socrates' description of dialectic as "eidetic counting" has no counterpart in the Stranger's description. For example, we are not told here to start with complexes and divide them into their distinct levels of formal constituents. One could say that the *Philebus* passage is not incompatible with the *Sophist* passage, but no more than this. Finally, if we compare the Stranger's account with Socrates' discussion of dialectic in the *Republic*, there is again no secure basis for taking the two versions of dialectic as the same and considerable reason for emphasizing their differences. I will mention only a few points here. In the *Republic*, dialectic is closely linked to the idea of the good, which provides a dimension of nobility or excellence to the ideas. The pure noetic vision of the good is said to serve as the paradigm for the just city (VII, 540a4ff). This suggests that, in the *Republic*, the ideas are ordered hierarchically, to exemplify the ranking of the sciences, arts, and activities of the citizens. No such reference to a "normative" hierarchy is present in the *Sophist*. Finally, Socrates speaks of dialectic as a kind of deduction by means of ideas alone, without icons or hypotheses (VII, 533a1ff), that is, as a deduction that "discharges its premises" by rising above the sensuous objects from which it starts and providing definitions of each being entirely through the use of ideas.

I shall not engage in a detailed study of the account of dialectic in the *Republic* for a previously stated reason. There is general agreement that this account is quite different from the Stranger's, although the reasons given for this difference are varied. One general conclusion seems to be uncontroversial. Nowhere in the dialogues does Plato give a detailed, nonmetaphorical account of dialectic as the central method of philosophy. To this, I add the following (to my mind critical) point: such descriptions of dialectic as we have, despite all references to λόγος, counting, and the exhibition of modes of combination and separation, place the main emphasis upon the intellectual perception of forms. There is no reason to accept the widespread view that, in his later dialogues, Plato drops this emphasis in favor of a type of linguistic analysis comparable to that employed by modern analytical philosophers. This is of course not to say that there are no "analytical" elements in Plato's dialogues. Neither is it to overlook the reliance upon intellectual perception in such analytical thinkers as Frege and the early Wittgenstein, with whom perhaps Plato, taken as a philosophical analyst, has the most in common.[14]

For whatever the reasons, Socrates' refusal to provide Glaucon with a literal and extensive account of dialectic in the *Republic* is the rule, not the exception, in the dialogues.[15] The Eleatic Stranger, following the passages just studied, summarizes the case as follows. Dialectic is "knowledge through discrimination of kinds, of the degree to which each is able to combine and to which it is not" (253d8–e2). Theaetetus agrees to this, as well as to the Stranger's assertion that we cannot attribute the dialectical skill to anyone but the man who philosophizes "purely and justly" (καθαρῶς τε καὶ δικαίως; 253e3–7). On this nonmethodological point, the Stranger is in complete agreement with the Socrates of the *Republic*. The free life requires not merely dialectic, but its pure and just employment. This passage strengthens our inference from the Stranger's remark at 246d7 that agreement by better men is more authoritative than agreement by worse men. In this sense, the distinction between the philosopher and the sophist is one of character. It is no doubt also plausible to suppose that sophists cannot practice dialectic; but even if they could, this would not suffice to make them philosophers.

As though in acknowledgment of the vagueness with which he has described the science of the free man, the Stranger says that now and later we will find the philosopher "in some such place," if we look for him. What we have stumbled upon is the region inhabited by the philosopher, who is hard to see clearly, even if his obscurity differs from the obscurity of the sophist. "The sophist runs away into the darkness of non-being, feeling his way by routine (τριβῇ), and he is hard to perceive (κατανοῆσαι) because of the darkness of the place" (253e8–254a3). As usual, the emphasis is upon the intellectual perception or identification of the sophist, as a living being, and not simply upon the construction of a definition. The philosopher is hard to see because he "always devotes himself through calculative thinking to the look of being" (τῇ τοῦ ὄντος ἀεὶ διὰ λογισμῶν προσκείμενος ἰδέᾳ). The philosopher cannot rest content with the looks of things (note the shift back from οὐσία to τὸ ὄν in conjunction with λογισμός). He cannot merely look, but must also "count" or explain to himself and to others what he has seen. However, thanks to the shining light of the region (of being), the philos-

14. For an extended discussion, see Rosen (1980).
15. Cf. *Republic* VII, 507a1ff, 509c7–10, 533a1ff.

opher is in no way easy to see: "The eyes of the souls of the many are unable to bear steadfastly the vision of the divine" (254a4–b1).

This passage thus confirms the importance of the theme of disguises introduced in the prologue by Socrates. The sketchiness of the Stranger's account of dialectic is presumably connected to the difficulty of perceiving the philosopher. It looks as though Theaetetus stands to the Stranger very much as did Glaucon to Socrates, at least on this crucial point. Whether or not Theaetetus is to be counted among the many, he is conducted to a definition of the sophist, but not to a definition of the philosopher. The Stranger's suggestion that perhaps we will look for the philosopher later, and with additional clarity, if we should still wish to do so, is never carried out (254b3–6).

Instead of pursuing the philosopher, the Stranger proceeds to the introduction of certain forms, called by him "most important" or "greatest," and thereby to the theme of combination and separation. Let me begin with a remark about terminology. In the stretch of text from 251d5 to the present point, there are (if I have counted correctly) twenty-one references to formal combination.[16] The Stranger uses fourteen different words (some of them differing only by a prefix) to designate this combination. Of these, seven are verbs or nouns which carry the sense of "communion" *qua* fellowship. The second most frequently used expression is that of "mingling." Also employed is "harmony" or "vocal agreement." The central theme of these passages is thus one of a community of equals. The term μέθεξις, normally translated "participation" or "sharing in," appears once, although it is implied in verbs or nouns for "mingling" and it appears regularly in the subsequent discussion of the alphabet of pure forms. I have already pointed out that the Stranger uses two distinct paradigms, those of spelling and musical composition, as though they were the same. If one form "mingles with" or "shares in" another, then the integrity of each distinct form is violated.

Presumably the use of expressions for "sharing in" is one of the principal pieces of evidence that contributes to the popularity of the "predicationalist" interpretation of the "greatest kinds." I grant, and in fact emphasize, the ambiguity in the Stranger's terminology. However, I continue to think that his intention is to use the paradigm of mingling as though it exhibits the same formal relation as the paradigm of spelling. This is certainly the manner in which he conducts his exposition, and, as I have argued and will argue further,

16. 251d5, e8, e9; 252a9, b1, b3, b6, d2, d7, e2; 253a2, a6, a8, b2, b9, b11, c2, e1; 254b7–c5.

to take him in the sense of the "predicationalist" interpretation is to give primacy to the "mingling" paradigm, which leads to results exactly opposite to those demanded by the doctrine of pure forms. In brief, it leads to a dialectical logic, or one within which forms are "looks" of a self-differentiating totality, a totality within which each look is continuously being transformed into the others. This apart, the "predicationalist" doctrine is incoherent in its own right and leads to the suppression of the form *being*, or to its replacement by two senses of "is," namely, that of identity and that of predication. On this reading, "participation" or "sharing in" becomes the standard sense of all combination verbs, but at the price of dissolving the distinction between the relation of forms to one another, on the one hand, and between the forms *being* and *sameness*, on the other. I shall have more to say on this in what follows. Here I conclude that the Stranger's terminology is inconsistent, as to some extent are his paradigms. But this reflects an internal inconsistency in his doctrine, not an intention to develop an Aristotelian doctrine of predication. The internal inconsistency is that the pure forms are described, if they are to "mingle" or "have a share" in one another, as intrinsically distinct, yet cannot be so conceived or described.

The Stranger recommends that we conduct our discussion by means of the "greatest" forms, rather than by all of them, in order to avoid confusion (254c1–4). I wish to make two other points of terminology here. First, the Stranger uses the terms γένη and εἴδη interchangeably in this section. "Kinds" or "forms" are here the same. The second point concerns the word μέγιστα, which could be translated either as "greatest" or "most important." After considerable reflection, I have come to the conclusion that it makes no difference which of these translations we employ. The "importance" of the forms to be considered lies in the frequency of their appearance within combinations and separations. They are, however, hardly the "most important" or "greatest" in an exclusive sense; one might argue that terms like "one" and "many" stand on a par with the examples chosen by the Stranger.[17] But whether we choose "greatest" or "most important," it is essential to observe that the eidetic alphabet of these forms cannot possibly include all forms or formal combinations. To take the critical example, *if* there are forms corresponding to "flies" and "sits," these cannot plausibly be elements in the alphabet of greatest kinds. The members of the alphabet are all marked by extreme generality. They are the simplest constituents of intel-

17. Cf. *Parmenides* 136a4ff and *Theaetetus* 186a2ff.

ligibility. What flies is, is the same as itself, other than every other, and so on. Most seriously, it is an instance of change, and so, I would argue, cannot possibly be an independent formal element. The distinction between the greatest kinds and "forms" in other, derivative senses, will become critical when we shift to the analysis of false statements.

The Stranger informs Theaetetus that we must first consider "what sort" (ποῖα) each of these greatest kinds is. The Stranger seems to be inviting us to define the pervasive forms, but his procedure shows that this is not a correct assessment. The Stranger will answer this question merely by pronouncing a name with respect to each form. Our second task is to consider what power each of the most important forms has to commune with the others (ἔπειτα κοινωνίας ἀλλήλων πῶς ἔχει δυνάμεως; 254c4–5). The term "power" is used with as much plasticity in the Platonic dialogues as are terms like εἶδος and οὐσία. In the Sophist, there have been three principal uses assigned to δύναμις: at 219a4–7, to designate the primary subject of diaeresis; at 247d8ff, in the definition of "being" or "beings" (247d6, 247e3), attributed to the improved (247c3) materialists; and now here as before at 251e8 and 252d2, in expressions for the combination of forms. In the last three cases, the Stranger regularly joins δύναμις with κοινωνία or ἐπικοινωνία.

Nothing is said by the Stranger to suggest that these uses of δύναμις are synonymous. I myself believe it would be a mistake to attempt to force a univocity of sense onto these passages, comparable to the mistake committed by those who see a "unitary" or "average" conception of being in the Sophist. If it is correct, as I think, to maintain that Plato never reduces to unity the various senses of being in the Sophist and elsewhere, then it is reasonable to allow for a variety of kinds of power. This suggestion gains added weight when we recall the well-known fact that δύναμις and φύσις are often used interchangeably by Plato. Any attempt to find a link between the present use of δύναμις and the other two must begin by resolving the following problem. Is the "power" of combination resident within the forms or external to them? Neither alternative provides us with a satisfactory basis for explaining κοινωνία. As I have already noted, if the form is itself a power, it loses its "phenomenological" nature as a look; in addition, it is transformed into a dynamic process of "actualizing" a given look, rather than into a look which exerts and suffers, as in the definition of being at 247d8ff. If the power "belongs" to the form, this seems to compromise the elemental purity of each form. Differently stated, on this interpretation, there is an underlying and unifying force within each form that is other than the form *qua* look. But why does this force combine in some cases and separate in others? Once this question is thought through, I suspect, the result is neo-Platonism, perhaps via the way station of the divine demiurge of the *Timaeus*. And this result seems to follow even more speedily if the power is held to be external to the forms.

My best guess as to the Stranger's intention is this: "power" means "nature". The Stranger is saying only that some forms are capable of combining and others are not. These combinations and separations (which latter are themselves effected via combinations with *otherness*) articulate the structure of intelligibility, of which, when we turn to analytical thinking, only determinate segments are visible to each cognitively focussed view. To say this is not to rule out the possibility that the Stranger intends to be making an oblique comment on κοινωνία in his reference to the divine whole. However, we must be careful, in reflecting upon this possibility, not to confuse the divine οὐσία with the atomic τὸ ὄν of the μέγιστα γένη.

To come back to the Stranger's present investigation, we are now attempting to determine whether it is possible to talk about non-being "as though it is," even though it "genuinely is not" (ὄντως μὴ ὄν), without suffering any harm. As the Stranger rather modestly puts it, we may not be able to do this with full clarity, given the present mode of investigation (254c5–d3). This implies, like the previously cited remarks by Socrates to Glaucon, that on another more intimate occasion, the Stranger might speak more fully. After this qualification, the Stranger identifies *being, rest,* and *change* as "the greatest" of the forms with which we shall be concerned (254d4–6). The term "greatest" was used previously to refer to all the examples to be chosen. It is possible that this second use of μέγιστα means that *being, rest,* and *change* are the most important of the set of examples of "greatest" *qua* most pervasive forms. What we must emphasize, however, is not this but the fact that the three aforementioned forms are introduced by the Stranger, and accepted by Theaetetus, without any argument whatsoever. They have only to be mentioned, as it were, for us to see their importance. Nothing even remotely resembling diaeresis or (if it is distinct from diaeresis) dialectic is employed to establish the distinctness of these forms. Neither is there any elaborate analysis of the logical or ontological status of the forms under discussion. Finally, let us note that the Stranger uses τὸ ὄν, and never οὐσία, to refer to the eidetic letter *being*. The term οὐσία appeared last in the general discussion of being, change, and rest at 251c8–e9. It will occur next at 258b2, not

as the name of the letter *being*, but in order to emphasize that a part
of *otherness*, in antithesis to and in combination with *being*, "is"
genuinely.

The next conclusion has already been examined by us. *Change*
and *rest* do not mingle with one another, whereas *being* mingles
with both. We have therefore three distinct forms (254d7–13).[18]
Change and *rest* each "exist" or (better) "possess being," but we
cannot say "*change* is *rest*." Hence we must be able to say "*change*
is not *rest*," by which we mean that the two forms are distinct, are
not the same form. We are not denying that "*rest*" is a predicate of
change, in the statement's *grammatical* analysis. But grammatical
syntax is based upon ontological combination. However, let us not
get ahead of the Stranger's analysis. He goes on to say that of the
three forms, each is other than the other two but the same as itself.
He then asks whether *sameness* and *otherness* are two additional
forms, always mingled with the original three from necessity? Or
do the expressions "same" and "other" actually refer to one of the
original three forms without our noticing it? "Perhaps," replies
Theaetetus (254d14–255a3).

Why is Theaetetus in doubt here? His hesitation, I think, is far
from unreasonable. If "same" refers to a distinct form, namely,
sameness, then no other form, including *being*, is the same as itself
by virtue of its intrinsic nature. By insisting upon the distinctness
of *sameness* and *otherness* the Stranger implies, although he does
not state explicitly, that his greatest forms are not "things." They
are differing looks of things. In a thing, and by extension in a form
conceived as an independent thing, it would be impossible to distinguish between the "sameness" of the thing and its "thinghood" or
being. This is not an easy point to make, and no matter how it is
made, it contains a grave danger. The distinctness of the looks of
being and *sameness*, to stay with this example, seems to be reasonable only so long as we do nothing more than pronounce the names
of these elements. The moment we consider the nature of each element, however, it is no longer possible to keep the elements separate. Nothing can be said about *being*, beyond pronouncing its name,
without making use of the other pervasive kinds.

The Stranger goes on to convince Theaetetus that neither *rest* nor
change can be *otherness* or *sameness*. To give just one example, if
rest were *otherness*, then *change*, as other than *rest*, would in fact

---

18. Detel (1972), p. 79, distinguishes here between the senses of "is." His analysis
is substantially the same as that of Frede and Owen.

become *rest*. The other cases follow analogously. Hence, whatever form we say combines jointly with *rest* and *change* must be distinct from each (255a4–b7).[19] Theaetetus is again not sure whether *sameness* and *being* are two distinct forms or one. The Stranger convinces him that they are two forms by an argument parallel to the preceding one. *Rest, change,* and *sameness* each combine with *being*. If the names "being" and "same" do not refer to (σημαίνετον, "point out") distinct forms, then to say that "rest is" or that "change is" is to say that "rest is the same" or that "change is the same." In this way, the Stranger establishes that *sameness* is a fourth in the list of "greatest" kinds (255b8–c7). He is about to turn to *otherness*. In so doing, he will face squarely the problem of non-being.

---

19. The ὅτιπερ at 255a4 refers to a form, not to a "predicate" common to *change* and *rest*.

SCENE FIFTEEN

Non-Being

(255c8–259d5)

We have now distinguished four formal elements or greatest kinds. It is time to decide whether "otherness" is the name of a fifth such element, or whether "the other" and "being" are to be understood as two names for the same form (255c8–11). This brings us to the passage which was the starting point for Frede's study, part of which we analyzed in the previous scene: "I suppose you agree that among the beings [τῶν ὄντων], some are always spoken of with respect to themselves [τὰ μὲν αὐτὰ καθ' αὐτά] and some with respect to others [which are distinct from themselves, τὰ δὲ πρὸς ἄλλα]" (255c12–13). Before we interpret this statement, let us translate the rest of the Stranger's point. Having elicited Theaetetus's agreement to the previous remark, he continues: "The other is always with respect to another, is it not?" "Yes," Theaetetus agrees. "It would not be so, if *being* and *the other* were not altogether different" (εἰ γε τὸ ὄν καὶ τὸ θάτερον μὴ πάμπολυ διεφερέτην, 255d1–4). The same speech continues as follows: "for if 'other' shares in both these forms, as 'being' does, there would be a sort of 'other' among the others which is not relative to another" (ἀλλ' εἴπερ θάτερον ἀμφοῖν μετεῖχε τοῖν εἰδοῖν ὥσπερ τὸ ὄν, ἦν ἄν ποτέ τι καὶ τῶν ἑτέρων ἕτερον οὐ πρὸς ἕτερον; 255d4–6).

The expression "shares in both these forms" in 255d4–6 refers to the pure forms *being* and *otherness*. But the "other" (θάτερον) of which the counterfactual speaks is an instance of a member of a pair of existing things considered as other than its partner. This "other" is not the form, which could not be taken as sharing in itself (and similarly with the "being" in ὥσπερ τὸ ὄν). The Stranger says that the situation described in 255d1 would not be so unless *being* and *otherness* were distinct forms. We can then reconstruct the meaning of 255d1 as follows. The look "other" is explained exclu-

269

sively by the form *otherness*, and not by the form *being*. This is because instances of *being* can be said to be αὐτὰ καθ' αὑτά, in the expression of 255c12–13. Contrary to the Frede-Owen hypothesis, the entire passage is confirming the view that "*a* exists," where "exists" means "possesses being," is a complete statement. However, "*a* is other" (where "is" is not taken as the existential sign, but as a superfluous particle belonging to "other," which could be rewritten "others") is not a complete expression. This is because instances of *otherness* are among those beings which are always spoken of πρὸς ἄλλα. To be "other" is necessarily to be other than something else.

Two further points should be made about this passage. First, as has been regularly observed, the Stranger shifts from speaking about a pure form to speaking about its "image" or exemplification in "beings" or "things" without explicitly distinguishing between the two. He does this because, by his own doctrine, there is no genuine distinction between them. Thus 255d1 can be taken to refer either to properties or to forms without any change in the meaning of the passage as a whole. There is no reason to supply λέγεσθαι in the passage, as Frede does, by importing it from 255c12–13. For purposes of clarity, I have placed 'other' and 'being' in single quotes in translating 255d4–6, simply to indicate that these function as names of images or forms. The Stranger is constructing a contrary-to-fact conditional as part of his argument that *otherness* and *being* are distinct forms. The "doubling" of *otherness* is required in order to show that the property corresponds to just one form, namely, *otherness* (and not also to *being*). Second, we cannot infer from the fact that we "speak about" beings that the form properties of beings are predicates. The grammatical analysis of "*a* changes" or "*a* is other than *b*," for example, must distinguish whether *a* and *b* stand for pure forms or "beings" in the sense of instances of forms. In the latter case, each instance will necessarily participate in several forms, since, to mention only the "most important" examples, whatever exists as an individual in the sensuous world must be, be the same as itself, and be other than every other. Finally, there is no doctrine of predication in Plato, and certainly none in the middle section of the *Sophist*. The controlling metaphor is that of combination, of "being-there-together."[1]

The conclusion to the speech we have been analyzing is as fol-

---

1. Cf. Gadamer (1980), p. 148: "Plato's *logos* is not Aristotelian predication. Here no specific *hypokeimenon* is presupposed to which a determination is added as a predicative attribute. On the contrary, in Plato the *logos* is thought of essentially as a being-there-together, the being of one idea 'with' another."

lows: "As it is, it is unqualifiedly the case for us that whatever is other is necessarily this specific nature with respect to another" (νῦν δὲ ἀτεχνῶς ἡμῖν ὅτιπερ ἂν ἕτερον ᾖ, συμβέβηκεν ἐξ ἀνάγκης ἑτέρου τοῦτο ὅπερ ἐστὶν εἶναι; 255d6–7). There is exactly one form of otherness. But the look of otherness is "double" in the sense that it cannot show itself in less than two things, whether these be forms or instances of formal combinations. The duality of otherness is thus intrinsic to the form qua look. This is not true of being, change, and rest. The statements "a is," "a changes," and "a rests," however odd they may look, are all complete or well-formed expressions when they refer to the combination of a form with, or the participation of an instance in, a distinct form. But "a is other" (or "a others") is not. This is surely what the Stranger intends to say. One might quarrel with him on a number of points. For example, why should we not argue that the property of "othering" is as complete as the property of changing, resting, or even existing? Or again, is not "othering" a version of changing? To say that what changes does so in a given respect while retaining its identity is to say that what changes also combines with, or better, participates in, the form sameness. But the changing qua changing is necessarily "othering" (in normal English, becoming other). So at least it could be said.

In order to understand the Stranger's position with respect to otherness, we must remember that he is on the way to a resolution of the problem of non-being. It will be part of his resolution not to hypostatize "not"; that is, he will deny that "being" (or being) has a contrary (or "opposite"). In one sense, then, "not" must be explained as a syntactical particle to which no form corresponds. But in another sense, this is impossible, since the Stranger requires forms to provide meaning. The semantic force of "not" will thus be derived by him from otherness. Despite the assurances of some scholars to the contrary, the Stranger does have a "complete" use of "is," as I have now explained at length. This use cannot be negated; at least, the Stranger never deals with this problem. He never deals with nonexistent "things" because (to put the point somewhat awkwardly) for him, there are no such things. I am not contending that he would not understand statements like "Socrates does not exist." The absence of such statements follows from his primary concern with "exists" in the sense of "possesses being" or "combines with being." But the analysis of statements like "Socrates does not exist" would present grave problems for the Stranger. This is because he wants to explain "not" by way of a form. The form he chooses is otherness. So "not to be" means for him "not to be F," where ultimately F is a form or combination of forms (in the case of instances). But "not to be F" must in turn mean "to be G," where G is ultimately a form, or formal combination, entirely distinct from F. If Socrates does not exist, then he does not participate in the form *being*. In this case, however, he participates in no forms at all. He is not "other than" an instance of *being*. The doctrine of forms provides no basis for explaining the meaning of the statement "Socrates does not exist." Nor, for that matter, does the meaning of "Socrates is dead" spring readily to the eye, given the Stranger's doctrine.

In sum: since we wish to avoid speaking of nonexistent things, or to put it positively, since anything at all combines with or participates in *being*, "not" must be explained by means of the available network of pure forms. The obvious choice is *otherness*. "Not to be this" is instead "to be that." Hence *otherness* must be a double look, or what would today be called a two-place relation. This conclusion gives rise in turn to a second question: What about *sameness*? Contrary to the contemporary procedure, the Stranger takes "sameness" as a complete look. This is misunderstood by those who replace "sameness" by "identity" and explain that, in turn, as one sense of "is." As I have shown in detail, this destroys the distinction between the two forms *being* and *sameness*. When the Stranger says that each form is the same as itself, he is in fact denying that form F is "related" to any other form, *qua* same; hence his insistence that *sameness* and *otherness* are two distinct forms. If *sameness* were a two-place relation, it would contain *otherness* in its intrinsic nature; and this would violate the separateness of the two forms. The Stranger sees no need to consider "sameness" as a reflexive relation (for example, as "$F = F$"); we may infer that this would introduce duality from his standpoint. However we might analyze it, the expression αὐτὸ δ' ἑαυτῷ ταὐτόν (254d13) is for the Stranger a way of saying that the form *sameness* is a distinct form, which provides a distinct look, and which is complete in itself. That is, "*a* is the same" is a complete expression, whereas "*a* is other" is not.

This same point bears upon the expression αὐτὰ καθ' αὑτά in 255c12–13. Can we not follow Owen here and take it to be referring to the "identity" use of "is," as in "A is A"? To do so is to take "same," as Owen puts it, "as a grammatically incomplete predicate."[2] However, there are no passages in the text of the *Sophist* in which "same" is said to be an incomplete predicate. The only expression of which this could possibly be said is "other" or (in

2. Owen (1971), pp. 256–57.

Owen's translation) "different." I will not repeat all the reasons I have given for the impermissibility of reducing *being* to the copula and the "is" in "is identical to." Nevertheless, there is a real problem here, and one which no doubt encouraged Owen (and Frede, who with some variations follows him on this point) in his interpretation.[3] The problem lies in the Stranger's use of "same" in what appear to be two distinct senses. Sometimes he uses it as a reflexive pronoun, in speaking of things or forms apart from other things or forms. But at other times he uses it to refer to the property or form *sameness*. It is, I think, clear that the Stranger has the following distinction in mind. Let us restrict ourselves to forms for the sake of simplicity. The form *being* stands apart from every other form. As so standing apart (namely, as *being* and nothing else), it is "*being* itself." However, as not merely standing apart, but as "the same as itself," it combines with *sameness*. I think that this is an error on the Stranger's part. One cannot think or speak of the property supplied by *being*, except as *that same property*, the "property" or "form itself." This becomes clear from the Stranger's attempt to refer to forms "in themselves" and yet as independent of the form *sameness*. The fact is that the Stranger's doctrine breaks down at this point. It cannot be rescued by the importation of the "identity-predication" distinction. This importation leads to a new doctrine, not to the correct formulation of the Stranger's doctrine.

In Frede's version of this argument, to speak of a form αὐτὸ καθ' αὑτό is to say, not that it "exists" (combines with *being*), but that "form X is x," where "___ is x" serves to designate the essence of the form. According to Frede, x thus designates the same property, whether it is applied to a form or to the individual x's. I think this expresses a sound insight; it is developed by Frede into an argument against the charge of self-predication.[4] But the insight is contained within an erroneous interpretation of the formal combinations as

---

3. Frede (1967), pp. 29ff.
4. Ibid., p. 33. For an excellent rebuttal of the charge that Plato is guilty of the fallacy of self-predication, cf. Marten (1967), e.g., p. 218. Speaking of the statement that the idea of the great is itself great, Marten says: "Das synthetische Verhältnis der Prädikation ist bei Platon im Horizont von Teilhabe, Gemeinschaft, und Anwesenheit zu suchen. Um eine Selbstprädikation ausdrücklich zu machen, hätte Platon etwa formulieren müssen: Die Grösse 'selbst' hat an sich selber Anteil, steht mit sich selbst in Gemeinschaft, ist sich selber gegenwärtig. Dergleichen Wendungen finden sich nicht." [The synthetic relation of predication is to be sought in Plato in the horizon of sharing, community, and presence. In order to make an explicit self-predication, Plato would have had to say something like this: Greatness "itself" shares in itself, stands with itself in community, is present to itself. Such expressions are not to be found.]

predications. The Stranger never says that "form X is x." Further-more, forms do not possess "essences." If we are going to use this Aristotelian word, let us say that they *are* essences, or better, na-tures. The decisive objection to Frede's interpretation is that, like Owen's, it is misled by the Stranger's erroneous distinction be-tween the reflexive pronoun and the form *sameness*, as well as by the genuine insight that "*a* is" is an incomplete expression when used in any other sense than "combines with" (or "participates in") the form *being*. Frede's interpretation fails to make clear how "_____ is x" could be neither a case of self-predication nor the expression of a predicate distinct from the form X. It amounts to the subsump-tion of αὐτὸ καθ᾽ αὐτό cases under πρὸς ἄλλο cases, in which, for "x is y," we let x equal y. This in turn is based upon the modern anal-ysis of identity, which is not to be found in Plato's text.[5] It cannot be an accident that Frede, in presenting his argument for the intro-duction of "is$_1$" in the sense just explained, introduces no evidence from Plato, but cites Aristotle three times.[6]

For the Stranger, then, the form *otherness* serves to detach or dis-tinguish one form from another. He does not explain exactly how *otherness* is itself "other" than the remaining forms, any more than he explains how *being* possesses being or *sameness* sameness. To this we may add that *otherness* exhibits a nature or power that is reminiscent of the image. If *otherness* is other than the other forms by virtue of itself, and if "other" is a two-place relation, then *oth-erness*, as a unique and separate form, is intrinsically related to some distinct, separate form. As itself, *otherness* is also not itself. Its look is blurred. It seems to possess non-being within itself in a way that is not explicable as due to combination with itself.

Theaetetus, however, raises none of the above objections. And so the Stranger concludes that "the nature of otherness" (τὴν θατέρου φύσιν) is a fifth among the forms and "penetrates" all of them; "for each one is other than the rest not through its own nature, but by sharing in the look of *otherness*" (διὰ τὸ μετέχειν τῆς ἰδέας τῆς θατέρου; 255d9–e7).

The Stranger is now ready to state certain conclusions about the five forms thus far distinguished. The first of these has been dis-cussed before, since it is regularly cited and subjected to conflicting analyses by those who assert or deny that the Stranger employs "is" in an existential sense.[7] The passage runs from 255e11 to 256a1. We

5. Frede (1967), pp. 31–32, 35, and especially 58.
6. Ibid., pp. 31–33. Cf. Seligman (1974), p. 79.
7. For a defense of that thesis, cf. Ackrill (1971) and my discussion in the Prologue.

have agreed that change "is altogether other than *rest*" (. . . κίνησιν, ὡς ἔστι παντάπασιν ἕτερον στάσεως). Hence, "it is not *rest*" (οὐ στάσις ἄρ' ἐστίν), "But it 'exists' by sharing in *being*" ("Εστι δέ γε διὰ τὸ μετέχειν τοῦ ὄντος).

According to Owen, what is traditionally translated as "change exists" or "change is" is either elliptical for "change is with respect to something" or fragmentary for "change is different from rest."[8] Frede presents an extremely complicated analysis, employing numerous other passages, based upon the presupposition that "change is" cannot be allowed to stand, inasmuch as, for Plato, "*a* is" must always be completed as "*a* is *b*," where *b* may be the same as *a*, or the "essence" of *a*, where *a* is a form. I have already pointed out that Frede is right in those cases where *a* is a sensuous individual or instance of a formal structure, but not itself a form. In the present case, however, a different analysis is required. I would agree in part with Frede's view that "change is" means that *change* (in my notation) "shares in" *being* (*das Seiende*). That is to say, whereas this cannot be understood as a predication, and certainly not as an identity, it is not semantically exact to see the statement as "existential" in the usual sense of that term. However, Frede is prevented from accepting the sound translation "*change* shares in *being*" because he takes the "is" in "change is" to be a copula, instead of the Stranger's expression for "shares in *being*." In other words, the "is" in the literal statement is for Frede the sign of "shares in," and hence may mean that, in his terminology, the form *change* has the essential property "change."[9] But this cannot be correct, since, as I have already shown, it assimilates the *relation* between forms into the form *being*. But κοινωνία, μέθεξις, and so on, are not synonyms for *being*. There is unquestionably a problem here about the exact sense of formal combination, communion, or sharing. That problem is not resolved, however, by suppressing the independence of the relation from its relata.

Frede thus arrives at the following interpretation of 255e11–256a1: (1) *Change* is different from *rest*; therefore, (2) *change* is not, namely *rest*; and (3) *change* is, namely different.[10] The Stranger does not say that "*change* is different," however; nor could he, even on the Frede-Owen hypothesis, for *change* is not identical with "difference" or (as I call it) *otherness*. Hence "is different" must itself be completed by another term, for it is a "two-place predicate." Are we to assume

8. Owen (1971), pp. 254–55.
9. Frede (1967), pp. 45, 55–56.
10. Ibid., p. 56.

that the Stranger has merely repeated in step 3 in a cryptic form what he already stated fully in step 1? This labored analysis is in fact entirely unnecessary. It is also impossible, since it both suppresses *being* and leaves us with an incomplete predication. The correct analysis is the obvious one: the Stranger expresses himself, not elliptically, but exactly, when he says that *change* "is, through sharing in *being*." In the phrase "change is," "is" is not a copula, but the name of *being*. The phrase "through sharing in *being*" explains the sense of "is" in the preceding phrase. One may therefore conclude that "change is" is a well-formed expression, but that it is not an "existential" statement in the usual sense of that term.

We may now proceed to the remainder of the Stranger's conclusions.

In the section from 256a2 to 256a9, there are three sentences to be translated and interpreted. The first is: Αὖθις δὴ πάλιν ἡ κίνησις ἕτερον ταὐτοῦ ἐστιν. The Stranger wants to distinguish between *change* and *sameness* (and so the second sentence reads οὐ ταὐτὸν ἄρα ἐστίν). This distinction can be made because *change* shares in (combines with) *otherness* "with respect to" *sameness*. (I shall comment on the phrase "with respect to" shortly.) However, this distinction does not alter the fact that *change* is "the same" by sharing in *sameness*, as do all things (Ἀλλὰ μὴν αὕτη γ'ἦν ταὐτὸν διὰ τὸ μετέχειν αὖ παντ' αὐτοῦ). This passage contains difficulties which we have seen previously. The second of the three Greek sentences exhibits very clearly a feature of all three, namely, that there is a tacit reference throughout to *being*. The form *change* must combine, not merely with *otherness*, but with *being*, in order to be separated from *sameness*. This is the semantical "deep structure" of the sentence "then it is not the same," where "it" refers back to *change*. This sentence is certainly ambiguous; but the Stranger is not negating an existential "is," as some would have it. By his own fuller analysis, the "not" here refers to *otherness*. Furthermore, the "is" could not here be understood either as identity or as predication. *Change* is not identical with *sameness*, nor does it admit, as a form, of the property "change." A denial of identity takes place, as indicated, via *otherness*. As for a "negative predication," to say that a form does not have a property is just to say that it does not combine with the form responsible for that property, but tht it does combine with *being*. The "is" in "then it is not the same" cannot be assimilated into, or taken as, the copula of predication, because then there would be no reference to *being* as independent of the relation covering the pertinent forms. Finally and conclusively, if "same" were

NON-BEING 277

a predicate, then it would be false to say that "change is not the same," since the form *change* is the same as itself.

There is, however, a more serious difficulty in this passage. In the third sentence, the Stranger uses the pronoun αὕτη to refer back to ἡ κίνησις, or *change*, which, he says, is "the same" (ταὐτόν) because it, like everything, shares in "sameness" (αὐτοῦ refers back to ταὐτόν). The problem is this: if *change* is not "itself" independently of *sameness*, then it will not be an independent form capable of combining with *sameness*. But if it is "itself" independently of *sameness*, what does it gain by so combining? The Stranger might reply that there is no "prior" and "posterior" in the world of forms, and that the "selfhood" of *change* is precisely the result of its eternal combination with *sameness*. But if these combinations are eternal, what sense does it make to speak of the forms as independent? Furthermore, if this combination is eternal, then all of them must be.

I want to put this complex point as simply as possible. The nature of each form, as well as our ability to refer to its combinations, and hence to carry out rational discourse of any kind, depends upon its positions within what will later be called the "web of forms." On the other hand, the visibility or discursive accessibility of each form as "itself" depends upon our capacity to pick it out from its various positions within the web. This in turn requires us to say that we can see the pertinent relation binding each form to the others. We must be able to refer to each form "with respect to" each of the others. How is this possible?[11] If all combinations are eternal, that is, simultaneously present, then the combination of one form "with respect to" another particular form is not the same as the global relation of combination. The answer cannot be that we arrive in each case at the appropriate relation by analysis. This is because the analysis itself depends upon our apprehension of the relations in question. The Stranger's entire presentation makes this last point clear. No "analysis" takes place; instead, assertions are made about forms "with respect to" one another, and Theaetetus agrees in all the appropriate places, with a minimum of explanation. To judge by some of the secondary literature, the Stranger would have to be in

11. Van Frassen (1969), pp. 490ff, speaks of a different problem, namely, what it means to say that an individual participates or does not participate, in a form by virtue of what it is or is not. He seems to conflate the combination of forms with the participation of instances in forms. Nevertheless, the expression "in virtue of," when taken to apply to forms, is the same as my expression "with respect to." The sense of this expression is not explained by formal combination.

the process of instructing Theaetetus in advanced set theory. Instead, he simply calls Theaetetus's attention to the pertinent relations.[12] But if we are supposed to understand him to mean that we arrive in each case at the pertinent relation by way of discursive analysis (just as we arrive at the correct spelling of a word by following a "rule"), what is the distinction between the discursive analysis and the form(s)? If the forms are actualized by discursive analysis, then they are not forms but "possibilities." In this case, what is the standard for recognizing that we have actualized a genuine possibility? What counts as "genuine" here, *other than the discursive analysis*?

The Stranger's third conclusion is that *change* "is and is not" the same, but in two different senses. When we say that *change* "is the same," we do so because of its sharing in *sameness* with respect to itself (διὰ τὴν μέθεξιν ταὐτοῦ πρὸς ἑαυτήν). When we say that it "is not the same," we do so through its communion with *otherness*, by which it is separated from *sameness* and made, not that, but other (256a10–b5). I can be very brief here, as no new problems arise in the present conclusion. The expression "change is the same" appears only in indirect discourse. Again we have to distinguish between its grammatical form and its semantical analysis. Grammatically, it is a well-formed expression as the Stranger uses or conceives of it. Nevertheless, in analyzing it, the Stranger has to say that *change* is "the same as" itself. This in turn means that the form *change* combines with the form *sameness* "with respect to" itself, and so gives rise to the problems discussed above. The solution is not to take "the same as" as a two-place relation, because the property of selfhood must be furnished directly by *sameness*. Hence "itself" is an ambiguous amalgam of *change* and *sameness*. In other words, "*change* is identical to *change*" is an incomplete analysis of the sense of the original, a fact concealed by the shift from "the same as" to "is identical with." The "is" in "is identical with" must tacitly refer to the form *being*; it cannot be a copulative particle of the identity expression.

The Stranger then makes a fourth conclusion: if "*change* itself" (αὐτὴ κίνησις) partook somehow of *rest*, there would be nothing odd in saying that it was at rest (256b6–c3). This passage provides us

---

12. Owen (1971), p. 238, n. 31, makes in passing a closely related point when he observes that "difference from" is not a rule of verification, since if it were, this "would make falsification an interminable business." Cf. p. 245, n. 42. Owen, however, raises no question about how we see, in any given case, that X is different from Y; i.e., how we distinguish this from all the other relations into which X and Y enter.

with an excellent example of the problem of "same" and "self." The Stranger wants to talk about *change*, not about *change* as combined with *sameness*. He could, of course, have left out αὐτή in this particular instance. But by using it, he shows us the nature of the problem: a pure form cannot even be pure unless it is itself, apart from other forms and even the form *sameness*. However, the passage has stimulated discussion for a different reason. The Stranger cannot be referring here to changing things. He must presumably mean that the form *change*, as a distinct and independent form, is "resting," or remaining the same as itself, and in that sense one might be able to say that it partakes "somehow" (πη) of *rest*. If this is what he means, the assertion is still puzzling, since it amounts to a blending either of *rest* and *sameness* or of *change* and *rest*.

Consequently *change* is other than *otherness*, *sameness*, and *rest*. So it is in a way not other and other (256c5–10). We should pause for a moment over the expression ἕτερον τοῦ ἑτέρου, "other than *otherness*." What is the semantic analysis of this expression? To be "other" than form *F* is to combine with *otherness* with respect to *F*. But if *F* is *otherness* "itself" (not to repeat that puzzle), how can a distinct form, say *G*, combine with *otherness* except with respect to a third form *H*, distinct from *F* and *G*? If *otherness* is a two-place relation, which we may represent as 0 (*x,y*), surely we cannot allow one of the variables to be replaced by *otherness* itself? A relation cannot be one of its relata.

In conclusion six, the Stranger shows that we must fearlessly insist that *change* is also other than *being*. Hence *change* "is not" *being* and "is" *being* (256c11–d10). In other words, *change* combines with *otherness* with respect to *being*; yet it must simultaneously combine with *being* "with respect to" itself.

It is therefore necessary, according to the seventh conclusion, that non-being "is" (τὸ μὴ ὄν . . . εἶναι) "with respect to" (ἐπί) *change* and all the kinds. "For the nature of *otherness* works" (ἡ θατέρου φύσις ἀπεργαζομένη) "in all of them to make each other than *being*, hence" to make them "not being" (or "not to be a thing"; οὐκ ὄν). "Thus we may correctly say that all of them are not" (that is, are not things; οὐκ ὄντα) "in the same ways" (κατὰ ταὐτά); "and again, since they share in *being* [τοῦ ὄντος], that they possess being and are [εἶναι τε καὶ ὄντα]" (246d11–e4).

All the aforementioned difficulties in the Stranger's conclusions coalesce in this climactic assertion about non-being. Non-being "is" because it is the work of *otherness*. Incidentally, the verb "works" may possibly be connected with the previous definition of οὐσία as "power." If this is so, then φύσις is equivalent at 256e1 to δύναμις. Hence, when we say that one form "shares in" another, perhaps we should be understood as saying that the power of one form shares in the power of another, thanks to the relation of combination (in which what "works" or exercises power remains independent). This gives rise to other problems, such as that of the inner complexity of forms. A form cannot be a power, as I noted previously. A look, and the power of a look, are two distinct features of a complex entity. Second, I used the term "things" in my translation to bring out the fact that the Stranger "reifies" being to the extent that he considers it as a form.[13] These points apart, then, to say that a form "is not" is to say that it combines with *otherness* "with respect to" *being*, something which it can do precisely because it combines with *being* "with respect to" itself. And this is in turn an abbreviation for the fuller point, namely, that each form "is not" any of the others (not just *being*), thanks to the same combinations. Again, the expression "in the same ways" (κατὰ ταὐτά) applies the property of sameness in a very obscure way. The Stranger means that form *F* is not form *G* thanks to form *otherness* (and in the background, *being* and *sameness*, to mention just these two). So "the same" here refers to the combination of each form with *otherness*. In each case we have the same combination. Are these to be counted as instances of sameness contributed by the form *sameness*? This would seem to blur the distinction between forms and combinations (that is, between relations and relata).

Perhaps I should make one very brief additional point here, in order to avoid compromising an earlier conclusion. The expression "form *F* is" is complete in a sense that the expression "form *F* is not" is not complete. We can restate the former, albeit awkwardly in English, as "form *F* be's" (and so, "form *F* exists"). But we certainly cannot paraphrase "form *F* is not" in such a way as to obtain a sense, except by adding at least one form: "form *F* is not form *G*."

And so the Stranger has come at last to non-being. He is about to explain the sense of "non" by translating it into the quite distinct expression "is other than," where "is," we must remember, plays two roles. First, it refers to *being* as the tacit but necessary element in all formal combinations. Second, "is other than" must be replaced by "combines with *otherness*." To that extent, we may accept the contention that "is" does in certain contexts play the role

---

13. Cf. Manasse (1937), pp. 20, 37, 52, 56. The logicizing of the ideas (as Manasse puts it) carries with it the consequence that they are no longer prior to all analysis, and more important, to all combination.

of "combines with" or "shares in." But in this sense, it is not a name of *being*. Whether in Greek or in English, "is" plays a variety of roles, and it is certainly the task of the philosopher to sort these out and to keep their senses distinct from one another. When I deny that ontological combination is predication, I am certainly not suggesting that the only sense of "is" is ontological. I am instead distinguishing between the syntactical "is" as it appears in expressions like "form *F* is other than form *G*" and the ontological "is" that is a name for *being*. In grammatical terms, this is tantamount to defending the "traditional" view that, in the *Sophist*, "is" has three senses: identifying, predicative, and existential. However, I would add a fourth sense, which signals formal combination.

We may now continue with the Stranger's account of non-being. "With respect to each of the forms, *being* is many, whereas non-being is boundless in amount." Theaetetus agrees (256e5–7). There has been some controversy about the Stranger's meaning. I take him to be saying that there are a finite number of relations between *being* and the other forms, since the elements in an ontological alphabet must themselves be finite in number. On the other hand, non-being is not a genuine form; not all instances of non-being can be explained as instances of otherness. There is thus no way in which to count its "relations" to the forms. He goes on to remind us that *being* is other than all others (τῶν ἄλλων; 257a1–3). Given the context, "others" presumably refers to the other forms. The Stranger then adds: "*Being* is not in the same amount that the others are; for not being these, it is itself one, and the number of the others is not boundless" (257a4–7). Again, I take "these" and "the others" to refer to forms. The unity of *being* depends upon its independence from the other forms, which are of a finite number. Strictly speaking, each instance of non-being at the level of forms must be an instance of being. This consideration could lead us to suppose that the Stranger is referring to boundless "predicates" of a subject being.[14] Interpretations of this sort, however, take us away from the level of the greatest kinds, and in addition raise the problems which beset the "identity-predication" reading. I think it is simpler and more in harmony with the text to take "non-being" here in an informal sense, as a pseudoform, and so as unable to "bind together" its own instances.

The Stranger, after encouraging Theaetetus to persevere in this consequence of the communion (κοινωνίαν) of forms, then brings

14. Owen (1971), p. 254. Crombie (1963), p. 508, has a variation of this approach.

up a crucial point in his doctrine: "Whenever we say 'non-being' [τὸ μὴ ὄν], we do not speak of something opposite to being, but only other [οὐκ ἐναντίον τι λέγομεν τοῦ ὄντος, ἀλλ' ἕτερον μόνον]." Theaetetus does not understand (257a8–b5). At 250a8–9, we agreed that *change* and *rest* are entirely opposite to one another; hence they cannot combine. But *being* has no opposite, since each form necessarily combines with *being* (and therefore, all instances of forms must ultimately participate in *being* as well). The Stranger rules out a form of pure nothingness; in this important sense, he commits no parricide with respect to Parmenides. As I have already noted he is therefore led to search for some other form by which to account for the "work" of "non." Pure nothingness is thereby suppressed in favor of negation, and negation is explained in two ways or steps. First: to say that something not-is *p* amounts to asserting that it is non-*p*, or (as we could tentatively say), that it is *q*, where *q* is "other" than *p*. This compressed explanation of the syntactical function of "non" must be expanded in the present context, since we are speaking of forms only. To say that form *F* is not form *G* is then, as we already know, to say that form *F* combines with *otherness* with respect to form *G* (and with *being* and *sameness* with respect to itself).

Some commentators insist upon reading "is-not" or on applying the negation to the verb "to be" (which they take as a copula) instead of to the form (which they take as a predicate). This controversy is largely meaningless from our standpoint, since the semantic analysis of the sentence puts the emphasis upon the separation of one form from another by means of a third. At best, the "is-not" reading brings out the fact that "is" has no opposite, and so that the negation is actually shifting us over to *otherness*. The "non-*G*" reading brings out the fact that *otherness* is shifting us from form *G* to some other form, namely, *F* itself: it is *G* which is other than *F*. What we need to recognize is not the syntactical location of the "non" (or "not"), but that it functions by way of the form *otherness*, and that its work is rather peculiar. All it accomplishes is to tell us that form *F* is the same; that is, that it combines with the form *sameness* with respect to itself. There is, of course, no explicit reference to *sameness* in negative statements about forms. So, in saying "form *F* is not form *G*," we have not at all succeeded in saying what we mean, given the Stranger's analysis. I take it that I do not need to repeat my analysis of the problems contained in "with respect to itself."

We saw a moment ago that Theaetetus does not understand what it means to say that "non-being" is not the opposite of "being" (the

name of *being*). Given the Stranger's analysis of negation, it is hard
not to sympathize with Theaetetus. If "F is not G" means that F is
some form other than G, since F cannot be any form but itself, "F
is not G" means "F is F." In other words, it is not enough to interpret "F is not G" as the negation of an identity statement. To do this
is not even to approach the Stranger's doctrine. This doctrine has as
its goal the elimination of "not" from our semantical analysis of the
meaning of the given statement. There is no way to avoid the conclusion that, for the Stranger, a negative identity statement about
forms is in fact an affirmative identity statement. To be accurate, "F
is not G" can mean either "F is F" or "G is G." I suggest that this is
counterintuitive. The Stranger has not only not introduced a prototypical version of the distinction between identity and predication. He has failed to capture the intuitive or plain sense of "not."
He fails because he starts from the assumption that meaning derives
from forms. This assumption will not lead us to an understanding
of "not," even if it should be the case that the "predicationalist"
interpretation is right and there are as many forms as there are predicates. Whereas there is no form (in the Stranger's sense) of non-
being and no "positive" contrary or opposite to *being* (this says the
same thing as the first clause), "not" continues to refer to a primitive *absence of form*. I leave this point as an objection to the Stranger's procedure, as I have argued it out elsewhere.[15]

It is enough for us to see that the Stranger's doctrine will not work
in its own terms. The preceding paragraph contains one more difficulty internal to the Stranger's teaching. That teaching requires us
to take a negative identity statement as either or both of two affirmative identity statements. As a consequence, *otherness*, which
provides the "power" of "not," does its work by cancelling itself out
of the very explanation it is supposed to be providing. It transforms
itself, in the course of that explanation, into *sameness*.

The Stranger now tries to remove Theaetetus's failure to understand with an example. His example does not concern any of the
forms thus far introduced, and about which we have been speaking
for so long. As I understand this passage, the Stranger puts to one
side the "greatest kinds" temporarily, in order to make things easier
for Theaetetus. When we say that something is not great, we may
mean either that it is small or that it is intermediate. According to
this example, then, "great" does not have a unique opposite. By
analogy, we should expect that *being* does not have a unique oppo-

15. Cf. Rosen (1980) and Kojève (1972), p. 82.

site. This is hardly the same as to say that it has no opposite at all. In slightly different terms, whereas the intermediate is partway between the great and the small, non-being would seem to be analogous neither to the intermediate nor to the small, assuming that the great is analogous to *being*.

However, the Stranger draws the following moral from his example: "Whenever we are told that negation [ἀπόφασις] signifies the opposite, we shall not agree; but we shall agree to this only, that the μή and the οὐ disclose something other than the name to which they are prefixed, or rather than the things referred to by the negated names" (257b6–c4). Verbs, as well as nouns, count as names; this passage thus leaves open both "not-is" and "non-G" as correct negations. The Stranger seems to be speaking very generally, in keeping with his example of the great, the intermediate, and the small; τῶν πραγμάτων ("things") presumably refers to anything at all, not merely forms. And again, forms are themselves classified as "things." The eidetic alphabet blurs the distinction between principles and their domain. In other words, *being* is a "thing" within the whole, not the principle of wholeness. In sum, a negative statement about anything whatsoever, when correctly analyzed, states that a thing *p* is in fact some other thing. It thus becomes obvious that the Stranger's analysis will not cover negative existential statements.

The Stranger turns next to the following point: "It seems to me that the nature of *otherness* [ἡ θατέρου . . . φύσις] is chopped up into small bits, like knowledge." Not surprisingly, Theaetetus again fails to understand (257c5–9).[16] We must distinguish between the nature of *otherness* and the examples by which the Stranger tries to make that nature easier to grasp. *Otherness* is unlike the other "greatest kinds" in that it has a fragmented interior. The other forms exhibit their look within a single "thing." This is true even of *sameness*; if *F* is the same as itself, "sameness" is visible in *F* alone. But *otherness* requires a minimum of two "things" in order to exhibit its look. The Stranger offers four analogies to this "internally fragmented" property of *otherness*. The analogies turn upon the case of knowledge, the beautiful, the great, and the just. It should be noted that the Stranger does not identify these four as "greatest kinds."

---

16. Cf. *Republic* III, 395b3ff: φαίνεταί μοι εἰς σμικρότερα κατακεκερματίσθαι ἡ τοῦ ἀνθρώπου φύσις. This ambiguous metaphor leads to unsatisfactory results with respect to both human nature and ἡ θατέρου φύσις. In both cases, a certain violence is done to the unanalyzable, in order to enforce a technical resolution of a problem. It would be risky, but hardly unthinkable, to speculate upon a deeper link between human nature and the nature of *otherness*.

They are intended to assist Theaetetus because they are more accessible, and this means easier to analyze, than the "greatest kinds"
themselves. The Stranger concentrates upon the first two examples,
and we shall do the same.

Knowledge, like *otherness*, is one. Whether or not it is a form in
the technical sense, "knowledge" is a family of kinds of knowledge.
Each "part" (μέρος, not εἶδος) has a name of its own; thus there are
many τέχναι and ἐπιστῆμαι (257c10–d3). So too with the "parts"
(μόρια) of *otherness*; the unity is not dissolved by the multiplication
of parts, or so the Stranger claims. Theaetetus remains dubious
(257d4–6). It is striking that the Stranger speaks of "parts" rather
than forms here; in other words, *otherness* is a unique form. Despite
its peculiar interior, it cannot have other forms as structural ingre-
dients.[17] This apart, the analogy between *otherness* and knowledge
seems to be quite tenuous. To "know" science S_1 is not in fact to
know science S_2. One might also question whether there is an analogy between the sense in which each particular science or art is
"knowledge" and the sense in which each pair of distinct terms exhibits *otherness*. Geometry is not medicine, yet both are "parts" of
knowledge. *Change* is not *rest*, but both are forms; they are not
primarily, but only secondarily, "parts" of *otherness*.

The Stranger shifts to his second example. There is, he says, a
"part" of *otherness* which "stands in contrast to" (ἀντιτιθέμενον
cannot by hypothesis mean here "is opposed to") the beautiful.
Theaetetus is able to give the name of this part: "For that which in
each case we call not beautiful [μὴ καλόν] is the other of nothing
else than the nature of the beautiful" (257d7–11). Again, it is irrelevant whether "the beautiful" is the name of a pure form. Since
otherness combines with all fundamental forms, it thereby combines with all "things," in the comprehensive sense of the term.
Beautiful things, taken collectively, are coordinated by *otherness*,
not with a vacuous "family" of nonexistent things, but with a "family" of things that are beautiful. The Stranger does not identify the
name of this coordinate family. If we are to proceed by analogy with
his original example of the great, there are presumably two such
families, namely, the plain and the ugly. These two examples suggest the following objection. Whereas it is true that the "not large"
may be the small or the intermediate, it is also true that the opposite of the large is the small, just as the opposite of the beautiful is
the ugly. The Stranger's explanation of negation thus makes it un-

17. *Statesman* 262a8: in diaeresis, we must not divide a μόριον that is not an εἶδος.

suitable as the basis of the logical conception of negation in the standard sense. We have just seen that "is-not" does not signal negative predication, but rather the combination of *being* and *otherness*. To this we can now add that "non-*p*" is ambiguous; its sense depends upon the context of discussion. The Stranger is not negating a variable and thereby implying the assertion of its complement. He is negating a definite term, in the present case a form, but without necessarily implying that the form is to be replaced by its "complement." We are dealing here with the names of individual forms, not of sets defining predicates. There are no logical complements to individual things; forms do not have opposites. To put this in one more way, if "other than" is to provide us with a completely general explanation of "not," the senses of negated sentences cannot be dependent upon the ontological type of the negated variables; they cannot be dependent upon the factual or contextual terms of the statement we are attempting to formalize. In the case of "Platonic negation," however, we do have such dependence. The Stranger, so to speak, is once more seen to be a relevance logician.

The Stranger then asks: "Does the not beautiful come about as follows, that some other [part] of a family of things is separated and coordinated with respect to some [part] of things?" (257d10–e5). Theaetetus agrees at once with this ambiguous statement, which has stimulated controversy among interpreters. Since there is some question as to the exact meaning of this passage, it would be unwise to build too heavily on it. Fortunately, it is not necessary to do so, as we have the Stranger's meaning from the context. The relation between the beautiful and the not beautiful is that of coordination (ἀντιτιθὲν) between the two "separated" (ἀφορισθὲν) but not opposed parts of a "family" (γένους). I take this last term as a cryptic reminder that "beautiful" and "not beautiful" are sensibly contrasted with respect to individuals of the same kind.[18]

I referred above to "platonist negation" as characteristic of relevance logic. Let me try to make this point a bit more fully. It bears, of course, on those negative statements which are not directly about formal combinations. In all the remaining cases, negation is a syntactic operation of reference shift, rooted semantically in the form *otherness*, which must therefore carry out its work directly upon language, as will be stated later by the Stranger. However this is accomplished, when we negate *p*, we assert only that the "subject" of our negative statement has an unspecified property *q*, which is

18. For a different interpretation, see Lee (1972), pp. 278–79.

coordinated to, but not the opposite of, although distinct from, *p*. The shift in reference to be accomplished depends upon what we are talking about, upon the context of discourse, and upon our intentions. 'Consequently, despite the "work" of *otherness*, the various coordinated properties cannot be eternal combinations of forms. To say that everything "shares in" *otherness* is thus to say that everything can enter into a negative statement, but nothing more than this. It is not true that every statement we utter is the exhibition of an eternal structure of forms. There is then a difference between the "work" of forms like the so-called greatest kinds, at least in the case of *being, sameness,* and *otherness,* and properties like "sits" and "flies," which, on the predicationalist reading, are also the names of forms. The aforementioned greatest kinds are always ingredient in the nature of everything. But the same individual—for example, Theaetetus—may sometimes be sitting, sometimes walking about, and (under special circumstances) even sometimes "flying" (as in an airplane).

I myself do not believe that "sits" and "flies" are the names of forms. But those who think otherwise must grant at a minimum that they can only be "forms" in a sense distinct from that in which the "greatest kinds" are forms. Surely no one will maintain that "Theaetetus" is the name of a form.[19] So apart from those forms which are ingredient in his nature, either as a thinkable thing or as an instance of the form *human being* (if there is such a form), the forms in which Theaetetus will "participate" will depend upon the context, whether of his experience or of our discourse about him. It is therefore impossible to formalize "platonist negation." Reference shifts induced by negation are not between complementary terms. Whereas "ugly" is the opposite of "beautiful," the complement of "beautiful" ("non-beautiful") may or may not be equivalent to "plain." One can of course write "non-*p*" whenever a negated name occurs in a Platonic text. But nothing useful, and something quite misleading, will have been accomplished by so doing. More generally, the semantical work of *otherness* is incomplete; we also require the context in which it is applied.

The Stranger goes on to emphasize that both elements coordinated by negation share equally in *being,* the not great and the great, the not just and the just, and so on. "The nature of *otherness* has shown itself as belonging to the beings" (τῶν ὄντων οὖσα). That is,

---

19. No Platonist, that is, unless one includes neo-Platonism under that rubric. As a sample of the literature, see Blumenthal (1966).

otherness combines with *being*, and so, is a "thing" or entity (another instance of the regular confusion between principles and things). The "parts" of *otherness* therefore also possess being (by virtue of sharing in *being*; 257e6–258a10). And in general, "the antithesis [ἀντίθεσις] of the nature of a part of *otherness* [ἡ τῆς θατέρου μορίου φύσεως] with the nature of *being*, when these are contrasted with each other, is no less, if it is right for me to say so, ousia than is *being* itself; for it signifies not the opposite [ἐναντίον] to *being* but only this: other than *being*" (258a11–b3). "Most manifestly so," Theaetetus agrees (258b4).[20]

When we say of a "part" of *otherness* that it "is not," we are apparently saying that the part lacks being (and so, by extension, that it does not share in *being*). This is impossible, however, since everything shares in *being* through the mediation of the network of forms of which it is an instance. Therefore, the referent of the negated name, as θέμις requires us to say, belongs as much to ousia as does the form *being*. So we have here a clear distinction between οὐσία and τὸ ὄν, in which the former is the comprehensive term. The forms must be elements (because they are "things") within the whole, whose name is presumably ousia, the divine being (and hence the reference to θέμις).

We have, then, found non-being, which, as coordinate with being, combines with *being*, and may be called "non-being itself" (τὸ μὴ ὄν . . . αὐτό), even though it is not, as taken apart from *otherness*, a genuine form. We can therefore dare to say that non-being no more lacks ousia than does anything else, and that it has a nature of its own (τὴν αὐτοῦ φύσιν ἔχον). Whatever is, is, and whatever is not, *is* not (since it shares in *being*). So too with non-being. However, the Stranger then raises a question which requires special consideration. Are we to count non-being as "one form among the many things" (ἐνάριθμον τῶν πολλῶν ὄντων εἶδος ἕν; 258b8–c5)? There are three possible interpretations of this query: (1) Is non-being a "greatest kind" in itself? (2) Is non-being in fact the form *otherness*? (3) Is non-being a pseudoform, or a collection of instances sharing the property that their names are negated in some statement? The Stranger is here comparing non-being with the great, the beautiful, the nongreat, the nonbeautiful, and so on. If we take εἶδος in its technical sense, all these, including non-being, will be "greatest kinds," and in the cases of the negations this is surely ruled out by the Stranger's own doctrine. But once we exclude this sense of εἶδος,

---

20. Cf. Manasse (1937), p. 26, on ἐναντίον τοῦ ὄντος.

there is no reason to apply it to the great, the beautiful, and so on, any more than to the nongreat, the nonbeautiful, or any other negation. Whereas non-being is in fact explained by the work of the form *otherness*, it is not quite the same to say that non-being "is" the form *otherness*. I therefore understand εἶδος in a nontechnical sense in this passage as the only reading that corresponds to the Stranger's overall doctrine.[21]

We are now entering into the final stretch of the Stranger's resolution of the problem of non-being. In the remainder of this scene, which has already been unusually long and unavoidably complex, I will consider only those elements of the text from 258c6 to 259d8 in which new points are made or some new formulation of a previously made point occurs.

Let us first look at 258c6–d7, where the Stranger claims that we have gone beyond the limit set by Parmenides, who forbade us to think that "non-beings are" (εἶναι μὴ ἐόντα; the quotation is from Parmenides himself). It is true that we have investigated the forbidden thought, and in so doing, given an account of "what the form of non-being is" (τὸ εἶδος ὃ τυγχάνει ὂν τοῦ μὴ ὄντος). I have already commented upon the use of εἶδος in what must be a nontechnical sense with respect to non-being. What needs saying here is that the Stranger has in fact verified the injunction of Parmenides; both thinkers forbid us from treating pure nothingness as a genuine form, or in other words as a letter in the eidetic alphabet. Non-being is a form in the derivative sense that it is a name for otherness, which is exhibited by the form *otherness*. This same point is reiterated at 258e6–259a1: "We long ago said good-bye to any opposite to *being* ... " Whether we were right to have done so is another matter.[22]

At 259a2–6 the Stranger says, "*Being* and *otherness* pass through all things and through each other" (τό τε ὂν καὶ θάτερον διὰ πάντων

---

21. At 258c1–3, the Stranger says that we have found that "the great is great" and "the beautiful is beautiful." Frede (1967), pp. 30ff, takes these as forms on a par with the greatest kinds, and explains away self-predication by an interpretation of "the great is great" that amounts to this: "the form 'great' exhibits greatness just as do individual great things" (my paraphrase). I find this highly implausible, since it blurs if it does not suppress the distinction between forms and instances. But it is also unnecessary, since the statements are better explained as identity statements.

22. Cf. Crombie (1963), p. 513: Plato may be thinking of "the absence of all positive predicates" or "total characterlessness." Again: "It would not be altogether impossible to wonder whether we might not need to postulate the existence of that which totally lacks character to be that in which character inheres. *Chōra* in the *Timaeus* comes dangerously near to this." See also Aristotle, *Physics* 192a6–16: "Plato spoke of that in which properties inhere as τὸ μὴ ὄν." Cf. *Parmenides*, hypotheses III–IV.

καὶ δι' ἀλλήλων διεληλυθότε). This may be taken together with 258d7–e3: "Each part of *otherness* which is contrasted to *being* is itself genuinely non-being" (ὄντως τὸ μὴ ὄν), and therefore an εἶδος. So *being* and *otherness* are coextensive; hence, every "part" of *otherness* is "contrasted" with *being*; in short, *otherness* as an integral form is entirely responsible for non-being. The same thing is said in slightly different words at 249a6–b1: "*Otherness*, partaking of *being*, is [or "exists" in the special sense] through this partaking, yet is not that in which it partakes but another; and since it is other than *being*, it must be non-being, as is entirely clear" (τὸ μὲν ἕτερον . . . ἐξ ἀνάγκης εἶναι μὴ ὄν). The εἶδος of non-being is not some "negative form," but *otherness*. The "parts" of non-being are not formal parts of *otherness*, nor is non-being as a whole a formal part of the form *otherness*.

A corresponding point holds good for *being*. It participates (entirely) in *otherness*; thus each being is negatable. And *being* is negatable in the sense that it is none of the other forms. I remind the reader that in each case, to say that "*being* is not form *G*" is just to say that *being* is the same (as itself) and form *G* is the same (as itself). Since *being* is radically independent of all other forms, and remains such even in combination with distinct forms, it follows that "there are myriads upon myriads of things that *being* is not," which is to say that *being* is neither any of the other forms, nor (as a form) is it any of the instances of the forms. The converse is not so simple. Everything is, *qua* participating in (or combining with) *being*. But everything is not in the countless senses in which each thing may be negated (259b1–7).

The Stranger closes his summary with good advice to all of us. Whoever doubts our "oppositions" (that is, our analysis) must either produce something better than what we have said or be condemned by us as lacking in seriousness. This is a quality which must not be confused with pleasure in eristics (259b8–d8).

SCENE SIXTEEN

False Statement

(259d6–264b8)

TRANSITIONAL REMARKS

We are about to shift from the ostensible resolution of the problem of non-being to the analysis of false statement. Let us pause for a moment in order to gather our thoughts about the discussion thus far. The problems of non-being and falsehood emerged from our attempt to define the sophist. In the Stranger's portrait, the sophist is a fantasm of the philosopher (and by extension of the wise man, under whose name he conceals himself). He produces inaccurate images of knowledge which dupe the young, or those who lack experience in the apprehension of beings. However, the Stranger's picture of the sophist itself seems to be a fantasm, since it shows the latter as if he were a specious geometer, shoemaker, carpenter, and so on. As also emerges from other aspects of the Stranger's presentation, the genuine problem of sophistry turns upon the distinction of better from worse, upon the ends to which the arts and sciences are addressed, not to the veridical or specious exercise of those arts themselves. If the sophist produces fantasms, these are of wisdom, not of τέχνη. Stated as concisely as possible, the sophist defines wisdom as perspectivism. Taking sophistry in the deepest sense, it is an anticipation, not of the modern Enlightenment, but of Nietzsche.[1]

Even, then, if the Stranger should succeed in distinguishing between true and false statements about beings, in the sense that classifies them in accordance with their looks or kinds, this will not be enough to define, let alone refute, sophistry. It remains to be shown that, with respect to human intentions, there is a distinction between true and false statements, or, if there is such a distinction,

1. Cf. Kube (1969), pp. 60, 114.

that it is the same distinction as in the case of statements about "looks" or likenesses. In our own day, this problem is known as the hermeneutical circle. The same point can be put in a different way. Even if we could develop a satisfactory technical definition of truth (one thinks here of Tarski's so-called truth definition), it remains to be determined whether there is an original corresponding to discursive icons about the good life. "Snow is white" may be certified as true because we have access to the whiteness of snow. But is there any analogy between white snow and the good life?

This is the general problem of sophistry, which does not emerge clearly and distinctly from the Stranger's technical obfuscation. In saying this, I do not mean to imply that the problem of non-being or falsehood is itself specious, but only that the Stranger fails to present an accurate account of the relation between these problems and the problem of sophistry. There is also a very deep puzzle in the Stranger's doctrine of forms and copies, which, if it cannot be resolved, must compromise his definition of sophistry. An accurate image is said to look like, yet not to be, the original form. Yet, in the case of a successful copy of a formal look, there seems not to be any such difference. Despite the claim that there is an "ontological" difference between the original and the image, with respect to the look *qua* look, no such difference is visible. Ontological originals then become suspect, and gradually succumb to charges that they are "invisible substances" or "superfluous theoretical entities." The result is that we are left with nothing but the erstwhile "images," that is, the statements or symbolic representations of formal structures. The images have been transformed into the originals. And this is the doctrine of sophistry.

It would seem, then, that we are faced with a dilemma. Either we grasp the original directly, in which case images are superfluous and there are no false statements. Or we do not grasp the original directly, but only via images, in which case there is no evident criterion for distinguishing between accurate and inaccurate copies, other than images themselves, and we have fallen into a vicious circle. On this alternative, there are once more no false statements. To this dilemma, we can add the following point. Even granting the distinction between originals and images, the "look" of the original must be present in the fantasm as well as in the icon. For if not, then the fantasm will not be a distorted copy of that original. It will be the copy of some other look, and in that sense, an icon.

The Stranger's attempt to explain away "the altogether not," on the same basis of the doctrine of forms, is in my opinion also a failure. The sense of "nothing" cannot be explained by a doctrine of counting, referring, and enforcement of the principle of noncontradiction. The reason for this is not in my opinion obscure or difficult to state. There is indeed no form contrary to the form *being*, but this is because "nothing" is not the name of a form. The Stranger's account of non-being as negation, or as a "power" of *otherness*, could almost be described as algebraic. "Not" seems to be a kind of permuting function. But permutations are possible only with distinct elements. Elements are "distinct" because each one is not the other, and not because, when speaking of a given element in a negative statement, we are actually referring to some other element. In the traditional expression, *omnis determinatio negatio est*. As one could also put this, being is already a negation. There is, then, nothing surprising about our inability to "refer" to a "nothing" which is distinct from every being, and yet imagined to be a kind of pseudo-thing.

In sum, one may distinguish at least two senses of "not." The first sense is that of a total absence of determinations. The second sense is that of the difference between one determination and another. The Stranger's explanation of this "difference" is that of a form which relates the two determinations by distinguishing them. But the application of the form *difference* (*otherness*) presupposes (logically, not temporally) two distinct determinations to which it may be applied. If this presupposition is not honored, then the ostensible pure form *otherness* is assimilated into the nature of the determinations themselves. But if the presupposition *is* honored, then the "difference" between two determinations is not the same as the "being" of each determination *qua* determination. The "being" of the determination is already a "negation" or limitation, *not a difference*. Perhaps I should add that the preceding remarks are in no way incompatible with such products of analytical thought as mathematical logic. The primitive status of negation in logic (even when concealed within something like the stroke function), if one were actually to think about it instead of merely listing rules for its operation, points us in the same direction. The rule defining the use of "not" is already permeated with negativity. However, this is not the place to develop such notions.[2]

THE STRANGER'S EXPLANATION OF FALSEHOOD

A false statement, on the Stranger's account of things, "pretends" to be an icon. A true statement, on the other hand, *is* an icon: it

2. Cf. Rosen (1980) for some steps in this direction.

preserves the proportions of the original(s). The word λόγος means not simply "speech" but (among other things) "ratio." There are, of course, true as well as false speeches. But if we reserve the word λόγος for a true speech (which Plato frequently does), then the sense of "ratio" brings out very well the intrinsic reference to proportions. At the same time, this presents us with a problem. A λόγος, when used in the narrower or technical sense just distinguished, can refer either to the original proportion or ratio of forms or to its discursive icon. This is in turn connected to the previously noted difficulty of how to distinguish between the original "look" and the same look as copied in an accurate image (here, statement). We shall have to keep these points in mind as we work our way through the next section of the *Sophist*.

Those who attempt to separate everything from everything lack breeding and "musical" cultivation as well as philosophy. To insist upon comprehensive separation would be to dissolve all ratios (πάντων λόγων), whether in things or in speech (259d8–e7). We have, then, defeated the "separatists" (as we may call them) at "the propitious moment" (ἐν καιρῷ). According to the Stranger, we did so in order to establish that λόγος "is one of our families of beings" (ἡμῖν τῶν ὄντων ἕν τι γενῶν εἶναι; 260a1–6).[3] On the face of it, this seems to be an unmistakable claim that λόγος is one of the "greatest kinds." Such a claim would seem to make sense in view of the Stranger's intention of extending the work of *otherness* to discourse. Nevertheless, there are difficulties involved in accepting the obvious sense of the passage. If λόγος means here "ratio" *qua* combination of formal looks, then it must include ratios of original forms as well as of words (since such a look is to be found in both dimensions). But a ratio of forms is a compound of simple elements, and not just a simple element. In other words, it must be a "segment" of the web of forms, not a distinct and simple form. On the other hand, if λόγος means "discourse" here, then statements or icons are elevated to the level of ontological form. The "look" of the family of linguistic expressions must itself then be a linguistic expression.

We can avoid this dilemma by assuming that the Stranger is here using γένος in a loose sense, very much as he did εἶδος with respect to non-being. I myself think that this is what the Stranger ought to be doing. There is, however, no way to prove it, and such an inference is at best a guess. Either, then, the Stranger is speaking loosely here, or he has (presumably inadvertently) committed himself to a

3. Cf. Wiehl (1967), p. 201, n. 113.

doctrine with vitiating consequences. One thing is certain. If λόγος is one of the "greatest kinds," then the term must mean "ratio," not "discourse." Those who take λόγος as a pure form may wish to argue that it is necessary to do so in order to derive the explanation of falsehood from the explanation of non-being as the work of *otherness*. However, I do not believe that this is necessary. A statement cannot be falsified by a direct combination with *otherness*. It is not words (or names) but forms which combine with forms. False statements must therefore be subjected to analysis in order to isolate an ultimate "infrastructure" of pure forms, within which *otherness* functions in such a way upon the forms named by the words in the statement as to falsify the statement.

In other words, falsehood requires us to distinguish, not merely between names and forms, but also between formal combinations and the participation of spatio-temporal individuals within such combinations. Let us briefly consider an example. The statement "Theaetetus flies" contains two names woven together in such a way as to produce a falsehood. But it is not a fantasm of the weaving together of two forms, *Theaetetus* and *flying*. It is noncontroversial that "Theaetetus" is not the name of a form. The individual named "Theaetetus" must participate in a combination of such forms as are named by "rational," "animal," and the like; but he must also participate in forms like *being, sameness, otherness, change,* and *rest*. The name "flying" is controversial. Many commentators take it as the name of a form. I have already indicated why I do not. To those reasons, one may add this consideration. If forms correspond to every possible predicate, then they must be infinite in number. We will have forms like *scratching, tickling,* and *giggling,* but also like "____ is a centaur" and other impossibilities. Such an understanding of the Stranger's doctrine confuses it with Husserl's phenomenology of essences, according to which the intended content of each act of consciousness is an eternal essence.[4]

Fortunately, for my present point we need not decide one way or the other whether "flying" is the name of a form. Even if it is, the

---

4. This is, I think, the net result of interpretations like those of Ackrill (1971), p. 207, who shifts from forms to concepts, and Detel (1972), p. 93, who infers from 256e5f that there are infinitely many forms. For Husserl, cf. *Ideen* I (1975), Paragraph 2, p. 12, for the attribution of a *Wesen* to each contingent real individual, "ein rein zu fassendes Eidos," which "steht nun unter Wesens-Wahrheiten verschiedener Allgemeinheitsstufe." There is an interesting parallel between Husserl's "adequate" and "inadequate" intuitions of essences and the Stranger's distinction between icons and fantasms. Cf. *Ideen* I, Paragraph 3, pp. 13–14, and finally p. 15: a *Wesensanschauung* is of that which can be the subject of true or false predication.

name "Theaetetus" does not combine with it. Of course, the point
here is not merely that the individual Theaetetus does not combine
with a certain form, but that he does not participate in it. Theaetetus is not flying. He must then participate in the form *otherness*
"with respect to" the form *flying*. It is thus the form *otherness* which
combines with the form *flying*. So the plausibility of the Stranger's
account of falsehood, if it has any, does not depend upon our taking
λόγος as a form, capable of direct combination with *otherness*.

To come back to 260a1ff, we need to establish the nature of λόγος,
since if we were deprived of it through its comprehensive lack of
being (μηδ' εἶναι τὸ παράπαν), we would lose philosophy and would
be unable to say anything. This consequence follows whether the
Stranger is thinking primarily of λόγος as "ratio" or as "discourse,"
but the stronger conclusion is plainly that, without λόγος as ratio,
there would be nothing to talk about. Nevertheless, Theaetetus does
not understand why we must now reach an agreement about *logos*
(260b3–4). The Stranger replies as follows. We found previously that
non-being was "one family among the others" (ἕν τι τῶν ἄλλων γένος
ὄν), scattered amongst all the beings (260b5–9). As was previously
explained, the Stranger must be referring to *otherness*, if γένος means
"greatest kind." Otherwise, he is using γένος informally, to collect
together all instances of non-being; and this is unlikely, if only because he said previously that these instances were "unbounded." I
take this passage as a consequence of the Stranger's previous identification of non-being with the entire form *otherness*.

To continue, our next task is to determine whether non-being
mingles with belief and λόγος (which I take to mean "discourse"
here; 260b10–11). If it does not, then everything is true. If it does,
then belief and λόγος can both be false. For to think or say "the
things that are not" (τὰ μὴ ὄντα) is to produce the occurrence of
falsehood in discursive thinking and speech (ἐν διανοίᾳ τε καὶ λόγοις;
260c1–5). The next knot to be unravelled is this: if "non-being"
names *otherness* and λόγος means "discourse," then has the Stranger not invited us to determine whether *otherness* combines with
discourse, and so with names rather than forms? There is no need
at all to take such a line of interpretation, which conflicts with the
previous stages of the Stranger's doctrine. Non-being, whether
understood as the form *otherness* or the syntactic consequences of
the work of that form, enters into discourse by way of its effect upon
the forms to which the names in the statements of discourse refer.
"The things that are not" is not easy to understand on the Stranger's
account of things. It certainly does not refer to non-being (*other-*

ness). Neither can it refer merely to separations of formal elements. In the first place, false statements are not exclusively about pure formal combinations, as we saw in the case of Theaetetus. But whether false statements are about forms only, or about individuals and forms, in what sense do they say "the things that are not"? Strictly speaking, of course, there are no such things; there are only "the things that are." To be a not-thing is to be something else, as it were. Take the false statement "*change* is the same form as *rest*." This statement is false, but it is not about nonexistent beings. It is about forms, which it claims to bring into a combination that cannot obtain. So "the things that are not" means "things other than those about which we speak," and in the case of the example, the "things" in question are not forms but combinations or relations of forms. The false statement thus gives an inaccurate "ratio."

One might be initially inclined to take τὰ μὴ ὄντα as instances of *otherness*, but this will not do, because all things are instances of *otherness*. Differently stated, whatever is such an instance, *is*. To say that it "is not" is either meaningless or incomplete; it can only "not be" in relation to something else for which it is mistaken by the speaker. We thus end up with the analysis of the previous paragraph. But further, it turns out that a false statement is primarily a psychological act, just as it was in the *Theaetetus*. The forms play a part in the analysis of a false statement because, when we are speaking about them, it is their relations that we get wrong. Yet, the forms do not themselves explain why or how we go wrong about those relations. There is no purely formal analysis of falsehood. The same result could be obtained by starting with a sentence like "Theaetetus flies." I leave the details as an exercise for the reader.

The intrinsic ratios of forms cannot be "false" because they are what they are, regardless of how we perceive them. A false statement, as we have just seen, is an erroneously constructed copy of a ratio. But of what ratio is it a copy? Not of an obtaining ratio, since then the statement would be true. But not of a nonobtaining ratio, since there are no such ratios, that is, there are none such at the level of the originals or pure formal combinations (and separations). Nonobtaining ratios occur only at the level of discourse. Yet we do not seem to be in a position to certify them as nonobtaining, and hence as false, simply by comparing them with obtaining or ontologically genuine ratios. How do we arrive at the statement that "the form *change* is the same as the form *rest*"? Certainly not by perceiving the forms in their obtaining relations or ratios. It looks very much as though a false statement is not a copy at all, not an image in the sense of an inaccurate representation of an original, but an invention, that is to say, *an original* in a sense quite distinct from that of forms. What I am suggesting here, of course, is not that this is the Stranger's intention. I mean to suggest that this is an unintended consequence of the explanation he does in fact offer. Only by taking false statements as "originals" can we make sense of the claim that a fantasm seems to look like the original, but does not. Unfortunately, if false statements are "originals" because not copies of formal ratios, then the refutation of the sophist falls to the ground.

The Stranger goes on to remind Theaetetus that if falsehood exists, so too does deception, in which case "all things must be full of images, icons, and fantasms." The sophist, on the contrary, denies the existence of falsehood. According to the Stranger, this amounts to the acceptance of a radical separation between non-being and ousia (260c6–d4). In fact, the sophist's position would be better put as a denial of ousia. However, since we have now shown that non-being shares in being (τοῦ ὄντος), perhaps the sophist will modify his battle plan by claiming that some forms (τῶν εἰδῶν) share in non-being, but others, including λόγος and belief (δόξα), do not. This would enable him to deny the existence of the image-making art and hence of fantastics, in which we said he is to be found. For if λόγος and belief do not share in non-being, then there can be no falsehood (260d5–e3).

In this passage, the Stranger uses his own terminology to express the sophist's alternatives. He takes it for granted that the sophist must accept the doctrine of forms, and therefore the distinction between originals and images. As we have seen, this is asserted rather than argued. It is worth noting that the sophist does not have to deny the "existence" of forms. He need only interpret them as "perspectives," and so, as existing for those who believe themselves to see them. In any event, we are now going to inquire into the nature of λόγος, belief, and fantasy (φαντασία), in order to see that each communes with non-being. This will enable us to verify the existence of falsehood and to imprison the sophist therein, if he is guilty. If he is not, then we must set him free and look for him in another family (γένει; 260e3–261a3). The term "fantasy" appears here for the first time; it is apparently used as a synonym for "image" rather than for "fantasm" only. A "fantasy" is a "seeming," what appears to be, but is not (an original).

It is important to emphasize that if λόγος is a pure form, it cannot commune with non-being in the same way as do belief and fantasy. A form is separated from another form by its combination with oth-

erness. It does not thereby itself become that which seems to be, but is not, some other form. This error takes place in us, through the mediation of images, both perceptual and discursive. On the other hand, if λόγος is discourse, then it is on a par with belief and fantasy in the sense that the names of which it consists may be erroneously combined by us. Falsehood does not exist at the level of pure formal combination. If it did, this would amount to the hypostatizing of non-being, or to admitting a form that is the contrary of *being.*[5]

Theaetetus expresses his exasperation at the sophist's capacity to erect one defensive screen after another.[6] He is sufficiently moved to utter his longest speech in the dialogue (261a4–b4). The Stranger encourages him with military metaphor. Theaetetus must be brave. We are making a small advance at each stage of the campaign. If one's spirit were to fail him under these circumstances, what would he do if no progress were visible or if retreat were necessary? Perseverence or spiritedness is required to capture a city, and the same is true in philosophical investigation. Now that we have passed the main problem of non-being, the remaining tasks will be easier and smaller. Theaetetus replies that the Stranger's rebuke is nobly stated (261b5–c6). Passages like this are not mere literary ornamentation. They illustrate the necessary connection between nobility of character and λόγος in the philosophical nature. In order to be free, one must be spirited or brave, as we should have learned from the discussion of the philosopher-soldiers in the *Republic.*

We turn first to λόγος and belief (fantasy is ignored), in order to determine more clearly whether non-being touches them, or whether both are entirely true and neither is ever false (261c6–10). We begin with names (ὀνόματα), asking about them what we asked previously about forms and letters. Do all unite with each other, or none with any, or some with some? The answer, says Theaetetus, is plain: some unite and others do not (261d1–7). The Stranger takes Theaetetus to be saying something like this: names spoken in sequence (ἐφεξῆς) in such a way as to "point out something" (δηλοῦντα τί) unite. Those which signify (σημαίνοντα) nothing as a sequence, do not unite (261d8–e2). This is the basis of the Stranger's understanding of language. There is no "fitting together" of a property element in a "sub-

---

5. David Lachterman calls my attention here to *Republic* V, 476a4–7, which indicates that, for Socrates, the κοινωνία of multiple forms produces the φαντασία of manyness. Perhaps the eidetic counterpart of falsehood is for Socrates the multiplicity of forms, which leads to the apparent compromising of the individuality of each form.

6. Cf. *Statesman* 279c4ff for the significance of προβλήματα.

ject" (Aristotle's ὑποϰείμενον) to produce a new complex unity in which elements are no longer independent. I see no reason to attribute a doctrine of predication to the Stranger. "Names" (which cover verbs as well as nouns) combine and separate, just like forms. The proper combination points something out: with caution, we can say that it "refers," provided we recognize that it may refer to what is now called a "sense," and not only to its "extension." Nothing is said about particles, logical connectives, or any expression other than names. The analysis of "not," however, shows us that, for the Stranger, to "mean" is ultimately to be backed up by a form or a formal structure. In Aristotelian predication, there is a substratum that "receives" or "dispenses with" properties (more accurately, these are "present" or "absent" within an οὐσία). In Platonic combination, the ultimate constituents of intelligibility are atomic forms, which stand together or apart, but which do not "receive" one another within themselves, despite the terminology of "sharing" and "participating." To "share" is to combine "powers," but not to make one power from two. At least this is the case with the "greatest kinds." So too with names: they stand together or apart. They combine, but they do not "blend" or lose their independent identities. And it is certainly false to think of some names as "values" of functions.

A statement is a ratio, in the extended or metaphorical sense of the term, of names. In order to be significant, it must "reflect" or "image" a ratio of things (ultimately, of forms), regardless of whether each name in the statement is the name of a form. As we saw in our analysis of the Frede-Owen thesis, it is essential not to take formal combination for a form. "Sharing" or "combining" is not a form but a ratio of forms. We are inclined to think of the ratio itself as a form; for example, as a relation. The Stranger, however, does not identify relations as forms; instead, he thinks of them as "objects" corresponding to abstract nouns. In the language of the paradigm of the alphabet, the ordering of letters that constitute a correctly spelled word is not itself a formal letter. To take the crucial case, "being," despite its participial form (τὸ ὄν), functions as an abstract noun. To take it as a two-place relation "___ is ___" is thus to distort fundamentally the Stranger's doctrine. There are no "gaps" in the nature of *being*. Only in the case of *otherness* is such an approach at all plausible; and the fact that it is so is a sign of the difficulties within the Stranger's doctrine.

Previously, I raised the question: How can the Stranger distinguish between the look of an original and the same look as reflected in an image? We may now suggest an answer on his behalf. In the case of true statements or icons, the look is the same. What differs is not the look but the medium, so to speak. For the Stranger, the difference between verbal representations of looks and the looks themselves is obvious, not something requiring proof. Unfortunately, the suggestion does not take us very far toward an explanation of the difference between true and false statements. It will not do to see a quasi-Tarskian doctrine of truth in the *Sophist*, whereby we check the truth of "Theaetetus flies" by looking to see whether Theaetetus is flying or not. If this were all that were involved, then of course the doctrine of forms and images would be entirely irrelevant. The Stranger is not concerned to verify the empirical fact reported by a statement, but to explain the *meaning* of the statement. He is not interested in a "truth-conditional semantics." For him, the falsehood of "Theaetetus flies" must be derived finally from the semantic support of "not." And this, as we know, is the form *otherness*. The Stranger's task is thus to explain the function of forms with respect to combinations of names. This requires that names refer to forms. Yet in a false statement, names *cannot* refer to forms in the required sense, as we have seen on more than one occasion. Hence the Stranger fails to explain falsehood.

This failure is independent of the question whether, each time the Stranger uses words like εἶδος and γένος, he is to be understood as introducing a pure form *qua* "greatest kind." I have already argued that this cannot be the case, but that is a separate point from the question of whether the Stranger's doctrine of falsehood is acceptable. Coming back to his account of language, the Stranger next introduces a "twofold family" (διττὸν γένος) for pointing out ousia with the voice: these are nouns and verbs (261e3–262a2). The sign for deeds (ταῖς πράξεσιν) is called a "verb," whereas the sign for those who perform the deed is called a "noun."[7] The Stranger divides words initially in terms of deeds, but finally on the basis of things, and *not* on the basis of speeches or grammatical functions (262a2–8). The family of nouns and verbs derives its meaning from οὐσία, and not vice versa.

Theaetetus fails to grasp immediately why a λόγος cannot consist of a sequence of nouns alone or verbs alone. He may be thinking of

7. Cf. Cornford (1935), p. 306, and Manasse (1937), pp. 39ff. Manasse emphasizes that throughout this section, beings underlie predicates, and that the distinction "meaningful/meaningless" is prior to that of "true/false" in the case of statements. This is substantially the same point I make in the text concerning the distinction between meaning and truth value. Contrast Uphues (1973; reprint), p. 51. For Plato, thinking is identified as speaking but not vice versa. Hence ὄνομα and ῥῆμα cannot be the same as "subject" and "predicate," which are terms of thinking.

geometry, in which there are no deeds. In any case, the Stranger provides various examples involving animals, just as, much earlier, when explaining what he meant by "everything," he began with examples of living things. Unless they mingle together, nouns alone and verbs alone do not stand together as λόγος. They indicate neither action or inaction nor "the οὐσία of what is or is not" (οὐσίαν ὄντος οὐδὲ μὴ ὄντος). The Stranger here distinguishes between activity and things; he uses the term "ousia" in connection with the latter only. This is another sign of his "thing ontology," except to the extent that he implies a difference between things and οὐσία itself. A λόγος, here a "statement," is then the smallest unit of significant speech, namely, a "web" (συμπλοκή) of a noun and a verb (262a9–c7).[8]

We can draw a very important inference from this little passage. The shortest meaningful statement points out either an action or inaction, or that something exists or does not exist. Since the latter pair can be done by the combination of just one noun and one verb, the Stranger is presumably sanctioning the existential use of "is" in well-formed statements like "Socrates exists." Second, the Stranger holds to the "Fregean" thesis that the statement is the smallest unit of meaning. Third, to name is not the same as to point out; this is the basis for the distinction between sense and reference.

Theaetetus again requires clarification, and the Stranger responds with an example. The shortest statement, for instance "man learns" (ἄνθρωπος μανθάνει), concludes something (τι περαίνει) about something that is, was, or will be (262c8–d6). Theaetetus grasps the point, and is thus able to accept without difficulty the claims that each statement must be about something (τινὸς εἶναι) and of a certain quality (ποιόν τινα). In other words, we cannot make statements about nonexistent things, and each statement must be true or false. By a "nonexistent thing," I do not mean a fictional object, but rather something which has no share in being. The Stranger does not develop a doctrine of fictional objects; we find no counterparts in the Sophist to such contemporary favorites as "Santa Claus does not exist." This is not to say that the Stranger would have an easy time in dealing with such cases. Presumably he would explain them in a way similar to his brief account of dream images (266b10ff), that is, as consisting of fragmented reflections of existing things.

We come now to one of the most discussed sections of the dia-

8. David Lachterman suggests an alternative reading of οὐσίαν ὄντος οὐδὲ μὴ ὄντος as in apposition to πρᾶξιν οὐδ' ἀπραξίαν. In addition, he notes that verbs are said to be "mingled" (κεράσῃ) with nouns.

logue. The Stranger confirms its importance by requesting close and united attention. He is about to utter a properly constructed statement, and asks Theaetetus to identify the person about whom it speaks. Let me underline that, throughout this passage, the Stranger speaks exclusively of persons and actions. He never speaks of forms. The example he gives is quite short: "Theaetetus sits." Theaetetus sees quite easily that the statement is about himself (262e10–263a5). But then the Stranger gives a second example: "Theaetetus, with whom I am now talking, flies." Theaetetus says that no one would say otherwise than that this statement is also about himself (263a6–10). The Stranger makes clear in the second statement to which Theaetetus he refers, where he does not do this in the previous example ("Theaetetus sits"). This is because his interlocutor is in fact not flying. Hence, without the explanation, the sentence, given the Stranger's previous doctrine of forms, would not be about Theaetetus at all. In other words, a purely grammatical or logical analysis does not provide by itself the meaning of a false statement. We require also what would be called today "contextual" information, or information about the speaker's intention.[9]

The Stranger now introduces the distinction between truth and falsehood. He gets Theaetetus to identify the first statement as true, and the second as "somehow" (που) false. The true statement tells "the things that are about you" (τὰ ὄντα ὡς ἔστιν περὶ σοῦ).[10] The false statement says "things other than things that are" (ἕτερα τῶν ὄντων). So "it says of the things that are not, that they are" (or "it speaks about the things that are not as though they are"; τὰ μὴ ὄντ' ἄρα ὡς ὄντα λέγει). Positive and negative existential statements would seem to qualify for inclusion if the first translation is right, although it remains unclear how the Stranger would explain the meaning of a negative existential. Furthermore, in this discussion, truth and falsehood are ascertained by virtue of our capacity to determine "how things are" or "how they are not." If the Stranger really believes that there is a connection between the doctrine of forms and the analysis of falsehood, then he must intend to make a distinction between meaning and truth value. We determine that "snow is blue" is false by looking at snow. So too we determine that "Theaetetus flies" is false by looking at the proper Theaetetus.[11] But the determination of the truth value of "Theaetetus flies" is not a semantic analysis of

9. Cf. Cornford (1937), p. 312, and *Euthydemus* 285d.
10. Cf. Detel (1972), p. 100, and Keyt (1973), pp. 288ff. Alternative translation: "The things that are as they [truly] are concerning you."
11. Cf. Sprute (1962), pp. 58–59.

the meaning of "Theaetetus flies," that is, of falsehood. Unfortunately, the Stranger makes no such explicit distinction (263a11–b10).

There follows a second account of the work of false statements. In this passage, there is a disputed manuscript reading that requires a brief discussion. The two best manuscripts, B and T, yield the following sense: a false λόγος states "what genuinely is, but is other than what is with respect to you" (ὄντως δέ γε ὄντα ἕτερα περὶ σοῦ). Burnet, Fowler, and Wiehl accept the correction of Cornarius, which changes ὄντως to ὄντων. The sense is accordingly that a false λόγος states "things which are other than those things concerning you" (263b11). Frede retains the readings of B and T (ὄντως). He infers from this that our passage in its entirety makes clear that "in the case that something is actually different, is already contained, that it is₁ actual"; in other words, that it is identical to itself (p. 58; for "is₁" see III' on p. 18). If this means that even a false statement must correspond to, or exhibit, an actual formal structure, the question arises as to what forms are involved in a statement like "Theaetetus flies." Earlier (p. 43), Frede observes that the συμπλοκὴ εἰδῶν applies to "Theaetetus flies" as a combining between a predicate concept and the form of an existent ("zwischen Prädikatsbegriff und der Form des Seienden"). It is not clear to me what this could mean except that "___ flies" is a predicate concept and that "Theaetetus" is the name of a form of an existent. So, too, on page 44: "The fact that in each case something existent will be expressed, provided only that a form is attached to a predicate, makes it initially possible to define false statements in such a way that through them, something will be expressed as existent which is not existent; for something must be existent [seiend sein], in order to be able not to be existent."

If I have understood Frede correctly on this point, I would agree with him in part: not to be this is actually to be that. But I see no reason to hold that the συμπλοκὴ εἰδῶν is intended by the Stranger to underlie false statements. In fact, we are given just one example of a false statement, "Theaetetus flies," and, on Frede's analysis, there must be a form corresponding to the individual named "Theaetetus." This seems to be an undesirable consequence of failing to distinguish between the doctrine of formal combination on the one hand and the analysis of false statement on the other.

The Stranger's doctrine cannot be saved, not even by the desperate measure of transforming Theaetetus into a form. So regardless of whether we read ὄντως or ὄντων, a false statement cannot be connected to a relevant formal structure. Let us continue with the Stranger's words. "We said that many things are, and many are not, with respect to each thing" (263b11–13). The second of the two statements about Theaetetus is said about someone. If this "someone" is not Theaetetus, then it is no one else; in this case, the statement is not a λόγος at all (263c1–12). This proves, incidentally, that the statement is not about a form *Theaetetus*. So much for examples. The Stranger moves directly to his definition.

Let us first try to translate the definition as literally as possible. "When things are so spoken about you [περὶ δὴ σοῦ λεγόμενα] that the other is spoken as the same and things that are not as things that are [μέντοι θάτερα ὡς τὰ αὐτὰ καὶ μὴ ὄντα ὡς ὄντα], it seems that such a synthesis, brought about from verbs and nouns, has produced in all respects what is genuinely and truly [ὄντως τε καὶ ἀληθῶς] false λόγος (263d1–4). The definition is formulated in terms of what is said about Theaetetus. I do not believe that we should disregard this fact entirely, and move directly to a general definition. There is a distinction between false statements about spatio-temporal individuals and false statements about forms. However, perhaps enough has already been said about this. Second, we may ask whether there is a significant distinction between speaking the other as the same and speaking of things that are not as though they are. With respect to our example, the first presumably means that we say that Theaetetus flies, whereas "flies" is other than "sits," which last is what he is doing. The second, however, seems to come to the same thing; it means that we speak of Theaetetus as if he were flying, which he is not. Third, it should be noted that whereas a false λόγος must be a fantasm, it is referred to as "genuinely and truly" what it is. As I noted previously, the Stranger does not distinguish the "degrees of reality" of originals and images. Finally, there is no reference to forms anywhere in this account of false statement. The entire section hangs upon a connection between λόγος and non-being. If non-being is *otherness*, however, the connection is between this and the remaining "greatest kinds." We may also suppose that other forms share in the power of *otherness*, and thereby provide the intelligible substructure to the statement "Theaetetus flies." Neither Theaetetus nor the "deed" of flying is itself in direct combination with the form *otherness*.

It is plain, the Stranger continues, that discursive thinking, belief, and fantasy are families (γένη) arising in the soul as both true and false. We note that φαντασία returns to the discussion, and that λόγος is replaced by διάνοια. Burnet, following Stallbaum, excises γένη although it appears in both *B* and *T*. I see no reason to follow him. Certainly "families" cannot mean here "greatest kinds." On this assumption, διάνοια would be a pure form, synonymous with λόγος, instead of a psychic power. This does not seem to require extensive refutation, any more than does the hypothesis that a form corresponds to belief or fantasy.

We can now summarize this very sketchily developed doctrine. Non-being "touches" belief and speech (261c6–9), and it does so at the level of pure forms, which are either themselves the referents or make up the deep structure of the objects referred to by the names woven together within λόγος. Some names combine in a significant way and others do not, "just as in the case of the forms and letters" (261d1ff). The analogy between formal structure and linguistic structure is combination. Names are the "atomic elements" of significant statements. Nothing is said after 261c6ff to explain the sense in which non-being "touches" discursive thinking. This is true even if we follow the view that the words θάτερα ὡς τὰ αὐτά at 263d1–4 are a reference to *otherness*, a view which I reject. Nothing is ever said to explain how forms and names "combine," if that is the proper term to apply here. If we try to apply the doctrine of formal combination to the present problem, what is the correct analysis of "Theaetetus flies"? It can only be this: the form *Theaetetus* communes with the forms *being* and *otherness* so that *Theaetetus* (is distinct from *otherness*, and hence) is the same (via combination with *sameness*); so too for *flying*. But this is absurd.

Perhaps we should run through the inapplicability of the predicationalist interpretation one more time. Suppose it is claimed that our false statement should be analyzed as follows: "*Flying* is erroneously predicated of Theaetetus." Then what is *flying* predicated of? We have already noted that this question seems to lead Frede to be committed to a form named "Theaetetus." If so, this is to take an Aristotelian first substance for a Platonic form. We should also observe that "erroneously" is just a concealed version of "falsely," which has not been removed, and so not explained, by the analytical process. If we eliminate "erroneously" as well as the thesis of a form named "Theaetetus," then we might as well eliminate the thesis of a form named *flying*. The falsehood of "Theaetetus flies" then follows directly from looking at Theaetetus. And so the predicationalist analysis of the statement "Theaetetus flies" may be an acceptable piece of grammar, but it has no more to do with the truth or falsity of the statement than does the combinatorial interpretation.

The Stranger's analysis boils down to this. A false statement says either (1) that what is, is not, or (2) that what is not, is. In both cases, it says something "other" (263b7, 263d1). In fact, the Stranger gives an example of the second case only. He does not analyze statements like "Theaetetus is not sitting." So we restrict ourselves to what he does say, namely, that he has explained "Theaetetus flies." This statement evidently says that what is not, is. After all, Theaetetus is not flying. But this means that what is, is not. So either we have to accept negative facts, or we are forced to begin, again, to analyze "Theaetetus is not flying." This is a true statement that says either that what is not, is not, or that what is, is, depending upon how one explains the "fact" that Theaetetus is not flying. If we reject negative facts, then, it very much looks as if the correct analysis of "Theaetetus flies" is "Theaetetus is not flying." I doubt whether many readers will take this as a successful piece of analysis.

The remainder of this scene contains a brief account of the previously mentioned faculties of the soul. To begin with, "διάνοια and λόγος are the same." However, διάνοια is an inner dialogue between the soul and itself, occurring without speech (263d10–e6). Λόγος therefore refers here to speech, not to ratio. As such, it is the stream of sound that flows from the soul via the mouth. The distinction between affirmation and negation applies to λόγος, but it can occur silently within the soul, κατὰ διάνοιαν, "by way of διάνοια, in which case it is called δόξα (263e7–264a3). This seems to mean that there is a distinction between thinking and judging. When we arrive at a δόξα by way of sense perception (and not via thinking alone), this is correctly called a "fancy" (φαντασία; 264a4–7). Since these can be true or false, we must not identify them with "fantasms." After summarizing these definitions, the Stranger infers that the defined terms are all akin to discourse, and hence some of them must be sometimes false (264a8–b4). The Stranger does not mention νόησις or intellectual perception. However, he begins his next sentence with the verb κατανοεῖν. He asks whether Theaetetus "perceives" that they have discovered false judgment and discourse sooner than they expected. "I perceive it" (κατανοῶ), Theaetetus replies (264b5–8). Unfortunately, something has gone wrong on the discursive road from the vision of pure looks to the perception of the meaning of falsehood.

In the preceding pages, I have taken the Stranger's technical doctrines with the utmost seriousness and have subjected them to close analysis, together with those views according to which these doctrines represent a new and crucial stage in the evolution of Plato's thought. The result of this analysis is that the doctrines are a technical failure, and that they do not represent a radical shift from the ostensibly "immature" or metaphysical Platonism to a new and substantially more sophisticated anticipation of Fregean and post-

Fregean concepts. It is a separate question whether either the Stranger or Plato puts forward these doctrines seriously or ironically. To this question, I will give a separate answer, one which follows from the Prologue to this study. In my opinion, it would be going too far to say that the technical digression in the *Sophist* is merely an elaborate Platonic joke (as some have also suggested about the second half of the *Parmenides*). I prefer to say that Plato was experimenting with a technical resolution to the problems of non-being and falsehood and at the same time was indicating in the ways discussed in the Prologue that a technical resolution to these problems is not feasible. In other words, Plato is both presenting a plausible philosophical accusation against Socrates, by means of the persona of the Stranger, and himself refuting that accusation. As I put it earlier, the *Statesman* is the Stranger's recantation. None of this, however, deprives the experiment in the *Sophist* of its technical interest. It was necessary to work through the details in order to persuade ourselves that at least this technical solution is a failure. By the same token, our criticism of the predicationalist thesis was also necessary, in order to show that the "late" Plato was not a prototypical version of a Fregean or post-Fregean analytical philosopher. And, to the extent that the Stranger is such a prototypical version in the *Sophist* (namely, someone who defines fundamental philosophical problems in a technical manner, in order to obtain a technical solution), we can now see that his "technicism" renders him indistinguishable from the sophists themselves. This is certainly not to condemn τέχνη. It is rather to assert that Plato's conception of philosophy is exhibited by his dialogues altogether, and not by a heap of fragments selected on the basis of principles that are not to be found in those dialogues.

Diaeresis Concluded

(264b9–268d5)

After this lengthy detour, we are now ready to conclude the diaeresis of image making, and will then have captured the sophist (264b9–c6). We distinguished initially between icons and fantasms, but we did not then know which kind the sophist makes. This puzzle led in turn to dizziness, induced by the denial of falsehood, and so of icons, images, and fantasms (264c7–d2). We have now presumably seen that non-being "touches" λόγος, and so, that falsehood in fact exists, whether in the form of λόγος or judgment (δόξα), as something which purports to be, but is not, the original (264d3–6). False statements were thus connected with image making and fantasm making at 260d5–63. Hence we can now conclude that "imitations of beings" (μιμήματα τῶν ὄντων) exist, and that "an art of deception can arise from this disposition."

It should be noted that the Stranger does not explicitly identify falsehoods as fantasms. The sophist is an imitator of beings (235a1) and hence an image maker. Since fantasms are inaccurate copies, it is assumed that the sophist manufactures fantasms rather than icons. However, icons are also marked by the property of not being what they resemble. It might be thought that icons identify themselves as images whereas fantasms do not. Of course, speeches, whether icons or fantasms, cannot be mistaken for things themselves. But if fantasms implicitly deny or are constructed upon the explicit hypothesis that denies the existence of pure forms, they may be construed as claiming to be, not spatio-temporal things, but original interpretations of the value of such things.

At 260d5–e3, the fantasm-producing segment of the image-making art is identified as the mode of sophistical deception. The sophist, however, denies that his productions can lead us into falsehood. In order to make sense of the sophist's claim and follow the Stranger's advice of always stating our opponent's thesis in the best possible way, we must distinguish between images of things or beings and imitations of judgment. The sophist does not pretend to be a carpenter or a geometer. He does not produce inaccurate copies of houses or geometrical proofs. Instead, he produces judgments, and he trains us in the art of persuading others to accept our judgments. It could be argued that this is a more plausible doctrine than that by which the Stranger attributes non-being, and hence the capacity to produce falsehood, to *all* images at 236e1–237a4 and again at 264c7–d6. Let us restrict ourselves here to discursive images. Non-being "touches" the dimension of pure forms thanks to the power of *otherness*. It is transmitted into discourse, on the Stranger's account, because discourse consists of combinations of names which refer, either directly or indirectly, to forms. A false statement says "what is not." This can only mean that it says something "other." But other than what? We cannot even say in all cases: other than the speaker's intention, for the speaker may "believe" or "judge" that he is speaking in accord with his intention. This may be countered by the claim that the forms which he combines, or the predications he asserts, do not "in fact" obtain. But that is a matter of fact or truth value, not of semantics or meaning. A failure to draw this distinction leads to the suppression of the doctrine of forms. But to draw that distinction is to show that the Stranger has not explained falsehood.

The Stranger demonstrates neither the nature of images nor the existence of false statements. He takes both as given. Whereas this is perhaps defensible, the point is that these assumptions are never legitimately connected to the doctrine of forms. If "not to be" is in fact "to be," but merely to be "other," this will not do as an explanation of falsehood. The fact that a statement says something "other" than what it "seems" to say is not enough to make it false. The "other" sense may be a superior version of the truth of what the sentence, on its surface, says poorly. Furthermore, a sentence *cannot* say something "other" than what it seems to say. A sentence says what it says: for example, "Theaetetus flies" does not say "Theaetetus does not fly." In sum, "otherness" is not falsehood. In a false statement, there is a gap between what is said and things themselves (whether objects or forms). This gap cannot be entirely plugged with the work of *otherness*. The gap exists within the nature of images as images, not simply in fantasms. The image is not, precisely with respect to what it shows itself to be: *the look*. To deny this is to deny the distinction between original and image, and so once more, it is to deny the doctrine of forms.

It is easy to show that the Stranger has not explained the nature of the image. We may grant that an image "is not" its original because of the work of *otherness*. But this still leaves "likeness" unexplained. The image cannot be "like" the original thanks to the work of *sameness*. The "is" in the "is and is not" property of the image cannot be that of identity; so the predicationalist analysis gets us no closer to an account of the nature of likeness. We might try the desperate expedient of positing a pure form of *likeness*. The Stranger does not himself take this turn, and for a good reason. If there were a form *likeness*, it would contain within its nature the "is and is not" property, and so be analyzable into *being* and *otherness*. On the other hand, if "likeness" is not a form, but a property of the spatio-temporal world (and hence of language), in what sense is it false? Is it not rather true that some things are like others? Once likeness is removed from the context of the relation between original and image, who is to say that what I judge to be "like" is not, but only seems to be?

With these difficulties established, let us return to the diaeresis. We need to divide the family of image making, retaining always the righthand segment and so staying in communication with the sophist until we have stripped him of whatever he has in common with other image makers, thus leaving only his peculiar nature. We will then display this nature, primarily to ourselves, but next, to those who are most akin to our method (264d7–265a3). It would seem to follow from this that we will not make a public display of our analysis.

The following diaeresis is either number 6 or 7 (excluding the diaeresis of the angler), for reasons noted previously.

STEP ONE: According to the Stranger, we initially divided τέχνη into production and acquisition (265a4–6). The sophist "disguised himself in the forms" of acquisition, such as hunting, contests, and merchandising. The term ἐφαντάζεθ' implies that the sophist does not belong in these forms. So by the Stranger's own account again, the previous diaereses were mistaken. We ourselves may prefer to believe that they provided us with accurate portraits of the sophist's intricate nature. The Stranger now disregards the results of the previous diaereses, and begins again with a division of production (αὐτὴν τὴν ποιητικήν) into two parts, since mimesis produces images but not things themselves (265a7–b3).

STEP TWO: At 219a10, ποίησις was said to consist in (1) farming or the care of living bodies, (2) the care of tools, and (3) mimesis. We are now concerned with mimesis only. The Stranger divides this into divine and human mimesis. Theaetetus does not understand,

and the Stranger explains. We must decide whether to follow "the belief of the many" (τῷ τῶν πολλῶν δόγματι) by saying that nature produces animals, plants, and lifeless bodies constructed in the earth "from some spontaneous cause, without productive intelligence" (διάνοια). Or shall we rather say that they have been produced by a divine demiurge who works with λόγος and knowledge? Theaetetus admits that he wavers between these two judgments and often changes his mind. "But looking at you, and understanding that you believe them to come into being owing to god, I also adopt this response" (265b8–d4). "This belief of the many" presumably refers to the judgments of the majority of philosophers. The Stranger proposes that "the things called 'natural' have been produced by a divine art," whereas the things constructed from these by mortals are produced by a human art. "Correct," says Theaetetus (265d2–6).

STEP THREE: Divine and human production are each divided into two further parts. In each case, there is a making of originals (αὐτο-ποιητική) and of images (εἰδωλοποιική; 265e8–266b1). Animals, including humans, and all constituents of natural things, are made by god (266b2–5). Images corresponding to each of these are made by "daimonic contrivance" (δαιμονία . . . μηχανῇ). This is not clear to Theaetetus. The Stranger explains that these images include dreams and the spontaneous fantasms (φαντάσματα) of daylight, such as shadows and mirror images (266b6–c4). We note that εἶδος is used at 266c3 for "image." Theaetetus agrees and says that there are two corresponding works of divine production. These are not given technical names (266c5–6). In the case of human art, man makes either the original (for example, a house; αὐτουργική) or an image (εἰδωλο-ποιική). We may observe that a painting is called "a kind of human dream produced for those who are awake" (266c7–d4). Theaetetus agrees (266d5–7).

STEP FOUR: Since falsehood "genuinely exists" (ὄντως ὄν), we are now able to divide image making into eikastics and fantastics (266d8–e5). It is not clear whether falsehood obtains in both cases or in the latter only.

STEP FIVE: We bypass divine mimesis and divide the fantastic art of humans into the tool-working kind and the kind in which the producer is himself the tool. Theaetetus does not understand (267a1–5). The Stranger has in mind the imitation of another person's figure or voice; we can leave to someone else the task of naming tool working (267a6–b3). I note the following difficulty. At 235c2 and 235d1, mimesis was identified as a branch of poetics and seemed to be the same as image making (εἰδωλοποιική). At 265a10–b3, this definition was in effect repeated. But now mimesis is defined as a segment of human fantasm making.

STEP SIX: Mimesis has two parts, depending upon whether it occurs with or without knowledge of what is imitated. The man who copies your bodily figure must "know" or "perceive" you (the Stranger has now shifted from εἰδότες to γιγνώσκων); that is, he must be acquainted with you (267b4–c1). The Stranger turns next to "the schema of justice and all of virtue." As Theaetetus agrees, many who are ignorant of virtue, but have some opinion about it, strive zealously to make this supposed virtue appear in themselves (267c2–7). So the Stranger, of course, assumes that there are "original" virtues, or what must presumably be called "forms." The Stranger takes the imitation of virtue as paradigmatic for those who copy with or without knowledge. There are many such, not identified by those lazy predecessors who neglected the division of families by looks (τῆς τῶν γενῶν κατ' εἴδη διαιρέσεως; 267c8–d7). The Stranger takes (what he calls) the rather daring step of introducing two names, one for "imitation rooted in opinion" (δοξομιμητικήν) and one for "a kind of investigative mimesis" that functions on the basis of knowledge (τὴν δὲ μετ' ἐπιστήμης ἱστορικήν τινα μίμησιν; 267d8–e3).

STEP SEVEN: The Stranger distinguishes between imitators who doubt their own knowledge and those who do not. The latter are called "simple" and the former "ironical" imitators (267e4–268a8).

STEP EIGHT: Two kinds of ironists show themselves to the Stranger. "I see one kind that ironises in public before many people in long speeches, and another that ironises in private using short speeches to force his partner in dialogue to contradict himself" (268a9–b5). The upshot of this is to identify the public ironist as a popular orator (δημολογικόν) and the private ironist (who cannot be wise, since he was said to be ignorant) as "the altogether genuine sophist" (τὸν παντάπασιν ὄντως σοφιστήν; 268b10–c4).

One must be unusually obtuse not to see and wonder at the Stranger's own irony. The culmination of the hunt for the sophist is to identify Socrates as a practitioner of that art. This is not to say that the coincidence between Socrates and the just-defined sophist is perfect. But the fit is sufficiently close to vindicate our initial suspicion that the Stranger has come to Athens to level an accusation against Socrates. The charge, of course, is one that will be admitted by Socrates in the *Apology*. He ignores political rhetoric and contradicts in private by means of short speeches in dialogue, while at the same time claiming that he knows only that he does not know.

SUMMARY: The Stranger concludes the dialogue by binding together the name "sophist" as before, "weaving it together from the end to the beginning" (268c5–7). In fact, the diaeresis itself proceeded from the beginning to the end. So too with all the previous summaries, except for diaeresis 4 (or later, 5). In the summary of that diaeresis, the distinction between money making and garrulity is omitted in such a way as to blur the difference between Socrates and the sophist.

Here is the Stranger's final summary: contradicting, ironical, opining, mimetic, maker of fantasms, a human producer who has been defined in speeches as a juggler (or wonder worker; 268c8–d2). This summary blends together the steps of the diaeresis, in reverse order, with an earlier rhetorical characterization of the sophist. It also omits the distinction at 267a1ff between using tools and using oneself as a tool. To the very end, the sophist's nature seems to resist exact enumeration.

"Whoever says that the genuine sophist is of this family and blood will speak most truly," the Stranger concludes. Theaetetus has the last word: "Altogether so" (268d3–5).

In the *Theaetetus*, Socrates says that the sophists, like all his predecessors save Parmenides, are members of the army led by Homer. They are all poets or "world makers." Sophistry is the production of the world in accord with the measures or ratios laid down by human perspectives. The Stranger's new teaching, on the contrary, is intended to lay bare the eternal structure of the one and only world. However, one may still ask whether this unique world is itself a "construction" in the image of the philosopher. In the *Philebus* (28c6), Socrates says that wise men all agree that pure intellect (νοῦς) is our king of heaven and earth, thereby exalting themselves. He does not say, but we may well ask, whether the philosopher is not the original of the image of god.

EPILOGUE

I

The *Sophist* is a philosophical drama, or in its own terminology, a peculiar blending of production and acquisition. As such, it is a musical artifact, designed by the soul to contribute to the care of the soul. The dialogue thus bears a limited analogy to bread and clothing, which are constructed by the body to contribute to the care of the body. However, there are at least two fundamental differences between philosophical music on the one hand and products like bread and clothing on the other. The first difference turns upon the interiority or self-reflexive nature of discourse. One may attempt to deny the philosophical significance of interiority by identifying philosophy as a certain kind of propositional discourse which is by its nature public or external. As an example of such discourse, one might cite the conceptual articulations embodied in diaeresis, or the division and collection in accordance with kinds. We have now seen that these conceptual articulations of the sophist are human products, the functions of which are relative to the interior experience that constitutes the basis of our humanity. There is no point in defining that basis, since definitions are concepts, and the senses of concepts are finally determined by individual human beings, who talk to themselves and to others. This talk is in one sense exterior or public, but only because it can be contrasted with interior understanding, which the Eleatic Stranger regularly appeals to under a variety of names.

One reason why many contemporary philosophers believe it irrelevant to speak of interiority is because they do not take seriously the philosophical relevance of the soul. Instead, they speak of the intellect or mind. For the Eleatic Stranger, however, there can be no

315

intellect except where there is soul. For our purposes, the difference between the intellect and the soul can be stated as follows. The propositional artifacts produced by the intellect, and to the extent that the intellect is identified with these artifacts, the intellect itself, can be modelled by a machine. Apart from the fact that a model is an image rather than an original, we note that there is no machinelike model of the soul. From the Stranger's standpoint, to speak of a "living" machine would be an absurdity. Nevertheless, if machines are alive, then, again from the Stranger's standpoint, they have souls. But the perception of the soul, in both the subjective and objective senses of the genitive, is not the same as the conceptual grasp of propositions.

Let me put this in slightly different terms. Those who oppose introducing talk about interiority into philosophy will claim that philosophical discourse is essentially public. Suppose we grant this claim for the moment. It is nevertheless true that public discourse, as distinguished from ideological chanting, is not spoken by the public but by individuals. Public discourse originates in private speech, or in the use of a public language for productive thinking. A λόγος is not simply the sum of its semantic and syntactical elements, but a ratio of these elements produced by an individual thinker. This ratio has an ambiguous nature. Suffice it to say that, by the argument of the Stranger, a distinction must be made between the ratio as an original and the discursive copy of that original. It may be true that the original ratio has a universal signification. But the fact remains that, as copied within a discursive proposition, the ratio also acquires a signification that is relative to the private intention of the speaker. To overlook this is to be naive, not technically competent. The private significance of the ratio, once it becomes public in its own right, is then an element in the reservoir of public knowledge. It retains its dual status as both public and capable of being put to private use.

Here is an example of the point I have just made. I can know the significance of some proposition for another person or community of persons, without accepting or even understanding that asserted significance. Some individuals are immune to the significance of science or universal speech, and this is not infrequently true of scientists and other experts, whom we then call, depending upon the rhetorical inflection they give to their immunity, either "tough-minded" or disillusioned. In the extreme case, we call them nihilists. Indeed, a truly universal speech would seem to be deaf to its own significance, since it is not speech but the individual speaker who hears. This individual is sometimes deaf to the distinction between the content of universal speech and the significance he attaches to it. In this case, there arises the self-contradictory situation in which science declares both its complete neutrality to human value and its nature as the ultimate human value. Such is the case in the *Sophist*, as is plain from the Stranger's identification of diaeresis as the distinction of like from unlike and of dialectic as the science of the free man.

If, then, philosophy is universal enlightenment, it is the individual who must be enlightened, for if the public is not a community of enlightened individuals, it can only be a mindless crowd. This philosophical thesis is understood by the sophist, who attempts, as Socrates claims in the *Theaetetus*, to derive a public doctrine from the primacy of private perception. The incoherence of the sophist's effort is due, not to the irrelevance of privacy, but to a failure to identify stable elements of perception. A stable element is not necessarily one that is publicly accessible. What must be publicly accessible is the language within which one speaks, to oneself or to others, about the nature of this element. Even if it were true that language constitutes the nature of all stable elements, privacy would remain in the multiplicity of languages. The striking feature of "Platonism," in the sense of the regular implication of Plato's dialogues, is this: philosophy is analogous to sophistry in that both root genuine publicity in a kind of private perception. We can negotiate translations from one language to another by virtue of our perception of elements that are not constituted by any language whatsoever. The forms of the Eleatic Stranger, as the elements of intelligibility, have a public and indeed universal significance precisely because of their direct accessibility to the eye of the soul, an accessibility that cannot be mediated by, but is the basis of, public discourse.

Whereas propositions are, or may be, public, life is both public and private. Contemporary emphasis upon propositions is a consequence of the separation of philosophy from life. As such it is closely connected to, if not at bottom identical with, the attempt to define life in public or universal terms. The least one can say is that if philosophy does not concern itself with life, life will soon put an end to philosophy. This is how we must understand the Platonic thesis that philosophy is a way of life, a thesis given melodramatic expression in the *Republic* in the daydream of the philosopher-king. At the same time, it should not be forgotten that too public a concern by the philosopher for life may lead to his death, as is described melodramatically in the *Apology*. Thus Socrates recommends that the philosopher should be indifferent to human beings or aspire to death, but also that the philosopher must know the nature of every human being and accommodate his discourse accordingly.

Some of my readers will assume that the preceding paragraphs have been addressed to the relation of epistemology and psychology. However, this is not my intention. Epistemology and psychology have no existence beyond the walls of the seminar room (unless one counts their ghostly manifestations in public life as a form of existence). They, like the seminar room itself, are constructions of a more fundamental activity that is at once too transparent and too obscure to be expressed in such terms. Other readers may classify my remarks as a consequence of a literary existentialism. Once again, I must demur. Existentialism is a product either of the modern university or the cafe, neither of which institutions is visible in, let alone equivalent to, the Platonic dialogue. That my remarks are literary, on the other hand, is no more and no less true than that the remarks of, say, Rudolph Carnap and Donald Davidson are literary as well. Philosophers of the analytical persuasion, while not entirely insensitive to style, have been unduly reticent in commenting upon their own rhetoric, however freely they condemn the rhetoric of others. Those of us, humble or famous, who write for the public, are all litterateurs. The serious question is one of pertinence. Which literary genre is appropriate to the discussion of a Platonic dialogue? It is impertinent to offer a response to this question if one begins by ignoring the visibility of the dialogue as a public artifact.

I now come back to my opening comparison. The first difference between a dialogue and a loaf of bread is that the function of the bread is detached from the question of its significance. I can articulate universal propositions of a publicly confirmable nature about the role of bread in human life (including references to the famous instinct of self-preservation). However, I must answer for myself the question whether life is worth living. It is entirely secondary whether or not the public agrees with that answer. For the public, to paraphrase Proust, is not a waste product, but nevertheless an accumulating excretion of each individual's effort to answer the aforementioned question. The function of a Platonic dialogue, however, is not detachable from the question of its significance. Its function will vary directly with the significance we attach to it. This can be said of bread only to the extent that it becomes a "character" in a philosophical dialogue. There are then, no universal propositions of a publicly confirmable nature about the role of philosophical, and so

Platonic, dialogues in human life. I can put this in a slightly different way. Plato's "secret teaching" is secret, not because of an intentional concealment of opinions (these are easily detected), but because of the very nature of philosophical opinions, which conceal themselves or their referents even as they are being formulated and so brought out into the open.

This last contention will remind some readers of Heidegger's ontological thesis concerning the concealment of being. My point is that the Heideggerean doctrine is anticipated in the Platonic dialogues. There is nothing anachronistic in this statement. It does carry the deeper implication that what Heidegger calls the history of metaphysics is a misleading if not altogether false account. This, however, is a topic for another discussion. My remark about the nature of philosophical opinions is based upon the same everyday experiences that underlie contemporary science, mathematics, and indeed, every domain of intellectual activity. I shall begin my discussion of this point by stating the second fundamental difference between philosophy and bread. At a certain level of analysis, it is easy to distinguish between the natural constituents of bread and their technical modification. In the case of a philosophical work like the Platonic dialogue, the distinction is not so easy to make.

The problem raised by the attempted distinction may be articulated into the topics indicated by the titles of the three acts of the present study. Does the soul possess a power that enables it to distinguish between originals and images? Are forms like wheat and rye? If so, does the dependence of grain upon human cultivation imply a similar dependence of the elements of thought upon the process of thinking itself? Is every articulation of human experience already a modification of an original that is inaccessible apart from human production? Those for whom the senses of things are produced by language, since they do not go quite so far as to assert that things are also linguistic productions, admit of a separation between sense and reference which is an unself-conscious version of Kant's distinction between concepts and the *Ding an sich*. Of course, Kant's concepts must be filled with sensations, but the intelligibility of sensation (and of the schematizing of concepts) is conceptual. Concepts are neither things nor the paradigms of things. But they are the medium through which things become accessible to us, and though accessible these things are inaccessible except through that medium.

We cannot, at the level of ordinary experience, be satisfied with the assertion that the essence or look of wheat is human labor. After all, man does not plant a project of his intentional activity. Seeds may be food for thought as well as for the body, but they are not thoughts. Why then should we be satisfied with the metaphysical thesis that senses, or the essences of sensible assertions, are provided by the language or the history of the language in which those senses are normally expressed? One might be tempted to reply as follows. The seed can be perceived by the body before it is planted or modified by labor. The sense, however, can be perceived only in its linguistic realization, and language is a tool by which we construct, that is, produce, senses. Such a reply begs the question, since it does not exclude the possible distinction between perceiving with the assistance of language and producing entities. I have already noted that we still need to account for the relation between produced linguistic entities and material beings. For example, we need to explain how it is possible for mathematics to serve as a tool in the explanation of the structures and functions of nature. Whereas sets, and arguably even natural numbers, may be inventions of the mathematician, does it make sense to say that gravity and molecular motion are the invention of the physicist?

It will be replied to this that mathematical physics, or modern science, is an expression of the western European linguistic *Lebensform*. I regard this as a vacuous response. Those who live in ignorance of the laws of gravity and thermodynamics are not living in some other world (except in a metaphorical sense); they are living in ignorance. What we require is an explanation of why the western European *Lebensform* is adequate to an explanation of the work of the world, whereas nonwestern forms of life either produce no such adequate account, or else do produce parts of such an account. In either case, what counts is a perception of the unity of the world and the relative value of the various things we can say about it. To take only one example, Babylonian creation myths are not about some world other than the world studied by modern science. These myths may have brought out some interesting aspects of our common world that are not accessible to modern science. But that is a mark of the diversity within unity, not of the diversity of worlds. To be told that science is a consequence of our life form is to be told that, finally, science is on a par with Babylonian creation myths. For these, too, are consequences of a life form, and how are we to choose between life forms? In fact, such a choice is relatively simple, since once we perceive the diversity of life forms, we are in a position to understand the superiority of one to another. To say that this understanding is again a consequence of one's own life form is to speak truly. But it casts no light upon whether one's own life form enables one to speak truly.

I have chosen the example of modern science because it illustrates better than any other example two closely connected points. The first point is that philosophers and sociologists of science are today infected with a very deep crisis due to the influence of the doctrine of linguistic horizons and life forms. The second is that this crisis arises from the denial of the philosophical (and hence scientific) relevance of extralinguistic interiority or privacy, that is, from the denial of extralinguistic standpoints like those of the intellectual perception, not of Platonic ideas of objects, but of sense and significance. The extralinguistic standpoint of the speaker is coordinate to the integrity of the natural world, which is of course not radically independent of, but is accessible to, the speaker in its deeds. I would not deny that the interpretations (the scientific theories) of these deeds are human artifacts. And I have myself insisted upon the origin of the significance of the work of the natural world in the human individual. Since significance means "significance for man," where else could it originate (if we exclude references to divine revelation as lying outside the horizon of philosophy)? But human beings are themselves products of the work of the natural world, which, as a world, is something more than atoms in the void. Platonism, again understood as the regularly implied doctrine of the Platonic dialogues, holds that nature provides human beings with an ordering of significance. This implication can be stated as a doctrine of natural ends. I regard this as an overstatement, however, because it implies that the order is immutable and without exception; even further, it suggests that the natural ends are accessible to us in such a way as to permit us to decide unambiguously in any instance what to do or say. Even a casual familiarity with the Platonic corpus should suggest that, despite the confidence with which the Eleatic Stranger speaks of dialectic, the dialogues contain no such doctrine of natural ends. What they do contain is the basis for all sensible experience, including that of science, and even of modern science. Even when we go altogether beyond the more or less directly visible looks of everyday life, it is these directly visible looks that serve as nature's guide. And whether we call ourselves philosophers or scientists, we must go beyond these natural looks. The deepest problem in Plato is whether, in so going beyond them, we thereby discover that they are not natural but artificial. This is the problem of whether we can distinguish between philosophy and sophistry. But it is also the problem of whether even sophistry in its original form can be distinguished from nihilism. The sophist, after all, also makes certain claims about human nature. Once these claims are "relativized" to Greek history or political life, the triumph of sophistry is its own disappearance.

II

Mathematics does not simply prove theorems; it results in airplanes and nuclear energy. Zen Buddhism, for example, does neither of these. In itself, this does not prove the superiority of mathematics to Zen Buddhism. What it shows is that if we behave, and hence talk, in different ways, the results will be different. To a Platonist (in the sense in which I am using this term), this is not an argument for relativism, but rather for the stability of nature. We still have to decide what to do, and hence, what to say. But there is a basis for making this decision. This brings us to a deeper aspect of the problem. If the stability of the world cannot be explained by the thesis that the world is just talk, can we talk "about" the stability of the world without blurring the distinction between the originals and their linguistic images? What does "about" mean in this context?

In some ways like a contemporary of ours, the Eleatic Stranger seems to take his bearings by language. However, he does so because language is publicly accessible, not because privacy is irrelevant. To the extent that the distinction between philosophy and sophistry corresponds to the distinction between stability and instability, and so depends upon the stability of distinctions, philosophy cannot be merely talk about talk. Indeed, philosophy is not merely talk, but (to quote the Eleatic Stranger) the talk of the free man. If freedom is mere talk, then the distinction between philosophy and sophistry disappears. I leave it open whether or not anyone is free. My point is that freedom is not "about" anything, in the sense that a proposition is about a thing, a relation, or a state of affairs. Freedom is an original, not an image. This is why we refer to freedom as an ideal. It becomes actual, if at all, in human life. Thus, for example, "freedom of speech" refers to an absence of human restraint on what may be said by a living speaker who, as unrestrained, lives freely. But this is not the Stranger's point. He means by "free speech" the λόγος or rational analysis based upon (but not necessarily limited to the discussion of) pure ontological forms. Speech of this sort does not free us from the constraints of our political environment. It frees us from the interior and largely private dissolution engendered by sophistry.

I say "largely private" because freedom is a condition of the soul; but, as λόγος, it is mediated by language.

Freedom, then, understood as dialectic, is in the first instance talk about ontological originals. We have noted the following dilemma. If λόγος is an image, then there is no purely discursive access to originals. But if λόγος is itself the originals, in the sense of ratios or proportions, then there is no independent domain of originals serving as the basis for the distinction between accurate and inaccurate speech. In this case, all speech is "accurate," because whatever we say, the proposition exhibits precisely the ratio or proportion of its own structure. The Stranger certainly rejects the second of these alternatives. In order to resolve the dilemma, he must do something more than to embrace the first alternative. He must also provide us with a discursive account of intellectual perception. No such account is ever presented, nor could it be. An account of perception is either the original or an image. If it is an image, we require an independent perception of the original, in order to decide whether the image is an icon or a fantasm. To say that it is the original seems absurd, for how could perception be discourse? If it were, rival accounts of the object of perception would be possible, and these could be evaluated only on the basis of a direct, nondiscursive perception. It therefore seems that the dilemma cannot be avoided.

The basis of the "technical" problems discussed in the *Sophist* is thus the relation between the public and the private. Ontological forms, like numbers and geometrical figures, are intrinsically public in the sense that they present one face or look to everyone. However, this very publicity, since it is mediated by language, produces differing accounts of the looks in question. And this raises a fundamental question concerning the intrinsic simplicity of elements like pure forms, geometrical figures, and numbers. Perhaps that initial perception of simplicity conceals a deeper and unfathomable complexity. Perhaps the "one face" of elements of intuition is a mask concealing an intricacy equal to that of the sophist. If this is so, then science and even mathematics become human constructions based upon fantasms or inaccurate images of intrinsically inaccessible originals. The Stranger argues from the unexamined assumption that the "letters" in his eidetic alphabet are intrinsically simple and directly accessible in their simplicity. We can therefore state the fundamental aporia of Platonism in terms of the Stranger's procedures as follows. The aporia is not one of metaphysical profundity but, so to speak, of radical superficiality. This formulation covers not just the perception of formal elements but also our apprehension of the general looks of everyday experience. Whereas Socrates criticizes the sophistical doctrine of relativistic perception, neither he nor the Eleatic Stranger ever demonstrates that we directly perceive, and so correctly identify, beings like sophists, or for that matter, trees, horses, or human beings. The ultimate looks of things, the eidetic letters, show themselves directly on the surfaces of things. But the surfaces of things look different from different perspectives, and the ultimate elements are themselves mediated or differentiated by our efforts to analyze or even to describe them accurately.

There is, then, a double obstacle to λόγος or perfect speech. Such a speech is possible within carefully limited contexts. But the more rigorously we try to construct a fundamental and comprehensive ontology, the more we become entangled in the shifting multiple looks of sophistry. The more we shift our attention from a narrow concern with the details of the Stranger's analysis of non-being or falsehood and take in the entire dialogue, the more patent is Plato's recognition of this double obstacle. Philosophy, as portrayed in the *Sophist*, and in the entire Platonic corpus, is not a doctrine but a problem. The dramatic or human face of the problem is how to distinguish between the philosopher and the sophist. But the problem of the human face corresponds with poetic exactitude to the technical problems of being and non-being, truth and falsehood, original and image. It is the intelligibility of these technical problems that provides us with the best verification of the visibility of simple looks. The fact that there seem to be no solutions to these problems does not alter our capacity to see what the problems are. The Stranger, exactly like Socrates, takes this visibility for granted. One could perhaps say that, for Socrates, if sophistry were truly trimphant over philosophy, there would be no problems. Whether this is right or not, it is clear that the Stranger develops a positive doctrine that goes beyond anything put forward elsewhere by Socrates. To the extent that this positive doctrine is intended as a punishment of Socrates' excessive reticence, we are entitled to conclude that the failure of the doctrine is equivalent to the rescinding of the punishment. Whatever Plato's personal views, Socrates gains an acquittal before the bar of philosophical justice by remaining silent in the presence of the Stranger. This silence is compatible with, and is in fact verified by, the excessive loquacity in the *Apology* that leads Socrates to his death.

The problem of speech and silence is introduced very early in the *Sophist*, in distinct but related ways. It is intrinsic to the question of the philosopher's "fantasms" or disguises, and also to the transi-

tion from the private possession of πράγματα to the common agreement upon names, which is in turn a pivotal aspect of the production of discursive images. We cannot penetrate the philosopher's
disguises, nor will there be a philosopher beneath the disguises, unless we are able to negotiate successfully the transition from things
to names. This, as we have seen, depends upon a distance between
things and names, a detachment of the one from the other, or a zone
of silence that enables us to distinguish between icons and fantasms. If the distinction is entirely verbal, then common agreement
upon names is a production of convention, neither the discovery nor
the analysis of nature. In sum, there is no purely discursive distinction between icons and fantasms, and therefore, no epistemic or
commonly acceptable definition of the distinction between the philosopher and the sophist.

From this standpoint, the "non-being" or death of Socrates is an
existential metaphor for the logical or ontological aporia of non-
being. Socrates dies, not because of an ironical concealment of his
positive doctrines from the Athenian people, but because of an exact and explicit statement to them of who (not what) he is. There is
no common agreement between the city and the philosopher, who
is unable to present a commonly acceptable doctrine. In the absence
of such a doctrine, Socrates becomes indistinguishable from the
sophist. Whereas both lack genuine knowledge, Socrates apparently
lacks also the art of public persuasion. Socrates' regular qualification, that he knows that he does not know, is a sophisticated and
sophistical-sounding grace note to a destructive frankness that challenges the common definitions upon which political life depends.
The sophist, on the other hand, disguises himself with the image of
the city itself: man, and hence νόμος, is the measure of all things.
Socrates' failure to resolve this problem is analogous to the Stranger's failure to resolve the problem of non-being. Both disguise the
original problem by transforming it into another problem. The un-
bridgeable disjunction between philosophy and politics is transformed by Socrates into the philosophical superiority of death to
life; and death is always available. But this is a sophism by Socrates'
own insistence upon the fact that philosophy is a way of life. Socrates' positive doctrine is precisely that philosophy is not a doctrine
but a way of life, and this not in a common or public sense, but in a
private one. Even in caring for his friends, Socrates cares primarily
for himself.

The Stranger comes to punish Socrates for his unspeakable hybris.
This punishment takes the form of a positive doctrine that can (os-

tensibly) be stated publicly with no harmful consequences, because it seems to have no political implications. But the technical doctrine is inadequate by its own technical standards. First, the Stranger transforms the problem of nothingness (τὸ μηδαμῶς ὄν) into the different and subordinate problem of negation. Second, his insistence upon the apolitical nature of his method, and so the implication that the results of this method are apolitical, are falsified by his inability to keep sharply distinct the criteria of like/unlike and better/worse. Third, if it is true to say that technical doctrines have no political implications, then the distinction between philosophy and politics has not been bridged but reinforced. The praise of genuine freedom as dialectic is an intrinsic rejection of the Greek conception of political freedom as guaranteed by the preservation of and obedience to the laws of the city. Philosophical freedom is once more freedom from νόμος. This point is made much more explicitly by the Stranger in the *Statesman* than in the *Sophist*, but it is plain enough from the *Sophist* as well.

In what precedes, I have not been arguing that it is impossible to distinguish between the philosopher and the sophist, but rather that there is no public basis for validating that distinction. Indeed, the philosopher cannot define himself to another philosopher, nor for that matter to himself. However, he does not need to do so, nor, I would hazard the guess, does he make the effort. Philosophers do not define themselves. If Plato teaches us anything, it is that philosophers identify themselves, through speeches and deeds, by the nobility and comprehensive eros of their souls. Similarly, sophists identify themselves, not by the invalidity of their arguments, but by the weakness of their souls. Noble speech is of course a striking testimony of a noble soul, but nobility is not reducible to validity.

The reader may protest that to speak of nobility is to invoke a criterion far vaguer than that of intellectual power. I am not certain that this is right. We perceive the one as easily as the other; and whereas intellectual power can be applied to base ends, nobility of soul cannot. The point, however, is that Plato, and specifically the Eleatic Stranger, with all his confident (or perhaps exaggerated) praise of logical analysis, insists upon the fact that the genuine philosopher possesses a noble soul. The Stranger as much as Socrates establishes (although he does not demonstrate) the connection between formal ontology and care of the soul. The dialectician, in a way reminiscent of Spinoza, is free in his articulation of necessity. At a still more comprehensive level, despite the Stranger's acceptance of nature as god, there is an unexplained bifurcation in his account of being. *Ousia*, the divine and hence ensouled totality, cannot be the same as the atomic form *being* (ὄν). What we may with caution refer to as the transcendence of *being* by *ousia* is the positive version of the transcendence of non-being by nothingness. Definite speech, which obeys the principles of reference, enumeration, and noncontradiction, is rooted in definite looks. Comprehensive being, however, possesses every look, whereas thoroughgoing nothingness has no look whatsoever. In both cases, the result is an absence of definiteness.

A careful consideration of the Stranger's technical doctrines leads us to the hypothesis that excessive definiteness transforms itself by an inner necessity into self-contradiction. If Socratic eros, the impulse toward a perfect life, leads inconsistently to death, the Stranger's formalist dialectic, carried to its logical extreme, ends in silence. The suggestion naturally presents itself that in order to avoid these extremes, eros and formalist dialectic must mediate one another. This suggestion is in fact enacted in the Platonic dialogue. The dialogues are not proofs but exhibitions of philosophical freedom. No one can prove that he is free. The best one can do is live *as if* one were free. It is in this sense that Socrates refers in the *Phaedo* to the ideas as the most stable hypothesis, and in the *Philebus* to the fact that philosophers conceive of god in their own image. But this is also the basis for the sophist's implicit critique of philosophy. Freedom is not the same as, but it depends upon, the grasp of the whole in λόγος (and hence the Hegelian doctrine of the whole as *Begriff*). I have suggested that the sophist lacks the comprehensive eros of the philosopher. At the same time, I have urged, with reference to the Platonic dialogues, that comprehensiveness, whether in eros or λόγος, leads to nothingness (and hence the Nietzschean doctrine of man's radical finitude). One could therefore suggest that the first principle of sophistry is the denial of the whole.

More specifically, the sophist agrees with the identification between the whole and the all, that is, between unity and the sum of its parts, but then asserts that this sum cannot be counted. Man, on this view, cannot count on the whole; he can count only upon himself. From this standpoint, one could regard the history of philosophy as the gradual triumph of the sophists over Plato. To leave the point at this cryptic formulation, however, would be quite misleading. We must not make the mistake of accepting Plato's rhetorical refutations of sophistry as adequate to the difficulty of the problem. Plato could object to the sophist that the vision of the whole provides us with the only stable basis for self-understanding, and that the rejection of the whole leads to man's dissolution or multiplication into all looks (all "world views"). The deepest sophistical countercharge is that the Platonist deceives himself by living *as if* the unity of the whole both transcends and unites the uncountability of the all. This is not a charge to be taken lightly. It must be understood, and in understanding it, the Platonist grasps his responsibility to assimilate and come to terms with modern philosophy. He thereby admits the possibility of giving up his Platonism.

The power of sophistry, in the extended sense I am giving to the term, is plain from the crucial denial, attributed to the sophist by the Stranger, of images. In the *Theaetetus*, Socrates develops his denial into a doctrine of perception; in his version of sophistry, things are as we perceive them. In other words, there is no detachment of πράγματα from sense perception, hence no mediating or copying of originals by images. In the *Sophist*, the same doctrine is presented in terms of the arts: whatever man produces is an original. Some originals are more powerful than others, but with respect to specific human desires or intentions. The self-claimed power of sophistry is precisely to be able to persuade others to submit to the sophist's desires or intentions. If sophistry is true, then, in the extended sense, the doctrine is that of forcing nature to submit to the will and intellect of man. Since the Stranger has not provided us with an adequate account of originals or images, he has not refuted sophistry by his own requirements.

What, then, does the *Sophist*, if not the Stranger, show us? At the level of everyday life, it is easy enough to distinguish between the philosopher and the sophist. At that level, the philosopher is noble and the sophist is, if not quite base, a critic of the efficacy of philosophical nobility. The deeper we go, however, the more difficult the distinction becomes, and the harder it is to preserve one's love of nobility, especially if one accepts the exclusive criterion of λόγος. The distinction is, so to speak, an image of the detachment of originals from images, and so, of being from non-being. But the Stranger will not permit this latter detachment, since it nullifies the program of a comprehensive λόγος that he makes explicit in his praise of the ostensibly universal method of diaeresis. Λόγος (unlike poetry) depends upon the detachment of things from discourse, yet it attempts to assimilate things into discourse. In this sense, λόγος is self-contradictory.

This contradiction is repugnant to Platonism, but it arises at the level of both practice and theory. We can thus express it in two complementary ways. First: the restricted eros of sophistry leads to the subordination of theory to practice, and thus to the exaltation of political life. At the same time, however, the comprehensive eros of the philosopher is itself an implicit assertion of the unity of theory and practice, which, as the *Republic* shows, requires to be actualized in a political form that, rhetoric aside, subordinates philosophical freedom to political necessity. Second: whatever is valuable in human life depends upon the transparency of the distinction between philosophy and sophistry. But transparency is at once too fragile to endure without and to survive the application of discursive analysis. One thinks here of Hegel's demonstration of the mediation or contradiction intrinsic to immediate experience, as well as of Wittgenstein's unending effort to "deconstruct" the metaphysical tradition as part of his Sisyphean effort to return to ordinary, transparent discourse. At another level, the history of science and mathematics illustrates the same dilemma. The transparency of the continuum dissolves upon analysis into dialectical antinomies turning upon discovery and creation, or what the Stranger calls acquisition and production.

These antinomies are no excuse for irrationalism. They are not a condemnation of analysis but the illuminating expression of its deepest nature and limits. Inconsistency arises when our ambitions exceed our grasp. It is often said that there is a technical solution to every technical problem. If this is true, the fact remains that the foundations of technical thinking cannot be technical in the same sense. The resolution of an antinomy at one level leads to its reappearance at another level. In mathematics, those limitations intrinsic to formalism can themselves be expressed in formal terms, but this does not remove their limitative nature.

The aforementioned aporiai, the relation between theory and practice and the elusiveness of transparency, are the main themes of Plato's *Sophist*. One may say that they are the warp and woof of every Platonic dialogue, and that the profundity of the *Sophist* lies in its treatment of the most pervasive issues. But it has to be understood that these issues are not those of identity and predication, nor even, if we take them in a narrowly technical sense, of non-being and falsehood. Technical problems of this sort are like threads in the pattern of an intricate oriental rug. At first sight, the pattern is transparent in its power to move us. A closer look reveals individual motifs and figures that play a role in the overall effect. In order to appreciate the rug properly, one must move one's attention back and forth from the details to the comprehensive pattern. And if it is possible to talk of verbal expressions of visual intricacy, how we formulate the overall pattern is quite different from the sum of our views of specific motifs and figures.

Essentially the same procedure obtains in the reading of a Platonic dialogue. The overall pattern is first visible as the transparency of everyday life. This transparency is on the one hand too obvious to seem profound, and on the other, impossible to grasp conceptually except by way of a study of the details. But it is also true that our access to the deepest technical problems, whether theoretical or practical, is by way of the surface transparency of everyday life. Our very concern with technical detail thus turns us back to the general context, and what was initially obvious now becomes intricate and obscure. We realize that the "given" is at one and the same time the concealed. To take the case in point, an everyday life articulated by philosophers and sophists is hardly primitive, nor can we identify it straightforwardly as "natural" in an unproblematically regulative sense. I am far from sanguine about our capacity to draw a thoroughgoing distinction between nature and history, nor do I accept the thesis that a given historical epoch provides the norm for human conduct. I can even grant that every manifestation of a natural phenomenon is by means of a temporal or historical perspective. Nevertheless, despite these admissions and others that might be made, something visible and crucial remains: the temporal or historical perspectives themselves, to begin with.

The transparency of the Platonic dialogue, the avenue of entry, is in fact not a natural but an artistic phenomenon. However, the content of the artistic production claims to be natural in this sense. The drama of human beings who *attempt* to distinguish between philosophy and sophistry is paradigmatic for our comprehension of any philosophical teaching. Those admirers of Plato who would wish us to return to the Greek polis have missed his point. The polis, as presented by Plato, is an artistic example of how the distinction between nature and history emerges from history itself, not as fully made, but as the paradigm of history. It is of entirely secondary interest whether Plato regarded the Greek polis as theoretically superior to other forms of political organization. Even if he did, that is a contingent opinion, open to argument, and does not go to the root of the serious political question: man's attempt to philosophize.

The beginning is not the end, any more than the way up is the same as the way down. The given is the *fact* of philosophy (τὸ ὅτι), not the "what" (τί ἐστι) of philosophy. I made this point earlier by noting that philosophers do not define themselves, as do professors, for example, by stating their field of specialization. To say "I am a philosopher" is not even an identification, but an enigma or an act of hybris. Nor is the philosopher defined by a life form or historical perspective. On the contrary, history, whether understood as ἱστορία or *Geschichtlichkeit*, is defined by philosophy. Exactly the same can be said of science and mathematics. It is for this reason, not because of the supposedly radical historicity of truth or being, that the philosopher must be concerned with history, or with what Socrates refers to as the stories told by the ancients. The fact that philosophy originates in Greece does not mean that it is relative in its *application* to the linguistic history of the Greeks. If non-Indo-European languages lack terms for "being" or "nature," then they stand condemned by the philosopher as inferior to the Indo-European languages. Philosophy is not simply disinterested analysis; it is also punishment or justice. To analyze is to dissolve, and to discover the truth is to expose error. Discovery and exposure are not fully intelligible either as ontological or cybernetic procedures. They are human activities, and the basis of ontology and cybernetics is everyday life.

What one may call the archaeological or desedimenting study of the past is thus an abstract or sophisticated version of the dialectic of concealment and discovery intrinsic to any act of human consciousness. In the last analysis, the appeal of sophistry is rooted in the sophistical nature of intelligent life. The soul is both sophist and philosopher: sophist, because acquisition is also production; philosopher, because it perceives this unity and attempts to divide it into its constituent elements. Analysis without intellectual perception is destruction: perception without analysis is silence. The unsolved riddle of non-being lies in its eschatological nature: it is both before the beginning and after the end. And yet, it "is."

WORKS CITED

Ackrill, J. L. 1957. "Plato and the Copula: *Sophist* 251–259," in *Plato* I. *Metaphysics and Epistemology*, edited by G. Vlastos, pp. 210–222.

Allen, R. E. 1960. "Participation and Predication in Plato's Middle Dialogues," in *Studies in Plato's Metaphysics*, edited by R. E. Allen, pp. 43–60.

———. 1967. *Studies in Plato's Metaphysics*, edited by R. E. Allen. London: Routledge and Kegan Paul, 1967.

Annas, J. 1976. *Aristotle's Metaphysics, Books M and N*, translated, and with introduction and notes. Oxford: Clarendon Press, 1976.

Barker, A. 1978. "ΣΥΜΦΩΝΟΙ 'ΑΡΙΘΜΟΙ: A Note on *Republic* 531c1–4," in *Classical Philology* 73:337–42.

———. 1981. "Aristotle on Perception and Ratios," in *Phronesis* 26:248–66.

Becker, O. 1931. "Die diairetische Erzeugung der platonischen Idealzahlen," in *Quellen und Studien zur Geschichte der Mathematik, Astronomie, und Physik*, abt. 1, bd. 1, pp. 464–94.

Benardete, S. 1960. "Plato. *Sophist* 223b1–7," in *Phronesis* 5:129–39.

———. 1963. "Eidos and Diaeresis in Plato's Statesman," in *Philologus* 107:193–226.

Blumenthal, H. J. 1966. "Did Plotinus Believe in Ideas of Individuals?" in *Phronesis* 11:61–80.

Brandwood, L. 1976. *A Word Index to Plato*. Leeds: W. S. Maney & Son, 1976.

Burkert, W. 1959. "Στοιχεῖον: eine semasiologische Studie," in *Philologus* 103:167–97.

Cantor, G. 1932. *Gesammelte Abhandlungen*, edited by E. Zermelo. Berlin: J. Springer Verlag, 1972.

Carls, R. 1974. *Idee und Menge*. Pfullacher philosophische Forschungen, bd. 11. Munich: Berchmannskolleg Verlag, 1974.

Cherniss, H. 1962. *Aristotle's Criticism of Plato and the Academy*. New York: Russell and Russell, 1962. (Original edition, 1944.)

———. 1957. "The Relation of the *Timaeus* to Plato's Later Dialogues," in *Studies in Plato's Metaphysics*, edited by R. E. Allen, pp. 339–78.

Cornford, F. M. 1935. *Plato's Theory of Knowledge*. New York: Liberal Arts Press, 1957. (Original edition, 1935.)

———. 1937. *Plato's Cosmology*. London: Routledge and Kegan Paul, 1937.

Crombie, I. M. 1963. *An Examination of Plato's Doctrines*, II. *Plato on Knowledge and Reality*. New York: Humanities Press, 1963.

Dauben, J. W. 1979. *Georg Cantor. His Mathematics and Philosophy of the Infinite*. Cambridge, Mass.: Harvard University Press, 1979.

Deleuze, G. 1969. *Logique du sens*. Paris: Les éditions du Minuit, 1969.

Derbolav, J. 1972. *Platons Sprachphilosophie im Kratylos und in den späteren Schriften*. Darmstadt: Impulse der Forschung, Wissenschaftliche Buchgesellschaft, 1972.

Detel, W. 1972. *Platons Beschreibung des falschen Satzes im Theätet und Sophistes*. Göttingen: Vandenhoeck und Ruprecht, 1972.

Findlay, J. 1974. *Plato. The Written and Unwritten Doctrines*. New York: Humanities Press, 1974.

Frede, M. 1967. *Prädikation und Existenzaussage*. Hypomnemata, heft 18. Göttingen: Vandenhoeck und Ruprecht, 1967.

Gadamer, H. G. 1980. *Dialogue and Dialectic*. New Haven: Yale University Press, 1980.

Gaiser, K. 1963. *Platons ungeschriebene Lehre*. Stuttgart: Ernst Klett Verlag, 1963.

Gödel, K. 1964. "What is Cantor's Continuum Problem," in *Philosophy of Mathematics*, edited by P. Benacerraf and H. Putnam, pp. 258–73. Englewood Cliffs: Prentice Hall, 1964.

Gomez-Lobo, A. 1977. "Plato's Description of Dialectic in the *Sophist* 253d1–e2," in *Phronesis* 22:29–47.

Hegel, G. W. F. 1962. *Die Philosophie Platons*. Stuttgart: Verlag Freies Geistesleben, 1962.

Heidegger, M. 1982. *The Basic Problems of Phenomenology*, translated, and with an introduction and lexicon by A. Hofstadter. Bloomington: Indiana University Press, 1982.

Husserl, E. 1950. *Ideen I*. Husserliana, bd. 3. Amsterdam: M. Nijhoff, 1950.

Kahn, C. H. 1973. "*Language and Ontology in the Cratylus*," in *Exegesis and Argument*, edited by E. N. Lee et al., pp. 152–76.

Keyt, D. 1973. "Plato on Falsity: *Sophist* 263B," in *Exegesis and Argument*, edited by E. N. Lee et al., pp. 285–305.

Klein, J. 1968. *Greek Mathematical Thought and the Origins of Algebra*, translated by E. Brann. Cambridge: MIT Press, 1968.

———. 1977. *Plato's Trilogy: Theaetetus, The Sophist, and The Statesman*. Chicago: University of Chicago Press, 1977.

Kojève, A. 1972. *Essai d'une histoire raisonnée de la philosophie païenne*, II. Paris: Gallimard, 1972.

Koller, H. 1955. "Stoicheion," in *Glotta* 34:161–74.

Kosman, L. A. 1973. "Understanding, Explanation, and Insight in Aristotle's *Posterior Analytics*," in *Exegesis and Argument*, edited by E. N. Lee et al., pp. 374–92.

————. 1976. "Platonic Love," in *Facets of Plato's Philosophy*, edited by W. H. Werkmeister. Assen: Van Gorcum, 1976.

Kube, J. 1969. *TEXNH und APETH*. Berlin: Walter de Gruyter, 1969.

Lachterman, D. R. 1979. "Klein, Jacob, *Plato's Trilogy: Theaetetus, The Sophist*, and *The Statesman*," in *Noûs* 13:106–12.

Lafrance, Y. 1979. "Autour de Platon: continentaux et analystes," in *Dionysius* 3:17–37.

Lee, E. N. 1966. "On the Metaphysics of the Image in Plato's *Timaeus*," in *The Monist* 50:341–68.

————. 1972. "Plato on Negation and Not-Being in the *Sophist*," in *Philosophical Review* 71:267–304.

Lee, E. N., et al. 1973. *Exegesis and Argument*, edited by E. N. Lee, A. Mourelatos, and R. Rorty. Assen: Van Gorcum, 1973.

Leszl, W. 1970. *Logic and Metaphysics in Aristotle*. Padua: Editrice Antenore, 1970.

Lohmann, J. 1970. *Musike und Logos*. Stuttgart: Musikwissenschaftliche Verlags-Gesellschaft, 1970.

Macran, H. S. 1902. *Aristoxenus, The Harmonics*, translated, and with notes, introduction, and index. Oxford: Clarendon Press, 1902.

Manasse, E. M. 1937. *Platons Sophistes und Politikos*. Berlin: Druck Siegfried Scholem, 1937.

Marten, R. 1965. *Der Logos der Dialektik. Eine Theorie zu Platons Sophistes*. Berlin, Walter de Gruyter, 1965.

————. 1967: "Selbstprädikation bei Platon," in *Kant-Studien* 58:209–26.

Meinhardt, H. 1968. *Teilhabe bei Platon*. Symposion 26. Freiburg and Munich: Verlag Karl Alber, 1968.

Miller, M. 1980. *The Philosopher in Plato's Statesman*. The Hague: M. Nijhoff, 1980.

Mohr, R. D. 1981. "The Number Theory in Plato's *Republic* VII and *Philebus*," in *Isis* 72:620–27.

Moravcsik, J. M. E. 1962. "Being and Meaning in the *Sophist*," in *Acta Philosophica Fennica* 14:23–78.

————. 1973a. "Plato's Method of Division," in *Patterns in Plato's Thought*, edited by J. M. E. Moravcsik, pp. 158–91. Dordrecht and Boston: D. Reidel Publishing Co., 1973.

————. 1973b. "The Anatomy of Plato's Divisions," in *Exegesis and Argument*, edited E. N. Lee et al., pp. 324–48.

Orenstein, A. 1978. *Existence and the Particular Quantifier*. Philadelphia: Temple University Press, 1978.

Owen, G. E. L. 1953. "The Place of the *Timaeus* in Plato's Dialogues," in *Studies in Plato's Metaphysics*, edited by R. E. Allen, pp. 313–38.

————. 1971. "Plato on Not-Being," in *Plato I*, edited by G. Vlastos, pp. 223–67.

Peck, A. L. 1952. "Plato and the ΜΕΓΙΣΤΑ ΓΕΝΗ of the Sophist: A Reinterpretation," in *Classical Quarterly*, n.s. 2 (1952), pp. 32–56.

Prior, W. J. 1980. "Plato's Analysis of Being and Not-Being in the *Sophist*," in *The Southern Journal of Philosophy* 18:199–211.

Rosen, S. 1969. *Nihilism: A Philosophical Essay*. New Haven: Yale University Press, 1969.

——. 1979. "Plato's Myth of the Reversed Cosmos," in *The Review of Metaphysics* 33:58–85.

——. 1980. *The Limits of Analysis*. New York: Basic Books, 1980.

Ross, W. D. 1966. *Aristotle's Metaphysics*. Oxford: Clarendon Press, 1966. (Original edition, 1924.)

Sayre, K. M. 1969. *Plato's Analytical Method*. Chicago: University of Chicago Press, 1969.

Seligman, P. 1974. *Being and Not-Being: An Introduction to Plato's Sophist*. The Hague: M. Nijhoff, 1974.

Sprute, J. 1962. *Der Begriff der DOXA in der platonischen Philosophie*. Hypomnemata, Heft 2. Göttingen: Vandenhoeck und Ruprecht, 1972.

Stenzel, J. 1959. *Zahl und Gestalt bei Platon und Aristoteles*. Darmstadt: Wissenschaftliche Buchgesellschaft, 1959. (Original edition, 1924.)

——. 1961. *Studien zur Entwicklung der platonischen Dialektik von Sokrates zu Aristoteles*. Darmstadt: Wissenschaftliche Buchgesellschaft, 1961. (Original edition, 1917.)

Uphues, K. 1973. *Sprachtheorie und Metaphysik bei Platon, Aristoteles und in der Scholastik*. Herausgegeben von K. Flasch. Frankfurt: Minerva GMBH, 1973. (Original edition, 1882.)

Van Frassen, B. 1969. "Logical Structure in Plato's *Sophist*," in *The Review of Metaphysics* 22:482–98.

Vlastos, G. 1954. "The Third Man Argument in the *Parmenides*," in *Studies in Plato's Metaphysics*, edited by R. E. Allen, pp. 241–64.

——. 1965. "Degrees of Reality in Plato," in Vlastos, *Platonic Studies*, pp. 58–75.

——. 1971. *Plato I. Metaphysics and Epistemology*, edited by G. Vlastos. New York: Doubleday Anchor, 1971.

——. 1973. *Platonic Studies*. Princeton: Princeton University Press, 1973.

——. 1973. "An Ambiguity in the *Sophist*," in Vlastos, *Platonic Studies*, pp. 270–322.

Wiehl, R. 1967. *Platon. Der Sophist. Auf der Grundlage der Übersetzung von Otto Apelt*. Philosophische Bibliothek, band 265. Hamburg: Felix Meiner Verlag, 1967.

Williams, C. J. F. 1981. *What is Existence?* Oxford: Clarendon Press, 1981.

Zadro, A. 1961. *Ricerche sul Linguaggio e sulla Logica del Sofista*. Padova: Editrice Antenore, 1961.

INDEX OF GREEK TERMS

The Index of Greek Terms gives pivotal or explanatory passages for selected technical terms; it is not a complete listing of all occurrences of such terms in the text.

διακρίνω, 63–64, 118
δύναμις, 92–93, 101, 163, 217–20, 231, 241n, 265, 279–80

εἶδος, 6, 8–9, 170, 264, 288–89, 301
ἐπιστήμη, 91–93, 119n, 251
ἔργον, 86–89, 167

κοινωνία, 220, 275

λόγος, 9–10, 16–17, 40–41, 48, 55–56, 73–74, 87, 155, 251, 294–96, 316

μέθεξις, 221, 275

νόησις, 87

ὄν, 86, 180, 202, 218, 223, 243, 266

ὄντως ὄν, 194–95, 223
οὐσία, 8, 162, 185, 212–20, 223, 231, 241n, 243, 266, 279–80, 288, 327

πᾶν, 8, 166, 244
παράδειγμα, 91, 170, 196
πρᾶγμα, 86–89, 167

στοιχεῖα, 252–58

τέχνη, 10–11, 25–28, 91–93, 101–02, 158, 166

φρόνησις, 25, 46

ψυχαγωγία, 2, 20

INDEX OF PASSAGES CITED

Euthydemus 285d, 303

Gorgias 455d6ff, 27; 465a1ff, 27;
464b2ff, 27; 463d1ff, 27; 464c7ff, 27;
463a6–c8, 27; 452d5ff, 27; 454a6ff, 27;
452e9ff, 27; 465a5–6, 92; 464b2ff,
121; 520a6, 160

Parmenides 133a, 52; 135c8ff, 68;
128b7–e4, 68; 137b6–c3, 68; 130e1–3,
119; 132c12–133a7, 195; 132d–133a,
199; 144c4–6, 240; 155d3–e2, 240;
136a4ff, 264
Phaedrus 257b7ff, 1; 271a4–272b6, 2;
272b7–274b5, 2; 275c5–276a9, 3;
264c2–5, 84; 266b3–c9, 98; 270b1ff,
129
Philebus 39a1ff, 3; 15a–b, 51; 56d–e, 51;
59d, 51; 15a1ff–18d1, 71–83; 55d10–
e3, 92; 56d4ff, 92; 57a1, 92; 57e6ff, 92;
28d6ff, 93; 17c4–e6, 254; 17a6, 254;
17b3–4, 254; 56c4ff, 255; 28c6, 314
Protagoras 319a4, 11; 316d3ff, 26;
322c2ff, 26; 326c8–9, 26; 327a8–b1,
26; 316d3ff, 96; 358a1–b6, 105

Republic II, 376a5, 131; 376d9ff, 171;
381e8–383c7, 171; 459c2–d2, 171
Republic III, 392c6ff, 1; 402e3ff, 17;
394b9–c1, 18; 394e1–395b7, 19;
396a7, 19; 393b6–394b2, 19; 398a1ff,
104; 395b3ff, 284

Republic IV, 400d6–10, 70; 440e8ff, 94;
430e11–431b3, 103; 442c10–d3, 103;
428a11ff, 158
Republic V, 477c1ff, 220; 476a4–7, 299;
279c4ff, 299
Republic VI, 487a2–5, 16; 493a6ff, 160;
493a6ff, 172; 509b6–10, 212
Republic VII, 533b6ff, 22; 524d2ff, 48;
525c8–e5, 48; 529b3–5, 50; 526a1–7,
51; 522a3ff, 92; 536c2, 164; 530d6ff,
255; 540a4ff, 261; 533a1ff, 261;
507a1ff, 262; 509c7–10, 262; 533a1ff,
262

Statesman 308e4–311a2, 20; 257a1–
258b2, 21; 295a9ff, 25; 257c2ff, 69;
284c6, 85; 258b6, 93; 261e5ff, 97;
263e6–264b5, 102; 264d1–3, 102;
262c10ff, 111; 268b4ff, 115; 258b6,
119–20; 262c10ff, 128; 257a1–2, 129;
262a8, 285
Symposium 215b4–9, 63

Theaetetus 145b1–c6, 21; 145c1, 22;
146b1–7, 22; 143e4–144b7, 22;
183a4ff, 23; 152d1ff, 26; 146b1ff, 64;
144b10–c6, 69; 178a5–8, 95; 152c8ff,
96; 184c1ff, 119; 150a8ff, 129; 172a1–
c1, 138; 145d11–e6, 158; 179a–b, 162;
204a1ff, 164; 186a2ff, 241; 205a4ff,
253; 206d3–4, 254; 186a2ff, 264
Timaeus 48e–52d, 199; 30c5ff, 224;
36a1ff, 256

GENERAL INDEX

Ackrill, J. L., 31–33
Acquisition and production: of images, 14, 18; and philosophical arithmetic, 92; and diaeresis, 94–95, 116, 170–74; of sophistical wares, 110–11; making the whole, 165–66, 311–14
Adrastus, 255, 257
Alexander, of Aphrodisias, 197
Algebraic permutation, 293
Allen, Reginald, 34
Alphabet: of pure forms, 8, 30, 45, 135, 219–20; and diaeresis, 79–80; as paradigm, 248–51
Annas, Julia, 53
Antisthenes, 242n
Aristotle, 7, 48–57 passim, 70–71, 198; cited by Frede, 274; and predication, 300
Aristoxenus, 254–56

Barker, A., 257
Being: as produced, 4–7, 18; no science of, 16; and the copula, 30–33; senses of, 39–44; as ontological principle, 209; and power, 217–20; and being known, 220–22; identity and predication, 229–44; and non-being, 269–90; not a two-place relation, 300
Blending, 252, 256–58

Carelessness, accurate and inaccurate, 212
Carls, Rainer, 41–43
Cherniss, Harold, 34, 195–99
Combination, 243–44; and forms, 248–53; and dialectic, 259–63
Concepts, 6–7, 234, 241
Contests, 112–14
Contradiction, 176–79, 327

Cornford, F. M., 29–32
Correspondence doctrine, 148
Critical mythology, 205–08

Definitions, and images, 88
Deleuze, Gilles, 172
Diaeresis: and philosophical rhetoric, 2; as universal method, 8; and technical doctrines, 9–11; better and worse, 11; and pure forms, 31; as a formalism, 47–48; and mathematical formalism, 70–71, 85–86, 100, 106–07, 133–34; and the alphabet, 79–80; and music, 81–82; and hunting, 88–90; and natural joints, 98; varies as does the sophist, 107; disjunction in, 115–18; of diaeresis, 118–31; cannot distinguish originals and images, 120; and better–worse distinction, 122; multiplicity of, 132–43; pedagogical function of, 141; contradiction in numbering of, 142–43; compared to a fantasm, 157; and dialectic, 261
Dialectic: and freedom, 258–59; nature of, 259–63; and diaeresis, 261
Dialectical logic, 44–46
Disputation, 113–14, 160–64, 189
Dramatic perspective, 1–3
Dramatic phenomenology, 12–14

Eros, 20–22
Esotericism, 47, 49, 319; and secret hunting, 96–97
Existence: 229–44 passim; and logic, 232–33; and being, 271–72; and statements, 302

Falsehood: and being, 175–78; and discourse, 296–308

Fichte, J. G., 246
Formal ratios: cannot be false, 297–98
Forms. *See* Ideas
Frede, Michael, 29, 230–40, 269–76, 304–06
Freedom, 246, 322–23; and dialectic, 258–59
Frege, Gottlob, 4–5, 8, 262
Friends of the forms, 213–14, 220–25

Gaiser, Konrad, 46–47
Gaudentius, 256
Geometry, and the sophist, 10
Gödel, Kurt, 134
Good: and life, 167, 174; and pleasure, 176
Gorgias, 27
Gradational ontology, 194–95, 305
Greatest kinds, 31, 34, 49–57, 93; directly seen, 246; their nature, 264–68

Hegel, G. W. F., 44–45, 327, 329
Heidegger, Martin, 4–6, 319
Heraclitus, 99
Homer, 26, 62–66
Husserl, Edmund, 4–5, 295

Icons and fantasms, 65, 150–57; truth and beauty, 170–74; and false statement, 293–308
Ideas: knowledge of, 2; and predication, 7–9; combination of, 29–34; and syntactic predicates, 34–37; and mathematical formalism, 38–44; and pure numbers, 48–57; as formal ratios, 297–98. *See also* Alphabet, Combination, Greatest kinds
Identity: and predication, 269–90; not sameness, 272–74, 278
Image: and dramatic perspective, 2; dialogue as, 14–15; true and false, 14; icon and fantasm, 15–16; and pure forms, 149–50; nature of, 190–93; its nature unexplained, 311
Intellectual perception, 134, 241; in the *Philebus*, 77, 82; and accessibility of pure forms, 86–87; and dialectic, 260
Interiority, 315–16
Irony, 176, 308, 313–14

Joking, 166–68

Kant, Immanuel, 241, 319
Klein, Jacob, 49–57
Koller, H., 255

Lachterman, David, 219
Lee, Edward N., 197–200
Leszl, Walter, 200
Likeness, 120–21, 172–73, 311; nature of, 10–11; and truth, 176–77; and non-being, 186–87; and ideas, 187
Logic, irrelevant to sophistry, 139–41
Lohmann, Johannes, 255–56

Macran, H. S., 256–57
Materialists, 9, 212–20
Mathematical formalism: and Plato's technical doctrines, 5; none in the *Philebus*, 74–75, 78–79
Mathematical model, 46–47
Mathematical physics, 320–22
Mathematics: and positive teaching, 8; and drama, 9; and education of philosophers, 17–18; and music, 20; and dreaming, 22
Medicine and gymnastics, 122–26, 130–31
Mimesis, 311–14
Monism, 208–11
Moravcsik, Julius, 47–48
Music: and education of philosophers, 17–18; and diaeresis, 81–82; as a paradigm, 251–58

Naming, and predication, 243
Nietzsche, Friedrich, 141, 291
Nihil absolutum, 180–81
Noble and base, 13, 15
Noble soul, 326, 328
Non-being, 151–52; being of, 177–79; and predication, 181–82; and reference, 181–82; and enumeration, 182–83; discursively inaccessible, 183–84; and contradiction, 184; and mathematics, 185; and falsehood, 201–03

Odysseus, 62
Ontological "is," 281
Ontological perspective, 3–8
Ontologies, two distinct, 223
Ontotheology, 223
Opinion, 160–62
Oratory, 160
Original and image, 292; in true statements, 148–50
Originals: as produced, 14; look like images, 120
Otherness: and non-being, 269–90; as doubled, 270, 272, 274
Owen, G. E. L., 29, 195–99, 230–41, 270–75

Painting, and writing, 3
Paradigm-copy model, 195–99
Parmenides, 26, 240; and the Eleatic
  Stranger, 62; and Socrates, 68; and
  non-being, 180, 182–83, 201, 289;
  criticism of, 204–05, 282
Parricide, 204–05, 282
Perfect speech, 324
Phenomenology, 4–6; and historical per-
  spectives, 13
Philosophers, nature of, 16–18
Philosophical rhetoric: and writing, 1–4,
  9, 19; and sophistry, 26–28
Platonism, 5, 14–16, 18, 321, 328; shift
  to Aristotelianism, 192–93; and
  Hegel, 220
Pluralism, 206–08
Politics: and sophistry, 11; and philoso-
  phy, 103
Portrait sketcher, 147–50, 165–69
Predicates: and pure forms, 116–17,
  149–50; and ousia, 225
Predication: and ideas, 7–9; and imagery,
  195–99; identity and being, 229–44;
  and mingling, 263–64
Presence and absence, 215
Private and common, 69, 87–88, 317,
  323
Process ontology, 219–20
Protagoras, 26
Protarchus, 72–83 passim
Pure formal units, 72–83
Purification, of bodies and souls, 119–31
Pythagorean music, 255

Relevance logic, 178–79, 286
Routley, Richard, 178–79

Shame, 216
Socrates: and rhetoric, 2, 11, 27; and mimesis, 19; trial of, 23–24, 61–69; accused of sophistry, 24, 64; refutations
  of sophistry, 26–28; and Descartes,
  80–81; central criticism of sophistry,
  161–62; and music, 253–55; and dialectic, 261–63; as genuine sophist,
  313–14; his death, 325
Socrates and the Eleatic Stranger: meth-

odological differences, 8–10; interest
  in the soul, 11; relationship to Theaetetus, 20–21; technicism, 23–26;
  sophistry as art, 26–27; accusation
  and punishment, 61–69, 111–12; merchandising, 108; difference in their examples, 117–18; ignorance and punishment, 125–28, 130–31; ethics and
  technical analysis, 137–38; punishment, 325–26
Soul: and philosophical rhetoric, 2; as
  image of the whole, 15; articulation
  of, 97; merchandising of, 108–09; nobility of, 140; and intellect, 315–16;
  both sophist and philosopher, 331
Speech and deed, 84–85
Speech and silence, 324–25
Stricter and softer Muses, 206

Tame and wild, 102–05
Tarski, Alfred, 292
Technical: as opposed to literary, 1–3; in
  the narrow sense, 8–9; subordinate to
  sound judgment, 25
Theaetetus: and forms, 8; his nature,
  20–23, 63, 68
"Theaetetus flies," 295–96, 301, 303–07
Theo of Smyrna, 254–57
Theodorus, 62–67; his nature, 20–23
Transparency, surface, 329–30

Visual imagery, 188
Vlastos, Gregory, 35–38, 194–95, 198–
  99

Whitman, Walt, 141
Whole, 16; and all, 209–11; and power,
  231
Wisdom, 158–59, 164; two roots of, 246
Wittgenstein, Ludwig, 4–5, 132, 262,
  329
Wolf and dog, 131
Writing, and conversation, 3

Xenophanes, 206

Zeno, 62, 68